Volume 2

Country Walks

near London

Edited and designed by
Time Out Guides Limited
Universal House
251 Tottenham Court Road
London W1T 7AB
Tel   + 44 (0) 20 7813 3000
Fax + 44 (0) 20 7813 6001
Email guides@timeout.com
www.timeout.com

Updates, news & credits

Updates are published between editions of this book – if you would like an update sheet for the latest edition, send four first class stamps to Walks Book (II), 6 Blackstock Mews, Blackstock Road, London N4 2BT. Please also send in (or e-mail walks@albery foundation.org) any information about blocked paths, errors, changes or suggestions. Updates are also accessible on the internet at www.walkingclub.org.uk.

The **Nicholas Albery Foundation** (020 7359 8391) is the charity that benefits from bookshop, credit card sales and author royalties from this book. The Foundation's projects include: the Global Ideas Bank, with its compendiums of innovations and annual awards (www.globalideasbank.org), the Natural Death Centre (www.natural death.org.uk), and the Poetry Challenge (www.poetrychallenge.org.uk). Books available from the Foundation's secure online facility (www.globalideasbank.org/ bookorder.html) include: *Seize the Day, The World's Greatest Ideas, The Natural Death Handbook, Poem for the Day (One and Two)* and *Alternative Gomera*.

Walk checkers

The researchers are very grateful to all those who helped check the walks in this book: Faye Ainscow, Richard Bach, Timothy Bassett, Catherine Beer, Barbara Blake, Peter Boon, John A Borst, Marie-Lyse Boulet, Alan Brennan, Trevor Brice, James Broom, Miriam Burns, Bruce Campbell, Daniella Carrozza, Gabriella Carrozza, Cathy Charsley, David Chevance, Jane Clargo, Martine Collumbien, Kate Copeland, Tim Crowther, James Dixon, Tim Dixon, Ebru Dogan, Herman Douglas, Brigid Doyle, David Elliott, Janet Elliott, Sarah Elliott, Marian Farrugia, Ralph Fox, Samantha Fuller, Caroline Galea, Jon Gulley, Sheila Hale, Peter Hall, Tom Harding, Richard Harrod, Ralph Hawtree, Patricia Haygarth, Dave Hughes, Richard Jackson, Elisabeth Jeffries, Ainslie Johnston, Andrew Kennedy, Jayne Kennedy, Henrikje Klasen, James Lancaster, Alan Langridge, Bridgette Leach, Diana Leary, Corina Leong, Alun Llewelyn, Janice Long, Sinead Mhuircheartaigh, Irene Miller, Andrew Murphy, Sue Neale, Debbie Perry, Cliff Phelps, Vittoria Redoglia, Kate Roberts, Colin Ross, Susanne Rutishauser, Kaori Saito, Nick Saunders, Peter Savage, Ray Scraggs, John Sephton, Glynn Snow, Andrew Starling, Richard Stevens, Tim Sweetman, Anna Swinn, Jennifer Toynbee-Holmes, David Vernest, Carine Verwimp, Marion Watkinson, Alexi Weddernburn, Susannah Wight, Cheng Wood and members of the Sunday Section of the SWC.

The editor would like to thank the Nicholas Albery Foundation office team for their support; Jake, Katie and Luke for keeping him sane; all the walkers (especially David and Peter) for their hard work, patience and understanding; Jonathan Cox for additional material; and Sarah Guy and all at Time Out without whom this book could not and would not exist.

Other walking groups

The **Ramblers Association**, 2nd floor Camelford House, 87-90 Albert Embankment, London SE1 7TW (020 7339 8500/ www.ramblers.org.uk) was officially founded in 1935, having previously consisted of a federation of rambling groups dating back to the latter half of the 19th century. The RA takes decisive action on blocked, obstructed and overgrown paths, working with local authorities. This book would have not have been possible were it not for past and present efforts of the Ramblers Association.

The **Outsiders Walking Club** is a London-based walking club (www.outsiders.fsnet. co.uk), members of which have advised and contributed to helping with the walk checking.

All the walks in the book have been checked at least three times in the past year, but neither the editor nor publisher can accept responsibility for any problems encountered by readers. The maps are sketches only and not to exact scale.

Contents

Contents

Overview

WEST MIDLANDS

WARWICKSHIRE

WORCESTERSHIRE

GLOUCESTERSHIRE

OXFORDSHIRE

BUCKINGHAMSHIRE

BERKSHIRE

WILTSHIRE

HAMPSHIRE

SURREY

DORSET

WEST

ISLE OF WIGHT

Introduction

This book is a double tribute – to a uniquely beautiful corner of England; and to Nicholas Albery, a remarkable and creative individual.

It is sometimes said that the south-east corner of England is one big suburb – wall-to-wall housing from London to the sea. Equally, it is said that modern agriculture has destroyed all the traditional charm of the countryside.

In fact, as this book proves, nothing could be further from the truth. On these walks you will discover tranquil valleys, meadows strewn with wild flowers, ancient country pubs, quaint villages and woods that are carpeted in spring with bluebells and wood anemones.

A particular feature of this book, compared to the original *Time Out Book of Country Walks* (whose walks the authors all thoroughly recommend), is the large number of downland walks – particularly in the South Downs, but also in the North Downs and Chilterns. We have chosen these walks because of the unique beauty of the Downs: a very English kind of grandeur. Also included are several fine coastal walks and a couple with a literary flavour.

As in the original book, each of the walks starts and ends at a railway station, and have a lunch stop (usually a pub) and a tea stop (a tearoom where possible; otherwise a pub that is open in the afternoon and serves hot drinks). An innovation in this book, however, is that we have included short, and sometimes long, options for the walks. In this way we hope that the book will be suitable for walkers of all abilities, offering everything from a Sunday afternoon stroll to a full day-long hike.

Nicholas Albery

The unique individual to whom this book is dedicated is Nicholas Albery, self-styled social inventor, who created the original *Time Out Book of Country Walks*, and the basic format of walk directions and details that we have followed in this volume. One of Nicholas's most creative ideas was to include in his original book a self-organising Saturday Walkers' Club. Six years on it is still thriving, and its members devised the walks in this book.

Nicholas Albery's life would make an interesting book of its own. A leading light in the counter-culture of the late 1960s and early 1970s, he continued to develop new ideas and innovations through his life. His achievements include helping establish Frestonia, a housing co-operative that successfully declared itself independent of the UK to resist redevelopment; being the first person anywhere in the world to (albeit unsuccessfully) sue an oil company for environmental damage; and standing as a parliamentary candidate for the Ecology Party.

Nicholas's core enthusiasm, however, was what he called 'social inventions' – new non-technological ideas to improve society. The Institute for Social Inventions arose from this passion, as did its online arm, the Global Ideas Bank (www.global ideasbank.org), which continues to promote the central concept, creative problem-solving, to this day.

Projects that emerged from the Institute's hub include the Natural Death Centre, founded with Nicholas's wife Josefine, which gives advice on alternative and ecological funerals (www.natural death.org.uk), and the Poetry Challenge, a much-used fundraising format in which school pupils are sponsored to recite poetry by heart for a good cause (www.poetrychallenge.org).

The original *Time Out Book of Country Walks* was typical of the way Nicholas could combine the practical with a higher purpose. Practically it sprung out of his love of walking with friends and out of a medical condition that was helped by taking regular exercise. But by creating the Saturday Walkers' Club he also turned his enthusiasm into a virtual community of Londoners, who met, walked, talked and socialised. The club exists to this day, and all purchasers of this book are welcome to participate in it (*see p11*).

Tragically (and doubly so for a lifelong advocate of public transport), Nicholas was killed in a car accident in 2001 at the age of 52. The Saturday Walkers' Club and his walks have outlived him, however, and have proved a way for many people from all walks of life to discover the beauties of the English countryside.

This book is our way of continuing Nicholas's work, both by adding a new set of walks to the original volume and by supporting the projects Nicholas set up: all authors' royalties from this volume will go to the Nicholas Albery Foundation.

Getting to the walks

The walks in this book all start and end at a railway station. See the **Transport** section at the start of each walk for details of where to catch the train if starting from London. The **Saturday Walkers' Club** section in each chapter gives an idea of what time to set off from London if aiming to reach the recommended pub by lunch-time.

We have also given brief details in the Transport section on possible parking places near the start of the walks, but car drivers are advised to check this information locally. For non-circular walks, car drivers will also find brief details on how to get back to the start of the walk by public transport.

Having said that, the authors all heartily recommend leaving your car at home and using trains to get to the walks – and not just for the obvious environmental reasons. Firstly, despite their poor image, trains in the south-east are largely fast, reliable and convenient. Secondly, trains whisk you from the centre of London much faster than you can drive, and often drop you in the very heart of the countryside. What greater pleasure, for example, is there than getting off the train at pretty Southease station or at rural Stonegate or Pluckley?

For circular walks it is obvious what train ticket to buy: a day return to the station where the walk starts. On linear walks – from one station to another – you should, theoretically, get a day return to the station at the start, and then a single from the station at the end of the walk to the point where the return route intersects with the outbound one. In practice, our experience is that ticket inspectors often accept a day return to whichever station is furthest from London, particularly if you explain that you are doing a country walk between two stations.

The costs of travelling by train can be substantially reduced by using a railcard, such as the Network Railcard, which costs £20 and gives a one-third reduction on off-peak rail fares for you and three friends. For current details of all railcards (Family, Senior Citizen, Young Persons, and so on), see www.railcard.co.uk or ask in your local train station. Holders of other London travelcards should also note that you can reduce most fares by buying rail tickets from the edge of the outermost London fare zone for which your travelcard is valid.

The best place to get train information is from the Network Rail website (www.nationalrail.co.uk): click on the 'Planning Your Journey' icon for the timetable search page. Alternatively, you can call National Rail Enquiries on 08457 484950.

Be sure when travelling by train to check that there are no engineering works first. Sunday is the day most affected, but other days are not immune. Nothing spoils a nice day out like the dreaded words 'replacement bus service'. The best way to check for engineering works is simply to look up your proposed journey on the website above, or to call the enquiries number.

Take TimeOut to visit

field & trek

Established for over 30 years, Field & Trek is the UK's leading retailer of Outdoor Clothing and Equipment. We have 20 stores across the country, an award-winning mail order department and the UK's leading on-line outdoor store at www.fieldandtrek.com

10% off your next purchase!

The directions

One of the joys of Nicholas's original *Time Out Book of Country Walks* is the directions, about which one reviewer said 'We defy you to get lost'. Unlike some other walking books, these include absolutely all the information you need to follow a walk without having to refer to a map.

Having said that, we heartily recommend the excellent Ordnance Survey Maps, especially the Explorer series. A map can be useful for devising your own short cuts and on the (hopefully very rare) occasions when you miss the way.

Of course, if you are a confident navigator, you will not need all the detail provided in the text. For this reason, the essential directions are in italics. Experienced walkers should be able to follow the walks using just the italics, dipping into the detail when they are unsure.

Note that the seasons can make a difference to how easy it is to follow a walk. In summer, vegetation can obscure footpath posts or arrows on trees, and in winter, paths through woods can sometimes become confusing. Ploughed fields in winter also test navigational skills, while in summer you may have to decide whether to wade through a field of corn or walk around its edge. We have done our best to take all these factors into account when devising our walk directions, however, and give you as many navigational clues as possible.

At key points in the text we also provide compass bearings. This is not because we expect walkers to navigate the south-east of England with compass in hand like a polar explorer, but because there may be occasions, for example in a wood or when crossing a newly ploughed field, where you are unsure about your onward way. In these cases, the compass bearing can reassure you that you are on the right route.

The idea of using a compass sends many people into a blind panic, but in fact, it is not complicated. Simply align the needle of the compass with north

(usually helpfully marked by a red arrow on the compass base) and then face in the direction of the bearing given in the text using the numbers around the edge of the dial. This, and the instructions in the text, should make the onward route obvious.

Each chapter also includes a sketch map, with numbers – for example **[7]** – referring to points in the text, so that you can check your progress along a route. Where a turning is less obvious or complex, we alert you to that in the directions with a **[!]**.

When to walk (a walker's year)

A fine spring or summer day is the time when most of us think of a country walk, but the countryside of the south-east of England is delightful all year round.

In **winter** the weather is often by no means as bad as you might expect (or the weather forecast predicts). Nevertheless, you would be unwise to set off without a waterproof and, as paths are muddy in winter, proper walking boots with good treads are also recommended. Mud can make walks seem harder going than in summer.

Advantages of winter walks include the lack of leaves on the trees, which mean views open up that would otherwise be concealed, while January often features a period of fine weather, with frosty mornings and low golden sunlight. The pleasure of entering a warm cosy pub after a brisk morning's walk is also considerable. Please be courteous and take off muddy boots first, though.

Of course, in winter it gets dark early, so allow enough time to complete your walk, particularly if stopping for lunch. Not all of the walks in this book are suitable for winter for this reason. A good rule of thumb is that it takes an hour to walk three kilometres (two miles). It is a good idea to take a torch with you in case you miscalculate.

Spring truly starts in mid March, but from mid February there are early signs of it, with snowdrops in the woods and lanes. March brings yellow celandines and daffodils, the former carpeting some woodland floors and lane verges.

By April, wild flowers are bursting forth everywhere, and the grass is lush and green. The trees are still bare, however: an entrancing combination. The ground is also drying out, making picnics possible, or walking in trainers. White wood anemones and then bluebells come out in the woods, the latter around the last week of April (fading in early May). Many of these walks feature lovely bluebell woods, in particular the Hurst Green to Chiddingstone Causeway walk, and the Boxhill ending of the Guildford to Gomshall walk.

By this time, leaves are coming out on the trees and buttercups and other flowers make the meadows and downland pastures a botanist's delight. The long days in May and June also mean walks further from London are possible, making these months an ideal time to get out into the countryside

Summer is also a fine time to walk, but as June turns into July stinging nettles and other undergrowth reach their height. Nettles in particular are worth bearing in mind if you plan to wear shorts on a hot day (for example, on the Robertsbridge walk). Downland walks are less prone to nettles, but if the summer is hot, lack of shade can be a problem. At such times, woodland walks, such as the Wendover Circular, can be a pleasant alternative.

For many walkers essentials in the summer include a bottle of water and a hat, not to mention sun cream. It is amazing how burnt you can get when walking all day even in English summer sunshine. Heat also brings haze, so summer is not always the best time for views. On the other hand, you can swim in the sea, and the English Channel is a bearable temperature from mid July to well into September.

The first sign of **autumn** is when the blackberries ripen in August: you can find this wonderful wild fruit growing everywhere on these walks. Autumn is many walkers' favourite season, with cooler temperatures, softer light, and the landscape bathed in golden colour. Once the leaves turn – late September or October – woodland walks are especially delightful, particularly the Chiltern walks in this book. Leaf fall conditions seem to last longer and longer each year – right to the end of November in both 2002 and 2003.

Accuracy and updates

All walks in this book were checked at least three times during 2003, and all pub and attraction opening times and other such details have also been verified.

However, there will inevitably be the occasional error, as well as changes after publication. Common changes include collapsed stiles (some local authorities maintain them well: others don't) and footpath signposts falling over, being removed or getting covered by foliage. Also, fences are erected where none were before and vice versa. Pubs sometimes close or stop serving food, and rural tearooms, alas, are particularly liable to going out of business at short notice.

So if you spot such errors or changes, please let us know by emailing walks@alberyfoundation.org, or writing to Time Out Country Walks (II), 6 Blackstock Mews, Blackstock Road, London N4 2BT. You will receive a credit, if you wish, in any future edition of this book. You can also check the Saturday Walkers website www.walkingclub.org.uk to see if there are any updates to the book. The site may also contain alternative routes for the walks published here.

To ensure walks follow rights of way, we have relied on OS Maps, particularly the excellent Explorer series, and to the best of our knowledge all routes in this book follow public rights of way, permissive paths (paths where the landowner – usually the National Trust or a local authority – has given formal permission to use the path, but may withdraw it if they wish: such paths are usually marked on OS maps too) or common land. Still, it is impossible to guarantee this book is free of errors.

Our experience has been that the vast majority of rural landowners and inhabitants are perfectly friendly and accommodating to walkers so long as they keep to legitimate paths. Be civil to them and respect their rights and they are likely to do the same to you.

Saturday Walkers' Club

The Saturday Walkers' Club (SWC) is a self-organising group, independent of Time Out, that meets each week to do the walks in this book. All those who buy this book are invited – at their own risk – to join the club walks. This is an extension of the successful club based on the original *Time Out Book of Country Walks*.

The club works as follows:

• Using the rota on page 13, check which walk is to be walked that week: the walk numbers (and letters) refer to the Contents page.

• Then turn to the SWC section of the relevant walk to find out the recommended train for that walk. Take the nearest train before or after the time specified (if the difference is the same, take the later train). In the case of engineering work on the train line to any of the walks involving either a diversion adding 30 minutes to the journey or a replacement bus service, that walk will not take place.

• Where the walk is one of the Walk options, the train time is the same as for the main walk, unless otherwise specified.

• Club walkers can usually be found near the middle of the train. If you do not find them on the train, they will usually form an obvious group on the platform when you arrive at your destination. If not, try holding this book up to see if anyone responds.

• On the walks there is no leader and each walker is responsible for finding their own way. You are also free to split away from the group if you find the pace

too fast or slow or if those walking that day are not suited to your mood.

As this is a self-organising group, there is no guarantee that anyone will turn up for a particular walk, but experience from the club based on the original *Time Out Book of Country Walks* suggests that average numbers per walk will be from five to 15 people, sometimes more on a fine day.

As with the original edition, for this book we are proposing three different walks each week. Those new to the club might find it easier to start with the Main walk.

Main walk: This follows the walk as indicated in the rota. Thus, this group does both the standard walks in the book and also some of the variants – usually shorter walks for the shorter winter days, though sometimes also longer ones.

Vigorous walk: This group does the walks on the Saturday before the one indicated in the rota. Thus in 2004, it would do walk 15 on 3 April, not 10 April as in the rota: or on 12 June, it would do walk 8. [As this group will walk at a slightly faster pace than the main walk, it will do only the standard walks in the book – that is, the walk numbers without letters after them in the rota. In winter this means the group will meet every other week.]

Sunday walk: Saturday was chosen as a day for club walks because trains are more frequent, pubs less crowded and tearooms more likely to be open. Saturday trains are also much less affected than Sunday services by engineering works. Nevertheless, we recognise that some people might like to do a walk on a Sunday, and such folk should do the walks in the rota on the Sunday a week after they appear in the rota, or, in other words, eight days later than the date specified.

Thus, in 2004, the Sunday walk for 18 April would be walk 15, while for 19 September it would be walk 13c. (Note that in 2004 and 2005, at Christmas, the 'Sunday' walks will be on Tuesday 28th and Wednesday 28th respectively.)

The Great Escape

2004		2005		2006		2007	
Date	**Walk**	**Date**	**Walk**	**Date**	**Walk**	**Date**	**Walk**
3 Jan	16a	1 Jan	21	7 Jan	1b	6 Jan	16a
10 Jan	13	8 Jan	11a	14 Jan	4	13 Jan	13
17 Jan	6a	15 Jan	15	21 Jan	6a	20 Jan	6a
24 Jan	21	22 Jan	14b	28 Jan	17	27 Jan	21
31 Jan	12a	29 Jan	3	4 Feb	12a	3 Feb	12a
7 Feb	4	5 Feb	10b	11 Feb	14	10 Feb	4
14 Feb	27b	12 Feb	4	18 Feb	15b	17 Feb	27b
21 Feb	3	19 Feb	1b	25 Feb	8	24 Feb	3
28 Feb	12c	26 Feb	19	4 Mar	23	3 Mar	12c
6 Mar	14	5 Mar	12a	11 Mar	30	10 Mar	14
13 Mar	10b	12 Mar	2	18 Mar	27b	17 Mar	10b
20 Mar	8	19 Mar	20a	25 Mar	13	24 Mar	8
27 Mar	20a	26 Mar	24	1 Apr	20	31 Mar	20a
3 Apr	23	2 Apr	26	8 Apr	15	7 Apr	23
10 Apr	15	9 Apr	22	15 Apr	10	14 Apr	15
17 Apr	18	16 Apr	7	22 Apr	12c	21 Apr	18
24 Apr	16	23 Apr	9	29 Apr	5	28 Apr	16
1 May	5a+b	30 Apr	16	6 May	13c	5 May	5a+b
8 May	7	7 May	6	13 May	21	12 May	7
15 May	30	14 May	11	20 May	1	19 May	30
22 May	20	21 May	9	27 May	29	26 May	20
29 May	10	28 May	17	3 Jun	27	2 Jun	10
5 Jun	12	4 Jun	27	10 Jun	9	9 Jun	12
12 Jun	25	11 Jun	20	17 Jun	14	16 Jun	25
19 Jun	8	18 Jun	25	24 Jun	26	23 Jun	8
26 Jun	26	25 Jun	23	1 Jul	19	30 Jun	26
3 Jul	27	2 Jul	26	8 Jul	2	7 Jul	27
10 Jul	9	9 Jul	18	15 Jul	30	14 Jul	9
17 Jul	28	16 Jul	29	22 Jul	22	21 Jul	28
24 Jul	19	23 Jul	5	29 Jul	25	28 Jul	19
31 Jul	24	30 Jul	28	5 Aug	11	4 Aug	24
7 Aug	18	6 Aug	12	12 Aug	28	11 Aug	18
14 Aug	28	13 Aug	24c	19 Aug	7	18 Aug	28
21 Aug	29	20 Aug	10	26 Aug	29	25 Aug	29
28 Aug	24	27 Aug	8	2 Sep	23	1 Sep	24
4 Sept	6	3 Sept	30	9 Sep	12	8 Sep	6
11 Sept	13c	10 Sept	28	16 Sep	16	15 Sep	13c
18 Sept	22	17 Sept	11	23 Sep	28	22 Sep	22
25 Sept	1	24 Sept	9	30 Sep	25	29 Sep	1
2 Oct	11	1 Oct	1	7 Oct	22	6 Oct	11
9 Oct	8b	8 Oct	7	14 Oct	18	13 Oct	8b
16 Oct	17	15 Oct	5a+b	21 Oct	6	20 Oct	17
23 Oct	19	22 Oct	14	28 Oct	20a	27 Oct	19
30 Oct	12a	29 Oct	15b	4 Nov	24	3 Nov	12a
6 Nov	5	5 Nov	3	11 Nov	1a	10 Nov	5
13 Nov	14b	12 Nov	8a	18 Nov	13	17 Nov	14b
20 Nov	2	19 Nov	17	25 Nov	8b	24 Nov	2
27 Nov	1c	26 Nov	1c	2 Dec	2	1 Dec	1c
4 Dec	4	3 Dec	13	9 Dec	10b	8 Dec	4
11 Dec	15b	10 Dec	16a	16 Dec	21	15 Dec	15b
18 Dec	1a	17 Dec	18a	23 Dec	18a	20 Dec	1a
27 Dec	5c	27 Dec	5c	30 Dec	3a	29 Dec	5c
31 Dec	11a						

Wendover Circular

Whiteleaf and Pulpit Hill.

Start and finish: Wendover station

Length: 18.5km (11.6 miles). For shorter variations, *see below* **Walk options**.

Time: 5 hours 45 minutes. For the whole outing, including trains, sights and meals, allow 8 hours 30 minutes.

Transport: Two trains an hour (one hourly on Sundays) run between London Marylebone and Wendover (journey time: 46-52 minutes). For those driving, Wendover station car park costs £2 a day including Sundays, but there is a notice stating that it costs £15 to non-rail users. There is some street parking, and the public car park off the High Street by the library is free on Sundays.

OS Landranger Map: 165
OS Explorer Map: 181
Chiltern Society Map: 3
Wendover, map reference SP865077, is in Buckinghamshire, 7km (4.4 miles) south-east of Aylesbury.

Toughness: 7 out of 10.

Walk notes: This energetic walk serves as a fine introduction to the Chiltern Hills, first passing through woodland, then descending into hidden vales and fields before emerging out onto the Chiltern escarpment above Princes Risborough at a spot that commands panoramic views of the countryside below. After lunch in Whiteleaf, a pretty village with many ancient cottages, the return to Wendover goes through wooded valleys and hills. It continues along a fine open section of escarpment, with grand views north, before descending to the plains for a leisurely finish. This walk is particularly pretty in autumn when it is a riot of russet hues.

Walk options: Directions are given at the end of the main text that allow you to shorten the walk in three different ways (*see p23*).

a) Main walk via Cross Coppice short cut: You may reduce the length of the main walk by 5km (3.1 miles) to 13.5km (8.4 miles) by following the main walk directions as given until [3]. Then follow the Short walk directions and then pick up the main walk directions at [6].

b) Short walk from Wendover to Monk's Risborough: Follow the main walk directions to [5] and then pick up the directions at the end of the main walk text. This route is 11.2km (7 miles).

c) Short walk from Monk's Risborough to Wendover: Follow the directions at the end of the main text and then pick up the main walk directions from [5]. This route is 9.7km (6.1 miles).

For options b) and c) above, if driving, it is best to park at Aylesbury. Wendover and Monk's Risborough are on separate train lines, each being two stops along the line from Aylesbury.

Saturday Walkers' Club: Take the train nearest to 9.15am (before or after) from Marylebone. For the Short

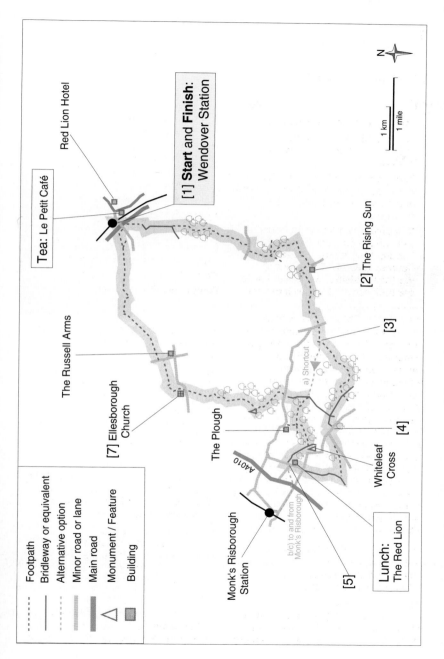

Red Lion Hotel

Tea: Le Petit Café

[1] Start and Finish: Wendover Station

[2] The Rising Sun

[3]

a) Shortcut

The Russell Arms

[7] Ellesborough Church

The Plough

A4010

Whiteleaf Cross

[4]

b/c) to and from Monk's Risborough

Lunch: The Red Lion

[5]

Monk's Risborough Station

N

1 km
1 mile

Footpath
Bridleway or equivalent
Alternative option
Minor road or lane
Main road
Monument / Feature
Building

View of Princes Risborough from the top of **Whiteleaf Hill**.

cut walk and the Wendover to Monk's Risborough walk take the train nearest to 10am. For the Monk's Risborough to Wendover walk take the train nearest to 10.30am.

Walk directions

[1] [Numbers refer to the map]
On leaving the ticket office of **Wendover station** *turn right up Station Approach. In 130 metres turn right at the T junction with Ellesborough Road to cross a bridge* over the railway line and Wendover Bypass. Once *over the bridge turn left* to go up a car-wide gravel track, indicated by a footpath signpost, your direction 140 degrees. Cross over a stile to the left of a metal fieldgate onto a car-wide gravel track following the line of some National Grid pylons. In 50 metres cross over another stile to the left of a metal fieldgate. *Turn half right* to go diagonally across a field, marked by a footpath signpost, your direction 200 degrees.

After 300 metres, *at the field boundary, cross a stile and turn right up a tarmac lane* with houses on the left, your direction 240 degrees. In 140 metres *turn left through metal gateposts* onto a signposted bridleway, your direction 140 degrees. After 70 metres the path curves to the right. In 60 metres continue up across a field between fences, your direction due south. In 200 metres, at the top of the field, ignore a bridleway to the right to cross a stile in front and continue in the same direction (due south), marked by a footpath arrow.

After 25 metres you pass under some mini pylon cables. Continue down to cross a stile in a dip after 80 metres. Go diagonally up across a field towards a wood, in the same direction. In 300 metres, *at the top of the field, go over a stile*, your direction 210 degrees, to follow a footpath *up into Coxgrove Wood.* In 120 metres you *pass a tree on your right with a yellow ahead and left arrow painted on it. In 15 metres the footpath forks three ways. Take the middle fork down to a stile*, your direction 170 degrees.

In 30 metres pass to the right of the redundant stile to emerge from the wood. Continue down across a field. In 120 metres *pass to the right of a redundant stile into a wood.* Ignore the paths immediately to the right and left and go up a footpath ahead, indicated by a yellow public footpath arrow, your initial direction 210 degrees. After 120 metres the footpath continues along the left-hand edge of the wood. In 60 metres pass round to the right of a redundant stile to *emerge from the wood and go up the left-hand side of a field,* your direction 170 degrees.

After 40 metres *cross into the next field. Turn right* as indicated by an arrow on a footpath post to go up the right-hand edge of the field, your initial direction 240 degrees. After 140 metres *pass round to the right of a redundant stile into a wood* of beech trees, your direction 230 degrees. In 250 metres continue straight on, ignoring a waymarked footpath down to the left. In 80 metres ignore a path up to the right and continue slightly downhill.

In 100 metres *cross a stile and turn up to the left,* your direction 160 degrees. After 60 metres *cross another stile and turn right to go up alongside a barbed-wire fence.* After 100 metres the footpath runs between houses and gardens. In another 100 metres, *at a footpath T-junction, turn left.* After 5 metres ignore a turning to the right to a road and continue straight ahead. In 70 metres you *turn right onto a lane, passing Old Ford Cottages,* Dunsmore, on your right.

In 40 metres go straight over at a crossroads, following a road signpost to Kimble and Princes Risborough, passing a duck pond on the left, your direction 290 degrees. In 80 metres *turn left to cross a stile to the right of a metal fieldgate. Take the left-hand footpath across the field,* aiming for a stile midway along the boundary fence opposite, your direction 200 degrees. (Do not head down the field to the stile at the bottom corner of the field.) Dunsmore Old Farm can be seen below on the right.

In 100 metres go over the stile to go down across the next field, your direction 210 degrees. After 70 metres cross a stile into the next field and continue in the same direction. In 150 metres go over another stile at the bottom edge of this third field. In 45 metres, *at the bottom of a small field* with a wood to the left, *go over a stile to reach a path T-junction* after 10 metres. *Turn left along a bridleway,* with the wood to your left and a wooden fence and field beyond to your right, your direction 170 degrees.

In 100 metres, at the end of the field on your right, *the path enters a wood* and forks three ways. Ignore the bridleways to the left and right to *continue straight ahead* on the middle footpath passing through a wooden horse barrier (staggered parallel barrier), your direction 130 degrees.

Continue through the wood on a footpath edged by young oak trees. After 250 metres a track joins from the right. Keep straight along this now car-wide track. After 300 metres, *at the corner of the wood, turn right up a car-wide track* on the right-hand side of a field, with a hedgerow on your right, heading towards a wood, your direction 260 degrees. In 250 metres, *at the top corner of the field, you enter a wood* (Little Hampden Common). Continue up in the same direction, marked by a white arrow on a tree. After 140 metres ignore a path to the left as the footpath winds up through the wood.

In 250 metres you emerge from the wood onto a lane directly opposite the **Rising Sun [2]**, the recommended lunch stop for the short cut walk. *If not stopping at the pub turn right up the shingle car-wide track* past a house on the left leading into a wood, your direction 330 degrees. After 40 metres *the track forks,* with an entrance sign to Hampden Manor ahead. *Fork left* off the shingle track, following a South Bucks Way sign up into the wood, your direction 300 degrees.

After 130 metres *fork left along the bridleway in front of a sign saying 'No Horse Riding On Common'.* After

15 metres *take a small footpath forking left off the bridleway*, your initial direction 200 degrees. In 100 metres you *emerge from the wood. Continue straight ahead* along the right-hand edge of a field, with a hedgerow on your right, your direction 240 degrees.

After 180 metres cross over into the next field through a gap in the hedgerow, marked by a yellow footpath arrow on a low post. Continue down in the same direction with the hedgerow on your left. After 150 metres, *at a dip, fork left up into a wood*, marked by a yellow footpath arrow. In 140 metres you pass a deep hollow on your left, your direction 310 degrees. 20 metres after this, *where the footpath forks, take the left, lower fork*, your direction west. In 140 metres you emerge from the wood into a field.

Follow a yellow footpath arrow on a footpath post down the left-hand edge of the field towards a converted farm (Dirtywood Farm), your direction 240 degrees. In 120 metres *ignore a yellow footpath arrow through a private garden. Veer right* to follow the 'Permitted Path avoiding private garden', your initial direction 300 degrees. After 200 metres *turn right down a driveway*, your direction 250 degrees. In 250 metres you *reach a T-junction with the main road, which you cross over*. Follow a metal footpath signpost to *continue straight ahead up a private (to cars) tarmac lane* through a wood. After 200 metres you emerge from the wood to continue along the lane, with trees to your left and a hedgerow and field beyond to your right.

In 100 metres the lane curves sharply to the left. **[3]** On your right is a yellow footpath arrow indicating a footpath straight ahead across fields.

[If you are intending to take the short walk refer to option **a) the Shortcut via Cross Coppice** walk directions at the end of this main section.]

Otherwise, for the main walk *follow the lane up and round to the left* as it becomes gravel, your initial direction 220 degrees.

There are woods on the left for 70 metres then open fields both sides as you go up towards a wood of conifers.

After 350 metres *at the edge of the wood where the road sweeps up to the right towards Solinger Farm, turn left to cross over a stile to the left of a double wooden fieldgate*. Continue straight ahead into the wood along a car-wide track, your direction 220 degrees. After 120 metres ignore a track off to the right to continue up the track, with a field visible through the trees to the right.

[!] In 250 metres, *where the track curves to the left, turn half right down into the trees along an easily missed narrow footpath*, marked by a white arrow on a tree to the right, your direction west. After 130 metres the footpath veers down to the right, passing a hollow on your left, your direction 320 degrees. In 40 metres you pass a short concrete post on your right, with a field to your right. In 200 metres, at the corner of the field to your right, a wire fence now runs alongside the footpath on your right. Continue up through the wood, your direction 260 degrees.

After 100 metres, *as the wire fence comes to an end at a T-junction, turn right uphill*, your direction 310 degrees. In 40 metres *continue straight ahead to emerge from the wood*, now with a fenced field on the left and trees to your right, as the path goes uphill and then flattens. After 450 metres you reach a crosspaths and just ahead to the right is a wooden hut with scaffolding and a satellite dish. Continue straight ahead along a car-wide gravel track towards a house, your direction 280 degrees.

In 240 metres *cross a stile to the left of a metal fieldgate and turn left along a driveway*, your direction 210 degrees. After 80 metres, *at a T-junction with a road* **[4]**, *cross over and turn right* along a grass verge. In 150 metres *at a road junction turn left* down a road signposted to Princes Risborough, your direction 250 degrees.

In 200 metres *where the road starts to descend more steeply downhill you*

X marks the spot

Whiteleaf is within a part of the Chiltern escarpment rich in historical and sacred sites, including Pulpit Hill fort (also on this walk) and Ivinghoe Beacon. **Whiteleaf Cross** is carved into the chalk hillside above the village. Alongside the cross are the remains of Neolithic and Bronze Age burial mounds. The cross rises above the ancient settlements of Monk's Risborough, Princes Risborough, Bledlow, Horsendon and Saunderton, settlements that are linked by the ancient Lower and Upper Icknield Ways. The existence of the Cross was first noted by the antiquarian Francis Wise in 1742, who proposed the theory that it had been constructed to commemorate a battle by the Saxon king Edward the Elder. The true origins of the Cross remain unknown to this day, and continue to be the subject of conjecture, speculation and legend. The site has recently been the subject of a major restoration project, which, as well as restoring the Cross to its former state, also uncovered artefacts from Roman times and the Bronze age.

pass a wooden fieldgate on your right
with 'Brush Hill Local Nature Reserve'
engraved on its top bar. *40 metres
after this turn right to enter the nature
reserve through a metal kissing gate
by a two-armed Ridgeway signpost.
Follow the downhill arm* along the
footpath, initially parallel to the road,
your direction 260 degrees. After 200
metres, passing a wooden bench on the
left, *go down some steps and through
a metal kissing gate to leave the reserve.*
Go down some further steps to enter
a shrubby wooded area and continue
downhill, your direction 260 degrees.

In 150 metres you reach a footpath
junction marked by a three-armed
footpath signpost. Continue straight on to
go down some more steps to emerge from
the wood through a gap in a wooden fence
after 20 metres. Continue down the left-
hand edge of the field, your direction 260
degrees. After 100 metres pass through
a gap in the hedge into an arable field.
In 200 metres *at the field corner you
reach a path junction marked by a three-
armed footpath signpost. Turn right*
onto the Icknield Way, a car-wide track
between hedgerows, your direction 50

degrees. Follow this track for 750 metres,
ignoring any turnings off, to *come out
to a crossroads.*

*Go over the crossroads and continue
along a tarmac lane* (Upper Icknield
Way), your direction 20 degrees. In
200 metres you reach the **Red Lion**
pub in **Whiteleaf** on your right, the
recommended lunch stop for the main
walk. Coming out of the pub, turn right
to continue down the Upper Icknield
Way. After 80 metres you reach a lane
(The Holloway) off to the left. **[5]**

[If you are taking option **b)** the
Wendover to Monk's Risborough
walk, refer to the directions at the end of
this main section.]

*Otherwise, in a further 60 metres turn
right up a tarmac drive to follow a public
bridleway signpost marked Icknield Way,*
your initial direction 100 degrees.

After 40 metres ignore a footpath
signpost pointing left to continue up the
tarmac lane, which in another 40 metres
becomes a narrow path up along the left-
hand edge of a wood. After 160 metres, *at
the top of this path, you reach a junction
with a car-wide track. Turn right uphill
into the wood* and keep to the left path

along the blue Riders route, your direction 200 degrees. (Ignore a fork immediately to the right along a green chain-link fence.)

In 25 metres the path veers left, with a wooden Buckinghamshire County Council Whiteleaf Hill sign on the right. After 250 metres go through a wooden gate to follow the Icknield Way sign onto a grassy area. In 70 metres you *reach a three-armed footpath signpost at the top of the hill.* To the right you can view Princes Risborough and beyond, with the **Whiteleaf Cross** (*see p19* **X marks the spot**) carved into the hillside below the wooden rail.

To continue the walk, *turn left to join the Ridgeway footpath,* your direction east. In 50 metres go through a wooden gate into a wood to join a car-wide track, which goes slightly downwards, your direction 80 degrees. After 180 metres you pass a short concrete post on the right as the footpath goes downhill more steeply. In 350 metres, at a crosspaths marked *by a four-armed footpath signpost, turn right to leave the Ridgeway,* your direction 110 degrees. *After 40 metres you cross another path diagonally and keep straight on along the lower left path,* your direction 100 degrees, gradually veering left and downwards.

After 200 metres *go down some wooden steps to reach a crosspaths. Continue straight ahead to the Cadsden Wood information board,* your direction 100 degrees. (For the recommended lunch stop for the Monk's Risborough to Wendover walk, take a short diversion here: Turn left along the level footpath, your direction 330 degrees. In 300 metres you cross a stile to reach the **Plough** pub).

At the board take the lower left track up into the woods, your direction 110 degrees. In 30 metres you pass a redundant stile on the left. In 140 metres *fork right up a footpath, marked by a yellow footpath arrow on a post* at the junction, your direction 140 degrees. *After 100 metres the footpath turns left,* your direction east, and winds upwards, before levelling and then going slightly

downwards to reach a stile after 300 metres near the edge of the wood. Cross this stile to *reach a crosspaths and turn left onto a bridleway,* your initial direction 20 degrees. After 450 metres the *bridleway leads out to a road* **[6]**.

Cross the road to turn half left onto the track opposite. After 20 metres turn right up a bridleway signposted Icknield Way to enter Pulpit Wood, your direction east. The path goes round to the right, initially parallel to the main road. After 80 metres *turn left at a crosspaths through a wooden horse barrier uphill,* indicated by a yellow footpath arrow on the post, your direction 70 degrees.

After 170 metres, *at the top of the steep incline, you reach a crosspaths. Turn left* onto an unmarked car-wide track along the side of the hill, your direction 310 degrees. In 150 metres continue straight on at a crosspaths, marked by a Pulpit Hill Fort sign on the right, your direction still 310 degrees. After 250 metres *turn right to follow a sign pointing up to Pulpit Hill Fort,* your direction 40 degrees. After 80 metres, *at the top of the incline, veer left to reach a white painted crosspaths symbol on a tree.* (This is the site of the remains of **Pulpit Hill Fort**.) *Fork left,* your direction 310 degrees.

After 15 metres, where the footpath forks, take the right fork, passing a large tree on your left with a white painted arrow. After 80 metres, *at a path T-junction, turn right to follow the footpath along the top edge of a hillside.* After 100 metres the footpath veers to the right away from the hill edge and goes between two posts at an opening in a barbed-wire fence. Continue down, your initial direction 40 degrees.

In 70 metres go over a crosspaths. After 30 metres go through a wooden kissing gate. In 40 metres you emerge from the wood and continue downhill, your direction 40 degrees. In 140 metres *you reach a field boundary. Veer left with a barbed-wire fence on your right* and a field beyond, your direction 350 degrees.

After 30 metres ignore a footpath signpost indicating the Ridgeway to the right and left to *cross a stile ahead. Continue straight on, keeping the fence on your right.* After 150 metres veer to the right to continue following the fence. After a further 100 metres, *immediately before the fence veers to the right, turn right over a stile.*

Head up the left-hand edge of the field, your direction 60 degrees. In 30 metres you go up into a wood and veer left. After 80 metres go over a stile to the right of a metal fieldgate. In 20 metres cross a tarmac road (the driveway to Chequers, the Prime Minister's official country residence) and continue on a car-wide track through the wood. After 130 metres you emerge from the wood to continue up an open area, with a mound/hillock to the right. In 160 metres, by a public footpath signpost, go down some steps to enter a lightly wooded area, your initial direction 40 degrees.

After 140 metres cross a stile to emerge from the lightly wooded area and continue on a narrow chalky footpath cut into the side of Beacon Hill. The footpath becomes less defined in the chalk as you *continue down towards Ellesborough Church*, which can be seen ahead (partially hidden by foliage in summer). After 300 metres, at the bottom right-hand corner of the field, go over a stile to cross the next field.

In 200 metres go through a wooden kissing gate at the bottom right-hand corner to turn right onto the main road (Ellesborough Road). After 20 metres cross over the road to enter the churchyard of **Ellesborough Church [7]**. *If not visiting the church, follow the public footpath through the churchyard*, keeping to the left of the church. After 50 metres go down some concrete steps and then through part of an old metal kissing gate to cross a stile after 30 metres.

Continue downhill and veer right, aiming for a stile in the right-hand corner of the field. After 150 metres cross the stile and then another after 10 metres to

continue along a tarmac lane with houses to the left, your direction 60 degrees. After 180 metres, *at a T junction, cross over a lane to follow a footpath* with a field to your left and houses to your right, your direction 80 degrees.

After 80 metres ignore a footpath off to the left to continue across a field. You can see Coombe Hill and its monument to the half right. In 220 metres go over a stile to continue along a narrow fenced-in footpath between fields, your direction 70 degrees. After 140 metres go over two stiles to continue towards some housing. In 100 metres *cross a stile to turn left onto a main road* to follow the yellow Aylesbury Ring footpath arrow on the stile, your direction 350 degrees. (If you wish to break off for a late lunch at the **Russell Arms**, turn right up the road, your direction 170 degrees. In 200 metres you reach the pub on your left.)

In 40 metres turn right to cross a stile to the right of a metal fieldgate, marked by a footpath signpost for the Aylesbury Ring, your direction 70 degrees. After 100 metres cross a stile to the left of a metal fieldgate to continue up a grassy track between fields. After 140 metres pass to the left of a metal fieldgate to continue uphill with a fence on your right.

After 250 metres, at the top right-hand corner of the field, cross a stile to go across the middle of a large flat field, following a yellow Aylesbury Ring footpath arrow, your direction 70 degrees. In 300 metres cross a stile into the next field and head across the field towards trees, your direction 70 degrees. After 160 metres go over a stile into the next field. Continue along the left-hand side of the field towards trees.

In 100 metres go over a stile into an orchard, keeping to the left-hand side. In 40 metres *go over a stile to the left of a large old house with tall chimneys* (Wellwick Farm). Go straight down the field to cross a stile after 120 metres. *Turn half right towards some farm buildings*, your direction 120 degrees. After 80 metres cross over a stile to the left of a metal fieldgate to leave the field. *Go through the farmyard and cross a tarmac lane* after 40 metres to enter a field.

Turn left to continue parallel to the road for 50 metres, your direction 60 degrees. *At a wooden telegraph pole turn right,* indicated by a yellow Aylesbury Ring footpath arrow, to follow a grassy path separating two fields in the direction of a large corrugated metal barn in the distance, your initial direction 140 degrees. In 60 metres the footpath veers left and then right.

After 300 metres you reach a hedgerow ahead. *Cross a stile to the left of the hedgerow and turn left to head towards a brick bridge in the distance,* your direction 60 degrees. Continue on the fenced path between fields, crossing four more stiles. In 250 metres, *after crossing the fourth stile, turn half right* to follow a yellow Aylesbury Ring footpath arrow diagonally across a field, your direction 110 degrees.

In 400 metres, at the corner of the field, you reach a mini pylon pole (with a transformer box) on the left and a yellow Aylesbury Ring footpath arrow. Turn half right to follow the arrow along the left-hand edge of the field, your direction 140 degrees. After 120 metres *you reach the entrance to Wendover Cricket Club on your left. If not wishing to take tea, turn left here* through the kissing gate for 100 metres to cross a stile and footbridge leading *to Wendover station.*

Otherwise, continue straight on along the track. After 180 metres the track joins the main road (Ellesborough Road). *Turn left to cross the bridge over the bypass and railway line towards* **Wendover**, down past Station Approach on the left and the **Shoulder of Mutton** pub on the left. After 100 metres you reach a small roundabout. Turn right along South Street to reach **Le Petit Café** or continue straight on for 200 metres to the **Red Lion Hotel**. (To see **Anne Boleyn's Cottages**, built on land given to Anne

Boleyn by Henry VIII as a marriage gift in 1533, continue down past the Red Lion to the Clock Tower at the mini roundabout and turn right up Tring Road. The cottages are on your left.)

After tea, to get to the station, turn left out of the café. In 100 metres pass by the Shoulder of Mutton pub on your right and turn right down to **Wendover station**.

Walk options

a) Short cut via Cross Coppice walk directions:

Follow the main walk directions to [3].

Continue straight ahead to leave the lane. Follow the footpath, marked by a yellow footpath arrow on a post, passing through wooden posts into a field, with a hedgerow on the left, your direction 280 degrees. In 300 metres continue into the next field, marked by a yellow Circular Walk footpath arrow. After 100 metres there is a wood (**Cross Coppice**) on your left. In 200 metres, *at the end of the wood, the footpath bears round to the left at the field corner. After 10 metres ignore a footpath to the left into the wood. Bear right to follow the footpath into the right-hand field of the two fields ahead,* your direction 280 degrees.

Continue along the left-hand edge of the field, your direction 270 degrees. In 250 metres, *at the corner of the field, follow the footpath through a gap in the hedgerow to cross a stile.* Go down through a wooded area, following a yellow Circular Walk footpath arrow, your direction 280 degrees. After 60 metres *turn right at a crosspaths* onto a signposted public bridleway. After 450 metres the *bridleway leads out to a main road.*

To continue the walk, *follow the main walk directions from* [6].

b) Short walk from Wendover to Monk's Risborough:

Follow the main walk directions to [5].

Turn left down the lane (The Holloway). *In 60 metres fork left down a fenced-in footpath.* After 100 metres go through a metal kissing gate to go diagonally down across a field, aiming for a metal kissing gate to the right of some wooden fencing (enclosing a children's swimming pool).

In 160 metres go through the kissing gate and continue along a fenced-in footpath. In 80 metres go through a metal kissing gate to *reach the main A4010. Cross over and turn left. In 40 metres turn right* down Mill Lane. In 600 metres, *just before the railway bridge, turn right* up Crowbrook Road. Monk's Risborough station is 150 metres on the left.

c) Short walk from Monk's Risborough to Wendover:

Coming off the single platform at Monk's Risborough station, *turn right onto a suburban road,* your direction 210 degrees. *After 150 metres, at a T-junction, turn left* onto Mill Lane, signposted Monk's Risborough. *In 600 metres, at a T-junction* with the main A4010, *cross over and turn left. In 40 metres,* immediately after Monk's Risborough Church of England School on your right, *turn right through a metal kissing gate* along a fenced-in footpath. After 80 metres go through a metal kissing gate into a field and turn half left up across the field aiming for the left-hand corner.

After 160 metres, at the field corner, go through a metal kissing gate to continue up a fenced-in footpath. In 100 metres the footpath leads out to a lane (The Holloway). Turn right up the lane. In 60 metres you reach a T-junction. If stopping at the **Red Lion** pub, turn right to reach the pub on your left after 80 metres. Otherwise turn left and *follow the main walk directions from* [5].

Lunch & tea places

Le Petit Café *6 South Street, Wendover, HP22 6EF (01296 624601).* **Open** 9.30am-4.30pm Tue-Fri; 9.30am-5.30pm Sat, Sun. **Food served** noon-3pm Tue-Sun. Serves tea and scones and simple cooked food. This is the suggested tea stop on the main walk.

Plough *Cadsden Road, Lower Cadsden, nr Princes Risborough, HP27 0NB (01844 343302).* **Open** 11am-2.30pm, 5-11pm Mon-Fri; 11am-11pm Sat, Sun. **Food served** noon-2pm, 7-9pm Mon-Sat; noon-2.30pm Sun. A short diversion from the walk route and 2.5km (1.6 miles) from the start of the Monk's Risborough walk, the Plough is the suggested lunch stop for the Monk's Risborough to Wendover option.

Red Lion *Upper Icknield Way, Whiteleaf, nr Princes Risborough, HP27 0LL (01844 344476).* **Open** noon-3pm, 5-11pm Mon-Sat; noon-7pm Sun. **Food served** noon-2pm, 7-9pm Mon-Sat; noon-2pm Sun. Located 10km (6.25 miles) from the start of the main walk, this pub serves wholesome food. There is a small beer garden at the front and back. This is the suggested lunch stop for the main walk. Booking is advised.

Red Lion Hotel *9 High Street, Wendover, HP22 6DU (01296 622266).* **Open** 7.30am-11.30pm daily. **Food served** noon-9pm daily. Serves tea and coffee as well as food.

Rising Sun *Little Hampden, nr Great Missenden, HP16 9PS (01494 488393/ 488360).* **Open** 11.30am-3pm Tue, Sun; 11.30am-3pm, 6.30-10pm Wed-Sat. **Food served** noon-2pm Tue, Sun; noon-2pm, 7-9pm Wed-Sat. Situated 4.5km (2.8 miles) from the start of the walk, the Rising Sun serves inventive food. It's a popular pub, seating about 25 inside, with a small beer garden at the front. This is the suggested lunch stop for the short cut option. Booking is advised.

Russell Arms *2 Chalkshire Road, Butler's Cross, HP17 0TS (01296 622618).* **Open** noon-3pm, 6-11pm Tue-Sun. **Food served** noon-2pm, 6-9.30pm Tue-Sun. A short diversion from the walk route and 2.5km (1.6 miles) from the end of the walk, this pub serves decent food.

Shoulder of Mutton *20 Pound Street, Wendover HP22 6EJ (01296 623223).* **Open** 11am-11pm Mon-Sat; noon-10.30pm Sun. **Food served** 11am-10pm Mon-Sat; noon-9pm Sun. Serves meals, plus tea and coffee.

Ellesborough Church, 3.5km (2.2 miles) from the end of the walk, is a nice alternative tea option. Tea and cakes are often served here from 2pm to 5.30pm at weekends during summer.

Saunderton via Bledlow Circular

Chinnor Hill and Bledlow Ridge.

Start and finish: Saunderton station
Length: 17.3km (10.8 miles). For a shorter walk and other variations, *see below* **Walk options**.
Time: 5 hours 20 minutes. For the whole outing, including trains, sights and meals, allow 9 hours.
Transport: Trains run hourly between London Marylebone and Saunderton (journey time: 42-51 minutes). For those driving, Saunderton station car park is free.
OS Landranger Map: 165
OS Explorer Maps: 171, 172 and 181
Chiltern Society Maps: 7 and 14 Saunderton (station), map reference SU813982, is in Buckinghamshire, 16km (10 miles) south of Aylesbury.
Toughness: 6 out of 10.

Walk notes: This walk through a peaceful part of the rolling Chiltern Hills has one or two steep hills, but the gradients are otherwise gentle and there are many fine views out over the valley and plain. The first part of the walk runs along the valley bottom before following the Ridgeway to lunch at Bledlow. In the afternoon you pass through a series of secluded valleys before reaching Radnage, and then go over Bledlow Ridge and back along the valley to Saunderton.

Walk options: Directions for the shorter variation are given at the end of the main walk text (*see p32*).

a) Short walk: You may reduce the length of the main walk substantially to 9km (5.6 miles) by following the main walk directions until point [3]. Then follow the Short walk directions, before picking up the main walk directions again at point [8].

Other options: You may combine the Saunderton via Bledlow short walk with the Saunderton via West Wycombe short walk (see Walk 3) for an 18.3km (11.4mile) walk. This walk takes the form of a figure of 8. With plenty of refreshment stops along the way, you may choose to start with either walk.

You can increase the length of the main walk by over 9km (5.6 miles) to 26.6km (16.6 miles) by combining it with the Saunderton via West Wycombe short walk. For the more ambitious, the walk may be lengthened by over 18km (11.25 miles) to 33.3km (20.8 miles) by combining it with the Saunderton via West Wycombe main walk. Both of these longer walks take the form of a figure of 8. You can start with either walk – there is no shortage of refreshment stops along the way.

Saturday Walkers' Club: Take the train nearest to 10.10am (before or after) from Marylebone.

Walk directions

[1] [Numbers refer to the map]
Coming off the London train on platform 2 at **Saunderton station**, go into the

station car park and *turn left* down Station Approach to reach a T-junction after 120 metres. *Turn right to head up a lane*, your direction 250 degrees.

In 270 metres the lane curves slightly to the right. **[!]** In 30 metres, just as it bends sharply to the left, *fork right and leave the lane*, passing a double metal fieldgate on your right, and follow a two-armed footpath signpost. In 5 metres you come out to the bottom corner of a field, where you *turn half right along the bottom edge of the field*, your direction 320 degrees.

In 150 metres, at the end of the field, *turn right and cross into the next field.* Keep straight on diagonally across the field, your direction north, merging with a hedge on your right after 100 metres. Keep to the right-hand side of the field. In a further 200 metres exit the field and continue along the side of a factory, with a chain-link fence to your left, your direction 340 degrees.

After 350 metres pass between two wooden posts to the right of a 2 metre-high metal gate, then *cross a lane* (Haw Lane) and continue along a footpath into the next field. Carry straight on across the middle of this field, your direction 340 degrees. In 450 metres you cross over into the next field. Continue straight ahead along the right-hand edge of the field, with a hedgerow on your right, your direction 330 degrees.

In 450 metres, at the right-hand corner of this field, continue straight ahead. *Pass between some farm buildings on your right and a thatched house on your left*, keeping straight on at a footpath post with a yellow arrow.

30 metres after the thatched house *the footpath comes out to a field. Pass to the left of a telegraph pole after 40 metres* and follow a not too clearly defined footpath, which veers to the right. Aim towards the right side of another telegraph pole (which on closer inspection has a yellow arrow on it), 70 metres distant, your direction 10 degrees. 40 metres past the telegraph pole cross a stile in the right-hand field corner **[2]** and *turn left along a quiet road.*

In 170 metres *turn left onto a signposted footpath, opposite Carpenter's House*, your initial direction 300 degrees. Follow this footpath between hedges. In 80 metres you come out into a field and continue along its left-hand edge, your direction 310 degrees. In 200 metres you pass around a National Grid electricity pylon.

In another 90 metres, at the corner of the field, follow the edge of the field round to the right. In 25 metres *turn left*, your direction west. In 10 metres cross over into the next field, passing a three-armed wooden footpath signpost on your right-hand side, *to join the Ridgeway* and continue straight up the left-hand edge of the field, your direction west.

In 200 metres, at the left-hand field corner, continue straight on up to go through a wooden gate after 20 metres. In 60 metres you reach a wooden kissing gate with a three-armed signpost. **[3]** [If you are intending to take the short walk refer to the **Short walk** directions at the end of this main section.] Otherwise, for the main walk go through the wooden kissing gate and continue along the Ridgeway up a steeper gradient, your direction 260 degrees.

In 110 metres ignore a stile on your left and *veer right as marked by a wooden footpath post with a yellow arrow and a Ridgeway acorn on it*, your direction 310 degrees. You are now on the level along the line of the ridge. In 220 metres you enter a small wooded area and in a further 20 metres you go through a wooden kissing gate. In 10 metres you emerge from the wooded area and continue along the top line of the ridge.

After 160 metres you start to go downhill through a wooded area. In 250 metres, at the bottom of the hill, you emerge from the wooded area and continue along the left-hand edge of a field, your direction 340 degrees.

In 80 metres, just before the corner of the field, *turn left and go through a metal kissing gate to continue straight ahead*

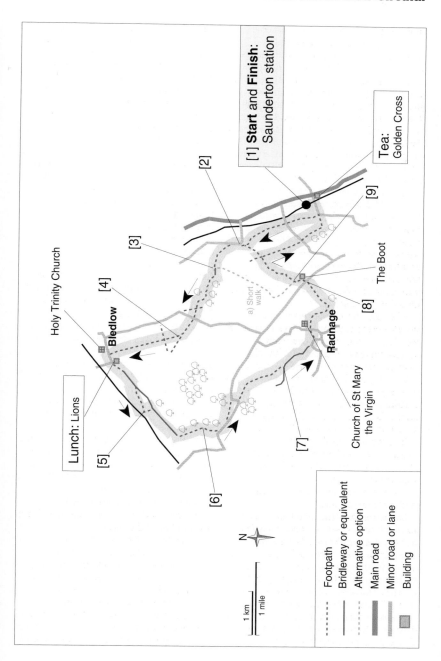

[1] **Start** and **Finish**: Saunderton station

Tea: Golden Cross

[2]

[3]

[9]

The Boot

Holy Trinity Church

[4]

Bledlow

a) Short walk

[8]

Radnage

Lunch: Lions

[5]

Church of St Mary the Virgin

[6]

[7]

N

1 km
1 mile

Footpath
Bridleway or equivalent
Alternative option
Main road
Minor road or lane
Building

across a field, your direction 280 degrees. In 140 metres go over a crosspaths marked by a footpath post. In 90 metres go through a metal kissing gate and into the next field. Turn half left diagonally across the corner of this field. In 130 metres go through a metal kissing gate to *come out onto a road*.

Turn left along the road for 10 metres and then turn right through a metal kissing gate. Continue along the left-hand edge of a field, your direction 310 degrees. After 200 metres ignore a stile on your left and continue straight on. In 20 metres *go left through a metal kissing gate into the next field and turn right. Continue in the same direction along the bottom right-hand edge of this field.*

In 200 metres turn right to cross over a stile [4], *leaving the Ridgeway*. In 5 metres cross a second stile. Turn half left down a footpath across a field towards a stile bordering a clump of trees, your direction 350 degrees. After 200 metres cross over the stile and go up for 30 metres through the wooded area. At the top go over a stile and into a field. Continue uphill in the same direction.

In 120 metres, at the upper edge of the field, cross a stile and then a car-wide earth track and another stile into a field. Continue straight ahead in the same direction, 350 degrees, along the right-hand edge of the field. In 400 metres, at the corner of the field, pass to the left of a redundant dilapidated stile and cross into the next field.

After 500 metres, at the right-hand corner of this field, go over a stile and continue along a fenced-in footpath until you *reach a road* after 60 metres and *turn left*. (Turning right here leads to the west entrance of **Holy Trinity Church** and, after a further 150 metres, you reach the entrance to **Lyde Garden**, a suitable **picnic** spot.) (*See p32* **Holy water**.) Continue along the road for 160 metres to arrive at the lunchtime pub, the **Lions**.

After lunch, coming out of the main entrance of the Lions, *turn left across a*

lane into a field, where you turn half left towards the far left-hand corner of the field, your direction 200 degrees. In 250 metres, *at the field corner, turn right onto a car-wide bridleway* (Swan's Way), your direction 220 degrees.

[!] After 350 metres, as the bridleway crosses a field boundary, *turn half right, taking an unmarked footpath diagonally across a field*, your direction 250 degrees. In 200 metres, on the far side of this field, you pass under mini electricity pylon cables and cross a stile to go along a fenced-in footpath, your direction 240 degrees.

In 200 metres follow the footpath round as it veers to the right and then to the left to cross a stile. Keep straight on across the field, ignoring a stile uphill to the left, your direction 260 degrees. In 70 metres cross over a stile and continue on, crossing two more stiles. In 50 metres you come out onto a tarmac driveway, passing a cottage on your left. After 30 metres cross over a stile [5] to the left of a double wooden fieldgate.

Turn left uphill along a car-wide earth track, following a bridleway signpost, your direction 120 degrees. After 50 metres you pass Ash Wain cottage on your left. Continue uphill under trees. In 150 metres you reach a junction with bridleway signposts left and right. *Turn right, signposted to 'The Ridgeway ¼ mile'*, your initial direction south. Continue uphill along this car-wide earth track. In muddy conditions you may prefer to take an intermittent footpath to the right.

In 300 metres, at a bridleway crossroads, *turn half right onto a car-wide level earth track*, rejoining the Ridgeway (marked by a signpost), your direction 240 degrees. In 170 metres you pass a metal gate entrance to a nature reserve on your left and after another 180 metres you pass a second metal gate entrance to the nature reserve.

After 220 metres, having come out of the wooded area and gone past a house on your left, you *reach a crosspaths marked by a four-armed signpost. Turn left uphill*,

The north tip of **Bledlow Ridge**.

your initial direction 130 degrees. In 80 metres the footpath forks. Take the right fork, your initial direction 170 degrees. In 30 metres continue straight ahead, as indicated by a white arrow on the left post of a wooden fieldgate to your right.

After 25 metres you enter a wooded area, the gradient now steeper, going up **Chinnor Hill**. In 200 metres you pass a tree on your right with a clear white painted footpath arrow pointing ahead. Continue uphill, following the white arrows, one after 160 metres on a tree on your left, another in a further 20 metres on a wooden post.

In 20 metres *follow the footpath as it veers half left*, passing a tree on your left with a white arrow, and go up some decayed steps. In 15 metres follow a white arrow on a tree and *turn half left, now with a wire fence to your right*. In 120 metres go through a wooden gate **[6]**,

and *turn right onto a lane* (Hill Top Lane), your initial direction 190 degrees. Continue along the lane for 350 metres until you reach a *T-junction with Red Lane. Cross over and turn left*, your initial direction 130 degrees.

In 150 metres, just past the entrance to Woodlands Farm on the left, diverge left from the road through a metal kissing gate, following a footpath signpost, your direction 130 degrees. In 10 metres you pass under mini pylon cables and in 60 metres cross over another stile. *Veer slightly right, to the right of a corrugated metal barn*, aiming for a wooden fieldgate, your direction 140 degrees.

Go through the wooden fieldgate and continue straight ahead, your direction 120 degrees, to cross over a car-wide track and pass around a farm building on your left. In 60 metres, at the far end of the building, turn left for 30 metres to reach

a car-wide earth track. Turn right along this track, your direction 110 degrees.

After 300 metres cross a stile to *come out onto a road and turn right* to go along the grass verge on the left side of the road, your direction 200 degrees. After 150 metres, *as the road curves right, turn left across a stile*, marked by a metal footpath signpost. Keep to the left-hand edge of the field, your initial direction 110 degrees. In 250 metres, at the left corner of the field, cross over a stile to enter some woods along a car-wide track.

After 150 metres, at the end of the woods, cross a stile to carry on down the left-hand edge of the field. In 400 metres, at the bottom corner of the field, cross a stile and continue straight up across the next field, gradually converging with its left-hand side, your direction 140 degrees. In 200 metres *cross a stile* **[7]** *to come out onto a bridleway, where you turn left,*

your initial direction 110 degrees. In 400 metres you reach a car-wide tarmac track and continue straight ahead, your direction 150 degrees.

In 400 metres, *at a lane T-junction, fork left down a lane*, your direction 120 degrees. In 110 metres *turn left at a two-armed footpath signpost*, your direction 60 degrees. In 25 metres cross a shingle drive to then go over a stile. Continue downhill across a field and then for 50 metres uphill. Cross a stile at the top corner of the field and come out to a lane T-junction. Continue straight ahead up the lane for 35 metres into the churchyard of **St Mary the Virgin**, Radnage.

After visiting the church turn left through the churchyard for 60 metres, *cross a brick stile and then immediately afterwards a wooden stile. Turn half right* across a field, your direction 110 degrees. In 80 metres go over a stile into the next field.

Continue in the same direction across the next field. In 70 metres *cross a stile and turn half right,* marked by an arrow on the stile, your direction 170 degrees. Head towards the corner of the field and cross a stile after 150 metres. Continue, with woods on your left, your initial direction south, as the footpath veers round to the left.

In 150 metres go over a stile. After 100 metres go over another stile to reach the corner of a narrow field after a further 20 metres. Ignore a stile to your left to cross the stile ahead. After 5 metres you pass on your right a field fence corner post with a white arrow and yellow public footpath arrow pointing ahead and a yellow public footpath arrow to the right. **[!]** After 2 metres *turn left up a footpath, marked only by a white 'C' painted on a tree to the right of the footpath,* your initial direction 350 degrees.

In 50 metres you pass a metal post on your right with a 'C' painted on it and a white arrow below the 'C'. Continue along the footpath. **[!]** After 10 metres *the path forks at a stub of a tree trunk ahead with a white band and a white arrow pointing to the right. Take the left-hand fork,* your direction 20 degrees, and continue up the hill to **Bledlow Ridge**.

In 180 metres the incline becomes less steep and, after a further 90 metres, *you reach a footpath junction where you turn right.* After 10 metres there is a fence and a field on your right; continue, your direction 60 degrees. In 350 metres cross a stile and then, after 150 metres, cross another stile to then go over the main road. **[8]** (If taking a late lunch, turn left and walk the short distance to the **Boot** pub.)

Continue straight ahead along a car-wide shingle driveway, which curves to the left. In 150 metres the driveway ends. Continue straight ahead along a footpath, your initial direction 310 degrees. In 100 metres you *reach the corner of a field with stiles to the left and right of a wooden fieldgate.* **[9]** *Cross the stile to the right* of the wooden fieldgate to

go down the right-hand edge of the field, your initial direction 10 degrees.

After 140 metres turn right through a metal kissing gate and then turn half left, directly downhill across a field, heading towards the right of some evergreen trees, your direction 40 degrees.

As you cross the brow of the slope, a metal kissing gate to the right of the evergreen trees becomes visible. *On reaching the kissing gate after 220 metres go through it and turn left* along the left-hand edge of the field. Follow this for 300 metres until you reach a metal kissing gate in the corner of the field in front of some farm buildings. *Go through the kissing gate and turn right along a driveway.*

After 150 metres *turn left at a T-junction,* marked by a three-armed signpost, and then follow the left-hand edge of a field on a car-wide tarmac public bridleway, your direction 340 degrees. In 60 metres, as the tarmac driveway ends, continue straight ahead along the car-wide earth track. After 100 metres ignore a stile on your left and continue straight on to reach a wooden footpath post in 70 metres *at a path junction. Fork right to go across the field,* your direction 60 degrees.

In 200 metres, having crossed the field, you reach a stile. *Do not cross the stile but turn right along the left-hand edge of the field,* your direction 140 degrees. After 200 metres you pass under some National Grid cables; in a further 80 metres cross a stile and continue in the same direction along the left-hand edge of the field.

In 600 metres you come out onto a lane (Haw Lane). *Cross the lane and then cross a stile* to go along the right-hand upper edge of a field. In 120 metres, at the corner of the field, continue straight on through a wooden kissing gate to the right of a stile and continue up the right-hand edge of this next field.

In 180 metres go through a wooden kissing gate to the right of a small stile and continue up in the same direction along the right-hand upper edge of the field. In 300 metres, at the top corner of this field, cross a stile and go through a wooded area for 20 metres to come out at the top corner of the next field.

The footpath leads diagonally down across the field, your direction east. (However, depending on the time of year and the state of the field, you may prefer to go down the left-hand edge of the field and then turn right at the bottom corner to go along the bottom left-hand edge of the field.) At the bottom corner of the field go through the hedgerow, passing a double metal fieldgate on your left, and then turn left to go down the lane for 280 metres to the T-junction with Station Approach.

For the suggested tea place, continue straight on under the railway bridge for 80 metres to the T-junction with the main road. *Turn right* to walk the short distance to the **Golden Cross**. After tea, retrace your steps to Station Approach and back up to **Saunderton station**.

Walk options

a) **Short walk directions**:
Follow main walk directions until [3].

Do not go through the wooden kissing gate. *Turn left along the car-wide earth track*, your direction 170 degrees. In

350 metres go through a wooden gate to the right of a metal fieldgate.

Continue down a car-wide earth track along the right-hand edge of the field, your direction 220 degrees. In 160 metres, at a path junction marked by a wooden post, continue straight ahead to reach another path junction after 40 metres, again marked by a wooden post. Continue up a car-wide earth track across the field in the same direction.

In 360 metres go through a fieldgate entrance and continue more steeply up across the field between fences to **Bledlow Ridge**. After 220 metres, at the top of the field, go through a wooden gate and continue along a car-wide shingle track. In 50 metres you pass a footpath post next to a bridleway signpost. Come off the shingle track and continue up a tarmac lane, your direction 210 degrees.

In 120 metres *take a footpath alleyway forking off to the left, marked by a two-armed footpath signpost*, passing to the left of a redundant stile, your direction 210 degrees. After 120 metres cross over a stile into a field. Continue down the left-hand edge, your direction south. In 100 metres, at the dip of the field, continue uphill for 20 metres to

Holy water

One of the finest churches in the area is **Holy Trinity**, **Bledlow**. It dates from the 12th century – only the nave survives from this structure, which once probably had transepts and a central tower. Of special interest are the nave arcades; they are fine examples of early 13th-century craftsmanship, and there's a 14th-century window and some interesting remains of medieval mural paintings in the north aisle. The church is open from 2pm until 5pm at weekends from Easter till the end of October.

Also in Bledlow, **Lyde Garden**, which can be accessed through a gate on Church End immediately east of the churchyard, is a beautiful water garden, and well worth a visit too. From the east side of the churchyard you can look down onto the Lyde, where water from eight springs merge. The closeness of Holy Trinity to the steep banks of the coombe has been immortalised in a local proverb yet to come true: 'They that live and do abide shall see the church fall in the Lyde.'

A shady stretch of the **Ridgeway**.

the corner of the field. Go through a wooden kissing gate and cross over a stile after a further 7 metres.

Continue, with a wooden fence on your right, your direction 150 degrees. After 180 metres you cross over a shingle driveway and continue straight on along a fenced-in footpath (backing onto gardens) in the same direction. In 100 metres continue along the fenced-in footpath, now between fields. After 250 metres cross over a stile to reach the corner of the field on your left, with the stile you have just crossed to the left of a wooden fieldgate and another stile to the right of the wooden fieldgate.

If you are not intending to take lunch at the Boot, you now follow the main walk directions from [9]. Otherwise, continue straight ahead along the footpath. After 100 metres the footpath leads out to a shingle driveway. Continue straight ahead and follow the shingle driveway as it veers to the right to come out to a T-junction after 150 metres. Turn right to walk the short distance to the lunch pub, the **Boot**.

After lunch, coming out of the main entrance of the Boot, *turn left to walk the short distance back to the T-junction, then turn left onto the shingle driveway.*

Follow the main walk directions from [8].

Lunch & tea places

Boot *Chinnor Road, Bledlow Ridge, HB14 4AL (01494 481499).* **Open/food served** noon-3pm, 6-11pm Mon-Sat; noon-4pm, 7-10pm Sun. The Boot serves good food and is the suggested lunch stop for the short walk option, 5.25km (3.3 miles) from the start of the walk.

Golden Cross *Wycombe Road, Saunderton, HP14 4HU (01494 565974).* **Open** noon-11pm Mon-Sat; noon-10.30pm Sun. **Food served** noon-2.30pm, 7-9.30pm Mon-Sat; noon-7pm Sun. This pub, close to Saunderton station, offers tea and coffee.

Lions *Church End, Bledlow, HP27 9PE (01844 343345).* **Open/food served** noon-2.30pm, 6-11pm Mon-Sat; noon-2.30pm, 7-11pm Sun. Located 7km (4.4 miles) from the start of the walk, this pub has an extensive garden and is the suggested lunch stop for the main walk.

Saunderton via West Wycombe Circular

Hughenden Manor and West Wycombe Caves.

Start and finish: Saunderton station
Length: 16km (10 miles). For a shorter version and other variations, *see below* **Walk options**.
Time: 5 hours. For the whole outing, including trains, sights and meals, allow 9 hours.
Transport: Trains run hourly between London Marylebone and Saunderton (journey time: 42-51 minutes). For those driving, Saunderton station car park is free.
OS Landranger Map: 165
OS Explorer Map: 172
Chiltern Society Maps: 7 and 12 Saunderton, map reference SU813982, is in Buckinghamshire, 16km (10 miles) south of Aylesbury.
Toughness: 4 out of 10.

Walk notes: This walk combines a fairly easy stroll in the Chilterns through a mixture of woodland and sloping meadows, with an optional visit to Hughenden Manor and West Wycombe Caves. The route heads south-east over the Chiltern Hills to Bradenham, and continues through Naphill Common and Flagmore Wood to Hughenden Manor. The route from Hughenden heads west across Downley Common to West Wycombe Caves for the recommended tea stop. After a brisk climb from the Caves up to the Dashwood Mausoleum, it is then an easy level stroll back into Saunderton.

Walk options: Directions for the shorter variation are given at the end of the main walk text (*see p43*).

a) Shortening the walk: You may reduce the length of the main walk by over 6km (3.75 miles) to 9.3km (5.8 miles) by following the main walk directions as given until [2]. Then follow the Short walk directions and pick up the main walk directions at [8].

Other options: You may combine the Saunderton via West Wycombe short walk with the Saunderton via Bledlow short walk (see Walk 2) for an 18.3-km (11.4-mile) walk. This combined walk takes the form of a figure of 8. With plenty of refreshment stops along the way, you may choose to start with either walk.

You can increase the length of the main walk by 9km (5.6 miles) to 25km (15.6 miles) by combining it with the Saunderton via Bledlow short walk. For the more ambitious, the walk may be lengthened by over 17km (10.6 miles) to 33.3km (20.8 miles) by combining it with the Saunderton via Bledlow main walk. Both of these longer walks take the form of a figure of 8. You can start with either walk – there are plenty of refreshment stops along the way.

Saunderton via West Wycombe Circular

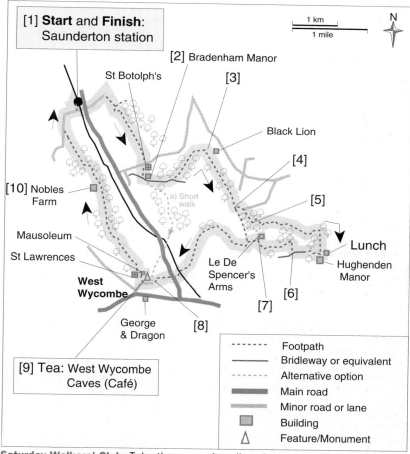

[1] Start and **Finish**:
Saunderton station

St Botolph's

[2] Bradenham Manor

[3]

Black Lion

[4]

[5]

a) Short walk

[10] Nobles Farm

Mausoleum

St Lawrences

West Wycombe

Le De Spencer's Arms

Lunch

Hughenden Manor

[6]

[7]

[8]

George & Dragon

[9] Tea: West Wycombe Caves (Café)

1 km
1 mile

N

- - - - - - Footpath
———— Bridleway or equivalent
- - - - - - Alternative option
████ Main road
████ Minor road or lane
▉ Building
△ Feature/Monument

Saturday Walkers' Club: Take the train nearest to 9.45am (before or after). For the short walk, take the train nearest to 10.15am.

Walk directions

[1] [Numbers refer to the map]
Coming off the London train on platform 2 at **Saunderton station**, go into the station car park and *turn left* down Station Approach to reach a T-junction after 120 metres. *Turn left down Slough Lane, passing under the railway bridge*, your direction 80 degrees.

In 80 metres you *reach the T-junction with the A4010. Cross over* and go along the right-hand side of Smalldean Lane, your initial direction 50 degrees. *After 150 metres* cross the goods entrance road to Janssen-Cilag Ltd on your right, then *turn right off the road and continue for 50 metres across a grass area towards a wooden gate*, your direction 60 degrees.

Go through the gate into a field and follow the permissive footpath round to the left (it runs parallel to Smalldean Lane on your left). In 300 metres you *reach a double metal fieldgate on your left. Turn right* to go along the permissive path across the field, your direction 140 degrees. In 350 metres follow the path to the right around the edge of a wood, then in 50 metres *go through a wide gap in the hedgerow into the next field and turn left uphill*, your direction 70 degrees.

In 40 metres go through a wooden kissing gate and continue up the left-hand edge of the field, in the same direction. *At the top corner of the field ignore a wooden kissing gate and follow the footpath round to the right*, along the top left-hand edge of the field, your direction south. After 300 metres, at the corner of the field, go through a wooden kissing gate to the right of a wooden fieldgate and continue straight ahead, your direction 140 degrees. After 20 metres you pass a 'No Riding' National Trust (NT) sign on your left. You are now on a car-wide earth track.

Continue down the track. In 350 metres you cross another car-wide earth track into the next field and pass three interlinked benches on your left. After 400 metres you cross a stile and continue straight ahead, your direction 160 degrees. In 30 metres cross another stile to the right of a wooden fieldgate, which takes you onto a car-wide earth track.

After 70 metres you *pass the entrance to Bradenham YHA on your left and come out onto Bradenham Woods Lane, with the church opposite*. Cross the road and *veer right along the tarmac footpath alongside the church wall*. In 30 metres you reach the lychgate entrance to the parish church of **St Botolph's, Bradenham**. If not visiting the church, continue straight ahead, your direction 190 degrees. After 50 metres you pass the entrance to Bradenham Manor on your left, with a 2 metre-high brick wall surrounding its grounds on your left.

15th-century houses in **West Wycombe**.

In 130 metres *bear left to join a car-wide earth bridleway*, your direction 120 degrees, and go up the bridleway, with the stone wall of Bradenham Manor still on your left. After 180 metres at the south walled corner of Bradenham Manor **[2]**, the bridleway curves round to the left.

[If you are intending to take the short walk refer to the **Short walk directions** at the end of this main section.]

Otherwise, for the main walk, *ignore a narrow earth footpath going straight ahead, marked by a white arrow on a tree, to keep left. After 7 metres the bridleway forks. Take the right-hand fork* up an initially tarmac car-wide track into a wooded area, your initial direction 60 degrees.

In 150 metres a car-wide earth track merges from the left. After a further 100 metres you emerge from the wooded area into a small opening. Continue straight ahead along what is now a car-wide shingle track, your direction east. **[!]** In 160 metres, *as the shingle track curves round to the right, turn half left across grass, your direction 40 degrees. After 15 metres you reach a bridleway path post with two blue bridleway arrows; take the right-hand fork*, your initial direction 30 degrees.

After 30 metres the path forks. Take the unmarked footpath half right, your direction 80 degrees. In 40 metres ignore a minor path forking off to the left, and continue along this footpath (which is parallel to the bridleway 30 metres to the right). After 35 metres you enter a wooded area. In 40 metres you *reach a path junction to bear half left*, your direction 50 degrees. In 25 metres you pass an electricity pylon pole on your left at the start of a mini pylon cable run.

Continue along the footpath that follows the route of mini pylon cables overhead. After 140 metres you pass under the mini pylon cables and continue straight ahead. In 20 metres, with a mini pylon cable post on your right-hand side, at the point where the pylon cables go off to the left, keep left and continue along the permissive path under the mini pylon cables, your direction 10 degrees.

After 80 metres along the path below the cables you pass a pond on your left. In 180 metres, still following the permissive path under the cables, you skirt to the right of another pond (often dried up in summer) and continue in the same direction, following the mini pylon cables. In 80 metres you pass a 'Bradenham' NT sign off to your left and follow the less distinct path, still under the cables, your direction 30 degrees (ignore a better defined path to your right). In 120 metres *you pass a mini electricity pylon pole on your right with a transformer box mounted halfway up; continue along the path tracking the cables*, your direction 20 degrees.

In 30 metres you leave the route of the mini pylon cables as the path turns off to the right into a wood, your initial direction 60 degrees. *After 50 metres you reach an unmarked path crosspaths. Turn half left* towards some wooden fieldgates at the entrance to a small yard, your direction 20 degrees. In 50 metres you *come out onto a car-wide earth track*, with the gates to your left leading into the small yard. *Turn right* along a car-wide earth track, your initial direction 120 degrees. After 100 metres you pass some houses on your left on the edge of Naphill; after a further 30 metres you *reach a two-armed public bridleway signpost.* **[3]**

If you are not intending to take the earlier lunch stop at the Black Lion, turn right, your direction 210 degrees, and pick up the directions at the asterisk **[*]** below. Otherwise, *for the earlier lunch stop, turn left, your direction 50 degrees. In 20 metres, at a three-armed footpath signpost, turn right* along a car-wide earth track, with houses to your left, your direction 150 degrees. *After 100 metres turn left* through a wooden gate leading into the garden of the **Black Lion**. After lunch, retrace your steps back to the two-armed public bridleway signpost [3].

[*] Go down the car-wide earth track, back into the woods, your initial direction 210 degrees. *After 70 metres, at a crosspaths, turn left*, marked by a path post with a blue arrow, your initial direction 130 degrees. (In muddy conditions you may prefer to take the intermittent official – unmarked – footpath 20 metres to the left; if you do this, ensure that you always keep sight of the bridleway, as this footpath meanders considerably and sometimes peters out.)

Follow this path for 1.4km (0.9 miles) until you reach a car-wide shingle track at [4] *below.*

In more detail: After 250 metres you go over a crosspaths. Continue straight ahead, ignoring any turnings off, your direction 160 degrees. In 500 metres you pass a footpath post on your right with blue bridleway arrows. After a further 200 metres you pass another footpath post; follow the blue arrow pointing straight on, your direction 150 degrees. In 300 metres you pass another footpath post on your left with a blue arrow pointing straight ahead and a yellow arrow pointing to the left. Continue forward, your direction 140 degrees.

After 60 metres ignore a fork to the right and go over a crosspaths, your direction 130 degrees; after 10 metres you pass a pond on your right. In 60 metres you pass under some mini pylon cables and in 20 metres reach a car-wide shingle track. [4] *Turn half left*, your initial direction 140 degrees. In 120 metres you pass the entrance to Rose Cottage on your left. After 60 metres *the lane curves to the left by a car turning area; leave the lane and continue straight on to the left of a redundant metal kissing gate into a wood*, your direction 120 degrees.

After 4 metres the footpath forks. [!] *Take the right fork*, your initial direction 130 degrees. In 80 metres you continue straight ahead, marked by a white arrow on a tree to your right, your direction 160 degrees. Follow the white arrows on the

trees. (Don't divert off to the larger path and clearing on your right.)

[!] In 100 metres there is an *easily missed yellow footpath arrow pointing left on the tree to your left.* [5] *Turn left* (just after the white arrow on a tree pointing straight ahead) your initial direction 50 degrees. After 7 metres continue straight ahead, indicated by a yellow footpath arrow on a tree on your left. Continue along this path, marked by faint and not-so-faint white blobs on the trees.

[!] After 60 metres, *where the footpath forks, take the right-hand fork*, your initial direction 60 degrees. Follow the path round for 30 metres and go through a metal kissing gate out of the wood and into a field. Continue for 60 metres down the right-hand edge of the field and *through another kissing gate to enter Flagmore Wood.* [!] *After 3 metres turn left to take a footpath downhill, near the left-hand edge of the wood.*

After 80 metres go through another metal kissing gate, *cross over a car-wide earth track and continue straight ahead uphill*, marked by a footpath signpost to Hughenden Manor, your direction east. In 5 metres you pass a 'Hughenden Estate, Flagmore Wood' NT sign on your left; *after 10 metres turn left up a permissive path*, your initial direction 30 degrees. *The path follows the edge of the wood.* In 250 metres you *reach the corner of the field on your left. Follow the footpath round to the left*, your direction 40 degrees.

After 40 metres you go over a crosspaths and in 60 metres turn left over a stile to leave Flagmore Wood. *Turn right* along the right-hand edge of the field, with Flagmore Wood on your right, your initial direction 120 degrees. In 60 metres, at the corner of the field, cross another stile and continue straight ahead. In 120 metres ignore a stile on your right leading back into Flagmore Wood and continue straight ahead along the footpath diagonally across a field. The footpath now diverges from the edge of the wood, but your direction is still 120 degrees.

West Wycombe Caves Café.

On the far side of the field *go through a metal gate and across a car-wide track to go through another metal gate*. Follow the permissive path across the field, your direction 80 degrees. Having crossed the field *go through a wooden kissing gate and continue down a footpath through Woodcock Wood*, your direction east. *After 80 metres you reach a crosspaths. Turn right*, marked by a blue woodland walk NT arrow on a footpath post, your direction 190 degrees.

After 300 metres go straight over a crosspaths, marked by a footpath post '2' on your left, your direction 210 degrees. In 30 metres, *at a footpath T-junction,*

turn left, your direction 170 degrees. After 30 metres you *come out to a car parking area. Continue straight ahead down through the car parking area*, your direction 170 degrees.

After 70 metres you pass an NT Hughenden Manor Estate notice board on your right; *continue straight ahead down a tarmac lane*. After 120 metres you pass through some wooden bollards. In 10 metres the lane curves to the left and 10 metres further on you pass by a wooden bollard. The **NT tearoom** is immediately to the left. After 20 metres, where the lane curves to the right, you reach the house and garden entrance to **Hughenden Manor**.

To continue the walk, *turn right outside the entrance to Hughenden Manor and follow the lane,* your direction 260 degrees. In 50 metres, *at a footpath signpost, continue straight down through a wood* along a bridleway marked to Downley. After an initial right-hand turn the path straightens out, your direction 330 degrees.

In 100 metres go straight over a crosspaths and continue down the bridleway. In 200 metres you *come out of the wood; continue on the level along a car-wide earth bridleway* between fences acting as a field boundary, your initial direction 280 degrees. In 350 metres you *reach wooden fieldgates on your left and right.* **[6]** *Turn right* through a metal gate to the left of the wooden fieldgate to go across the field, your direction 350 degrees.

Having crossed the field go through a metal gate by a wooden field gate. In 15 metres turn left at a crosspaths and go uphill along the left edge of a wood, your direction 240 degrees. Follow the white arrows on trees for 260 metres until you reach a footpath junction, marked by a footpath post on your right by a ditch. Continue forwards, marked by one of the yellow footpath arrows, your initial direction 230 degrees.

After 25 metres continue straight ahead as indicated by a white arrow on a tree on your left, your direction 240 degrees. After 80 metres *you reach a tree on your left with a white arrow pointing ahead and a white arrow off to the right. Turn half right,* your direction 290 degrees.

In 150 metres you *merge with a footpath from the right to turn half left,* your initial direction 260 degrees. In 10 metres ignore a kissing gate on your right and continue along the footpath. In 40 metres ignore a path to the right. After 20 metres *the path merges with another coming in from the left; keep right and continue up ahead,* your direction 320 degrees.

In 30 metres you *emerge from the wood.* Continue forwards. In 60 metres you go over a crosspaths and, in a further 30

metres, you pass a footpath post on your right with a yellow waymark arrow, your direction 350 degrees. *Fork right to pass through some bollards after 5 metres and turn left onto a shingle lane,* your direction 330 degrees.

After 140 metres you reach a footpath post. **[7]** *If not stopping at the suggested pub lunch stop, pick up the directions at the double asterisk* [**] below. *Otherwise, for the suggested pub lunch stop, continue straight ahead to reach* **Le De Spencer's Arms** *on your right after 130 metres.* After lunch, retrace your steps to the *footpath post* [7] *to turn right.*

[**] *Continue along the lane for 120 metres,* your direction west, ignoring any paths off. *The lane curves to the left* and in 50 metres *turn right by the entrance to a house, indicated by a public footpath signpost.* Go through a metal kissing gate into a field, your direction 290 degrees. Go along the right-hand edge of this field to then go through a metal kissing gate into the next field. Continue along the right-hand edge of this field.

At the corner of the field continue straight ahead, passing a double mini pylon post on your right to go down through a lightly wooded area into a valley, your initial direction 320 degrees. After 140 metres *at the bottom of the hill you reach a crosspaths. Turn left* along the valley bottom, your direction 260 degrees. In 350 metres the path reaches a tarmac lane.

Turn left up the lane. In 200 metres, *where the lane curves to the left, continue straight ahead, leaving the lane along a shingle track,* following a public footpath signpost, your direction 210 degrees.

After 70 metres go over a stile into a field. There is a view of the church of St Lawrence and the Dashwood Mausoleum, West Wycombe, ahead to the right. Go down across the field, your direction 190 degrees. At the bottom of the hill go through a gap in the field boundary and cross over a car-wide track and a stile into the next field. Continue along the right-hand edge of the field, initially uphill, your direction 210 degrees.

On reaching the bottom right-hand corner of the field continue straight on through a clump of trees for 15 metres and then into the next field; continue in the same direction, along the right-hand edge of the field. At the bottom right-hand corner of this field *cross a stile to the left of a metal fieldgate and go under a railway bridge.* Go through a wooden gate into a field and *turn half left and cross the field* to the main road (A4010), your direction 210 degrees.

Cross over the road and the stile opposite and go up the right-hand edge of the field, your direction 260 degrees. *After 200 metres turn right and cross a stile, then turn left* and continue up the left-hand edge of the next field in the same direction. In 150 metres you *reach the top corner of the field.* Continue forwards to the right of a redundant wooden kissing gate, *coming out onto a lane.* **[8]**

Turn left down the lane. After 30 metres the lane forks. If you are not having lunch at the recommended lunch place for the short walk (the George and Dragon Hotel), pick up the directions at the triple asterisk [***] below.

Otherwise, for the recommended lunch stop for the short walk, *continue straight ahead, bearing left down Church Lane.* In 150 metres the lane leads out *under an old house to a T-junction. Cross over the main road and turn right* to the **George and Dragon Hotel**. After lunch, coming out of the George and Dragon, *turn right and go back to the T-junction; turn left and back up Church Lane.* 30 metres before the junction with the upper lane, take the tarmac footpath that forks off to the left. In 40 metres you come out onto a lane and, after a further 50 metres, you *reach the driveway entrance of* **West Wycombe Caves**. Turn right to go up to the gates of the caves. Pick up the directions from [9] below.

[***] *Follow the lane round to the right to reach the driveway entrance of* **West Wycombe Caves** *after 90 metres. Turn right to the gates to the caves.* **[9]** The suggested tea place for the main walk is the **café** immediately past the gates. After tea, *come out of the gates to West Wycombe Caves and turn immediately right* along a footpath with wooden-pole fencing on the right, your direction west.

In 50 metres, *at the end of the fencing, you come out into the open to an unmarked footpath junction where you turn right* up a steep footpath, your direction 330 degrees. After 20 metres the path forks. Take the right fork and *continue up the steep footpath* in the same direction. In 70 metres, *at a path T-junction, turn right up some steps,* your direction 40 degrees.

After 30 metres, *at the top of the steps, turn left* towards the mausoleum and the church of St Lawrence, West Wycombe. At the **Dashwood Mausoleum,** *turn right to pass round the right side of the mausoleum into the churchyard of St Lawrence.*

After visiting the church of **St Lawrence** *turn right along a sand shingle track out of the churchyard.* Continue along the sand shingle track across a car park, your direction 350 degrees. You are heading towards Windyhaugh House, which is partially obscured by evergreens. At the edge of the car park leave the shingle track and cross the grass, continuing in the same direction as before. Go through some wooden bollards *and then bear to the left after 40 metres onto a car-wide earth track.*

From here the remainder of the walk follows this path in a northerly direction for 3km (1.9 miles) to a T-junction with Slough Lane, where you turn right for Saunderton.

In more detail: In 40 metres you pass Windyhaugh House (partially obscured by trees) on your right. After 80 metres you pass a footpath post on your left.

Hellfire!

Few historical figures have been the subject of as much wild and (largely) inaccurate speculation as **Sir Francis Dashwood** (1708-81). A wealthy and prominent public figure of the mid 18th century, Sir Francis built a grand house for himself, West Wycombe Park, in the early 1750s and rose to become Chancellor of the Exchequer and Postmaster General by the 1760s.

However, it was what he supposedly got up to in his spare time that caused his name to became notorious. Dashwood was a lifelong lover of classical architecture and mythology, but also a hard-drinking womaniser, who founded the Society of the Dillettanti to indulge the habits of like-minded aristrocrats (Dashwood had married into the aristocracy).

In 1746 he founded another, more controversial club, the Order of the Knights of St Francis, which was dubbed the Hellfire Club by those who believed that its members practised everything from satanism to drunken orgiastic partying. Yet the club counted such notable figures as the Earl of Sandwich, the Archbishop of Canterbury's son, the artist William Hogarth, the Prince of Wales and possibly Benjamin Franklin and Horace Walpole among its members. Originally the Order met in the George & Vulture public house in Cornhill, London, before moving to Medmenham Abbey, close to Dashwood's Buckinghamshire home.

Continue along this car-wide earth track ignoring any turnings off for the next 850 metres, your direction 330 degrees. When you reach a tree on your right with a white arrow pointing straight ahead, continue straight on, ignoring the fork off to the left after 10 metres, your direction now 350 degrees.

In a further 250 metres go over a crosspaths, marked by a footpath post, your direction 350 degrees. After 500 metres go through a wooden kissing gate, with a sign on it 'Footpath only – no bicycles'. Continue on a slightly narrower track, with a field to your left and woods on your right, your direction 340 degrees.

In the early 1750s Dashwood philanthropically provided work for the unemployed poor in the area in hollowing out **West Wycombe Caves**. Rumour had it that the Caves provided a suitably dramatic backdrop for the Hellfire Club's most outrageous depravities, yet the truth seems to be that Dashwood and his associates were mainly interested in a form of druidical paganism rather than anything as scandalous as sexually fuelled satanism. It seems that the stories of copulating monks and nuns, and the celebration of black masses over the bodies of naked aristocratic women, were the product of overactive imaginations.

The Caves can still be visited – their individual chambers and tunnels reach a quarter of a mile into the hillside, and include the massive Banqueting Hall, the Miners' Cave, the River Styx, and the Inner Temple, which is nearly 300 feet underground.

West Wycombe Caves
High Wycombe, HP14 3AJ (01494 533739/www.hellfire caves.co.uk). **Open** *Mar-Oct* 11am-5.30pm daily. *Nov-Feb* 11am-5.30pm Sat, Sun & bank hols. **Admission** £4; £3 concessions. **Credit** MC, V.

In 200 metres you pass the entrance to Nobles Farm **[10]** on your left as the track becomes a tarmac lane. After 500 metres the field on your left ends and you enter woodland, your direction 300 degrees. After 280 metres you go over a diagonal crosspaths, with a four-armed footpath signpost on your right, and

continue down the lane for a further 500 metres until you *reach a T-junction. Cross a stile to the left of a metal fieldgate and turn right onto Slough Lane,* your direction north.

In 240 metres *the lane curves sharply to the right; continue down the lane* for a further 280 metres until you reach the T-junction with Station Approach. For the suggested tea place for the short walk and late tea place for the main walk, continue straight on under the railway bridge for 80 metres to the T-junction with the main road. *Turn right* to walk the short distance to the **Golden Cross** (*see p33*). After tea, retrace your steps to Station Approach and make your way back up to **Saunderton station.**

Walk options

a) Short walk directions:
Follow main walk directions to [2].

At the walled corner of Bradenham Manor **[2]**, do not go round to the left along the car-wide track. Instead *fork to the right up the narrow footpath to enter a wood,* marked by a white arrow on the tree to the right at the start of the footpath, your initial direction 110 degrees.

In 15 metres continue straight ahead, following a white arrow on a tree. In 40 metres the footpath curves round to the right, as indicated by a white arrow on a tree. After 12 metres you pass a tree on your right with an arrow pointing ahead, your direction 170 degrees. **[!]** In 7 metres, *where the footpath forks, take the right-hand fork,* your direction 190 degrees.

Continue to *follow the white footpath arrows for the next 180 metres to then veer right as the narrow footpath joins a car-wide earth track,* your direction 130 degrees. In 140 metres continue straight ahead to follow the white arrow on a tree to your left along the car-wide earth track as it starts to go downhill, your direction 120 degrees.

In 50 metres you go over an unmarked crosspaths to start going uphill as the car-wide track narrows down to a metre width, your direction 140 degrees. After 140 metres you *pass a tree on your left with a white left-veering arrow and come out to a path T-junction after 7 metres. Turn left up a car-wide earth track*, your direction 130 degrees.

After 90 metres the car-wide earth track forks, marked by a two-way arrow on the tree just beyond the junction. Take the right-hand fork, your direction 190 degrees. [!] *In 350 metres, as the path curves round to the left, take the easily missed narrow footpath forking off to the right*, your direction south, marked after 5 metres by a white arrow on a small tree to the left of the narrow footpath.

In 200 metres you go over a crosspaths to continue straight on as the narrow footpath widens to a car-wide earth track and starts a gradual descent, your direction 170 degrees. After 60 metres *ignore the car-wide track as it forks downhill to the right and continue straight ahead on the narrow path*. In 10 metres you pass a tree on the left with a faint white arrow pointing ahead. In 40 metres the downhill gradient becomes steeper, your direction south.

Continue following the occasional white footpath arrows downhill as it becomes more densely wooded. After 300 metres the footpath continues downhill between fences. In 140 metres *you go through a metal gate to emerge from the woods* and then go down some steps *to cross the railway*. Descend some more steps and go through a second metal gate. *Turn half left across a field*, your direction 200 degrees.

Having crossed the field pass round to the left of a redundant squeezegate to *cross the main road* and then pass round to the left of another redundant squeezegate. *Turn half left up across a field*, your direction 200 degrees. After 500 metres, *at the top edge of the field, bear left* to continue along the top right-hand edge, indicated by a footpath post. In 100 metres, *at the top corner of the field, turn right and go round to the right* of a redundant wooden kissing gate *to come out onto a lane*.

You now follow the main walk directions from [8].

Lunch & tea places

Black Lion *Woodlands Drive, Naphill, HP14 4SH (01494 563176)*. **Open** noon-11.30pm Mon-Sat; noon-10.30pm Sun. **Food served** noon-2pm, 6.30-9.30pm daily. The Black Lion is located 4km (2.5 miles) from the start of the walk, and it provides a useful alternative early lunch stop.

George & Dragon Hotel *High Street, West Wycombe, HP14 3AB (01494 464414)*. **Open** 11am-2.30pm, 5.30-11pm Mon-Fri; 11am-3pm, 5.30-11pm Sat; noon-2.30pm, 7-11pm Sun. **Food served** noon-2pm, 6-9.30pm Mon-Sat; noon-2pm, 7-9pm Sun. The George & Dragon is the suggested lunch stop if taking the Short walk option; it's 5km (3 miles) from the start of this walk.

Hughenden Manor Stables Restaurant *Hughenden Manor, High Wycombe, HP14 4LA (01494 755576)*. **Open/food served** *Apr-Nov* noon-5pm Wed-Sun. *Nov-Mar* noon-5pm Sat, Sun. Located 7.5km (4.7 miles) from the start of the walk.

Le De Spencer's Arms *The Common, Downley, HighWycombe, HP13 5YQ (01494 535317)*. **Open** noon-3.30pm, 6-11.30pm Mon-Fri; noon-11pm Sat, Sun. **Food served** noon-2pm Mon-Thur, Sun; noon-2pm, 7-9pm Fri, Sat. Do book ahead if you want to eat at this pub, situated 9km (5.6 miles) from the start of the walk. This is the suggested lunch stop for the main walk.

West Wycombe Caves Café *West Wycombe Park, West Wycombe, HP14 3AJ (01494 533739)*. **Open** *Mar-Oct* 11am-5.30pm daily. *Nov-Feb* 11am-5.30pm Sat, Sun. This is the suggested tea stop, and is found at the entrance to the caves.

Chesham to Great Missenden

Through the Chilterns via Lee Common.

Start: Chesham station
Finish: Great Missenden station

Length: 15.5km (9.7 miles). For a short walk variation, *see below* **Walk options**.

Time: 4 hours 45 minutes. For the whole outing including trains, sights and meals, allow 8 hours 30mins.

Transport: The Metropolitan Line underground runs frequently to Chesham, changing at Chalfont and Latimer (journey time: 51 minutes from Baker Street). Trains back from Great Missenden to Marylebone run twice an hour (hourly on Sunday; journey time: 45 minutes).

If driving, it is recommended that you leave your car at Chalfont and Latimer station and catch the Metropolitan line one stop to Chesham. The return from Great Missenden is two stops to Chalfont and Latimer station (London-bound service).

OS Landranger Map: 165
OS Explorer Map: 181
Chiltern Society Maps: 3, 8 and 17 (most of the walk is on 17) Chesham, map reference SP961016, is in Buckinghamshire, 17km (11 miles) south-east of Aylesbury.

Toughness: 3 out of 10.

Walk notes: This walk makes for an easy day out from London. It starts in Chesham, the hustle and bustle of which is soon left behind for sloping fields, woods and hamlets. The route follows the Chilterns Link, but diverts at Herberts Hole to take a higher, southerly path. It then picks up the Chilterns Link again through to Ballinger Bottom and Lee Common, and so to lunch in the charming village called The Lee. After lunch the walk continues on a gently undulating course, before a gentle climb through woods up to Frith Hill and down a steep descent into Great Missenden.

Walk options: Directions for the shorter variation are given at the end of the main walk text (*see* p53).

a) Shorter walk: You may reduce the length of the main walk by 6km (3.75 miles) to 9.5km (5.9 miles) by following the main walk directions given until [5]. Then follow the directions before picking up the main walk directions again at [9].

Saturday Walkers' Club: Take the Metropolitan underground train nearest to 9.50am (before or after) from Baker Street underground station to Chesham, changing at Chalfont and Latimer.

Walk directions

[1] [Numbers refer to the map]
Coming out of **Chesham station** go straight ahead for 30 metres and then *turn left down Station Road*, your direction 290

degrees. In 80 metres, *at the bottom of Station Road, turn right* onto the Broadway, your direction 10 degrees. After 40 metres *turn left at the war memorial*. In 30 metres you pass the Broadway Baptist Church on your left. After a further 70 metres *cross over a zebra crossing to the left of a main roundabout.* Continue straight up a tarmac path *to enter a park.*

In 40 metres, *just past a small brick building on your right, turn left* along a car-wide tarmac path. Below on your left-hand side is Scottowe's Pond. After 250 metres, at the end of the car-wide tarmac path (with the church of **St Mary** further ahead), *turn right up a tarmac path* and follow a footpath signpost to Lower Pednor and Chartridge, your direction 290 degrees.

In 70 metres you pass Chesham Guides hut on your right. In another 40 metres, *immediately after passing the entrance to Chesham Bowling Club on your right, leave the tarmac path to go up a parallel earth footpath to the left.* In 80 metres you pass a footpath signpost on your right with a footpath arrow marked Chiltern Link and come out into a field. Continue straight ahead in the same direction along the left-hand edge of the field, with woods to your left. In muddy conditions you may prefer to veer right up the field and continue along the clearly defined path that runs about 40 metres parallel to the lower path.

After 500 metres, where the field comes to an end, head down into a lightly wooded area, your direction 300 degrees. After 80 metres *go over a stile* **[2]** *to take a footpath* marked by a footpath signpost arm 'Footpath – Radnor Road' *half left diagonally down across a field,* your direction 280 degrees. In 120 metres go through a wooden kissing gate and *cross a lane* to go through a second wooden kissing gate. *Take the left fork marked by a Chiltern Link signpost,* diagonally across a field, in the same direction 280 degrees.

In 250 metres go through a wooden kissing gate and veer left to cross a field, your direction due west. In 120 metres go over a stile to the right of a metal fieldgate and *turn right along a lane,* marked by a Chiltern Link signpost. *After 80 metres, just past a double wooden fieldgate, turn left up a bridleway,* marked by a metal bridleway signpost **[3]** (partially hidden by foliage in summer), your initial direction 280 degrees.

In 80 metres the bridleway enters a cutting and ascends more steeply. After 350 metres you pass double wooden fieldgates to your left and right as the bridleway levels out and runs parallel to a car-wide track on the left. (In muddy conditions it may be preferable to walk along this track.)

After 600 metres the bridleway comes out onto a car-wide track. Ignore a car-wide track down to the right and continue straight ahead. In 550 metres you pass Barnwood Farm on your right. Just beyond the farm pass to the left of a wooden gate and continue along a tarmac lane. After 500 metres, *at a T-junction with a white house (Little Hundred Orchard) on the left, turn right along a lane.*

In 60 metres ignore a footpath off to the left and continue slightly downhill. In 180 metres you pass a public footpath signpost on your left at the entrance to Redding's Farm. After a further 30 metres *turn right to enter a wood through a metal-chained squeezegate,* marked by a metal public footpath signpost. Go down through the wood, your initial direction 30 degrees. In 200 metres *leave the wood via another metal-chained squeezegate.* **[4]** *Turn left* along a car-wide earth track, your direction due west.

In 220 metres you *come out onto a lane* with a footpath signpost marked 'Chiltern Link' on your right. Follow this signpost to continue in the same direction along the lane, passing Wild Woods Cottage on your right.

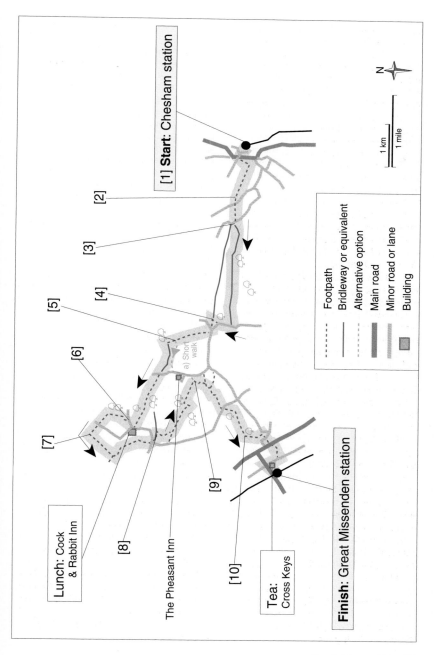

N

1 km
1 mile

..... Footpath
— Bridleway or equivalent
- - - - Alternative option
Main road
Minor road or lane
Building

[1] **Start**: Chesham station

[2]

[3]

[4]

[5]

[6]

a) Short walk

[7]

Lunch: Cock & Rabbit Inn

[8]

The Pheasant Inn

[9]

[10]

Tea: Cross Keys

Finish: Great Missenden station

In 40 metres turn right, marked by a Chiltern Link signpost to your left, and cross over a stile to go uphill along a fenced-in footpath, your initial direction 10 degrees. After 150 metres turn right over a stile (following a black arrow) and then left. In 130 metres, where the footpath joins a shingle lane, continue along in the same direction.

In 50 metres, *where the lane curves right, turn left across a stile* to the right of a metal fieldgate. *In 10 metres* pass a pond (often dried up in summer) on your right, and *turn right* to pass to the left of a redundant stile. *Continue along the right-hand edge of a field,* with a hedgerow on your right, your direction 350 degrees. In 260 metres go over into the next field, still with a hedgerow on your right. In 250 metres, at the right-hand corner of this field, *you reach a wooden kissing gate with footpath arrows ahead and to the left on its left post.* **[5]**

[If you are intending to take the shortened walk refer to the **Shorter walk directions** at the end of this main section.]

Otherwise, for the main walk, go through the kissing gate and continue down the right side of the field. After 50 metres *turn right over a stile to enter Bellows Wood. In 8 metres turn left,* marked by a black arrow on a tree ahead.

Continue down the footpath along the edge of Bellows Wood. *After 100 metres turn left,* indicated by a three-armed metal signpost. Continue along the lower right edge of the field, with a fence on your left. After 300 metres you pass a two-armed metal bridleway signpost on your left and enter a wooded area. Continue straight ahead and slightly downhill, your direction 290 degrees.

In 400 metres, *by a four-armed signpost on your left, continue straight on,* following the direction of the Chiltern Link, with a hedge on your right. Further on the bridleway curves round to the right *to come out to a junction directly in front of Rose Cottage,* **Ballinger Bottom** after 120 metres. *Turn left* along a shingle

car-wide track. After 50 metres you cross a road and a stile on the other side. *Follow a metal signpost for the Chiltern Link,* passing under mini pylon cables *to enter a wood,* your direction 330 degrees.

Continue through this wooded area. In 600 metres go over a stile to the right of a wooden fieldgate and *emerge from the wood into an open field.* This is **Lee Common**. *Continue in the same direction along the left-hand edge* of the field, with a hedgerow and woods on your left. *After 100 metres go through a wooden kissing gate,* passing under mini pylon cables, and continue in the same direction through a wood.

After 280 metres you emerge from the wood and veer right onto a shingle lane, your direction 300 degrees. In 200 metres you pass the entrance to Manor Gardens on your right. After 160 metres you reach a T-junction, with the **Cock and Rabbit Inn**, the recommended lunch stop, directly in front of you.

After lunch, *from the front entrance of the pub turn right* for 10 metres to the corner of the village green and then turn left along the road, your direction 10 degrees. In 35 metres, *at the corner of the green,* you pass the village war memorial on your left and *turn half right along the road signposted Lee Common,* your direction 70 degrees.

After 180 metres, *just past the entrance to some farm buildings, turn left to follow a footpath signpost* **[6]**, your initial direction 30 degrees. In 40 metres go over a stile and continue along the now fenced-in footpath gently downhill. In 100 metres go over a stile and continue in the same direction along the left-hand edge of a field with a hedgerow on your left. After 150 metres, at the left corner of the field, *go over a stile to enter a wood.* Continue along in the same direction along the left edge of the wood.

After 220 metres, *at a footpath junction* with a white arrow to the left and right on a tree ahead, *turn left,* your direction 315 degrees. In 180 metres ignore a stile on

The abbey habit

Great Missenden Abbey was founded in 1133 as a monastic house of the Arroasian (later Augustinian) canons, and in the 12th and 13th centuries was one of the largest Arroasian houses in England, primarily due to the benefactions of William de Missenden. It remained the centre of religious life in Great Missenden until 1538, when the abbey was dissolved under Henry VIII's Act of Suppression and converted into a country residence. Today, it is owned by Buckinghamshire County Council and is largely used by the council as a conference and training centre.

your right and continue straight on for a further 180 metres to *come out to a road. Cross the road and continue along a driveway* marked by a two-armed metal signpost on your right. *In 30 metres*, at the corner of a garden on your right, *veer right along the right-hand edge of the field*, your direction 320 degrees.

In 280 metres, at the right-hand corner of the field, you *enter a wood*. Continue in the same direction, ignoring a stile on your right after 15 metres. After a further 25 metres *turn left in front of a tree with a faint white painted arrow* **[7]**, your direction 230 degrees. In 160 metres you are now on the left edge of the wood with a field beyond.

After 120 metres you *emerge from the wood and cross a car-wide gravel track and a stile, taking you into a field.* Continue along the right edge of the field. In 150 metres you enter a small wooded area. After 20 metres you pass a small pond (often dried up in summer) on your left. In a further 20 metres you emerge from the wooded area. Continue on the footpath along the left edge of a field, your direction 230 degrees.

The **Chilterns**.

In 300 metres, *at the left-hand field corner* by a dilapidated footpath post on your left, *turn left to join the Chiltern Link*. Continue along the left-hand edge of the field with a hedgerow to your left, your direction 150 degrees.

After 140 metres you pass a small wood on your left. Continue along in the same direction, now along the right-hand edge of a field. In 250 metres at the end of the field you *cross a farmyard track* with a three-armed metal footpath post on your right. *In 10 metres go over a stile to the right of a metal fieldgate.* [!] *Continue straight ahead along a footpath running parallel to the upper side of a small embankment* (which acts as a field boundary) *to its right*, aiming just to the right of a clump of trees, your direction 160 degrees. (Ignore the Chiltern Link route diagonally across the field towards the houses to your left.)

After 200 metres cross over a stile, with a black arrow on its right-hand post, and continue in the same direction across a field. In 180 metres, *having crossed the field, turn right* at a white post. Continue *along a field boundary*, heading towards some houses on the far side of the field, your direction 210 degrees. In 250 metres, after crossing the field, the footpath leads out onto a car-wide track and after 35 metres you *come out to a lane. Turn left down the lane*, your direction 110 degrees. *After 60 metres you reach a triangular road junction.*

Cross over the road to take a car-wide bridleway on the other side, marked by a metal public bridleway signpost. Continue on through this tree arbour bridleway, your direction 120 degrees. [!] *After 250 metres* you pass two large wooden sheds on your left, just as *you emerge from the tree arbour. Immediately turn sharp right to cross a stile.* [8] Go along the left edge of a field, with a hedgerow on your left, your initial direction 250 degrees, passing under mini pylon cables after 20 metres. Continue along the footpath as it curves to the left with the hedgerow. [!] *After 200 metres the footpath diverges from the hedgerow to go diagonally across the field.* Head towards a stile to the right of a metal fieldgate in the corner of the field, your direction 140 degrees.

After 180 metres, *at the corner of the field, go over the stile.* Continue straight ahead across a field, *aiming for the right corner of a field jutting onto this field,* marked by a white-topped footpath post, your direction 120 degrees. In 300 metres, *at the corner of the adjacent field* marked by the white-topped footpath post, *pass to the right* of the corner of the adjacent field. Continue in the same direction, *now along the left-hand edge of the field,* with a hedgerow on your left. After 100 metres, at the corner of the field, cross a stile into the next field and continue straight ahead along the left edge of the field.

In 140 metres, at the corner of the field, *cross over a stile and continue straight ahead, crossing over another stile 7 metres further on. Go diagonally across a field, heading towards a wooden mini electricity pylon pole,* your direction east. In 180 metres, *having crossed the field, turn half right along the left-hand edge of the field,* with a hedgerow on your left, your initial direction 120 degrees. In 120 metres cross into the next field, passing a post with a footpath arrow on your left and a derelict stile on your left.

After 250 metres, at the left-hand corner of the field, cross a stile to the right of a metal fieldgate and pass a pond (often dried up in summer) immediately on your right. After 25 metres cross over another stile to the right of a metal fieldgate. Continue along the right-hand edge of a sports field, your direction 130 degrees. In 140 metres, *at the right-hand corner of the sports field, ignore a stile on your left to turn right,* your direction 210 degrees. In 20 metres go over a stile to the left of a metal fieldgate. **[9]**

15 metres further on cross another stile to the left of a metal fieldgate and *continue along the left-hand edge of a field,* your direction 220 degrees. *In 100*

metres cross a stile and turn left along the left-hand edge of a field. *In 25 metres, at the field corner, follow it round to the right,* your direction 190 degrees. *In 100 metres at the field corner cross a stile and turn right.*

Go along this footpath, your initial direction 250 degrees, with a wooden fence on your left, passing under mini pylon electric cables. *In 180 metres, at a wooden fieldgate* (marked 'Private') *on your left, turn right over a stile.*

Go along the left-hand edge of the field, your direction initially west, passing under mini pylon electricity cables after 100 metres. In 120 metres follow the field edge round to the left for 40 metres and then round to the right to resume the previous westerly direction.

After 220 metres, at the left-hand corner of the field, cross over a stile. Continue straight ahead towards a stile on the far side of the field. In 100 metres go over this stile and another after 20 metres before you *cross a road and a stile into a field.* Turn half left to cross the field heading towards a wood, your direction 190 degrees. In 180 metres go over a stile to *enter the wood* to follow a clearly defined footpath.

In 200 metres, at the edge of the wood, follow a white painted arrow on a tree and bear to the right to cross a stile and *emerge from the wood into a field.* Continue straight ahead for 10 metres and then *veer right along the left-hand edge of the field,* your direction 250 degrees. After 180 metres you pass under National Grid electricity cables as the footpath starts to descend.

200 metres further on cross over a stile and carry on downhill, your direction now 240 degrees. In 160 metres the footpath meets a wood on the right-hand side. After 50 metres cross a stile and continue downhill with a fence on your right-hand side.

In 70 metres, at the bottom corner of the field, go through a metal fieldgate. **[10]** (If the fieldgate is closed and locked go over the stile to its right and then after 10 metres the stile on the left)

Continue along the right-hand edge of a wood, with a fence on your right, in the same direction. After 40 metres *follow the footpath as it curves to the left and uphill* along the right-hand edge of the wood.

In 250 metres you *emerge from the wood*. Continue straight ahead along a fenced-in footpath. After 140 metres you *go through a wooden gate* onto a car-wide track and pass the entrance to Frith Hill Stables on your right, with concrete stallion heads on the brick gateposts. *In 30 metres turn right steeply downhill*, marked by a footpath post, your direction 250 degrees.

After 160 metres go through a pedestrian underpass under the A485 to continue downhill in a cutting. In a further 100 metres go through another pedestrian underpass under the A413 to arrive on the outskirts of Great Missenden. In 30 metres veer left along the road to the left-hand side of a green. In 80 metres *at the end of the green continue along the road as it curves to the right*.

After 250 metres you *reach a T-junction with the High Street. Turn right* along the High Street. After 250 metres you reach the **Cross Keys** on your left, the suggested tea stop. In 80 metres *turn left up Station Approach* and after 120 metres you come to **Great Missenden station**.

Walk options

a) Shorter walk directions:
Follow the main walk directions to [5].

Go through the kissing gate and turn left along the top left-hand edge of the field, your direction 260 degrees. After 300 metres, *at the left-hand field corner, go through a wooden kissing gate*. Continue along the footpath, with back gardens behind fencing to the left and woods sloping down to the right, your direction 290 degrees.

In 300 metres, *where the footpath forks* (marked by a wooden footpath post), *take the left fork, slightly uphill*, your direction

250 degrees. In 180 metres *you come out onto Chiltern Road. Turn right to reach a T-junction after 15 metres, where you turn left*, your direction south. After 140 metres you reach the lunch stop, the **Pheasant Inn** on your right.

After lunch, *from the Pheasant Inn* cross over Blackthorne Lane and *continue straight ahead along the left-hand side of a sports field*, your direction 200 degrees, initially passing a children's playground on your left. In 100 metres go through a gap between the hedge on your left and a cricket pavilion on your right. After a further 50 metres, *at the left-hand corner of the sports field, veer slightly left to continue straight ahead*, with a wooden fence on your left, your direction 210 degrees. In 20 metres go over a stile to the left of a metal fieldgate.

You now follow the main walk directions from [9].

Lunch & tea places

Cock & Rabbit Inn *The Lee, HP16 9LZ (01494 837540/www.graziemille.co.uk).* **Open/food served** noon-2.30pm, 6-11pm Mon-Sat; noon-3pm, 7-10.30pm Sun. Located 8km (5 miles) from the start of the walk, the Cock & Rabbit serves decent Italian food. It is the suggested lunch stop for the main walk.

Cross Keys *High Street, Great Missenden, HP16 0AU (01494 865373)* **Open** 11am-11pm Mon-Sat; noon-10.30pm Sun. **Food served** noon-3pm, 7-10pm Mon-Sat; noon-4pm Sun. This pub offers tea and coffee and is the suggested tea place. It also has a well-regarded restaurant should more sustenance be required.

Pheasant Inn *Ballinger Common, HP16 9LF (01494 837236).* **Open/food served** noon-2.30pm, 7-9pm Wed-Sat; noon-2.30pm Sun. Situated 7km (4.4 miles) from the start of the walk, the Pheasant offers inventive, though not cheap, food. It is the suggested lunch stop for those on the short walk.

Picnic: Lee Green, which borders the Cock and Rabbit Inn, and the edge of the sports field opposite the Pheasant Inn make good picnic spots.

Tring Circular

Ivinghoe Beacon and Chiltern woodland.

> **Start and finish**: Tring station
> **Length**: 17.6km (11 miles). For a shorter walk and other variations, *see below* **Walk options**.
> **Time**: 5 hours 30 minutes. For the whole outing, including meals and trains, allow 9 hours.
> **Transport**: Twice hourly trains run between London Euston and Tring (hourly on Sundays; journey time: 41-52 minutes). If driving, park at the large station car park at Tring.
> **OS Landranger Map**: 165
> **OS Explorer Map**: 181
> Tring, map reference SP951122, is in Hertfordshire, 13km (8 miles) east of Aylesbury.
> **Toughness**: 4 out of 10.

Walk notes: The first part of this route – following the Ridgeway along the Chiltern escarpment to Ivinghoe Beacon – is exhilarating, offering downland scenery as fine as anything on the South Downs. From the Beacon itself it seems as if you can see half of England on a fine day. Then, by way of contrast, you are plunged into ancient Chiltern woodland, lovingly preserved by the National Trust. Tea is at a NT kiosk on the Ashridge Estate, or in a tearoom in the stunningly pretty village of Aldbury. The paths are generally pleasant and easy underfoot, but note that on the Ridgeway the chalk paths can be slippery in the wet, and in the woods the paths are often very muddy in winter. All of the climbing is in the first half of the walk: the second half is all flat or downhill.

Walk options: Directions for the following variations are given at the end of the main walk text (*see p61*).

a) **Short cut from Ivinghoe Beacon to the Bridgewater Monument**: This option avoids Little Gaddesden by using a direct route to the Bridgewater Monument, and makes a shorter walk of 13.2km (8.3 miles).

b) **Extension from Aldbury to Berkhamsted**: This pleasant walk through ancient woodland can be used to extend any of the walks by 7.2km (4.5 miles).

c) **Short walk from Tring to Berkhamsted**: This walk goes from Tring direct to Aldbury and then joins the Aldbury to Berkhamsted extension above to make a short walk of 9.5km (5.9 miles).

Saturday Walkers' Club: Take the train nearest to 9am (before or after). If doing the **Short walk**, option **c)** above, take the train nearest to 10.30am.

Walk directions

[1] **[Numbers refer to the map]**
From the platform at **Tring station** *walk up the stairs and turn right along the footbridge*. Walk diagonally across the car park towards its entrance. *Emerging onto the road, turn right* along a pavement on its left-hand side.

In 110 metres ignore a road turning to the left signposted to Pitstone and Ivinghoe. 80 metres further on *turn left onto a concrete farm track signposted 'Ridgeway Bridleway'*, your direction 70 degrees.

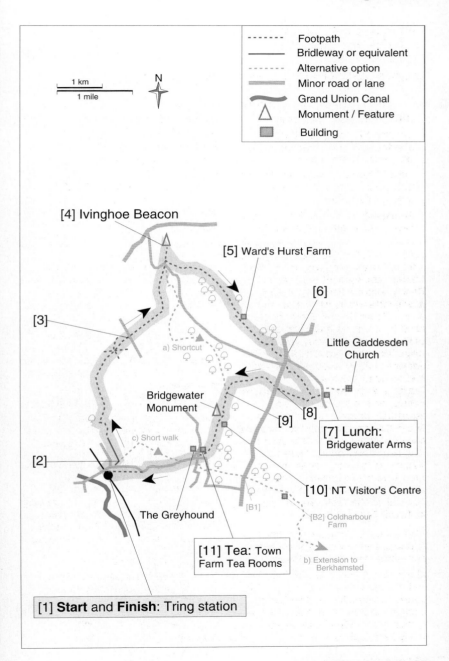

Footpath
Bridleway or equivalent
Alternative option
Minor road or lane
Grand Union Canal
Monument / Feature
Building

1 km
1 mile

N

[4] Ivinghoe Beacon

[5] Ward's Hurst Farm

[6]

[3]

Little Gaddesden
Church

a) Shortcut

Bridgewater
Monument

[9] [8]

[7] Lunch:
Bridgewater Arms

c) Short walk

[2]

The Greyhound

[10] NT Visitor's Centre

[B1]

[B2] Coldharbour
Farm

[11] Tea: Town
Farm Tea Rooms

b) Extension to
Berkhamsted

[1] **Start** and **Finish**: Tring station

The Ridgeway.

You now follow the **Ridgeway** *all the way to Ivinghoe Beacon.*

In more detail: In 50 metres, where the concrete track curves left to a farm, go straight on across the grass towards a white sign in front of a line of trees. *Pass through the metal gate just behind this sign* **[2]** *and turn left at a four-armed footpath sign,* your direction 330 degrees.

You are now on a broad bridleway. *In 500 metres, at a signposted crossroads, go right uphill following the Ridgeway sign,* your direction 10 degrees. In 50 metres pass a wooden barrier and a National Trust sign for Ashridge and Aldbury Nowers.

In 80 metres, just after the path enters the wood, ignore a smaller path to the left that slants back downhill, but in 10 metres *take the next left, once again clearly signposted 'Ridgeway',* your direction 330 degrees. Climb up two flights of wood-supported steps, ignoring a signposted footpath to the left at the top of the first flight.

[!] *At the top of the second flight of steps, turn half left,* your direction 310 degrees, following a yellow arrow and acorn sign on a post, ignoring a path that carries on straight upwards. In 75 metres ignore a smaller path slanting off to the left. In a further 20 metres pass a footpath post and climbs seven steps.

You now stay on this path, ignoring ways off, as it curves gently right up through the woods, and then levels out and descends slightly. In 750 metres *you reach a wooden kissing gate and exit the woods.*

[!] The Ridgeway sign appears to point up the grass slope here, but your onward way is actually the well-defined path more or less straight ahead, your direction 330 degrees, which passes to the right of a large tree and which initially climbs only very slightly. Ignore the footpath to the left of the tree that forks left downhill.

In 25 metres the path passes a low wooden barrier. In 280 metres, after passing two more wooden barriers, it comes out on the top of the ridge.

Go more or less straight on along the grassy top of the ridge, following a blue arrow on a post, your direction 20 degrees. This is **Pitstone Hill**, the first of many fine spots between here and Ivinghoe Beacon for a **picnic**. Ivinghoe Beacon is visible in the distance.

In 250 metres the path curves slightly right towards a low rounded hill 100 metres ahead. Follow the grassy path to the top of this. From the summit of the hill descend directly to the car park below, your direction 50 degrees. Cross the minor road beyond **[3]**.

[!] *The four-armed footpath sign here is confusing, though the route is obvious.* Ignore a Ridgeway sign that points right (also signposted as the Icknield Way Riders Route), *and keep STRAIGHT ON through the kissing gate,* your direction 50 degrees.

Beyond the gate keep straight ahead on a broad path along the right edge of a field, with a barbed-wire fence to your right. (This field used to be arable farmland, as you can see if you look closely: it is now being returned to its original downland state.)

In 500 metres, when the fence ends at a four-armed footpath sign, carry on straight up the hill in front of you on a broad grass path. In 200 metres the path becomes more stony. In 70 metres ignore a footpath sign that points directly up the steep slope ahead to a stile and instead *curve left up the main path on a broad shelf.*

In 100 metres, at the top of the hill, **[!]** *pass to the left of a five-bar gate with a stile to its left* (NOT over the stile or through the gate, as seems more obvious). Follow a distinct path along the very edge of the ridge, with a wire fence to your right. In 50 metres, *just past a gorse bush on your right, ignore a fork to the left to carry straight on,* slightly uphill, towards a wood of low hawthorn trees.

In 80 metres, just before you enter the wood, ignore a stile to the right. In 140 metres, *on the far side of the wood,* ignore a stile 15 metres ahead and instead *go straight on downhill*, keeping the fence on your right. In 70 metres, where your onward way is blocked by a fence, *go right through a kissing gate* on a path that goes uphill briefly before descending in 250 metres to the road.

Cross the road and take the left-hand of the two broad tracks ahead; that is, the one that starts on the left-hand side of the row of low wooden posts, your bearing due north.

In 70 metres, just over a low rise, a broad track forks right. Keep to the left fork, which goes over another hillock and into a dip before the final climb to **Ivinghoe Beacon [4]**. A map set in a stone plinth on the top of the beacon shows the whole 137-km (86-mile) route of the Ridgeway. There is also a trigonometry pillar.

[At this point, you can take option **a)** the **Short cut from Ivinghoe Beacon to the Bridgewater Monument** by following the directions at the end of the main walk text.]

Otherwise, to continue with the main walk: from the Beacon, *turn around and retrace your steps to the bottom of the dip*, your direction due south. Here, *rather than carry on over the next hummock, take the track that skirts it on the left-hand side*, marked by an acorn on a post. In 280 metres go straight across a crossroads with a car-wide track, 30 metres to the left of the road, following yellow and green arrows on a post.

In 40 metres, at another path crossroads, go left over a stile to the left of a rusty metal gate, following a green arrow marking the **Icknield Way**, *which you now follow to Wards Hurst Farm (point [5] below)*. Beyond the stile continue downhill along a broad grassy path, with a wire fence to your right, your direction 120 degrees.

In 120 metres ignore another stile ahead and instead *go right through a fieldgate, afterwards turning immediately sharp left again*, to follow the wire fence, now on

your left. *In 300 metres*, just after you pass another stile on your left, *three grassy paths diverge across an open field. Take the middle path* that contours the hill towards a footpath post 120 metres away, your direction 100 degrees.

At the footpath post ignore paths left and right and *keep straight on for a further 100 metres to a kissing gate to the left of a fieldgate*. Pass through the gate (marked with yellow and green arrows) and follow a broad car-wide track into a wood. In 450 metres the track plunges into a dense plantation of fir trees, still following yellow and green arrows, your direction 160 degrees.

After 120 metres in the fir trees *the path veers half left* to cross one row of pines before resuming its former direction along another avenue of trees. *In 40 metres it repeats the same trick*, veering half left and resuming its former direction.

In another 40 metres the path veers half left again and emerges into a more open area. There is a wooden fence of you. *Veer half right to follow the edge of the wood.* In 170 metres, 30 metres after a footpath post, *ignore a track forking right and instead keep more or less straight ahead* up the steep slope ahead on an initially indistinct path, with a wire fence to your left. Near the top of the hill small wooden steps confirm that you are on the right route.

As the slope eases the high wire fence to the left gives way to a lower barbed-wire one. 100 metres later cross a stile and walk straight ahead towards a rather ugly array of industrial farm buildings. This is **Wards Hurst Farm [5]**

In 50 metres, just before the buildings, turn right following a green arrow on a post (indicating the Ashridge Estate Boundary Trail). Pass a big cylindrical metal tank on your left and, in 70 metres, *just before you get to a corrugated metal barn, turn left following an arrow on a post.*

In 30 metres *turn left just before a high brick wall*, following a green arrow, through a gap between two brick farm

The view from **Ivinghoe Beacon**.

buildings and into a yard. *Turn sharp right here over a stile* and veer slightly left across the field beyond, your direction 130 degrees, to cross another a stile to the right of a metal gate in its left-hand corner.

Go straight across two more fields and stiles in the same direction. Beyond the second stile *converge with the edge of the wood to your left*. In 200 metres cross a stile to carry on along a car-wide earth track, still following the wood's edge. In 150 metres cross another stile and continue to keep to the edge of the wood.

You are now approaching a waterworks surrounded by a green mesh fence. *Cross a stile to the left of this*, still with the wood edge to your left, and keep straight on down an enclosed path. In 40 metres, *when the fence to your right ends, turn right*, your direction 170 degrees. In 50 metres you emerge onto a concrete car-wide track and, 20 metres beyond this, *turn left through a gate into a field*.

Turn half right across the field, your direction 140 degrees, following a yellow footpath arrow towards a white house with battlements in the distance. On the

far side of the field pass through a gate to emerge on the road, the B4506. **[6]**

Turn right along the road into the hamlet of **Ringshall**. Pass some pretty brick cottages on the right and in 120 metres ignore a road to the right signposted to Ivinghoe and Marsworth. *25 metres beyond this*, just after a driveway leading to a pumping station on the left side of the road, *turn left along a footpath to Little Gaddesden*, your direction 150 degrees.

In 10 metres pass through a kissing gate and go straight on, with the fence of a large garden to your left. In 150 metres follow the fence as it curves left towards a line of trees. *In 75 metres, where the garden ends at the line of trees, go right across a stile*, your direction 150 degrees. In 200 metres the path becomes a car-wide gravel track and then a concrete drive, and you pass a house to the right called Witchcraft Hill.

In 150 metres pass through a dark wooden fieldgate. *180 metres beyond this there is a slatted wooden fence on the left. Where the fence ends turn left at a four-*

armed footpath sign up a path which leads in 140 metres into the car park of the **Bridgewater Arms**, Little Gaddesden, the recommended lunch stop **[7]**. (Note that if you turn left a short way along the road in front of the pub you come to a **post office** that sells snack lunch items.)

An optional detour after lunch is to **Little Gaddesden Church**, which is set in the fields behind the village and contains the tomb of the Duke of Bridgewater. To get to it, *turn right out of the pub* along the road. *In 200 metres turn right onto a footpath and immediately fork right* towards the church, visible 400 metres ahead. Return to the Bridgewater Arms after visiting the church to continue the walk.

Otherwise, coming out of the pub *cross the road into the car park* and retrace the path that you came up before lunch: that is, go through a V-shaped stile and down a fenced path, which later passes between the gardens of houses.

In 140 metres cross a car-wide concrete track and go straight ahead down a path between gradually narrowing hedges. In 60 metres this passes three wooden posts and, in a further 60 metres, you emerge into woods.

Ignore a signposted path straight ahead and instead *go half right*, your direction initially 310 degrees, following a footpath that in 100 metres comes up alongside a golf course. Keep just inside the woods, with the golf course to your left and gardens to your right.

Ignore ways off and in 550 metres this path *brings you back to the main road, the B4506* **[8]**. *Cross straight over and carry on up a broad green pathway* through the heart of the woods.

In 100 metres ignore ways to the left and right, and in 50 metres do the same again: green arrows on posts point straight on. In another 250 metres another post has green arrows pointing ahead and right, but *go half left along another broad ride between trees*, your direction 270 degrees.

In 280 metres, just after a path merges from the right, ignore a fork left. 20

Water works

The most famous owner of the Ashridge Estate, across which much of the afternoon section of this walk passes, was Francis, 3rd Duke of Bridgewater (1736-1803). Known as the 'Canal Duke', his pioneering work in inland waterways is commemorated in the **Bridgewater Monument**, erected in 1832.

In 1759 Bridgewater employed engineer James Brindley to build Britain's first canal (which became known as the Bridgewater Canal) to transport coal from his mines in Worsley in Lancashire ten miles to Manchester (and later on to the Mersey). On its completion the price of coal in Manchester halved overnight. Brindley's innovation – a technique called 'puddling' – enabled the canal to travel in an aqueduct across the Irwell river valley. The aqueduct became the wonder of the age, and sparked a canal-building boom that lasted until the advent of the railways in the 1830s. Bridgewater himself is buried in the church of Little Gaddesden.

You can climb the Bridgewater Monument for fine views over the surrounding countryside (Apr-Oct 1-5pm Sat, Sun & bank hols). Ask in the tea kiosk opposite to get access if the tower is not open during these hours (it depends on how many volunteers the Trust has available on any given day).

metres after this, at a post with two green arrows on it, go straight ahead, ignoring broad paths left and right. In 150 metres go straight on at a path crossroads, your direction still 270 degrees. *In another 170 metres at a footpath post go left on a broad path, ignoring an arrow pointing straight ahead,* your direction 200 degrees. In 250 metres you come to *a junction with a car-wide gravel track, where you go left* **[9]**.

Stay on this path, ignoring all ways off, in 260 metres crossing a wooden bridge over a gully. 300 metres after this you come to the tall column of the **Bridgewater Monument** (*see below* **Water works**). Cross the green space to the wooden building ahead, which is the National Trust's **Ashridge Estate Visitors Centre**, which has some informative exhibitions about the surrounding area, and a **tea kiosk**, the first of two possible tea stops **[10]**.

Coming away from the tea kiosk, with the serving hatch behind you and the monument half right ahead, *turn left along a broad stony driveway* flanked on the right by parking spaces, your direction 220 degrees. *In 140 metres the parking area ends and a car-wide bridleway starts to descend the hill,* marked by a green metal bridleway sign to the left and green and blue arrows on a post to the right.

Ignoring all ways off on this bridleway brings you to the village of Aldbury.

But in more detail: *in 30 metres ignore a fork to the left* marked 'No Horses'. For the next 200 metres ignore other paths right and left until *you come to a major fork in the bridleway. Keep right downhill here,* your direction 210 degrees.

Again ignore ways off and in 200 metres the bridleway descends into a cutting. In 60 metres you pass houses on the left and *in 150 metres more you come to a tarmac road, where you turn right.*

In 70 metres you arrive in the centre of **Aldbury**, with a village pond ahead to your right, and the **Aldbury Village Store** to your left. **[11]** *Turn right on the road*

just before the pond and in 100 metres you come to **Town Farm Tea Rooms**, which is in the brick-and-timber beam building on the right, just past the **Greyhound Inn** on your left (which is a possible alternative if the tearoom is closed).

[At this point you can take option **b)** the **Extension from Aldbury to Berkhamsted** by following the directions at the end of the main walk text.]

After tea, *coming out of the tearoom, turn left* and walk back to the crossroads by the village pond. *Turn right beyond the pond, following a sign to Tring and Tring station.* In 100 metres you come to the churchyard on your right.

20 metres beyond the end of the churchyard ignore a footpath signed to the right, but in 40 metres, *10 metres before the road curves sharp right, go left through a metal kissing gate,* following a green footpath sign. *Turn right immediately to follow the hedge,* your direction 230 degrees initially.

In 150 metres the hedge ends and you are on a path along the verge of the road, with a wooden fence and an earth track on your left. In 100 metres the wooden fence becomes a white metal one for 70 metres or so. Where the fence ends veer left inside the field boundary, following a yellow arrow on a footpath post. Descend the hill, keeping the field boundary (an intermittent hedge) to your immediate right.

In 200 metres, at the bottom of the field, go through a gap in the hedge and cross a signposted bridleway. 20 metres later *turn half right through a gap in the fence to carry on diagonally across the field* on a permissive footpath towards its far corner. The white hotel just beyond Tring station can be seen ahead. At night, head for the right-hand end of the orange lights of Tring station. In 600 metres you reach the far corner of the field and the entrance to **Tring station** car park just beyond.

Walk options

a) Short cut from Ivinghoe Beacon to Bridgewater Monument:

Follow the main walk instructions from Tring to Ivinghoe Beacon, point [4].

From the Beacon, *turn right around and retrace your steps to the bottom of the dip,* your direction due south. Here, *rather than carry on over the next hummock, take the track that skirts it on the left-hand side*, marked by a post with an acorn symbol. In 280 metres this descends to a crossroads with a car-wide track. *Turn right up this for 30 metres to reach the road and go straight across, up a broad track*, your direction 210 degrees.

[!] *10 metres beyond the road, just after a footpath post with two green and two yellow arrows on it, turn left, broadly parallel to the road*, on a track that initially is not too distinct, your direction 160 degrees.

In 20 metres the path passes through bushes and starts to gently climb the hill. Ignore all ways off until *in 350 metres you come to a T-junction with a car-wide track* (just beyond a fork in the middle of which is a bush), *where you go half left*, your direction now 150 degrees. Ignore two tracks forking left shortly afterwards, to stay on the main track.

In 170 metres ignore a path to the right with a footpath post and curve left with the main track. This brings you to a grassy parking area, with the road directly ahead. *Turn right along the top of the parking area, parallel to the road*, your direction 160 degrees.

[!] In 220 metres ignore a footpath signposted to the right and instead *turn right down the car-wide track 20 metres further on, with a hedge to its left*, signposted 'Restricted Access, Clipper Down Cottage Only'.

You now stay on this broad track all the way to the Bridgewater Monument (apart from when you reach Clipper Cottage and have to pass to the right of it through a gate), a walk of about 50 minutes.

In slightly more detail: in 180 metres you pass a stile on your left and the path curves left. For the next 70 metres there are fine open views to the right and a path

merges from the right. You pass over a cattle grid.

600 metres further on you reach Fredwell Kennels, beyond which is Clipper Cottage. *Go through a gate to the right of the cottage*, with a faded National Trust sign on it indicating 'Permitted Footpath and Bridleway to Bridgewater Monument'. You now pass along the edge of the escarpment, in an area of fine ancient woodlands, for 1.6km (1 mile), at which point you pass an old wooden house to your right, marked with a National Trust sign for Ashridge [9].

250 metres further on you cross a wooden bridge over a shallow gully and, another 300 metres beyond this, you come to the **Bridgewater Monument**. The National Trust **tea kiosk** is just opposite, on the far side of the green. You now resume the main walk directions at point [10].

b) Extension from Aldbury to Berkhamsted:

Follow the main walk directions until point [11] or the route direct from Tring station in option c) below.

Emerging from the Town Farm Tea Rooms in Aldbury [11], *turn left* and walk up past the pond to the crossroads at the centre of the village. *Go straight ahead* down Trooper Road, following a sign to the Valiant Trooper pub. *In 120 metres, just after No.25, Sears Cottage, turn left up a signposted public footpath*, initially on a tarmac drive between houses.

In 60 metres you emerge into an open space with allotments (vegetable gardens). Go straight ahead across it on a grassy path. In 130 metres, *just before the fence at the top, go right following a footpath arrow*, your direction 200 degrees.

In the far corner of the allotments, just before you reach garden fences, turn left through a wire and wood gate, following a yellow footpath arrow. A fenced path between gardens brings you in 80 metres *to a road, where you turn left uphill*.

In 30 metres ignore a road to the right to continue uphill past a wood-sided house, called the Summer House, on your left. Just beyond it the road turns left and becomes a private driveway, and a *four-armed footpath sign indicates two paths continuing uphill, both signposted 'Chilterns Way'*. The right-hand fork climbs steeply to a wooden bench, but *your route is the left fork, signposted to Berkhamsted Common*, which turns more sharply left and immediately goes into the trees, your direction 50 degrees.

In 70 metres cross a road and go straight on up into the woods, again signposted Chilterns Way. You are now in a cutting, roughly on a bearing of 60 degrees. In 40 metres cross another cutting and keep on uphill, your direction now 20 degrees.

[!] *In 30 metres, as the path levels out slightly, go right, directly up the slope, at a tree with 'CW' on it and a curving white arrow* (less obvious in summer than in winter), your direction 90 degrees. *After 60 metres of steep climbing go straight ahead across a crosspaths to carry on up a well-defined gravel path*, your direction 120 degrees.

In 20 metres ignore a broad track to the left and a path forking left signposted 'No Horses'. In 80 metres you cross an earth driveway next to a house to the left and a 'Footpath only. No horses' sign. *Keep straight on here along a wide mud track* (easy to follow in summer when vegetation covers the forest floor: so wide as to be indistinct in winter when the forest floor is bare), following two blue arrows on a post, your direction 110 degrees.

In 300 metres *go straight across a crosspaths* marked by two blue arrows on a post *and in 50 metres veer slightly left with the main path*, now as wide as an A-road, your direction 90 degrees. 400 metres more brings you to the main road, the B4506 **[B1]**.

[**Special note in winter**: When you reach the road there should be a large open field behind high hedges just to your left, as well as a Chilterns Way sign.

On the far side of the road to the left is a row of tall pine trees. If this is not the case, *turn left on the B4506* until you reach this point]

On the far side of the road *three paths diverge from a small parking area*. One marked 'No Horses' forks left. Another follows a line of tall trees straight ahead. *But your onward path forks half right from the right-hand edge of the parking space, 20 metres to the right of a post with the blue arrows on it*, your direction 150 degrees. (This path is also marked 'No Horses', though in summer this sign can be hidden by nettles.)

Follow this path, initially on a very wide grassy ride between lines of trees. *In 250 metres you come to an old wooden footpath post on the right, easily missed amid the trees*. A faint path joins from the right. [!] 50 metres beyond this post the ways divide. The more obvious route is slightly left, bearing 90 degrees, *but your onward route forks right, bearing 120 degrees, heading into the trees*. [**In winter**, if in doubt at this point, veer half right through the trees and you will soon find the path along the forest boundary, which you can follow to Little Coldharbour Farm.]

In 250 metres cross paths to the left and right (more obvious to the left) and the forest boundary fence comes into view about 120 metres to your right, with open fields beyond. The path rapidly converges with the forest edge and *in 100 metres you merge with a broad path that is parallel to the fence*, about 30 metres inside the forest.

Keep straight on, parallel to the forest boundary on your right, your direction now 110 degrees. In winter the onward path is clear here: in summer, paths diverge left and right around foliage about 100 metres along the path, which can be a bit confusing, but keep always right, close to the forest boundary, and in 250 metres you come to **Little Coldharbour Farm** on your right.

Here the *path merges with the farm's*

driveway, a car-wide gravel track, to continue in roughly the same direction as before along it. In 200 metres a path marked 'No Horses' joins from the left and the track curves right. 90 metres after this *the track bends away sharply to the left to join a drive coming from a house to the right,* **Coldharbour Farm [B2]**. *Here leave the track and go straight on along a muddy bridleway,* your direction 150 degrees, *following an arrow on a post.*

In 150 metres fork right at a footpath post marked with four arrows and the number 47. In 150 metres this well-defined path comes out alongside a large open space to your left (a good **picnic** spot). Keep on the path just inside the forest edge. *In 170 metres, at a post covered in arrows, fork half right,* your direction 200 degrees.

In another 170 metres, *where the path comes to the forest edge, ignore a fork to the left and instead go right to cross a stile with a white arrow on it 10 metres ahead. Keep to the right-hand edge of the open field beyond,* your direction 220 degrees. In 120 metres pass through a wooden gap in a fence that is not visible until you get close to it and on into the next field, still with the hedge on your right.

After another 100 metres cross a stile, still keeping to the field edge, and in a further 130 metres *go over a stile into a wood,* signposted Alpine Meadow Nature Reserve. In 50 metres exit the wood and descend across a strip of grassland, your direction 170 degrees, before plunging back into the woods and down across a dip.

Climbing up the far side, *in 80 metres you come to a stile. Cross this, exiting the wood, and go right, steeply uphill,* following a yellow arrow and keeping the edge of the wood on your right-hand side, your direction 190 degrees. In 150 metres, as the slope levels out a bit, *cross a stile to the right of a rusty metal gate* and keep to the right-hand edge of the field.

In 300 metres, at the top of the field, go left, following a yellow arrow, your

direction 110 degrees. In 170 metres, in the far corner of the field, go straight on at a four-way path junction. You are now on a farm track, still on the right-hand edge of a field. In 400 metres follow this track half right along the edge of the next field, your direction due south.

In 150 metres, at a four-way hedge junction, *the track curves left, but your onward route is straight on, passing to the right of a stile in front of the hedge directly in front of you,* your direction 160 degrees. You are now descending through a large grassy field, with the hedge to your left and Berkhamsted visible ahead.

In 450 metres, at the bottom of the hill, *go through a metal kissing gate to the left of a double wooden fieldgate onto a sports field. Go left along the field edge.* In 140 metres *go through another kissing gate and turn right,* following a line of mini pylons, with a barbed-wire fence now on your right.

In 80 metres cross a stile to the right of metal fieldgate. You are now on a car-wide track, which in 80 metres comes out onto a tarmac road. In 180 metres you cross a stile to the right of two wooden fieldgates to emerge onto a suburban road, where you go half left downhill, your direction 200 degrees.

In 60 metres this merges with a busier road that comes in from the left. Keep straight on downhill towards the bridge visible in the distance, which is the railway line. The ruins of **Berkhamsted Castle** come into view on the left. In 120 metres you come to a mini roundabout. The back entrance to **Berkhamsted station** is just ahead to the right (London trains go from platform 4, the first platform you come to).

If you just miss a train, you might like to while away half an hour looking at Berkhamsted Castle: its entrance is 30 metres left from the mini roundabout. If you want to have something to eat or drink in Berkhamsted, it is only five minutes' walk to its High Road, which has cafés, pubs and restaurants. Go under the bridge to the left of the station entrance and on the far side turn right along Lower Kings Road. This curves left over the canal in about 100 metres and 200 metres further on brings you to a set of traffic lights, the junction with the High Road.

c) Short walk from Tring to Berkhamsted:

[1] From the platform at Tring station *walk up the stairs and turn right along the footbridge.* Walk diagonally across the car park towards its entrance. *Emerging onto the road, turn right* along a pavement on its left-hand side.

In 110 metres ignore a road turning to the left, signposted to Pitstone and Ivinghoe. 80 metres further on *turn left onto a concrete farm track signposted 'Ridgeway Bridleway',* your direction 70 degrees.

In 50 metres, where the concrete track curves left to a farm, go straight on across the grass towards a white sign in front of a line of trees. *Pass through the metal gate* just behind this sign and *cross a broad track* (signposted 'Ridgeway' to the left) [2].

Go up the small slope ahead and past a broken wooden gate. In 20 metres pass through a metal gate. In another 120 metres pass another broken wooden gate and go straight on, ignoring a path to the left marked by a three-armed footpath sign. In 140 metres you can see a golf course on your left and the village of Aldbury in the valley to the right.

In another 160 metres, at a three- and four-armed footpath sign, turn right through a wooden kissing gate. Go downhill on a path fenced off from a field, heading directly for the church tower. At the bottom of the field you pass through two metal kissing gates to pass to the left of a green corrugated metal barn.

At the end of the barn a kissing gate takes you into the field to your left, where you continue in the same direction as before, with farm buildings to your right. Pass a pond on your left and cross a stile

to the right of a rusted metal gate. *In 50 metres go through a wooden kissing gate and turn left onto the road.*

In 180 metres this brings you to the centre of the village [11], with the Aldbury Village Store on your right and a pond on your left. *Just past the pond, turn left.* The **Town Farm Tea Rooms** is the brick-and-timber building 90 metres along on the right, opposite the Greyhound pub.

[You now follow the **Extension from Aldbury to Berkhamsted** directions in option **b)** above.]

Lunch & tea places

Ashridge Estate Visitors Centre Tearoom *Ringshall, Berkhamsted, HP4 1LX (01442 851227).* **Open** *Late Mar-early Dec* noon-5pm Tue-Sun. As the name suggests, a useful Berkhamsted tea-stop.

Bridgewater Arms *Nettleden Road, Little Gaddesden, HP4 1PD (01442 842408).* **Open** 11am-3pm, 5-11pm Mon-Fri; 11am-11pm Sat; noon-10.30pm Sun. **Food served** noon-2.30pm, 6-9.30pm Mon-Sat; noon-8.30pm Sun. Located 11.2km (7 miles) from the start of the walk, this fine old country inn has a classy restaurant and offers cheaper bar meals at lunchtime. This is the suggested lunch stop for the main walk.

Greyhound Inn *19 Stocks Road, Aldbury, HP23 5RT (01442 851228).* **Open** 11am-11pm Mon-Sat; 11am-10.30pm Sun. **Food served** noon-2.30pm, 7-9.30pm Mon-Sat; noon-3pm Sun. This relatively upmarket pub serves lunch and is the suggested lunch place for the short walk option.

The **Town Farm Tea Rooms**, Aldbury, offers cream teas in a cosy room that feels like (and in fact is) the front room of a cottage. It is open year round until about 5.30pm. The village also has a shop, **Aldbury Village Store**, that is open until 5.30pm daily (until 7.30pm on Saturday and Wednesday). The **Bridgewater Monument** has a tea kiosk with inside and outside seating, open until 5pm March to December.

Picnic: Almost anywhere from Pitstone Hill to Ivinghoe Beacon is an excellent place for a picnic. A good picnic spot is also indicated in the Extension to Berkhamsted option after point [B2].

Henley via Stonor Circular

Hidden valleys of the southern Chilterns.

9.48 (?)

Start and finish: Henley station
Length: 21.9km (13.7 miles).
For a shorter walk, *see below*
Walk options.

Time: 7 hours. For the whole outing, including trains and meals, allow 10 hours 30 minutes.

Transport: Trains run hourly between London Paddington and Henley, changing at Twyford (journey time: about 1 hour). If driving, the railway station has a substantial car park that charges £2.20 a day.

Otherwise, you can try to park anywhere near Henley town centre. To start the walk, find the town's bridge over the Thames (there is only the one) and follow the directions from the point marked [*] in the walk directions.

OS Landranger Map: 175
OS Explorer Map: 171
Henley-on-Thames, map reference SU764823, is in Oxfordshire, 10km (6.25 miles) north-east of Reading.
Toughness: 7 out of 10.

Walk notes: Henley is normally thought of as a riverside town but, as this walk demonstrates, it is also on the southern edge of the Chiltern Hills, a charming area of hidden valleys, mixed woodland and farmland, and largely gentle slopes (although the main walk does have one substantial steep hill after lunch). The walk takes you up one side and down the other of the long valley leading up to Stonor, with plenty of charming views en route. Lunch is at a pretty and quiet pub in the village of Pishill, and the return is past hidden farms and through ancient woods into Henley, with its excellent tearooms. Note that this is a fairly full day out, and that tea is 11km (6.9 miles) from the lunchtime pub, so the main walk is only really practical from late February to late October. However, in winter, or if you fancy a later start, the shorter walk makes a pleasant alternative.

Walk options: Directions for both the following variations are given at the end of the main walk text (*see p74*).

a) Shorter walk: A short but pleasant walk up country lanes from the Rainbow Inn in Middle Assendon allows you to shorten the route to 14km (8.8 miles). This short walk still takes in several of the best sections from the morning and afternoon of the main walk. Pick up the directions at point [3] in the main walk text.

b) Stonor short cut: Alternatively, you can trim 2.5km (1.6 miles) off the main walk by using the short cut at Stonor, from point [4] in the main walk text. This short cut misses out the lunchtime pub, the Crown in Pishill, but, if you are relatively smartly dressed, you could have lunch at the upmarket Flying Pig restaurant at the Stonor Arms Hotel (*see p75*).

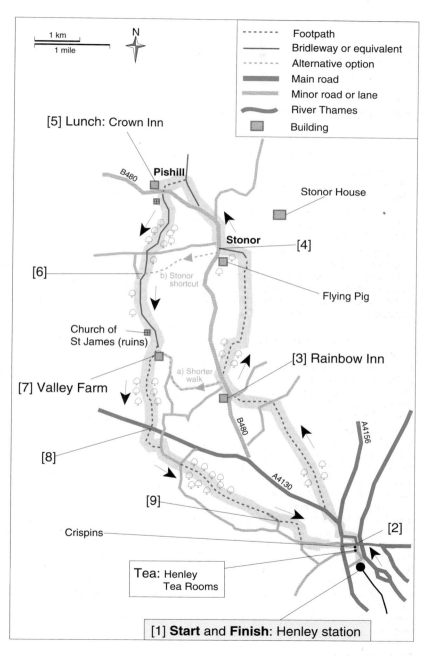

1 km
1 mile

N

Footpath
Bridleway or equivalent
Alternative option
Main road
Minor road or lane
River Thames
Building

[5] Lunch: Crown Inn

B480

Pishill

Stonor House

Stonor ——[4]

[6]——

b) Stonor shortcut

Flying Pig

Church of
St James (ruins)

[3] Rainbow Inn

a) Shorter walk

[7] Valley Farm

B480

A4156

[8]——

A4130

[9]——

Crispins——

Tea: Henley
Tea Rooms

[2]

[1] **Start** and **Finish**: Henley station

On Tuesdays, Thursdays and Saturdays there is one mid-morning and one afternoon bus from Henley railway station to Stonor, which is 9.7km (6.1 miles) into the main walk. (phone 01296 399500 for times). The easiest place to get off the bus in order to join the main walk is the entrance to Stonor Park.

Saturday Walkers' Club: Take the nearest train to 9am (before or after). If you are doing the short walk, leave an hour later.

Walk directions

[1] [Numbers refer to the map]
Coming out of **Henley station**, turn right down the station approach road, your direction 310 degrees.

In 50 metres *turn right at a T-junction*, immediately in front of the Imperial Hotel, your direction 50 degrees. You are now heading towards the Thames and a 'Boats for Hire' kiosk. In 120 metres *at the riverfront follow the road around to the left*, with the Thames to your right. In 100 metres ignore a road to your left (Friday Street) and keep on along the riverside. In another 110 metres *you pass the town bridge*. **[*]** *Continue straight on along the riverside*, passing the Red Lion Hotel on your left-hand side.

In 150 metres bear left with the road, away from the river. (Do NOT continue walking straight on into Wharfe Lane.) In 200 metres *turn right at a T-junction* with Asquiths Teddy Bear shop on the left-hand side, your direction north. In 100 metres ignore a private road forking right (which in any case is a dead end) and keep to the main road.

In another 80 metres, *at the second of two mini roundabouts, fork left*, signposted as the A4130 towards Wallingford, Nettlebed and Stonor Park. Keep walking along the right-hand side of this road. In 250 metres you *pass the Old White Horse Pub* on the right-hand side. 40 metres after this, just after the entrance

to Rupert House Playing Fields, *turn right on a footpath signposted 'Oxfordshire Way'*, your direction 350 degrees. **[2]**

You now follow the Oxfordshire Way until point [3] below.

In more detail: *follow the footpath uphill* between a chain-ink fence to the right and a barbed-wire one on the left. *In 250 metres this path leads into a wood.* Keep to the main path, ignoring minor paths off to the right. In 60 metres, after a bend to the right, the path curves sharply left, your direction initially 290 degrees. In another 170 metres, *at a metal kissing gate, continue straight on slightly uphill across an open field on a clear path*, keeping to the left of the nearest clump of trees, your direction 340 degrees.

Keep straight on through scattered trees. *In 600 metres pass to the left of a low farm shed and through a rusted fieldgate* (or an equally rusted kissing gate to its right). *Carry on along a farm track*, with a barbed-wire fence and a pig farm to your right, towards a large cedar tree, which can be seen at the end of the track, your direction 330 degrees.

In 430 metres *pass through a kissing gate to the left of a metal fieldgate*. Continue straight on along a tarmac driveway, in 15 metres passing through a white fieldgate marked 'Henley Park Private Road'. In 80 metres you pass a house on your right-hand side, and in a further 50 metres *the tarmac gives way to a gravel car-wide track*.

Keep on this track for 900 metres to a T-junction with a tarmac road, just past a pond and house to your left. *Cross over the tarmac road and across a stile*, signposted 'Oxfordshire Way'. Beyond the stile *follow the footpath as it veers slightly to the left across an open field, heading towards another stile to the right of a telegraph pole*, your direction west.

In 70 metres *cross over this stile* and continue onwards through the next field, following a path in the direction of the large wooden Turville Court Estate signpost. In 220 metres *cross over the next stile*, with a yellow Oxfordshire Way arrow on it, *and walk along a narrow path between two wooden fences.*

In 50 metres cross over a stile with a Chiltern Society yellow arrow on it to emerge into an open field. A fine view opens up of Middle Assendon village below and the Stonor Valley to its right, making this an ideal **picnic** spot. *Turn half right downhill, roughly towards the village below,* your direction west.

In 350 metres *pass to the left of a wooden fieldgate to carry on downhill on a tree-lined path.* In 180 metres *you come to a junction with a tarmac lane. Turn left here* into **Middle Assendon**. In 35 metres take the road to the right, merging in 50 metres with the main road, the B480. On the left-hand side is the **Rainbow Inn**, the lunch stop for the short walk. **[3]**

Continue walking up the B480 on the right-hand side. In 150 metres there are two roads off to the left.

[At this point, to follow the **Shorter walk**, option a), take the second road, signposted to Bix Bottom, then follow the directions at the end of the main walk text.]

To stay on the **main walk**, however, *ignore the two roads to the left* and carry on along the B480. *In another 200 metres take a signposted footpath off to the right,* uphill along a car-wide track heading towards an opening in the trees, your direction 20 degrees.

[!] In 200 metres, at the top of the field, *on entering the trees take the signposted footpath immediately to the left further into the woods,* following the direction indicated by a yellow Chiltern Society arrow on a post, your initial direction 350 degrees. In 500 metres *exit the woods over a stile into a field. Follow the left-hand edge of the field uphill,* with a hedge and barbed-wire fence to your left, your direction 80 degrees.

In 50 metres turn left with the field edge near a water trough. *In 90 metres pass through a wide opening* with a rusted metal fieldgate to its right and *continue*

straight on along a car-wide track with a hedgerow to your left, your direction 350 degrees. *Continue along this car-wide track for 1.3km* (0.8 miles), ignoring all ways off, *until you come to a farmhouse on the left-hand side.*

60 metres after the farmhouse *you come to a track crossroads. Go straight ahead through a double metal fieldgate* with four white arrows painted on it into a farmyard, your direction 350 degrees. In 100 metres, *on the far side of the farmyard, follow the track, keeping the woods to your left-hand side,* and ignoring the track off at the start of the woods.

In 130 metres, *where the track curves sharply round to the right, turn left down a path,* signposted with two blue arrows and a white signpost, your direction 310 degrees. Continue downhill, keeping a chain-link fence to your right.

In 500 metres pass through a metal fieldgate onto a road and into the village of **Stonor [4]**. [At this point, to follow the **Short cut via Stonor**, option b), follow the directions at end of main walk text.]

Alternatively, **to continue on the main walk to Pishill,** *turn right along the road into the village of Stonor,* your direction 350 degrees. Continue up this road. In 400 metres you pass the entrance to **Stonor Park** (*see p72* **Campion's champions**) on your right. In another 200 metres *ignore a road off to the right to Turville Heath and North End* and carry straight in the direction of Pishill, your direction 320 degrees

In 350 metres fork right onto a tarmac and gravel track, signposted 'Oxfordshire Cycleway', your direction 330 degrees, (though you can if you wish stay on the road for a further 1km/0.6 miles to get to the lunchtime pub slightly more quickly). Keep on this track, which climbs steadily uphill. *In 700 metres, as the gradient levels off, go left at a two-armed footpath sign,* following a footpath downhill along the left-hand edge of a field, your initial direction west.

In 200 metres, *at the far end of the field, pass through a broken metal gate* (hidden in a rather overgrown area in summer) *and on between wire fences*, with a pine wood to your right, following a white arrow on a post. In 150 metres *cross a stile and turn left onto a car-wide track*. In 40 metres, *at a T-junction with a road, go right*. 250 metres along this road you come to the **Crown Inn** in **Pishill**, the suggested lunchtime stop. **[5]**

After lunch, *come out of the pub and turn left*, retracing your steps along the road. In 200 metres *turn right up a car-wide tarmac lane signposted 'Oxfordshire Way and Church'*, your direction 170 degrees. In another 150 metres you pass the church on your right and the view opens out to the left. In 100 metres, *just before the track passes through gateposts and becomes a driveway to Chapel Wells, fork left onto a footpath marked with a white arrow* and 'PS22 OW', with a wooden fence to your right, your direction 150 degrees.

You now follow the OW (Oxfordshire Way) signposts till point [7] below.

But in more detail: in 70 metres, *where the path forks, take the left fork, marked 'PS17 OW'*, into a field. *Keep on the left-hand side of the field, downhill*, your direction still 150 degrees. In 60 metres a car-wide track merges from the right. *In 120 metres you cross a farm road and continue downhill more steeply*, still on the left-hand edge of a field. The path goes into a dip and starts to climb again and in 220 metres enters a wood.

Immediately on entering the wood you cross a car-wide track and keep uphill on a narrower path, which climbs steeply uphill through the wood, your direction 210 degrees. In 300 metres, *at the top of the hill*, there is an open area on your right and you *follow the white arrows on a clear path along the edge of the wood*. In 120 metres ignore a path merging from the left marked 'PS9', and keep straight on along the path marked 'OW PS17'.

In 50 metres ignore another path merging from the left. 70 metres beyond this, *where the path forks, follow 'OS PS17' to the left*, your direction 240 degrees. In 180 metres *you come to a road. Cross straight over and carry on uphill* on the Oxfordshire Way, following a white arrow on a tree, your direction due south, and ignoring a car-wide forest track forking immediately to the left.

In 180 metres, at the top of the hill, ignore a path (PS18) over the stile to the right and keep straight on along OW PS17. In 20 metres *you emerge from the wood and carry on slightly to the right across a field*, heading just to the right of a telegraph pole, which itself is to the right of a house roof, your direction 200 degrees.

In 160 metres, on the far side of the field, *turn left along the field edge*, curving right with it in 60 metres. 50 metres further on *exit the field down a grass path* between hedges to the left and a house garden right, your direction 200 degrees.

[6] In 50 metres, *at a T-junction with another car-wide track, turn right* through double black metal fieldgates. *After 20 metres on this track, at the start of a small green to your left* [!], *turn sharp left down a gravel path*, your direction 200 degrees.

In a further 15 metres, ignore a kissing gate to the right marked 'Nature Reserve'. Instead keep straight on, following the Oxfordshire Way sign. *In 600 metres, where the path forks, go right*, following SW26 OW (to the left is SW33). *This path goes steadily downhill for 700 metres until it meets a road at the bottom of the valley. Go left on this road*, signposted 'Oxfordshire Cycleway', your direction 140 degrees.

In 100 metres you pass the ruins of the church of **St James** on your right (you can pass through a gap in the hedge for a closer look; the church was abandoned in the 19th century). Stay on the road, ignoring a signposted footpath up a car-wide track to the right in 50 metres. In another 200 metres *you come to* **Valley End Farm**. *Turn right into the farmyard*, following the signposted footpath.

View from a Chilterns escarpment.

[7] In 15 metres *fork left in front of a farmhouse to a wooden fieldgate* 40 metres further on. 30 metres beyond the fieldgate, *merge with a car-wide gravel track from the left and keep on up it* along a field edge, your direction 220 degrees. **[!]** In 140 metres, *roughly halfway along the field, turn left over a stile* on a path that climbs steeply uphill to a line of trees, your direction 140 degrees.

In 100 metres, at the top of the hill, turn round for a fine view back over the valley. This is a nice **picnic** spot. *Cross the stile at the top of the hill and follow a path, with the wood to your right,* passing a metal fieldgate on your left and curving right with the path along the wood edge in 10 metres, your direction due south. *In 250 metres this path merges with a car-wide track* coming up from the field to the left. Keep straight on, your direction due south.

In 60 metres curve right uphill with the track. In 120 metres, just after entering a wood, *as the car-wide track curves right,* go straight on up a path, following the white arrow on a tree, your direction 190 degrees. In 180 metres, *on the far side of the wood, curve left with the path just inside the wood edge,* with an open field to your right, ignoring the squeeze gate ahead and still following the white arrows on the tree trunks.

In 200 metres, *at the end of the wood, follow the CW arrow out across the field,* heading for a grey transformer box on a mini pylon pole (or, alternatively, the right-hand end of the line of the rightmost of the houses ahead), your direction 190 degrees. In 300 metres, *on the far side of the field, pick up a garden hedge to your right and follow it* for another 40 metres down a broad green passageway between wooden fences for 50 metres *to a stile. Cross this, and the busy A4130* **[8]**.

On the far side of the A4130 *turn left for 25 metres. By a lay-by go right up a footpath,* signposted 'Chiltern Way Extension', your direction 220 degrees. *Follow a path between a hedge to the left*

Campion's champions

*and fence to the right to a stile in 50
metres. Cross this and carry on along
the left-hand edge of the field beyond,* with
a wire fence to your left, your direction
220 degrees.

In 120 metres a wood starts to
the left. **[!]** *80 metres after the wood
starts, and 20 metres before a fieldgate
ahead, go left over a stile into woods*
(concealed by vegetation in summer).
Go straight ahead through the woods,
at right angles to the fence you have
just crossed, your direction 110 degrees.
Note that there is **no clear path** here
and the more obvious way to the right
is not the correct one.

[!] In 100 metres *cross a stile that
is hidden by trees to leave the wood. Go
straight ahead across a special crossing
in the wire fence ahead* (this fence may
be seasonal/temporary) *and then half
right across the field to a stile at the left
end of a tile-roofed house,* your direction
120 degrees. In 110 metres *cross this
stile and turn left onto a lane,* passing
Benwells Farmhouse to the right, your
direction 100 degrees initially.

In 150 metres *you come to a road and
turn right.* In 450 metres you pass through
a small hamlet. *150 metres further on,
at a road T-junction,* where the road
to the right curves uphill into the trees,

There have been few more steadfast Catholic families in Britain than the Stonors. For more than 800 years Stonors have lived at **Stonor**, and through all that time they have never wavered from their beliefs, even during the turbulent times of the Reformation. The family played a key role in sheltering the Catholic martyr and (since 1970) saint **Edmund Campion** while he was on a secret mission for the Pope in 1581. Campion was captured and, under torture, revealed the help the Stonors had given him. He was hung, drawn and quartered at Tyburn, and various members of the family were arrested, fined and/or exiled.

The oldest parts of the current house date back to the late 12th century (and now house the tearoom and shop), while the chapel was built between 1280 and 1349. There are also Tudor features, though extensive remodelling took place in the Georgian period (the façade dates from 1749). The house hasn't changed substantially since the 18th century. Other attractions are an Italianate walled garden from the same period and the surrounding park, which supports a herd of fallow deer.

The entrance to Stonor Park is passed on the main walk, though the house itself cannot be seen except from the short cut of the main walk. Unfortunately, only superhumans would have the energy to complete the main walk and visit the house, so perhaps this is one to mark for a future visit or a very early start.

Stonor Park

Henley-on-Thames, RG9 6HF Stonor (01491 638587/www.stonor.com). **Open** (guided tours of house, chapel and gardens) *early Apr-June, 1 Oct-late Oct* 2-4.30pm Sun & bank hols; *July-Sept* 2-4.30pm Wed, Sun & bank hols. *Gardens only early Apr-June, 1 Oct-late Oct* 1-5.30pm Sun & bank hols; *July-Sept* 1-5.30pm Wed, Sun & bank hols. **Admission** *House, chapel & gardens* £6; free under-14s. *Gardens only* £3.50; free under-14s. **No credit cards**.

---

keep more or less straight on up a car-wide track, signposted as a bridleway, your direction 100 degrees.

[!] *In 25 metres, at the 'Lambridge Wood Strictly Private' sign, fork right off the track up an initially indistinct and unmarked footpath*, your direction 140 degrees (despite the private sign, this is a right of way). In 25 metres this crosses diagonally over a car-wide track (possibly seasonal or temporary). Beyond this *veer slightly left along a narrow path, heading for a white arrow on a tree*, 40 metres ahead, your direction 120 degrees. *Here, ignore a path to the right* and keep on the now more distinct path.

30 metres further on white arrows on trees left and right confirm you are on the right path, your direction still 120 degrees. *In 120 metres ignore a fork to the right (not signposted) but 50 metres further on fork right up a path marked by a yellow arrow on trees either side*, your direction 140 degrees.

Keep on this path, which is initially somewhat indistinct and meandering. Yellow arrows on trees confirm your route after a while, however. *In 260 metres cross a larger path* (signposted as path 11 to the left). *Keep straight on* (on path 25), your initial direction 130 degrees.

In 20 metres you pass another yellow arrow on a tree and keep on downhill. In 140 metres ignore path 27 signposted to the left and keep on path 25, your direction now 200 degrees. 25 metres beyond this *you approach the edge of the wood and turn left at a T-junction, keeping just inside the wood*, your direction 140 degrees. Keep on this car-wide track, with the wood edge to your right, ignoring all ways off.

In 500 metres you emerge into an area of new growth and keep straight on. In another 200 metres *you come to a stile and emerge onto a golf course. Keep straight on across the golf course* (watching out for low-flying golf balls), *heading to the left of a line of trees* 60 metres ahead, your direction 140 degrees.

When you get to the trees keep along their left-hand side. In 100 metres *pass two golf course tees on your right and keep straight on to the left of a row of much larger trees*, following a yellow arrow and soon picking up a gravel car-wide track. *In 250 metres veer slightly right onto a sandy-brown golf course path for 30 metres and then fork left off it to follow a car-wide track to the left of another line of trees.*

120 metres after this, *as the track curves right, keep straight on across a stile with yellow arrows on it.* Beyond the stile *keep straight on down a tarmac driveway between fences.* In 60 metres cross a stile to the right of a wooden fieldgate and, in another 20 metres, ignore a tarmac driveway to the left. In another 30 metres cross another stile to the right of a wooden fieldgate (if the gate is not open, which it usually seems to be).

Stay on the driveway and *in 400 metres you come to a wooden fence topped with razor wire* (the former home of Beatle George Harrison) *and the road bends right* **[9]**. *Go left here down a signposted footpath, with the wooden fence to your right*, your initial direction east. Turn left with this path in 200 metres *to come to a suburban road 40 metres later.*

Turn right along this road. In 180 metres go right uphill along Hop Gardens. In 400 metres you come to the main road, where you go left downhill (you can if you wish take the small quiet road to the left just before the main road, which also leads downhill to the marketplace). In 250 metres you come to the marketplace in the centre of **Henley**. Go straight on across this and on down Hart Street towards the church.

In 300 metres, just beyond the church and just before the town bridge, **Crispins** tearoom is on the corner to your right. To reach the station and the recommended tearoom, however, turn right along Thames Side (not signposted as such), passing the Angel Inn. The **Henley Tea Rooms** are 60 metres further along on the right.

After tea turn right following the road along the riverside. In 50 metres ignore the road to the right (Friday Street) and keep along the riverside. In 100 metres, at the Boats for Hire kiosk, *bend right with the road away from the river.* In 30 metres ignore Meadow Road to the left. In 90 metres, *opposite the Imperial Hotel, turn left up the approach road to* **Henley station**.

Walk options

a) Shorter walk:
Follow the main walk direction to point [3].

Having taken the second road, signposted to Bix Bottom, *follow this road gently uphill, turning sharp right with it in 500 metres.* Another 450 metres of minor curves brings you to a road T-junction, *where you go right*, your initial direction north. In 300 metres you pass two houses on your right (Keepers Cottage and Holly Hill Cottage).

Keep on the road for another 350 metres until you come to Valley Farm, Bix Bottom, advertised by a yellow sign to the left of the road. Ignore the concrete track into the farmyard immediately before this sign, but in another 40 metres, where the hedge to the left ends and just before a red-brick farm building, *go left up a signposted public footpath. Then resume the main walk directions after point [7] in the main walk text.* However, if you wish to visit the ruined church of St James, stay on the road for 250 metres, retracing your steps later.

b) Stonor short cut:
Follow the main walk directions to point [4].

To follow the short cut at this point, missing out the lunchtime pub in Pishill, *turn left on the road,* your direction 170 degrees. If you want to have lunch at the **Flying Pig**, continue on the road for another 80 metres. Otherwise, *in 20 metres turn right up a footpath signposted 'Chiltern Way and Maidensgrove 1 mile',* your direction 280 degrees.

In 50 metres cross a stile into a field and continue up a well-defined footpath, passing just to the left of a mini pylon pole after 50 metres. *In a further 150 metres cross a stile into the next field.* Continue uphill, your direction west, heading to right of a fenced-in clump of trees 70 metres ahead. After the trees end carry on in the same direction, slowly diverging from a fence you can see 30 metres to your left. After 50 metres you can see a stile leading into the wood.

If you turn around at this point there is a view of Stonor Park house. *In 250 metres cross this stile* and carry on up into the wood on another well-defined path marked with white arrows on trees, your direction 260 degrees initially. *In 450 metres cross a stile to emerge from the wood* and cross a field on a clear path, your direction 250 degrees. In 250 metres, at the far corner of the field, *turn left to exit the field* down a grass path, your direction 200 degrees. *You now resume the main walk instructions at point [6].*

Lunch & tea places

Crispins *52 Hart Street, Henley-on-Thames, RG9 2AU (01491 574232).* **Open/food served** varies; phone for details. On the corner of Hart Street and Thames Side, and immediately opposite the bridge in Henley, is an upmarket tea

alternative. It serves cream teas until around 6.30-7pm daily in the summer months, though it sometimes closes earlier in the winter or if custom is light.

Crown Inn *Pishill, nr Henley-on-Thames, RG9 6HH (01491 638364).* **Open** 11.30am-3pm, 6-11.30pm Mon-Sat; noon-3pm, 7-10.30pm Sun. **Food served** noon-2pm, 7-9.30pm Mon-Sat; noon-2pm, 7-9pm Sun. Located 10.6km (6.6 miles) into the main walk, this charming and friendly country pub has a peaceful garden and roaring log fires in winter. It welcomes walkers, but is quite popular, so if there are more than eight of you it might be a good idea to phone ahead. This is the suggested lunch stop on the main walk.

Flying Pig restaurant at the Stonor Arms Hotel *Stonor, nr Henley-on-Thames, RG9 6HE (01491 638866/www.theflying pigrestaurant.co.uk).* **Open/food served** noon-2.30pm, 7-9pm Mon-Sat; noon-5.30pm Sun. This is a fairly upmarket restaurant (not a pub), so you will need to be relatively smartly dressed (ie no shorts) and mud-free to lunch here. This is the suggested lunch stop on the Stonor short cut.

Henley Tea Rooms *Thames Side, Henley-on-Thames, RG9 1BH (01491 411412).* **Open** 9am-5pm daily. **Food served** 11am-2pm daily. Situated on the waterfront by the bridge in Henley, this place has plenty of tables and a nice selection of cakes and savoury items. Note that in summer closing time may be as late as 6pm or 7pm. This is the suggested tea stop on the walk.

Rainbow Inn *Middle Assendon, RG9 6AU (01491 574879).* **Open** noon-2.30pm, 6-11pm Mon-Sat; noon-3pm, 7-10.30pm Sun. **Food served** noon-2.30pm Mon; noon-2.30pm, 6-11pm Tue-Sat; noon-3pm Sun. The Rainbow Inn is 5km (3 miles) into the walk and serves pleasant home-cooked food. This is the suggested lunch stop on the short walk. Note that after lunch on the short walk, there is still 9km (5.6 miles) to go, so it is wise to leave the pub no later than 1.30pm in midwinter.

Picnic: the best spot on both the main and short walks is the hill before Middle Assendon, which has a superb panorama up the valley towards Stonor: this location is marked in the walk directions. Another possible picnic spot for the short walk is indicated in the text on the hill just beyond Valley End Farm (point [7]).

Henley via Hambleden Circular

The Thames, Remenham Hill and Hambleden.

Start and finish: Henley station
Length: 14.9km (9.3 miles).
For shorter variations, *see below*
Walk options.

Time: 4 hours 45 minutes. For the whole outing, including trains and meals, allow 8 hours 15 minutes.

Transport: Trains run hourly between London Paddington and Henley, changing at Twyford (journey time; about 1 hour). If driving, the railway station has a big car park (£2.20 a day). Otherwise, you can try to park anywhere near Henley town centre. To start the walk, find the town's bridge over the Thames (there is only the one) and follow the directions from the point marked [*] in the walk directions.

OS Landranger Map: 175
OS Explorer Map: 171
Henley-on-Thames, map reference SU764823, is in Oxfordshire, 10km (6.2 miles) north-east of Reading.

Toughness: 3 out of 10.

Walk notes: This pleasant and undemanding walk follows a completely different route from the Henley Circular walk in the first *Time Out Book of Country Walks*, though it shares the picturesque village of Hambleden for lunch. In the morning it follows the left bank of the river (wilder and less manicured than the right) along the stretch where the famous Henley Regatta is held each summer, before passing through pastures and woodland to Hambleden. After lunch, it follows the valley down to cross the Thames over the weir at Hambleden Mill and Aston, and then traverses the lower part of Remenham Hill to return to Henley for tea. Note that Temple Island Meadows on the riverside stretch of this walk is very marshy in winter: wear wellington boots or choose a drier time of year to do this walk.

Walk options: The simple variations below are marked in the main walk text.

a) Short cut to Hambleden: This short cut simply takes a more direct route to Hambleden village, reducing the walk by 2.1km (1.2 miles). This option occurs at point [3] in the main walk text.

b) Shortening the walk: There are hourly buses from Mill End, the hamlet next to Hambleden Mill (point [5] in the main walk text), back to Henley until 10pm daily (including Sundays), a journey of about ten minutes. This shortens the walk to 10.3km (6.4 miles). For bus times, call 0870 608 2608.

It is also possible to combine the start or finish of this walk with the corresponding section of the Marlow Circular walk (walk 8) to produce a Henley to Marlow or Marlow to Henley walk: see p92 of the Marlow Circular walk for details.

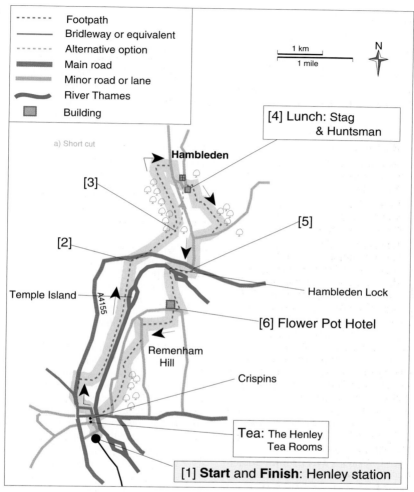

Legend:
- Footpath
- Bridleway or equivalent
- Alternative option
- Main road
- Minor road or lane
- River Thames
- Building

1 km
1 mile

N

a) Short cut

Hambleden

[4] Lunch: Stag & Huntsman

[3]

[5]

[2]

Temple Island — A4155

Hambleden Lock

[6] Flower Pot Hotel

Remenham Hill

Crispins

Tea: The Henley Tea Rooms

[1] **Start** and **Finish**: Henley station

Saturday Walkers' Club: Take the nearest train to 10am from London Paddington.

Walk directions

[1] [Numbers refer to the map]
Coming out of **Henley railway station**, *turn right down the approach road to the station*, your direction 310 degrees.

In 50 metres *turn right at a T-junction*, immediately in front of the Imperial Hotel, your direction 50 degrees. You are now heading towards the River Thames and a 'Boats for Hire' kiosk. In 120 metres, *at the riverfront, follow the road around to the left*, with the Thames to your right. In 100 metres ignore a road to your left (Friday Street) and keep on along the riverside. In another 110 metres *you pass the town bridge.* **[*]** *Continue straight* *on along the riverside* passing the Red Lion Hotel on your left-hand side.

In 160 metres bend left with the road away from the river. (Do NOT continue walking straight on into Wharfe Lane). *In 200 metres turn right at a T-junction* with Asquiths Teddy Bear shop on the left-hand side, your direction due north. In 100 metres ignore a private road forking right (which in any case is a dead end) and keep to the main road. In another 80 metres, *at the second of two mini roundabouts, fork right following the A4155* (where the left fork is signposted A4074 to Oxford)

Carry straight on along this road, passing Henley Rugby Football Club on your left in 100 metres. 80 metres further on, *just before a sign saying 'Marlow 8 miles' on the left-hand side, turn right through a metal fieldgate down a car-wide signposted footpath,* your direction 80 degrees. In 30 metres this path emerges into a playing field. *Keep to the right-hand edge of the field, with a green mesh fence to your right.*

In 100 metres keep to this fence (which increasingly becomes a hedge) even though the main path diverges left slightly towards a (locked) metal fieldgate. Keeping to the hedge brings you *in another 100 metres to a metal kissing gate,* 60 metres to the right of the fieldgate. Pass through the gate and *walk 30 metres further on to the river's edge, and then turn left along the river bank,* your direction 10 degrees.

Keep along the river (**Henley Reach**). *In 200 metres you cross a wooden bridge and continue straight on up a broad open space. In another 500 metres this open space comes to an end and your way seems blocked by trees. Your onward route is over a metal-and-wood footbridge to the right-hand edge of the trees* (this is somewhat hidden by nettles in summer). Beyond the bridge *you pass under a flint archway and over another footbridge into a field.*

You now continue along this path for around 2km (1.25 miles) until it

comes again to the A4155 (point [2] below). But in more detail:

Continue up the right-hand edge of the field with the river to your right (though at times it is screened by trees). In 100 metres cross another footbridge over a side canal, with a fine view left to a red brick mansion (**Fawley Court**). 15 metres after the bridge *pass through a wooden kissing gate* to enter **Temple Island Meadows**, an area of rougher vegetation that in late summer is gloriously overgrown with flowering plants, attracting numerous butterflies and insects. (**Note that in winter, this area is very wet and marshy.**)

Keep straight on, your direction 20 degrees, ignoring a footbridge immediately to the right. *In 200 metres pass through a wooden gate* to the right of a metal fieldgate and continue on along the right-hand edge of the field. *In 300 metres pass through another wooden kissing gate* and over a footbridge into the next field. On the right-hand side is **Temple Island** with its neo-classical folly.

In 80 metres, when you come level with Temple Island, *cross a footbridge over a ditch and in 100 metres another.* In the next field *the path now starts to gently diverge from the river bank,* passing between two telegraph poles in 100 metres and heading for the middle of the tree boundary another 100 metres further on. When you get to the trees *cross two wooden footbridges separated by 30 metres of wooden planking to emerge into another field.*

Continue in the same direction (due north) across this field, heading to the left of the rightmost of the trees in the middle of the field. In 150 metres *exit this field over another wooden bridge* with a car-wide crossing to its left. Keep straight on across the next field, your direction 20 degrees. In 100 metres *cross a tarmac driveway* and keep straight on. In another 120 metres *you come to a stile, which you cross to emerge onto the busy A4155.* **[2]**

Keeping up with the Smiths

Hambledon is famed as the cradle of cricket, but not this **Hambleden**. That village is in Hampshire, but its Buckinghamshire near-namesake is not without distinctions.

Its most distinguished former resident was **William Henry Smith**. In 1812 Smith's namesake father took over his family's modest newsagent's business on the Strand in London and greatly expanded it. His son became a partner in the firm in 1846, just as the coming of the railways presented a unique opportunity; the younger Smith secured the exclusive right to run book stalls in the stations.

Soon WH Smith was a household name and the family was wealthy. Smith junior became a Conservative MP in 1868 and rose through the ranks to be become First Lord of the Admiralty in 1877.

He was mercilessly lampooned by Gilbert and Sullivan in *HMS Pinafore* as Sir Joseph Porter, the admiral who'd never been to sea and who declared that 'A junior partnership is the only ship I have ever seen'.

'*I always voted at my party's call And never thought of myself at all*

Thought so little, they rewarded me So now I am the ruler of the Queen's navy.'

But such ridicule (he was popularly known thereafter as 'Pinafore Smith') did nothing to harm Smith's career – he later became Secretary of War, and at the time of his death in 1891 was Leader of the House of Commons and First Lord of the Treasury. Posthumously made Lord Hambleden, he's buried in the village churchyard.

Inside the parish church are several interesting memorials, including one to the family of Sir Cope D'Oyley, who died in 1633, on which his children are shown carrying skulls if they died before their parents. To the left of this tomb is an oak chest used by the Earl of Cardigan, commander of the ill-fated Charge of the Light Brigade, during the Crimean War.

Hambleden Mill stands a little way distant from the village, at a strategic point on the Thames, and was used for grinding corn until 1955. The associated weir was first constructed around 1420.

The village is owned by the family of the current WH Smith, though it was put up for sale in 2003 for a price of around £20 million.

Turn right on the A4155, following the tarmac footpath alongside it. In 150 metres you pass a half-timbered house on the left, and in another 100 metres, as the road curves right, an exclamation mark sign on the left-hand side of the road. 70 metres after this cross the road to *turn left up a car-wide track* (a signposted bridleway), your direction due north.

[!] *Immediately turn right through a kissing gate*, following a signposted public footpath into a small field, your direction

50 degrees. In 30 metres *cross a stile, a car-wide track and another stile* into a larger field. *Keep straight ahead across this field*, your direction 60 degrees, *aiming for a metal fieldgate* to the right of the start of a hedge 70 metres ahead. *Cross a stile 10 metres to the left of the fieldgate*. Ignore a stile to the right and instead *keep straight on uphill, keeping the hedge to your right*, your direction 60 degrees.

In 500 metres, *where the hedge ends, enter the woods via a wooden gate and continue on the path uphill*. In 5 metres ignore a faint footpath off to the right. In another 5 metres *cross over a wide path and continue up the hill in the direction of a fading white arrow on the tree*, your direction 70 degrees. Keep on uphill, ignoring all minor ways off. In 160 metres, *near the top of the hill, you come to a triangular junction.* **[3]**

[At this point, you can take option **a)**, the **Short cut to Hambleden**; if you are in a hurry to get to Hambleden for lunch, you can *keep straight on at this point, and the path leads in 500 metres to the village, shaving 2.1km (1.2 miles) off the walk*.]

To continue on the main walk, however, *turn left at the triangular junction*, your direction 320 degrees. *In 50 metres turn right at a T-junction*, just before which there is a faint white arrow on the tree to your right. You are now on a car-wide track that almost immediately curves left. *Continue on this track for 1km*. It first gently descends and then later climbs slightly before descending again. To the right through the trees there are fine views of Hambleden village in winter.

After 1km a car-wide track joins from the left. Keep straight on along this. *In 200 metres the track turns sharp right and comes to a track crossroads. Continue straight on* towards the cream house ahead, your direction east. In 250 metres *you come to a road where you turn right*. (Take care: though quiet, this road is busier than it looks at first. There is an intermittent grass verge to the left.)

In 300 metres *take a signposted footpath to the left over a stile into a field. Turn half right, heading for a stile to the left of a red-brick house*, your direction 140 degrees. (The direction is also indicated on a signpost to the right of the stile you have just crossed.) In 160 metres *cross this stile to exit the field and turn left on the road* into **Hambleden**, crossing over a brick bridge in 20 metres.

In another 30 metres ignore a footpath signposted to the left. 90 metres after this

Hambleden lock.

veer left into the churchyard of **St Mary the Virgin** through an opening in the wall. Keep straight ahead towards the church, curving left to its entrance in 60 metres. *Leave the church through the main entrance* between a row of yew trees and through the lych-gate. The **village store** is straight on to the right on coming out of the church, but your onward way is to *turn left*, your direction 60 degrees.

In 50 metres ignore a road to the left signposted to Pheasants Hill and Frieth. In 20 metres more you come to the **Stag and Huntsman** on your right, the recommended lunch stop. **[4]** *After lunch turn right out of the pub*, your direction east. In 20 metres ignore a footpath

signposted into the pub's car park and continue up the road, past a sign saying 'Private Road. Access only'.

In 100 metres turn right at the three-armed signpost down a car-wide gravel track, your direction 150 degrees. In 150 metres ignore a footpath signposted uphill to the left by a yellow arrow on a post. In another 350 metres *you come to a T-junction, where you turn left, uphill, still on a car-wide track*, following a yellow arrow on a post and a two-armed signpost, your direction east.

In 100 metres, just before a decaying wooden fieldgate, turn right, following a yellow arrow. In 10 metres a sign says 'Please keep dogs on lead'. Follow the direction of the yellow arrow, keeping the hedge to your right-hand side, your direction 170 degrees. In 200 metres *you enter a wood over a stile* with yellow arrows on it. *In 10 metres turn right at a yellow arrow-marked post and exit the wood through a metal kissing gate.*

Beyond the gate turn left, following the direction of the yellow arrow to the left of a kissing gate and a white wooden direction indicator behind towards the right-hand edge of a small line of trees on the far side of the field, your direction 120 degrees. To the right there is a fine view of the Thames Valley and much of the route you have followed to this point.

In 150 metres *exit this field through a metal kissing gate*. Keep to the left-hand edge of the next field, your direction 160 degrees. In 130 metres *exit this field over a wooden stile onto a tarmac road. Turn right down the road*, your direction 240 degrees. *In 500 metres, at a T-junction, turn left* following the sign to Henley and Marlow.

In 300 metres you come to the main road, the A4155, and the hamlet of **Mill End**. *Cross this very busy road with care and turn right*. In 20 metres you pass the **bus stop** for those wishing to end the walk here. **[5]** [See option **b**) in the **Walk options** at the start of this chapter.]

10 metres beyond the bus stop *you pass the entrance to Hambleden Marina, and 10 metres beyond this you turn left down a signposted footpath between houses*, your direction 200 degrees. This leads onto a tarmac driveway. *Walk straight ahead down this for 30 metres* towards a white metal fieldgate. *Just before the fieldgate turn right towards another white fieldgate, marked Hambleden Marina.*

Pass to the right of this and along a path between wooden fences, following white and yellow arrows. In 40 metres this brings you to **Hambleden Weir**. *Follow the metal walkway all the way across the Thames* (look back halfway across for a fine view of **Hambleden Mill**). When the walkway ends go down a concrete path for 20 metres and across the gates of **Hambleden Lock**. On the far side of the lock there is a three-armed signpost indicating the Thames Path.

(If you want a slightly easier, though not shorter, route back to Henley, you can turn right here and follow the river bank back to Henley, picking up the route at the point marked **[**]** below.)

To continue on the main walk, however, *turn left at the three-armed footpath sign*. In 15 metres *pass through a wooden kissing gate to the left of a metal fieldgate onto a tarmac lane*. (The river bank here is a very pleasant **picnic** spot: there is even a bench further up.) *In 150*

metres curve right with this lane, away from the river, at a three-armed signpost, your direction 190 degrees.

Continue on this tarmac lane for about 700 metres until you come to a wooden kissing gate to the right of double metal fieldgates. Carry on up the lane for another 30 metres until you get to a road, with a row of houses opposite. This is the hamlet of **Aston**. To visit the **Flower Pot Hotel**, a possible late lunch stop, turn left here for 40 metres. Otherwise, *turn right onto the road*, your direction 250 degrees. **[6]**

In 100 metres, at the 'Kill Your Speed' sign on the left-hand side of the road and just beyond the brow of the hill, *turn left over a stile* to the left of double metal fieldgates onto a permissive footpath, your direction 200 degrees. Continue uphill along the left-hand edge of a field onto **Remenham Hill**.

In 300 metres, *at the top of the hill, you emerge from a short wooded stretch to a T-junction* with a two-armed and one-armed signpost. *Go right here on a car-wide track* following a line of telegraph poles, your direction 250 degrees initially.

In 150 metres the trees end to your right, and in a further 80 metres another track merges from the left. Continue on across open fields for another 600 metres *to a wooden stile to the left of double fieldgates. Cross this and turn left onto a tarmac road*, your direction south. In 200 metres *turn right through an opening in the hedge just before a large oak tree* onto a signposted footpath.

Once through the hedge *go half left across a large field following the footpath arrow*, your direction 230 degrees. In 430 metres, *at the far side of the field, you come to the edge of woods and a four-armed footpath sign. Go straight on here* into the woods, your direction 190 degrees. Ignore all ways off. In 280 metres, *exit the woods over a stile.*

Continue straight ahead towards the tallest of a row of trees ahead, your direction 220 degrees, converging with a wooden fence to your right 100 metres later under the tall tree and at a three-armed footpath sign. *Continue straight on here down an avenue of trees* with a wooded slope to your right, your direction 170 degrees.

In 160 metres *cross a stile and descend onto the lawn of a large house.* 20 metres beyond the stile there is a public footpath sign pointing back the way you came. Immediately to the right on the ground is a touching plaque to Minty, a faithful dog. *Keep straight ahead, diagonally across the lawn,* your direction 210 degrees, with the house soon visible above you to the left, *heading for a stile in the hedge about 30 metres to the right of a wooden fieldgate in the far corner of the lawn* (a bush hides this stile in summer, but the bush is quite visible).

Once over the stile you join a car-wide track and continue onwards to the left-hand corner of the field. In 100 metres *exit the field through a wooden kissing gate to the left of double metal fieldgates. Cross over the road and through two wooden posts to continue along the left-hand edge of an open space,* joining a gravel track in 15 metres. 40 metres after this, *at a T-junction with a tarmac driveway, go left, passing through a gate to the left of double metal fieldgates.* The building to the right is the **Leander Club**, the prestigious Henley rowing club.

In 70 metres you come to the main road, the A4130. Here the Thames Path from Hambleden Lock merges from the right [**]. *Turn right on the main road across Henley Bridge and the River Thames.*

On the far side of the bridge **Crispins** tearoom is immediately ahead, but for the recommended tea place, the **Henley Tea Rooms**, *turn left* along Thames Side. The tearoom is 60 metres along on the right. *After tea turn right* following the road along the riverfront. In 50 metres ignore the road to the right (Friday Street), and keep along the riverside. In 80 metres, at the 'Boats

for Hire' kiosk, you *bend right with the road away from the river.* In 30 metres ignore Meadow Road to the left. In 90 metres, *opposite the Imperial Hotel, turn left up the approach road to* **Henley station**.

Lunch & tea places

Crispins *52 Hart Street, Henley-on-Thames, RG9 2AU (01491 574232).* Located on the corner of Hart Street and Thames Side, and immediately opposite the bridge in Henley, Crispins is a more upmarket tea alternative than the Henley Tea Rooms. It usually serves cream teas until 6.30pm or 7pm daily in the summer months, though tends to close early if custom is light.

Flower Pot Hotel *Ferry Lane, Aston, Henley-on-Thames, RG9 3DG (01491 574721).* **Open** 11am-3pm, 6-11pm daily. **Food served** noon-2pm, 6.30-9pm Mon-Sat; noon-2pm Sun. 10.6km (6.6 miles) into the walk is this homely, unpretentious place, serving food to match. There is a garden with hens and guinea-fowl pecking around it. If you intend to lunch here, start the walk at least an hour earlier – no later than 9am from London or 10am from Henley.

Henley Tea Rooms *Henley-on-Thames, RG9 1BH (01491 411412).* **Open** 9am-5pm daily. **Food served** 11am-2pm daily. On the waterfront just by the bridge in Henley, this place has plenty of tables and a nice selection of cakes and savoury items. This is the suggested tea stop on the walk.

Stag & Huntsman *Hambleden, RG9 6RP (01491 571227).* **Open** 11am-2.30pm, 6-11pm Mon-Fri; 11am-3pm, 6-11pm Sat; noon-3pm, 7-10.30pm Sun. **Food served** noon-2pm, 7-9.30pm Mon-Sat. 8km (5 miles) into the walk, this is a cosy and atmospheric village pub, with a blazing fire in winter and a garden in summer. This is the suggested lunch stop for the main walk (though note that meals are not served on Sundays).

Hambleden church serves teas in the churchyard on summer Sunday afternoons until about 5pm.

Picnic: The early riverside part of the walk is a fine picnic spot, as is the churchyard in Hambleden and the far (south) side of Hambleden Weir.

9.03 Paddington

Marlow Circular

Thameside meadows, wooded hills and a Georgian town.

Start and finish: Marlow station
Length: 19.4km (12.1 miles).
For shorter variations, *see below*
Walk options.

Time: 5 hours 30 minutes. For the whole excursion, including trains and meals, allow 9 hours.

Transport: Trains run hourly *9.3c* between London Paddington and Marlow, changing at Maidenhead (journey time: about 1 hour). For those driving, the obvious place to park is in Marlow; if you are not parking near the station, find the

High Street and pick up the walk in the text below. If you use a variation ending in Henley, there are hourly buses (the 328 or 329) back to Marlow until 10pm daily (for info, call 0870 608 2608). The buses go from Bell Street in the centre of Henley.

OS Landranger Map: 175
OS Explorer Maps: 171 and 172
Marlow, map reference SU855865, is in Buckinghamshire, 5km (3.1 miles) north-west of Maidenhead.

Toughness: 3 out of 10.

Walk notes: If all you know of the Thames is the grey muddy stretch that runs through London, you are in for a pleasant surprise on this walk. The Thames above Marlow is a lazy, tranquil river, which flows between pleasant meadows and overhanging trees, occasionally overlooked by fine old manor houses. The area is also known as a habitat for red kites – look up to see them hovering overhead. This walk follows the Thames path for the first 8km (5 miles), passing the ancient village of Hurley, little changed since the days when a Benedictine abbey stood here. Lunch is in Aston or Hambleden, both quaint riverside villages. By contrast, the afternoon takes you up over the wooded hills that frame the Thames Valley, and then back down into the well-preserved town of Marlow for tea. Note that much of the morning passes along the flood plain of the Thames and about once every winter this lives up to its name and the route becomes impassable.

Walk options: Directions, where needed, for the following variations are given at the end of the main walk text. *See p92.*

a) Marlow to Henley walk: From the Flower Pot Hotel in Aston (point [4] in the walk directions below), you can carry on into Henley, making a Marlow to Henley walk, for which there are two possible routes; either via Remenham Hill (13km/8 miles; 4 hours) or on along the river path (14km/8.7 miles; 4 hours 30 minutes).

b) Henley to Marlow walk: This walk uses the first half of walk 7 in this book, Henley via Hambleden Circular, as far as Hambleden, then joins the main walk at point [6]. It makes a walk of 14km (8.7 miles) and 4 hours 30 minutes walking time.

c) Marlow to Hurley (and back): A pleasant short excursion is to walk from Marlow to Hurley and back, lunching in Ye Olde Bell Inn in Hurley, and having tea in Marlow. The river path is easy to follow in the reverse direction. This is a round trip of

Marlow Circular

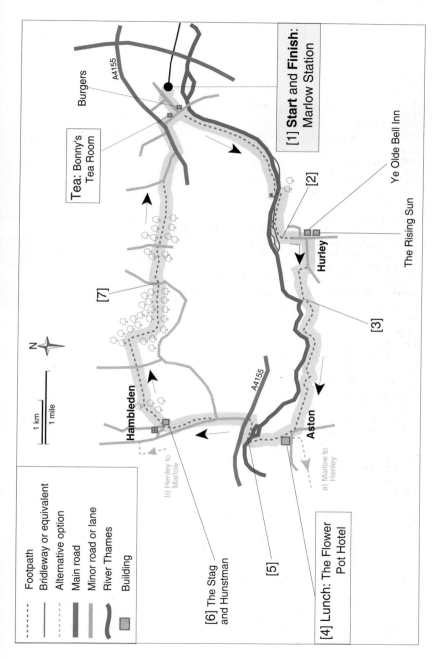

Legend:
- .... Footpath
- ———— Bridleway or equivalent
- -------- Alternative option
- ———— Main road
- ———— Minor road or lane
- ———— River Thames
- ▪ Building

N

1 km
1 mile

Burgers

A4155

Tea: Bonny's Tea Room

[1] **Start** and **Finish**: Marlow Station

[2]

Ye Olde Bell Inn

The Rising Sun

Hurley

[3]

[7]

Hambleden

Aston

b) Henley to Marlow

a) Marlow to Henley

[6] The Stag and Hunstman

[5]

[4] Lunch: The Flower Pot Hotel

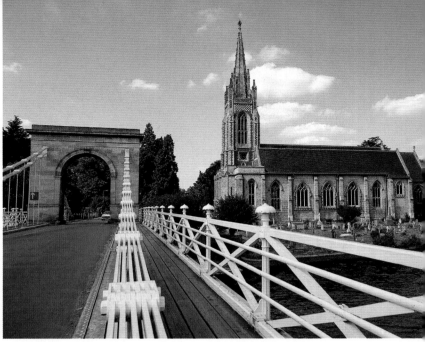

With its Georgian buildings and literary associations, the historic town of...

8.8km (5.5 miles), a leisurely 3 hours walking. Hurley is between point [2] and [3] in the main walk text.

Also, the buses which link Henley and Marlow (*see p84* **Transport** for full details) also stop on the A4155 just beyond Hambleden Lock, making it possible to end the walk at this point, 10km (6 miles) into the walk.

Saturday Walkers' Club: Catch the nearest train to 9am from Paddington. For the Henley to Marlow variation, see the train time in walk 7.

Walk directions

[1] [Numbers refer to the map]
From Marlow's diminutive station *walk along the platform, out past the small shelter, and straight ahead down the station approach.* In 30 metres a road merges from the right and in 70 metres you come to a *five-way road junction.*

Cross Lock Road to continue ahead along the main road to the right of the *Marlow Donkey pub,* your direction 240 degrees. (This is Station Road, though not signposted as such.) In 180 metres ignore Station Rise to the right and, a few metres after, Mill Road to the left. In 200 metres ignore St Peter Street to the left. In 70 metres *you come to a mini roundabout,* the junction with the **High Street** (which is the road to the right). *Cross straight over this junction and go half left into Higginson Park.*

Follow the car-wide tarmac path diagonally across the park, your direction 210 degrees, to the river, where you *carry straight ahead along the river bank. You now follow the riverside path, with the Thames on your left all the way to the bridge just beyond Temple Lock, a distance of 2.3km (1.5 miles).*

But in more detail: in 140 metres you leave the park (there is a nice view back of Marlow's church and bridge at this point) and in 300 metres you come level with **Bisham Church** on the opposite bank of the river. At this point cross a footbridge

... **Marlow** makes a fascinating place to start and end this walk.

over a side river, and in 100 metres another. After this second bridge you pass through a wooden gate and in 100 metres go through another into an open field.

The battlement-towered building across the river to your left at this point is **Bisham Abbey**. Keeping to the river's edge, in 300 metres you pass through a gate into another field, and in 300 metres do the same again. 100 metres after this you pass a stone memorial to a couple who used to organise the Marlow Regatta, and in 120 metres you pass through yet another gate. There is now a modern housing development across the river to your left. In 150 metres the path becomes a tarmac road and you are approaching a major weir in the Thames on your left. In another 150 metres you pass **Temple Lock** to keep straight on along the riverbank.

(Note that there is a public toilet by the cottage on the left-hand side of the lock.) There's a possible morning coffee stop here, the **Temple Tea Gardens** (open on fine days from March to September).

150 metres beyond the lock, turn left to cross over the river on Temple Footbridge. On the far side of the bridge, turn right to continue in your former direction, with the river now on your right. In 80 metres ignore a footpath to the left and continue on the river bank. In 100 metres pass through a gate into a field. (**Harleyford Manor** is the fine house ahead of you across the river at this point.)

In 250 metres pass through a kissing gate (or a metal fieldgate 25 metres to the left of it). Keep close to the river and in 80 metres *go right across a wooden footbridge onto an island in the river. ([!] If you are not right on the riverbank this bridge is hidden in summer by tall trees.) Turn left at the far end of the footbridge.* A sign announces you are at **Hurley Lock**. In 150 metres you come to the lock itself. Ignore a signposted footpath to the left over the lock and go straight on.

In 150 metres turn left to cross back over the river on a footbridge. **[2]** *Go left from the end of the footbridge, down steps* *and then ahead on a concrete path*, with a wall on your left. This brings you into the village of **Hurley**. In 50 metres you pass a house on the left and, in 60 metres, where the wall ends left and there is a triangular-roofed gate to your right, fork right, with a small green on your left. In 40 metres ignore a footpath sign that points right just before a large stone-walled building.

In 40 metres the **Hurley Farm Shop** is on your right (it is easy to miss, as it looks like the door of a house). 20 metres beyond this you come to another green. You pass the fine house of the Old Vicarage on your right and ignore a road turning to the left to keep straight on through the village. In 180 metres you come to **Ye Olde Bell Inn**, a possible early lunch stop. (If Ye Olde Bell Inn is full, there is another pub, the **Rising Sun**, 120 metres further on up the road; if you decide to visit it you will need to retrace your steps to Ye Old Bell Inn to continue the walk).

If you are not planning to stop for lunch at either pub, *turn right down Shepherds Lane, 10 metres before you get to Ye Olde Bell Inn.* (If you have stopped in Ye Olde Bell Inn, turn right out of the pub and then, in 10 metres, left down Shepherds Lane.) Follow this lane for 600 metres until you come to a signposted footpath to your right, just beyond a half-timbered house (Field House).

Turn right along this footpath, your direction 340 degrees, initially up a gravel drive and then, in 20 metres, where the drive turns right to the house, straight on through bushes for 30 metres more to a stile. Once over this stile you are walking along the left-hand edge of a field. In 200 metres this brings to another stile, which you cross and *turn left along a tarmac road.*

In 360 metres, at a crossroads (the road to the right is the entrance to a caravan park), where the onward road curves left, *leave the road to keep straight on along the right-hand edge of a triangular green space*, with the caravan park immediately to your right, your direction 260 degrees.

In 100 metres *you come to the far right-hand corner of the open space*, with a bungalow marked with the number 4 ahead of you, *and turn right through a gap in the hedge and then left to resume your former direction*, following a green footpath sign. In 30 metres you find yourself back on the riverside path, where you veer left **[3]**.

Almost immediately you pass to the left of a rusted fieldgate. You are now on a path with houses and bungalows to your left and boats moored to your right. In 200 metres you pass through a metal gate. In 140 metres, just before another, marked 'Private Road' and level with a house called Water's Edge, *fork right off the track*, following a yellow arrow on a path along the river's edge. In 40 metres pass through a wooden gate to keep straight on and, in 60 metres where the fence ends, ignore a footpath to the left to stay on the river's bank.

In 180 metres, 20 metres after passing through gateposts with no gate, *the path forks left through a wooden fieldgate into a field or right along the bank.* You can choose either route (the right fork merely follows a loop of the river round), but *the shortest is to fork left* across the field. In 220 metres you come to the river again and a three-armed footpath sign and *turn left through a kissing gate*, your direction initially 230 degrees. You now pass through a series of tranquil riverside meadows, keeping the river to your right all the time. In 350 metres you pass over a small footbridge flanked by two kissing gates. In 350 metres you pass over another bridge, this time flanked by stiles, and in 260 metres another bridge with kissing gates.

[!] *Beyond this third footbridge, leave the riverside and fork half left across a field* following a signpost for the Thames Path, your direction 240 degrees. *In 180 metres, you come to a three-way road junction*, where you go right, following a footpath sign, your direction 340 degrees. In 150 metres the road curves left and, in another 80 metres, it passes two houses on your right. Just beyond this *a track forks right through metal fieldgates but you go straight ahead*, your direction 260 degrees.

In 30 metres, *at a three-armed footpath sign, go right through a metal gate.* You are now walking towards a fine brick country house on the hill ahead. Keep to the left of the telegraph pole and in 60 metres pass through a metal gate. Beyond the gate, keep to the right of two saplings and carry on across the field, your direction 300 degrees. In 180 metres you pass through a wooden kissing gate. The fine house to your left is **Culham Court**. In 50 metres pass through a metal kissing gate and in 20 metres through another. In a further 20 metres go through a wooden kissing gate.

You are now in a big open field, which you cross in the same direction as before. To your right is a fine panorama of the Thames. In 350 metres *you pass through a wooden gate and in 40 metres you emerge onto a road* and continue straight on in the same direction as before. In 120 metres you come to a road T-junction, where you go right. In 60 metres you come to the **Flower Pot Hotel**, the first of two possible lunch pubs. **[4]**

[At this point, you can take option **a)**, the **Marlow to Henley** walk; see directions at the end of this main walk text.]

If you are not stopping for lunch *pass to the right of the pub, down Ferry Lane.* In 100 metres, by Ferry Cottage, *turn left off the road down a footpath. In 80 metres you come to a tarmac lane and go right along it.* Follow this road for 600 metres until you reach the river and then curve left with it for a further 150 metres, with the river on your right-hand side, to a kissing gate, the entrance to **Hambleden Lock**.

20 metres beyond the kissing gate you come to a three-armed footpath sign **[5]**, where you *turn right, crossing the lock by the lock gate* and keeping straight on beyond. This path soon curves round to the right and *crosses Hambleden Weir and the whole river on a metal walkway.*

On the far side walk up a tarmac path between fences to a driveway. Mill House is on your left. Turn left to follow a white arrow on the fence ahead and pass between Millgate Cottage (left) and Why Cottage (right) to a busy road, the A4155.

Cross the road with care and turn right. In 30 metres turn left up a road signposted to Hambleden, Skirmett and Fingest. (Note: if you want to take the **bus** here **back to Marlow**, the stop is the one just beyond this road junction: *see p84* **Transport** for bus details.)

Carry on up the road signposted to Hambleden. In 260 metres *there is a turning to the right to Rotten Row. Go through the metal kissing gate on the far side of this turning*, next to a sign indicating Huttons Farm, to walk straight on along a field edge, with the hedge on your left, parallel to the road you have just left. *In 500 metres pass through a metal kissing gate, cross a car-wide track and go through another metal kissing gate into the field beyond.* **Hambleden village** is visible on the far side of this field.

In 450 metres, near the top of this field, curve left through a metal kissing gate onto the road and then right across a stone arched bridge. In 50 metres pass the **Village Shop** on your left: the shop sells fresh cakes. Carry on past an old pump, with the church of **St Mary the Virgin** on your left. At the end of the churchyard, ignore the road to the left, Pheasants Hill, to carry straight on. The **Stag and Huntsman**, the second possible lunch stop, is a short way up this road on your right **[6]**.

Coming out of the pub, *turn right* (or keep in the same direction if not stopping for lunch) and carry on up the road, which is soon marked 'Private Road: Access Only' (it is, however, a public footpath), your direction 80 degrees. This road soon starts to climb a hill. In 100 metres ignore a car-wide track to the right. 10 metres later you pass the entrance to Kenricks house right. *In 180 metres the road becomes a path and climbs steeply up into woods.*

Stay on this path for 450 metres, ignoring all ways off, until it comes to the top of the hill and passes through a stile next to a gate to exit the wood. Beyond the stile go straight on, now on a car-wide track on the left-hand edge of a field. In 180 metres this path joins a tarmac lane coming from a house to the left. Keep straight on along this lane, your direction due east, for 500 metres until, just past a house on your right, *you come to a road.*

Cross over this road to continue straight ahead up a farm track on the right-hand edge of a field. [!] *In 300 metres, where the track curves left with the field edge, follow a path marked by a white arrow on a board straight on into the wood.*

Walk straight ahead into the wood for 220 metres, passing a white arrow cross on a tree and then a green arrow, and another white arrow cross. *10 metres beyond the second white cross and 40 metres before the forest edge ahead, turn right on a car-wide track,* your initial direction 140 degrees.

Stay on this track as it descends the hill and curves left then right. In 400 metres you come to the bottom of a small valley surrounded by pine trees, *where a track merges from your left-hand side. Continue to follow the valley bottom,* your direction 190 degrees. In 140 metres curve left with the valley bottom, passing a post with two yellow arrows. Ignore a path merging from the right and another diverging uphill right at this point.

Instead, continue to follow the broad track along the valley, ignoring all ways off, for another 1km until you pass through a green metal barrier, and come to a road. [7] *Turn right along the road and then, in 40 metres, turn left up a track,* signposted the Chiltern Way, your direction 70 degrees. In 10 metres cross a stile to the left of a metal fieldgate (note: this stile may be hidden by bushes in summer). Keep straight on, with a field edge to your right, and in 100 metres cross another stile. *60 metres after this, and 15 metres before a metal fieldgate, go right*

over a stile along a path fenced off from a field to your right. In 10 metres this curves right, your direction now 120 degrees.

In 400 metres cross a stile into a wood and, ignoring footpaths right and left, *follow the path straight up the hill ahead.* At the top of the hill, in 160 metres, veer slightly left, following white arrows on trees, *towards a road and car park 80 metres ahead.* Just before the road you pass a post with a yellow arrow on it. Go straight across the road and along a footpath onwards through the woods, still following signs for the Chiltern Way and with a Woodland Trust sign to the left of the path at its start.

[!] *In 50 metres, though the path appears to continue ahead across a small ditch, follow the white arrow on the tree to the right,* your direction 140 degrees. *Keep following the white arrows on trees through the wood* ([!] easier to see in winter than in summer, but in summer foliage on either side makes the route clearer) as the path curves left, crosses a ditch and eventually straightens out at a bearing of 100 degrees.

In 350 metres you come to two posts with yellow arrows on. [!] *Beyond the second post, at a footpath crossroads, keep straight on along a path that may initially be a bit hard to follow due to fallen trees,* your direction 90 degrees. In 20 metres another post with a yellow arrow to the right of the path reconfirms your route. *In 50 metres, at a junction marked by white arrows left and right on a tree, turn right onto a larger track,* your direction now 130 degrees. In 50 metres ignore an arrow pointing right to keep on gently downhill.

[!] *In 250 metres you come to the end of the wood. Go straight on, ignoring a large white arrow on a tree that points left just before the junction and two signposted footpaths to the right* (one over a stile, the other through a wooden squeeze gate). Keep straight on and in 15 metres pass through a wooden squeeze gate. You are now on a broad

Writers and religion

Most of the fine buildings in **Marlow**'s High Street and West Street are Georgian, but the town has an ancient lineage. It was already well-established in the days of the Domesday Book (1085), when it had 'twenty three copy-holders, one serf and one mill', as well as 'a fishery which yields 1000 eels'. At that time, Marlow was ringed by monastic foundations, and the remains of a 12th-century chapel (and crypt) can still be found at Widmer Farm. Bisham Abbey, which was given by Henry VIII to his divorced wife Anne of Cleves, and the village of Hurley, a former Benedictine monastery, are among the others passed on the walk.

Marlow's church was famously surrounded by marsh, prompting one churchwarden in 1777 to ask for money 'for a cast iron brazier wherein to make a large charcoal fire and warm the church in cold damp weather'.

Famous residents of Marlow include Mary Shelley, who lived in West Street for a year with her poet husband Percy Bysshe Shelley while finishing her novel *Frankenstein*. TS Eliot also came to Marlow to escape the bombing in London at the end of the World War I, and the town was home to Jerome K Jerome, whose novel *Three Men in a Boat* immortalised the pleasures of 'messing about on the river'.

---

path between wire fences, with an open field to the right, your direction due east.

In 220 metres *you come out of the trees into an open field and the path forks. Take the left fork* on a fenced path that descends into a dip and climbs out again, your direction 80 degrees. *In 320 metres you come to a wood and pass through this, veering left to reach the road* 100 metres further on. *At the road* (Bovingden Heights) *turn right* and in 30 metres ignore a road to the right (Spinfield Mount) *to carry straight on down the right-hand of two roads straight ahead* (they are in fact two halves of the same road, Spinfield Lane, but the right-hand one is the pedestrian route).

Keep to the right-hand side of the road. In 300 metres the two halves of the road merge. *60 metres beyond this, where the pavement ends, go down a tarmac path that diverges right from the road. In 30 metres this merges with a car-wide path to continue downhill.* In 30 metres the path becomes a road and in 200 metres it *descends to the main road, the A4155, where you go left.*

In 450 metres you pass the Lion, a modernised pub on your right, which more or less marks the start of the commercial centre of **Marlow**. *180 metres beyond this you come to a T-junction with an obelisk in the centre and turn right down a shopping street.* This is Marlow High Street.

Possible tea places (*see p92* **Lunch & tea places**) are **Caffe Uno** (80 metres down on the left), **Coffee Republic** (80 metres beyond this on the right), **Bonny's Tea Room** (50 metres further on the left) and **Burgers** (in a further 100 metres on the left, just before the church).

The way to the station is to turn left just before Burgers into Station Road. In 70 metres ignore St Peter Street to the right and in 200 metres more ignore Mill Road to the right and Station Rise to the left. 180 metres beyond this you come to a five-way road junction, with the Marlow Donkey Pub on your right: the way to the station is half right (Station Approach).

In 70 metres ignore a fork to the left into an industrial park and keep right: in about 40 metres, you come to **Marlow station**.

Walk options

a) Marlow to Henley walk:

This option uses part of the Henley via Hambleden Circular walk directions (walk 7 in this book) to return to Henley.

Follow the main walk directions until point [4].

Come out of the front (south) entrance of the Flower Pot Hotel and turn right (west) onto the road, which climbs gently uphill. In 40 metres you pass some cottages to the left and a car-wide concrete track leading to double metal fieldgates right. Keep straight on along the road here and pick up the walk directions in the Henley via Hambleden Circular chapter of this book at point [5]. This takes you over Remenham Hill and back into the centre of Henley.

The second option is to stay on the main walk route described above to point [5], but then remain on the river path instead of crossing Hambleden Lock. 4km (2.5 miles) of very pleasant riverside walking brings you to Henley's road bridge. The Henley via Hambleden Circular walk has details of tea places and how to get to Henley station. If you wish to return to Marlow by bus at this point, *see p84* **Transport**.

b) Henley to Marlow walk:
Follow the directions within walk 7 in this book, the Henley via Hambleden Circular, to lunch at Hambleden, and then follow the directions in the main walk text above from point [6]. This creates a Henley to Marlow walk.

Lunch & tea places

Bonny's Tea Room *59 High Street, Marlow, SL7 1AB (01628 471615).* **Open/food served** 8.30am-5pm Mon-Fri; 9am-5pm Sat; 1am-5pm Sun. Situated about halfway down Marlow's High Street on the left, Bonny's serves good home-made cakes.

Burgers *The Causeway, Marlow, SL7 2AA (01628 483389).* **Open/food served** 8.30am-5.30pm Mon-Sat. On the left at the bottom of the High Street just before the church, Burgers is (despite its name) an upmarket patisserie and tearoom.

Flower Pot Hotel *Ferry Lane, Aston, Henley-on-Thames, RG9 3DG (01491 574721).* **Open** 11am-3pm, 6-11pm daily. **Food served** noon-2pm, 6.30-9pm Mon-Sat; noon-2pm Sun. 9.2km (5.75 miles) into the walk, this homely, unpretentious place (more of a pub than a hotel) serves food to match. The bar is decorated with stuffed fish and there is a garden with hens and guinea-fowl pecking around it.

Stag and Huntsman *Hambleden, RG9 6RP (01491 571227).* **Open** 11am-2.30pm, 6-11pm Mon-Fri; 11am-3pm, 6-11pm Sat; noon-3pm, 7-10.30pm Sun. **Food served** noon-2pm, 7-9.30pm Mon-Sat. Located 11.8km (7.4 miles) into the walk, the Stag and Huntsman is a cosy, atmospheric old pub with a blazing fire in winter and a garden to enjoy in summer. Note that no food is served on Sundays.

Ye Olde Bell Inn *High Street, Hurley, SL6 5LX (01628 825881).* **Food served** *Bar* noon-2pm, 6-9pm daily. *Restaurant* noon-2pm, 7-9.30pm Mon-Sat; noon-2.30pm, 7-9pm Sun. This is a possible lunch choice if you are just walking to Hurley and back or as an early lunch option on the main walk. It is, in fact, a hotel, which serves food in its restaurant (though the 'smart casual' dress code would rule out most walkers) and bar meals. 120 metres further up the road on the left, the Rising Sun may also serve meals.

Other options: If you arrive later in Marlow (very likely on a spring or summer day), there are other choices. The local branch of **Coffee Republic**, on the right-hand side of the High Street about halfway down, stays open till 6pm. A little further back up the High Road is **Caffe Uno**, more of a restaurant in the evenings, but advertising itself as a café too. Marlow also has oodles of fine old pubs, some of which will almost certainly serve tea and coffee.

If you are returning to Marlow along the river from Hurley, the **Temple Tea Gardens** at Temple Lock is another possible tea stop: it is open roughly from March to September 'depending on the weather'.

Picnic: Almost anywhere in the first five miles of the walk would be an ideal place or a picnic. Marlow High Street (passed early in the walk) is the obvious place to buy picnic items; if you forget, the Hurley Farm Shop (actually a normal convenience store) in the village of Hurley can help you out. It is open 7.30am to 8pm daily.

Kintbury to Great Bedwyn

The North Wessex Downs, the Test Way and Great Bedwyn.

Start: Kintbury station
Finish: Bedwyn station

Length: 20km (12.5 miles). For a shorter walk and other variations, *see below* **Walk options**.

Time: 6 hours. For the whole outing, including trains and meals, allow 10 hours.

Transport: Trains run hourly (every 2 hours on Sundays) between London Paddington and Kintbury, changing at Reading or Newbury (journey time: 1 hour 10 minutes). Direct trains run back from Bedwyn to Paddington (hourly Mon-Fri, every 2 hours Sun; journey time: about 1 hour 25 minutes), but not on Saturdays (one train an hour), when you'll need to change at Reading. It is cheapest to buy a day return to Bedwyn. For drivers, it is best to park at Kintbury station and return to your car on the train from Bedwyn station (a 10-minute journey).

OS Landranger Map: 174
OS Explorer Map: 157 and 158 (most of the walk is on 158) Kintbury, map reference SU386672, is in Berkshire, 8km (5 miles) west of Newbury.

Toughness: 5 out of 10.

Walk notes: Though only an hour west of London by train, this walk has a decidedly West Country feel, far removed from the more manicured charms of the Home Counties. In the morning it passes through an idyllic series of woods and pastures, with largely gentle gradients. After lunch at a quiet country pub in Inkpen (the sort of place where the conversation at the bar is more likely to be about farming than the price of second homes), it then climbs up onto a long ridge, giving views as dramatic (and even more unspoiled) than any on the South Downs. The rest of the walk follows the Test Way, a broad track along the top of this ridge, before descending to the valley and the pretty village of Great Bedwyn.

Walk options: The walk can be shortened by taking shortcuts to two different points, both of which fall on the same bus route. At point [5] in the main walk text below, instead of crossing over the road, turn right to continue down the road for 1.6km (1 mile) to reach the Crown & Anchor (01488 668242), Ham, which shortens the walk by 6.2km (3.9 miles). Alternatively, at point [6] below, continue down the road for 1.8km (1.1 miles) to reach the Plough Inn (01672 870295), Shalbourne, which shortens the walk by 4.2km (2.6 miles). There is an infrequent 20 or 22 bus service from Marlborough to Hungerford via Bedwyn, which calls at the Plough Inn and the Crown & Anchor. (Bus enquiry line 08457 090899.) Alternatively you could order a taxi.

Saturday Walkers' Club: Take the train nearest to 9.30am (before or after) from London Paddington to Kintbury.

Walk directions

[1] [Numbers refer to the map] Coming off platform 1 from **Kintbury station** *turn left to head south down the right side of the road* past the Dundas Arms on your left. After 20 metres cross the roadbridge over the canal.

After 40 metres pass Millbank Road with Kintbury Mill on the right. In 50 metres the pavement goes up an incline with a handrail on the left-hand side. *At the top of this incline turn right at the partially hidden public footpath signpost,* your direction west, to walk up a tarmac car-wide path. In 10 metres you pass 'The Millers House' on your right.

In 30 metres the path narrows to a tarmac footpath called The Cliffs running between houses, your direction 260 degrees. In a further 150 metres, by a white house to your left, ignore a public footpath signpost on your right to continue straight ahead through an unusual wooden turnstile, *where you veer left up a lane,* your initial direction 230 degrees.

After 15 metres turn right as indicated by a public footpath signpost to enter a churchyard. Walk straight through the churchyard on a sand/shingle path between trees *to the gate at the far end.* Go through the gate to continue straight up an initially shingle path between houses, your direction 240 degrees.

In 120 metres you pass a public footpath signpost on your right as you *veer left onto a sand shingle driveway to reach a T-junction after 20 metres. Cross over the lane to continue on a tarmac driveway* that is slightly to your right called Titcomb Way.

In 25 metres fork right off the tarmac driveway along a grassy footpath between two wooden fences, your direction due south. After 80 metres the wooden fence on your right-hand side comes to an end and you pass through a redundant rusty kissing gate. The footpath now passes beneath an arbour of trees meeting overhead for the main part with the odd clearing.

After 450 metres, as the arbour ends, cross over a stile to turn right, and in 15 metres cross another stile to the left of a car-wide plank bridge. Turn immediately left to follow the footpath with trees on your left and an open meadow on your right edged with a wire fence, your direction 170 degrees. *In a further 150 metres at the end of the field turn right across a stile to walk up the left edge of the field,* your direction 200 degrees.

In 200 metres cross a stile with metal strips between the wood with a footpath signpost to the left. Continue straight ahead to follow this footpath along the right side of the field, your direction 210 degrees. *In 200 metres pass a footpath signpost on the right* to continue along the right side of the field. Pass by a wooden gate on your right after 40 metres to proceed straight down the right side of the field.

At the field corner turn right to go through a wooden squeezegate to the left of a metal fieldgate. Turn left up the lane as indicated by an arrow, your direction 170 degrees. After 40 metres pass by a public footpath signpost on your left pointing the way you are going and continue up the lane.

In a further 200 metres, as the lane turns sharply left, turn right on to a concrete car-wide track. Pass over a cattle grid by a wooden fieldgate to continue straight ahead, your direction west. In 80 metres the path dips to a bridge with low stone walls each side. After the bridge ignore a wooden single gate to the left to continue straight up the track.

In a further 100 metres, as the concrete car-wide track swings round to the left, go straight ahead to cross over a wooden stile into a field. *Veer slightly to your right to cross the field on a gently descending path, aiming for the bottom corner,* your direction 330 degrees. *In 80 metres go through an opening and turn left at a yellow waymark arrow.*

Kintbury to Great Bedwyn

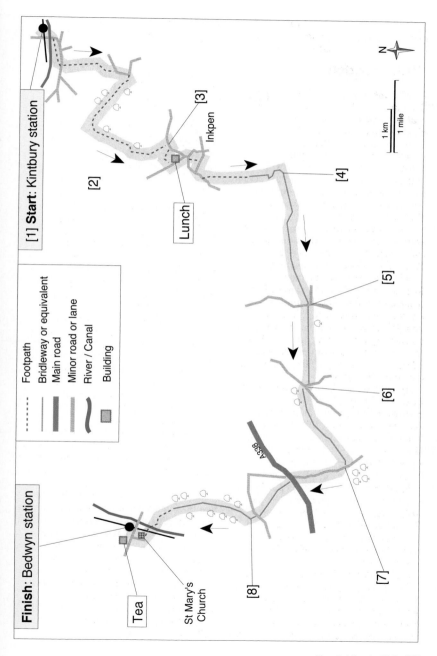

[1] **Start**: Kintbury station

[2]

[3]

Inkpen

Lunch

[4]

[5]

[6]

A338

[7]

[8]

Finish: Bedwyn station

Tea

St Mary's Church

N

1 km
1 mile

Footpath
Bridleway or equivalent
Main road
Minor road or lane
River / Canal
Building

Canal pleasures

This walk begins and ends at villages standing on one of the loveliest stretches of the **Kennet and Avon Canal**. The origins of this historic waterway lie in the dual threats of Atlantic storms and the French.

During the 18th and early 19th centuries Britain and France were frequently at war, and British cargo boats sailing between Bristol and London were often attacked by privateers. Unpredictable weather and the rugged south-west coast also took their toll on shipping, prompting the creation of an inland water route between the two cities.

The Kennet Navigation, stretching from the Thames near Reading to Newbury, was completed in 1723, while the Avon Navigation, from Bristol to Bath, opened in 1727.

However, the 91 kilometre- (57 mile-) long 'Western Canal Project', designed to link the two, wouldn't be built for another 90 years.

Work on the canal, engineered by John Rennie, started in 1794 and lasted 16 years (and came in three times over budget). Though most of the work was relatively primitive, back-breaking pick and shovel work, the result included a number of major engineering feats – including the almost half mile-long Bruce Tunnel, the beautiful neo-classical aqueducts at Dundas and Avoncliffe, and the Caen Hill flight of 16 locks (there are a total of 29 locks along a two-mile stretch of the canal).

The Kennet and Avon's glory days lasted just 30 years. Ironically, the canal was used to transport materials

---

Walk up the left side of the field for 20 metres following a wire fence to a stile in the left-hand corner. *Cross over the stile and go 6 metres up a potentially muddy slope to cross over another wooden stile.* Continue up this path through a few trees to enter an open field. *Follow the path with trees and wire fence to your left along the left edge of the field.*

In 130 metres cross a stile to continue on the footpath across the field towards a wooden fieldgate that can be seen on the opposite side 140 metres distant. At the bottom right corner veer to your right to cross a stile. Notice two waymarked paths, one footpath to the right and one veering slightly right. *Take the latter down across the field diagonally,* your direction 340 degrees.

In 100 metres *go over a plank footbridge to immediately cross over a stile and turn half left. Continue along a narrow strip of grassland with trees to your left,* hedge

and trees to your right, your direction 320 degrees. After 40 metres follow a public footpath post on your right with a yellow arrow to continue straight ahead. Follow the path along a narrow ditch to your right.

After 160 metres cross a two-plank footbridge and a stile with yellow public footpath signs to turn left along a footpath between young trees. In 200 metres the path passes through a redundant metal kissing gate to *come to a lane.* On your left is the entrance to a very grand-looking building, **St Cassian's Centre**, although there is no sign to indicate this.

Cross over the lane to go through another metal kissing gate by a public footpath sign. *Turn half left across the field,* your direction 290 degrees. After 40 metres you pass under mini pylon cables. To your left is a good view of St Cassian's Centre. In another 40 metres you pass a games field to your left.

that were used to construct the Great Western Railway. The opening of the London–Bristol rail line in 1841 killed off the commercial viability of the canal within a decade, and it rapidly fell into neglect and disuse.

Much of the canal has now been restored, thanks to the work of the Kennet and Avon Canal Trust (www.katrust.org). Today, the waterway is a popular route for leisure canal boats and its towpaths attract many walkers. The Trust is currently involved in a £29-million project to further restore the canal and secure its future for generations to come.

After 150 metres you *reach a crosspaths [2] with a four-armed public footpath signpost where you turn left,* your direction 250 degrees. *In 100 metres cross a car-wide concrete track to then go over a stile with a yellow footpath sign and continue straight ahead to cross a field. In 100 metres pass to the right of a redundant stile with a yellow arrow, your direction still 250 degrees.*

Follow the earth footpath straight ahead between trees, your direction 220 degrees. To your right is a downward-sloping meadow with scattered trees. Look out for banks of bluebells in spring. *In a further 250 metres cross a three-plank bridge over a dried-up stream with a handrail to your left to immediately cross a stile with a public footpath signpost. Cross the field half left and in 170 metres pass over the crossing place in the electric fence* (30 metres to the right of a metal fieldgate in the left corner), your direction 220 degrees.

Turn half left to cross the next field, with a tree encased by fencing to your right, *to cross a wooden stile in the left-hand corner. Cross a wooden footbridge to turn right along a tarmac car-wide track,* following a yellow public footpath arrow, your direction 240 degrees.

You are now at Balsdon Farm. *Follow the tarmac car-wide track round to the right after 80 metres.* After 30 metres the car-wide track veers to the left past the farmhouse, the tarmac now giving way to grass and concrete. *Continue on this track passing through a wooden gate,* marked 'Private Rd Public Footpath only' on the other side.

In 50 metres the track meets a T-junction with a five-armed public footpath sign to your right by a shingle patch. *Turn half left to go down a car-wide grassy path* between two wooden fences, your direction 190 degrees.

In 180 metres where the fences end, cross a wooden stile ahead with a yellow

Countryside near **Kintbury**.

footpath arrow pointing half left. Take the path passing down through trees after 5 metres. After 10 metres *cross a three-plank footbridge over a stream. Veer to the right uphill for 5 metres* to cross a wooden stile ahead with a yellow footpath arrow pointing half left. *Then walk up the right edge of the field* with a wire fence to your right, your direction south.

In 200 metres you cross an unusual corrugated stile to continue along the right edge of the field. After 400 metres you go over another one of these stiles with a two-armed public footpath signpost. *Turn right to walk down an out-of-condition car-wide track.* In 40 metres follow a public footpath sign on your right to continue on the track, now veering slightly to the right.

In another 40 metres cross a stile to the right of a metal fieldgate to reach a junction with a tarmac lane **[3]**, with a black and white Tudor-style cottage straight ahead. *Turn right at this T-junction and after 40 metres cross a lane bridge over a stream to immediately turn right over a stile onto a footpath.*

In 50 metres cross a stile to walk along the bottom right edge of a field with a wooden fence on your right and an attractive house beyond. On reaching the corner of the field cross an unusual stile to *follow the path round sharply to the right over a bridge* with stone walls each side crossing a stream.

Continue on the path with a wooden fence now on the right, another stream to your left. After 80 metres *cross a concrete footbridge over a stream* with a small cattle grid at both ends of the bridge. The path now becomes a dirt track going uphill to a wooden public footpath signpost.

[!] *Take the path to the left going up a bank*, your direction 240 degrees. *In 5 metres you come to a wire fence and cross over a stile to your right* that may be overgrown with nettles. *After 5 metres turn left*, your direction 220 degrees, and *walk up the left-hand side of field with a barbed wire fence to your left.*

In 100 metres, at the field corner, pass through an opening that was once a gate with a public footpath sign on the field post *to take the path straight ahead past a greenhouse to your left*. There are houses backing onto the left-hand fence and trees to your right.

After 20 metres the path becomes a shingle lane. Continue straight ahead for 50 metres to *come to a T-junction with a tarmac lane. Turn left down the lane*, your direction 150 degrees, and in 150 metres cross an old bridge over a stream. In a further 40 metres you come to the **Swan Inn, Lower Inkpen**, the suggested lunchtime stop.

Turn left from the pub to continue up the lane in the same direction. After 60 metres *at a Give Way sign at a triangular lane junction turn right on to the lane signposted to Combe and Ham.* In 30 metres continue along the lane as it curves to your right, signposted Ham and Shalbourne. After 50 metres pass a thatched red-brick cottage on your right.

In 20 metres turn left to follow a public footpath signpost, your initial direction 200 degrees. After 20 metres *cross a stile with a public footpath yellow arrow* pointing straight ahead. Cross the upper left side of a field, soon with a barbed wire fence to your left, to reach the field corner.

Cross over a dilapidated stile and walk across the field in the direction of houses straight ahead, aiming for a metal fieldgate with a high wooden stile to the left of the gate. *Cross over the stile to turn right down a tarmac lane.*

In 120 metres, *at a T-junction turn left, still on the lane marked Ham and Shalbourne.* After 200 metres *turn left onto a car-wide track* following a footpath signpost, your direction 150 degrees, heading towards a metal fieldgate 80 metres ahead.

Go through a metal squeezegate to the left of this metal fieldgate to continue straight ahead with open fields to your right. After 100 metres the path begins to veer to the right just after a public footpath signpost on your left, your direction now 200 degrees. Follow this grassy car-wide track with trees to your right-hand side.

As the trees on your right come to an end, continue, now with open fields on both sides, towards a row of trees straight ahead of you, 600 metres distant. As the path reaches the trees pass a public footpath and bridleway signpost to your left and continue straight ahead on a dirt footpath with trees on both sides.

After 500 metres curve left with the path at a public footpath signpost to go through a gate opening. Turn right up a grassy slope, your direction 170 degrees.

In 50 metres turn left onto a fairly indistinct bridleway, your direction now 100 degrees. Still continuing uphill on this path you can enjoy fantastic views to your left. After 300 metres and still ascending the bridleway curves to the right. Follow the path to the top of the hill until it shortly comes to a T-junction with another path where you veer right, your direction 230 degrees.

In 30 metres you pass a wooden gate and a bridleway post with a blue arrow on your left to carry straight on. *Follow the path for 100 metres to the field corner to cross over a stile to the right of a metal fieldgate.* **[4]** *Turn right onto a car-wide track, your direction west. You are now on the Test Way, which you follow to Botley Down.* [7]

But in more detail: Keep on the car-wide track with fabulous views off to your right. Sections of this path are potentially muddy in wet weather, but after a while this improves as the path begins to descend between gorse bushes. After 1.1km (0.7 miles) pass by a strange square grey metal object enclosed by fencing on your left.

As the path continues to gently descend, fine views extend from the right round to straight ahead. After a further 1.1km (0.7 miles) from the square grey metal object pass under mini pylon cables. 30 metres after passing under the cables the path veers slightly to the right as it descends more steeply. There are beautiful views now straight ahead and open fields to your left.

In 300 metres, as the path continues to descend through beautiful open countryside you pass by a stile on your right. *After 350 metres the car-wide earth track comes to a T-junction with a road* where a post to your right is marked as a byway in both directions. This road is about 3km (1.9 miles) from where you joined the Test Way.

Veer right at the road for 20 metres to a T-junction with another road. **[5]** Cross over the road straight ahead with care to rejoin the Test Way, which at this point is a car-wide earth track bridleway, your direction west. Continue on this car-wide earth track ignoring a way off to the right after 30 metres.

After 500 metres from the road the car-wide track again becomes potentially muddy. In summer trees and bushes on both sides of the path provide some shade. After 400 metres the trees end and you pass through a rusty metal fieldgate as the path continues through open countryside with views again to the right and also off to the left in the far distance. After 400 metres you pass a dilapidated barn to your right to continue on the car-wide earth track.

After 300 metres go through a metal fieldgate and in 10 metres *come to a T-junction with a tarmac road* **[6]** where you veer right slightly downhill. After 25 metres rejoin the Test Way on your left at a byway sign by a metal gate, your direction west. This is about 1.5km (0.9 miles) from the last road.

Go through the gate onto a potentially muddy byway. After 80 metres, passing through many nettles in summer, notice a beautiful big old tree on the left. After another 300 metres pass through a metal fieldgate to leave the wood, exposing fine views again to the right. There are now trees to the left and open fields to the right. When the trees end in 180 metres, there is a wire fence to the left.

In 1km (0.6 miles), as the path gets near to the woods ahead, it veers to the right with a barbed-wire fence to the right, just before some National Grid electricity cables. *In 60 metres the path leads down a T-junction with a road* **[7]**, *where you turn right.*

[If you don't want to walk along the road cross over it and to take a path up into a wooded area (the entrance to which is often overgrown in summer): in 15 metres *turn right along a path parallel to the road* through the woods with the road 15 metres down to your right. After 25 metres the path forks. *Take the left fork uphill away from the road.* In 50 metres you come out into a field with National Grid cables 30 metres to your left. *Turn*

right along the right-hand edge of the field, your direction 350 degrees. After 350 metres the track leads down to the road. Cross the road to continue along the grass verge on the right hand side.]

[!] Although the traffic should not be heavy, it does tend to be fast so extra care should be taken. 1km (0.6 miles) after leaving the Test Way you come to a busy crossroads with the A338 at a Give Way sign. *Cross over the A338 and turn left along a grass verge* towards Salisbury, your direction 230 degrees. *After 100 metres turn right at the public bridleway sign,* your direction 320 degrees, to cross an arable field.

After 200 metres you come to a field boundary and a waymarked post with two blue arrows. Carry straight on in the same direction towards an isolated tree 30 metres ahead to your left. *After another 300 metres turn right to follow the field boundary, then left after 5 metres.* You are now in a field with a hedge of trees to the right and a large white house clearly visible ahead across the field, your direction 290 degrees. Diagonally to your left you can see a windmill on the horizon (this is Wilton Windmill).

At the end of the field you come to a tarmac road, where you turn right. Almost immediately you pass ornate gateposts on your left with concrete dogs on top. *10 metres past these gates turn left through a gap in the hedge to walk up the left edge of a field* towards trees, with a fence to your left, your direction 290 degrees.

Follow the fence round to your left as the path narrows to a grassy track with the fence of the house to your left, later veering away from the house and fence up into the woods. After 80 metres the path comes out of the woods into the open to reach a crosspaths. **[8]**

Turn right onto a shingle path following a sign to Great Bedwyn. In 5 metres go through a wooden gate with a sign saying 'Bedwyn Brail' on the fence to your right. Follow the car-wide track through woodland, with wonderful displays of bluebells on both sides in season. After 400 metres, at a three-armed signpost, continue straight ahead, passing unusual stone benches to your left.

As the path continues it follows a line of tall fir trees to the left in what appears now to be a nature trail. After 300 metres the path veers to the left as it leaves the trees behind to emerge into more open countryside. The path then veers to the right to pass an old storage shed with a green corrugated iron roof on your right. After 180 metres you again enter woodland. In 400 metres you come to a staggered crosspaths marked by a four-armed public footpath signpost to your right. Carry straight on, signposted 'Gt. Bedwyn'.

After 190 metres the path now comes out into an open area. Continue on the car-wide grass track, your direction 350 degrees. *After 100 metres the path forks. Take the left fork, your direction 320 degrees, to enter woodland after 50 metres.*

As the path enters the wood it dips down and grass gives way to a dirt track. Follow the path as it winds around up and down, taking care not to stumble on the many tree roots. After 200 metres the path leaves the woodland, emerging into the left-hand corner of a field. *Continue ahead up the left-hand side of the field, with trees to your left.*

Continue straight to the far left-hand corner of the field past a redundant wooden stile on your left to go straight ahead down the left edge of the next field, with a hedge to your left. After 180 metres the path veers right down towards the Kennet and Avon canal and the River Dun.

A bridge over water can be seen diagonally down to your right. Follow the path down to this. *Pass through a wooden gate to cross the bridge over the canal. After 15 metres cross a small bridge over the river to go though a white picket kissing gate to cross a railway line. Go through another white picket kissing gate to cross a field* for 60 metres towards a wooden squeezegate adjacent to the churchyard wall of St Mary's, Great Bedwyn.

Go through the squeezegate and after 10 metres turn right into the part of the churchyard nearest to the church. Go straight ahead for 70 metres towards the churchyard gate opening into the road. *Turn right at the road* and cross over to pass a very unusual post office-cum-stonemason on your left-hand side. It is worth stopping here to read some of the memorials to past residents, many of which are very amusing.

Continuing up the road pass by a notice on a post to 'press button to operate fountain' and soon you will see the **Cross Keys Inn** *straight ahead at a T-junction. To get to the station, turn right at this T-junction,* onto the road marked 'Shalbourne & Oxenwood' and continue down this road where you will find the station after 50 metres on your left-hand side.

Lunch & tea places

Cross Keys Inn *16 High Street, Great Bedwyn, SN8 3NU (01672 870678/www.the xkeys.com).* **Open** noon-3pm, 6-11pm Mon-Fri; noon-11pm Sat, Sun. **Food served** noon-3pm, 6-11pm Mon-Fri; noon-11pm Sat; noon-3pm Sun. Meals, snacks, tea and coffee are available at this pub, which is the suggested tea stop for the end of the walk.

Dundas Arms *Kintbury, RG17 9UT (01488 658 263/www.dundasarms.co.uk).* **Open** 11am-3pm, 6-11pm daily. **Food served** noon-2pm Mon, Sun; noon-2pm, 7-9pm Tue-Sat. A pub at the start of the walk, with a lovely garden, a small river on one side and the Kennet and Avon canal on the other. Steak and ale pie-type meals are served in the bar; more elaborate food is available in another light-filled room.

Swan Inn *Craven Road, Lower Green, Inkpen, RD17 9DX (01488 668326).* **Open** 11am-2.30pm, 7-11pm Mon, Tue; 11am-2.30pm, 5-11pm Wed-Sat; noon-10.30pm Sun. **Food served** noon-2pm Mon-Fri; noon-2.30pm Sat, Sun. Located 6.5km from the start of the walk, this pub with a beer garden is owned by local organic beef farmers, who use mainly organic ingredients in their trad menu. Sandwiches are also available. Groups of more than eight should phone to book. This is the suggested lunch stop for the walk. There is a farm shop attached.

Alton Circular

Gilbert White's Selborne and Jane Austen's House.

Start and finish: Alton station
Length: 21km (13.1 miles). For a shorter walk and other variations, *see below* **Walk options**.
Time: 6 hours 30 minutes. For the whole outing, including trains and meals, allow 10 hours.
Transport: Two trains an hour run between London Waterloo and Alton (one hourly on Sunday; journey time: about 1 hour 10 minutes). For those driving, Alton station has a pay car park, which currently costs £3.60 a day. There is also a free car park near Kings Pond (join the walk at the crossroads marked [*]), or you can park anywhere in the centre of Alton and walk to the station to start.
OS Landranger Map: 186
OS Explorer Map: 133
Alton, map reference SU723397, is in Hampshire, 8km (5 miles) south-east of Farnham.
Toughness: 4 out of 10.

Walk notes: The quiet corner of Hampshire through which this walk passes seems like the kind of countryside in which nothing much has ever happened. Yet in the late 18th and early 19th century it inspired two famous writers – Gilbert White (the celebrated naturalist) and Jane Austen. After a section over wide upland fields to East Worldham, the walk first plunges into the delightful arcadia of woods, hangers and hidden pastures that surround Selborne, about which White wrote his famous *Natural History*. From here it crosses wooded Selborne Common and gentle ridges of downland to Chawton, the home of Jane Austen for the last eight, and most productive years, of her life. On the way you can reflect on Austen's remark in *Persuasion* that two villages only three miles apart 'will often include a total change of conversation, opinion and idea'. Though only a few miles apart, even today Chawton and Selborne seem like different worlds.

Walk options: Directions for the following variations are given at the end of the main walk text (*see p112*).

a) Short cut from Selborne to Farringdon: You can miss out Selborne Common and cut 1.6km (1 mile; about half an hour's walking) off the main walk. Follow the main walk directions until point [4], then follow the shortcut directions before picking up the main walk text again at point [5].

b) Short walk to Chawton: This follows a 5.6-km (3.5-mile) direct route from Alton to Upper Farringdon, a possible lunch stop, from where it is a further 3.4km (2.1 miles) to Chawton. It picks up the main walk directions again at point [5], which makes a total walk of 11.8km (7.4 miles).

The main walk is also remarkably well served with **buses**, which enable you to shorten it in many ways; for example, to have more time at Gilbert White's or Jane Austen's house. For times for these routes, call 0845 121 0180.
    From Monday to Saturday (not Sunday) the number 72 bus from **Alton station to Selborne via Chawton** has at least two morning and three afternoon services. The last bus back to Alton is currently around 5pm.

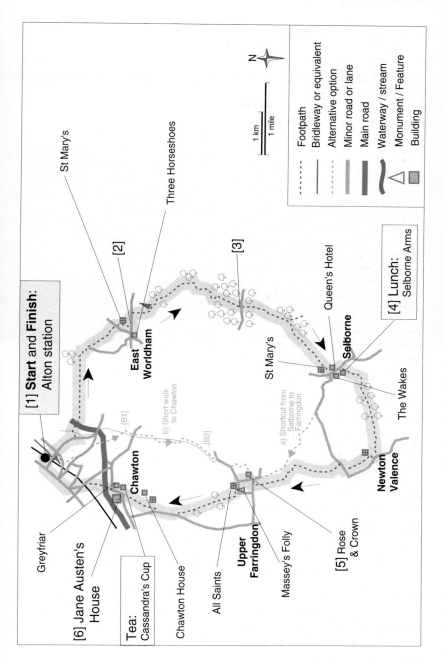

Alton Circular

N

1 km
1 mile

Footpath
Bridleway or equivalent
Alternative option
Minor road or lane
Main road
Waterway / stream
Monument / Feature
Building

St Mary's

Three Horseshoes

[2]

[1] **Start** and **Finish**:
Alton station

East
Worldham

[3]

Queen's Hotel

St Mary's

Selborne

[4] Lunch:
Selborne Arms

The Wakes

Greyfriar

[6] Jane Austen's
House

Tea:
Cassandra's Cup

Chawton

Chawton House

All Saints

Upper
Farringdon

Massey's Folly

[5] Rose
& Crown

Newton
Valence

b) Short walk
to Chawton

[B1]

[B2]

a) Shortcut from
Selborne to
Farringdon

The countryside around **Alton**.

This bus stops outside the Selborne Arms in Selborne and Jane Austen's House in Chawton. On Monday to Friday there are also at least five buses a day from **Alton to East Worldham**. On Saturday there are only two afternoon buses, however, and no buses at all on Sunday.

Using these buses you can vary the walk length and structure by, for instance, starting at East Worldham (point [2]), returning from Selborne by bus (thus doing only the first half of the main walk), starting at Selborne (thus doing only the second half of the main walk) or by catching a bus to Alton from Chawton.

Saturday Walkers' Club: Take the train nearest to 9am from London Waterloo to Alton. If doing the **Short walk to Chawton**, take the train nearest to 10am.

Walk directions

[1] [Numbers refer to the map]
Exit **Alton station** through the main entrance on platform 1. *Turn left out of the station*, your direction 230 degrees. In 60 metres, just after a sign points left to Hangers Way, *descend steps to the road* (Paper Mill Lane, though not named as such here). *Cross the road, and turn left.*

You now stay on the Hangers Way all the way to Selborne, but though waymarked, the twists and turns of the route are not always obvious. Close attention to the directions below is recommended. (A **hanger**, incidentally, is a woodland on a steep slope, from the old English word 'hangra': there are some fine examples as you approach Selborne.)

In 40 metres, pass under the railway bridge, and keep straight on up the main road, the B3004, ignoring side turnings.

200m after the bridge, and after a short steep climb, there is a busy crossroads. [*] Keep straight on, down what is now Wilsom Road, following a sign to Bordon. In 140 metres a light industrial estate starts on your left, partly screened by trees in summer. In another 130 metres, at the end of the estate, ignore a turning left to Omega Park, which is also signposted to the Household Waste Recycling Centre.

120 metres after the Omega Park turn go left downhill on a tarmac drive that in 10 metres becomes an earth footpath. Like many Hangers Way turnings, this is signposted on a post to the right of the path, but not very clearly. In 130 metres the footpath curves right, and in 60 metres comes to a stile. Go up an embankment and *cross the busy A31 dual carriageway* with care.

The onward path, again waymarked, is to the right of the electricity pylon on the far side of the road, your direction 100 degrees. Go up across a large open field following a line of pylons. In 120 metres *cross a stile, and in 5 metres curve left for 20 metres through the field boundary* to emerge into a higher field, where you *go right, resuming your former direction* (100 degrees) with the field boundary now on your right and a steep slope (**Neatham Down**) uphill to your left.

Follow the field edge for 380 metres, and *at the far end of the field go down through a gap* (partly hidden by trees and defended by about 20 metres of stinging nettles in high summer) into the next field, a vast open expanse. Go straight ahead across this field, heading for the right end of a clump of trees (**Monk Wood**) on the top of the ridge ahead, your direction east. In 350 metres you pass under the first of two sets of electricity pylons, and 50 metres later keep straight ahead at a four-armed footpath sign, still heading for the corner of Monk Wood ahead.

In 220 metres, *when you reach the corner of Monk Wood, turn left along the far side of it,* following a green arrow and a footpath sign, your direction 50 degrees.

In 40 metres *turn right at a two-armed signpost* to walk between two unfenced fields away from the woods towards more power lines and a clump of trees, your direction 120 degrees.

In 150 metres, *directly under the power lines, the path merges with a car-wide track* coming from the right to head towards the trees. In 20 metres ignore a footpath signposted left and *follow the car-wide track into the trees.* In 200 metres you pass a house on your right with an unusual round extension to it. Leave the track at this point to *cross the stile immediately to the left of the house and turn right beyond it onto a tarmac drive.*

In 20 metres, just beyond the front of the house, turn left at a footpath sign, your direction 120 degrees, down a tarmac drive for 10 metres and then along the right-hand edge of a garden. In 30 metres, *at the end of the garden, cross a ditch on a plank bridge and turn right along the right-hand edge of a field* with a wire fence to the left.

In 60 metres you pass another house to the right and in 30 metres more enter a wooded area. The path veers slightly left and comes in 50 metres to a *gap in a wood fence that leads into another large open field. Go straight ahead across this field,* towards the left-hand edge of the houses on the horizon, your direction 150 degrees.

After 300 metres the path follows a car-wide earth track for 80 metres to a three-armed footpath sign. Keep straight on here, leaving the track that veers right to some circular roofed barns. In 180 metres *you come to a tarmac lane, where you go right.*

In 40 metres, after passing two houses on the left, slant left up a tarmac path, with more houses on its left. In 80 metres *this path curves right along the side of the churchyard* of **Church St Mary, East Worldham**, and turns into a lane. If you want to visit the church (which contains the tomb of Philippa, wife of Geoffrey Chaucer), the entrance is 30 metres along on your left. If not, *carry on down the lane for another 120 metres to the main road,* the B3004.

For an early lunch stop, turn right here for 200 metres to the **Three Horseshoes** pub. Just before this, on the left, is the bus stop. However, *if not stopping for lunch, turn left onto the B3004.*

[2] Follow this busy main road. In 100 metres it starts to descend and you can glimpse an extensive vista of fields ahead of you. In 120 metres more, just before the Old School House on the left-hand side of the road, *there are two concrete tracks to the right. Take the right-hand (upper) one,* which is waymarked for the Hangers Way (note the sign is not very visible in summer).

In 70 metres you pass a large corrugated metal barn on your left, and after this you can see the rounded shape of **King John's Hill** to your left, with a large pond in front of it. *60 metres after the barn turn left through a metal fieldgate* following a footpath sign onto a grassy path that slants downhill towards a clump of trees on the right-hand side of the field and to the right of the pond, your direction 160 degrees.

[!] *At the bottom of the field, in 200 metres and just BEFORE a metal fieldgate into the next field, turn left towards King John's Hill,* your direction east, following a green arrow on the gate. In 15 metres you cross a stile and a plank bridge. The pond is now on your left. In 30 metres *you have to climb a metal fieldgate* (there should be a stile to its left, but at time of writing this had collapsed).

[!] *50 metres beyond the gate, roughly at the end of the pond, veer right following a green Hangers Way arrow on a post* to contour around the hill your direction 140 degrees. In 30 metres you pick up a line of trees, which you follow for 150 metres to a metal fieldgate on the edge of a wood.

[!] *Do NOT go through the fieldgate, but turn left just before it,* following a green arrow on a post, your direction east. Follow the wire fence on your right-hand side for 50 metres *to a stile in the corner of the field. Cross this and continue straight on downhill* along a car-wide grass path through the woods, your direction 170 degrees.

In 200 metres *cross a barrier of three logs to emerge into an open field.* Keep to the left-hand edge of this field for 70 metres to *cross a plank bridge with a stile at either end.* On the far side of this carry straight on across the field towards a line of trees, your direction 140 degrees.

In 250 metres *cross a stile and plank bridge into* **Binswood**. 10 metres later, *where paths fork, both quite faint, keep right,* your direction due south initially, following the right-hand edge of a clearing. You now pass through an area of mixed woods and small clearings for 250 metres, keeping roughly due south if the path is indistinct, before *emerging on the right-hand edge of a much larger clearing.*

Keep on this right-hand edge and in 100 metres *look out for a green arrow on a post where the path curves right to a metal fieldgate in 10 metres or so. Go through the wooden kissing gate* to the right of the metal fieldgate and on down the woodland path beyond, your direction 260 degrees.

At first you are in dense woodland but *in 50 metres an open field is visible through the trees to the right.* **[!]** *40 metres after this turn left off the path across a plank bridge,* following a green Hangers Way arrow on a post, your direction south initially. In 160 metres *cross a stile into an open field and go half right* following a green arrow, your direction 210 degrees.

In 180 metres *cross another stile and carry straight on into a wood* on a clear wide path between tall pine and oak trees, your direction 250 degrees. **[!]** *In 140 metres, about halfway up this path, turn left at a footpath post (not easily visible in summer)* following a green arrow, your direction 150 degrees.

In 60 metres, you come out into a clearing, with *a large brown pond to your right. Follow the edge of this,* curving right in 70 metres *to enter a gloomy pine wood* 30 metres later, your direction now 250 degrees. In 40 metres this path merges with a path from the left to become a car-wide track, and in 50 metres more *comes* to a T-junction and a two-armed footpath sign, *where you go left* onto a car-wide track, your direction 140 degrees.

[!] *In 40 metres turn right off this track directly uphill into a wood,* following a green Hangers Way sign, your direction 240 degrees. In 70 metres the path curves left and continues to climb. In 250 metres it flattens out and 50 metres later passes a house off to the right.

40 metres further on you pass through a gap in the fence to the gravel driveway of the house, and in 10 metres more come *to a tarmac lane* [3], *where you go right,* uphill, your direction west initially.

In 80 metres at a lane T-junction go left, following the Hangers Way sign, your direction 140 degrees. In 30 metres you pass a house, High Candovers. 20 metres beyond it *fork right on a car-wide gravel track,* your direction due south.

Stay on this car-wide track, ignoring ways off. In 100 metres, after passing some houses, there are open fields to your left and to your right a steep tree-covered slope – a fine example of a **hanger** (*see p104*). After 500 metres the open fields end to the left and there are woods both sides.

[!] *After 400 metres in the woods you see an open field to your right through a metal gate. Turn right off the car-wide track and approach the gate* and you will see a stile to the left of it with a two-armed footpath sign beyond it (in summer both stile and the Hangers Way sign next to it may be hidden by foliage until you're almost upon them).

Cross this stile. Beyond it go left diagonally downhill across the field, following the footpath sign on the two-armed footpath sign and passing to the right of a telephone pole, your direction 230 degrees.

In 170 metres you pass a fenced pond on your right and 50 metres beyond this *cross a stile to the left of a open metal fieldgate, following a green arrow, and carry on along a car-wide earth track,* your direction 250 degrees. In 40 metres ignore a track forking right and keep on the main track following the wire fence on your left. In 120 metres you pass through a former gateway with a redundant stile to its right, and 70 metres on *you cross a further stile into an open field.*

King John's Hill.

Turn left, downhill, towards a large pond, your direction due south. [!] *In 100 metres, just before a metal fieldgate and the pond, go right over a stile* with a green arrow on it and over a plank bridge and straight up the hill ahead, your direction 260 degrees.

[!] *In 80 metres do not go through the gate or over the stile into the woods but turn left before them to follow the wood's edge, with a wire fence to your right*, your direction due south.

In 150 metres *go through a wooden kissing gate and keep straight on* along a clear earth path, your direction 240 degrees. After 50 metres in the woods you emerge to find yourself on the right-hand edge of a fine open valley, the

Austen's powers

Though her novels are set elsewhere, **Jane Austen** was always a Hampshire lass at heart. She was devastated when her father retired in 1801 as vicar of Steventon, the small north Hampshire village where she was born, and moved his family to Bath. Jane hated Bath and wrote nothing during this period. Worse, when her father died four years later, she, her sister Cassandra and their mother were left with little money and no home.

It was Jane's brother Edward who finally came to the rescue. He had been adopted by the wealthy but childless Knight family, and so had inherited the Great House at Chawton (now Chawton House, which was recently opened as a library of women writers of Jane Austen's time). Edward found his sisters and mother a 17th-century house in the centre of the village, and they moved there in July 1809.

Jane was delighted by 'our Chawton home', and immediately started writing again. *Mansfield Park*, *Emma* and *Persuasion* were all written here, and it was while living in Chawton that she first won acclaim as a novelist when her youthful novels – *Pride and Prejudice*, *Sense and Sensibility* – were at last published.

Alas, Jane's happiness at Chawton was shortlived. In 1817 she fell ill with a mystery illness, and died in Winchester, where she had gone for medical treatment. Because she was the daughter of a clergyman, she was buried in the north aisle of Winchester Cathedral. Cassandra and her mother remained in Chawton for the rest of their lives, and are buried in the churchyard around the back of the church of St Nicholas, which, like the Great House, is passed on this walk.

The house is now run by the Jane Austen Trust and contains various items connected with Jane and her family, including some of her jewellery and the table at which she used to write. Jane kept the hinges of the door to this room deliberately unoiled so she could conceal her work if anyone came in, writing novels not being considered a suitable profession for a lady.

[Note that, as the house closes at 4pm, it may be wise to do the shorter walk, or use a bus option to ensure a visit.]

Jane Austen's House

Chawton, Alton, GU34 1SD (01420 83262/www.jane-austens-house-museum.org.uk). **Open** *Dec-Feb* 11am-4pm Sat, Sun; *Mar-Nov* 11am-4pm daily. **Admission** £4; £3 concessions; 50p 8-18s. **Credit** MC, V.

Long Lythe mentioned by Gilbert White ('lythe' is a Saxon word for a steep slope).

Keep along this clear path for 350 metres before it plunges into woods for 50 metres. At the end of the woods go through a kissing gate, ignore a path to the right up a valley marked by a three-armed footpath sign, and pass through a second kissing gate to keep straight on along the main path.

In 160 metres *you pass a house on your left*, and in 40 metres you *cross a wooden bridge over a stream. Beyond this the path forks. Take the right fork*, your direction 240 degrees, passing just to the left of an oak tree and bench in 40 metres. After this the path climbs steeply uphill and as you climb the **Church of St Mary, Selborne** comes into view on the hilltop ahead.

In 80 metres, at the top of the hill, *enter the churchyard by a kissing gate*. Cross it for 80 metres to reach the entrance to the church (right). After visiting the church, exit *the churchyard and walk 40 metres across* **The Plestor**, the village green, *to the busy main road*, the B3006.

At the road turn left, and in 20 metres on the right is the entrance to **Gilbert White's House**, a possible lunch stop. However, the recommended lunch stops are the **Queens Hotel**, 40 metres beyond the museum on the left, or the **Selborne Arms**, 80 metres beyond that on the right. (The **village shop** is between the two of them on the right). **[4]**

If you want to end the walk in Selborne and get the bus back, the **bus stop** is right outside the Selborne Arms (which is also the side of the road to be standing on for buses to Alton).

[After lunch, if you are in a hurry to get to Chawton to visit Jane Austen's House or have tea, or if you would like to avoid the steep climb onto Selborne Common, you can at this point take option **a)**, the **Short cut from Selborne to Farringdon** (directions at end of main walk text).]

To continue on the recommended slightly longer Selborne Common route, however, turn right out of the Selborne Arms or the Gilbert White Museum, or left out of the Queens Hotel, and *just beyond the Selborne Arms*, by a red phone box, *turn right up a tarmac lane*, signposted National Trust Selborne Common.

In 30 metres the lane forks. Take the footpath straight ahead between the two forks in the lane, signposted 'Footpath to the Zigzag and Hanger'. This is fenced off from an open field to the left. *In 250 metres pass through a wooden kissing gate and fork left up the first in series of steps*. This is the famous **Zigzag Path** cut by Gilbert White and his brother in 1753. *Follow the zigzags all the way to the top*, a long stiff climb, but with increasingly dramatic views.

At the top ignore a minor path leading right from a metal bench (which in summer is barely visible anyway) and *walk past the bench to turn right on the car-wide earth track beyond*, your direction 270 degrees. In 30 metres ignore a track diverging right. You are now on **Selborne Common**, which today is largely wooded. The Common was much more open in Gilbert White's time, and has only become more overgrown since grazing stopped in the 1950s. The National Trust is now trying to restore it to its former appearance.

In a further 70 metres pass through a kissing gate to the left of a wooden fieldgate. There is a notice here with information about Selborne Common. *Stay on the car-wide track across the Common, ignoring all ways off, for 750 metres until you come to a large open space to your right* (200-300 metres across: much larger than earlier, small clearings on the route).

Near the far end of this *fork left on the main track into the woods* (the more obvious way to go in any case), your direction 230 degrees, ignoring a less distinct car-wide track that keeps to the clearing edge. In 330 metres, at a four-armed footpath sign that marks a crossroads with a wide bridleway, *go straight on and carry on through a wooden gate to the right of a wooden fieldgate 20 metres beyond*.

Keep straight on after the gate on a car-wide track with open fields visible through the trees to the right and left. *In 500 metres this brings you to a road where you turn right* following a sign to Farringdon and Alton. This is the village of **Newton Valence**.

In 30 metres, past a war memorial and with a pond to your left, go right up a driveway signposted 'To the Church'. This is also marked 'PRIVATE DRIVE' but is a right of way.

It is worth going to the end of this drive to see the church and the fine vicarage to its right, but *your onward route is to turn left 60 metres after the start of the drive, where the stone wall ends left, and just before a gravel drive forks off to a house left,* down a path whose start is marked by two log stumps and an easy-to-miss three-armed footpath sign, your direction 320 degrees.

Follow this path with an uncultivated field left and a hedge to the right. In 70 metres the hedge ends and you carry on across an open space that is quite overgrown in summer, with an unhedged field to your right, your direction 320 degrees. In 80 metres *you pass through a metal kissing gate, cross a road, and pass through another metal kissing gate to carry on downhill,* your direction 320 degrees

Keep to the bottom of the shallow valley that develops, roughly following a line of trees to the left. In 350 metres you come to a fence and a gap blocked by two wooden bars. Cross this (sliding the top bar aside to get through) and in 20 metres go across a stile to the right of a white cottage and the left of a rusted fieldgate.

20 metres beyond this *you come to a tarmac lane where you go right.* In 100 metres, 40 metres before some red-brick houses on the left, *turn left down a car-wide farm track* (possibly through double metal fieldgates; but they have the air of being permanently open), your direction 310 degrees.

In 20 metres cross a stile to the left of a metal fieldgate and keep on the track, following a footpath sign. The track goes

gently downhill and then curves right uphill. In 550 metres ignore a track forking left into the next field by an electricity pylon to keep straight on, with the hedge on your left.

In 80 metres the two arms of the track merge again and a wood starts to your right. Carry on uphill along the track. In a further 170 metres, *just before a gap into the next field, and level with another electricity pylon on your right, go left at a two-armed footpath sign along the field edge,* your direction 300 degrees.

Follow this field edge, with a tree and bush field boundary to your right, for 200 metres as it curves round to the right, into a dip and up again, and then round to the left. 50 metres after the left turn ignore a faint vehicle track that crosses through into the next field to the right and continue following the field boundary (the path at this point may be faint to non-existent along the edge of an arable field).

In 100 metres more, *where the tall trees and bushes come to an end to your right and give way to a more conventional-sized hedge, veer right through a gap in the hedge,* following an old two-armed footpath sign.

Cross the field diagonally towards a post just about visible on the far side, your direction 340 degrees. (If in doubt, aim between a clump of trees on the horizon left and a pylon right). In 100 metres pass this post and carry on in the same direction across the next field.

In 200 metres, at the far edge of this second field, you *cross a bridleway at a point marked by a four-armed footpath sign. Keep straight over a stile in the same direction as before,* 340 degrees. You are now on an open down, with an extensive view in front of you. *In 250 metres cross a stile and in 100 metres another, descending into a cutting. Turn right here, downhill.*

In 200 metres you come to a road and the village of **Upper Farringdon**, *where you go right.* In 120 metres you come to a T-junction, and the **Rose and Crown** pub is ahead of you. Turn left at this T-junction down Crows Lane. (If you visit the Rose and Crown, turn right out of the pub garden onto the road to continue the walk.)

[5] *In 300 metres, at a T-junction, go left down Church Road.* **All Saints Church, Upper Farringdon** soon appears to your right and just beyond it on your left, **Massey's Folly** (an ornate red-brick building designed and built by an eccentric vicar). In 150 metres, *when you come level with Massey's Folly* and at the end of the churchyard, *go right up a gravel track.*

In 20 metres, at a two-armed footpath sign (against a tree) go straight on (signposted 'Right of Way'). *40 metres further on, at a T-junction, go left on a car-wide tarmac drive,* passing a barn on stilts on the left in 20 metres.

Pass various barns and in 80 metres you come to a *gravel track crossroads.* (There is a playground with a high wire fence to your left.) *Go right here, uphill,* your direction 340 degrees. Keep straight on along this track, first uphill and then into a wood. In 500 metres, *where the wood ends, keep on along the left-hand edge of an open field.*

In 200 metres, *where the track turns right along the far edge of the field, go straight on into a wooded area.* In 80 metres *cross a stile and keep straight on,* downhill and diagonally across the field, towards a metal trough in the far corner of the field, your direction 330 degrees.

In 300 metres, in the far corner of the field, *do not cross the stile to the busy road (the A32), but cross over a stile to the right* to follow a permissive path parallel to the road, your direction 10 degrees, with the parkland of Chawton House to your right and the road to your left.

In 200 metres cross another stile. *In 140 metres, where your way is blocked by metal barriers, go left across a stile into a wooded area.* Turn right on the far side of the stile and in 30 metres *you emerge onto the old Gosport Road,* now blocked off to traffic.

Carry on along this road all the way to the centre of **Chawton**. In 200 metres you pass a metal barrier in the road, and 30

metres after this you can turn right along the drive to **Chawton House** to visit the church of **St Nicholas** if you want.

Otherwise ignore this turning and stay on the road for a further 400 metres until you come to a T-junction with a Give Way sign. The red-brick building on the far side of the junction is **Jane Austen's House** (*see p102* **Austen's powers**). **Cassandra's Cup**, the recommended tea stop, is opposite, and the **Greyfriar** pub next door. [6]

After visiting these places you have a choice. You can end the walk here by taking the bus from the bus stop 5 metres beyond Jane Austen's House (for details, *see p112* **Walk options**).

Turn left out of Jane Austen's House (or right out of Cassandra's Cup or the Greyfriar) and walk down the main road of the village. In 250 metres, where the road curves right, go straight on up a dead-end road. In 80 metres, where the road ends, go down concrete steps to the left-hand side of it, to cross under the A31 in an underpass.

On the far side of the underpass ignore a lane to the left and go straight ahead down a wide empty road (the former main road, now bypassed). In 400 metres you come to a roundabout: go straight on and under a wide metal railway bridge (NOT the arched brick railway bridge to its left).

Stay on this road, initially along the right-hand edge of a green, and then along an urban road. In 700 metres, by the White Horse pub left, and where the traffic-bearing road swings right uphill, keep straight on along the High Street. In 250 metres you pass the Swan Hotel on the right, a possible late tea stop. In another 180 metres you come to a mini roundabout, and keep straight on.

In another 150 metres, at the end of the shopping zone and with the Magistrates' Court to your right, you come to a larger roundabout. Go straight on, passing the Alton House Hotel right in 120 metres. 30 metres beyond the hotel turn right up Paper Mill Lane. The entrance to Alton station is 40 metres up on the left.

Walk options

a) Short cut from Selborne to Farringdon:

Follow the main walk directions to point [4].

[4] After lunch in Selborne, *turn left out of the Selborne Arms or the Gilbert White Museum, or right out of the Queens Hotel,* your direction 320 degrees. 40 metres beyond the Gilbert White Museum, turn left down Gracious Street.

In 170 metres turn right with the road, ignoring a footpath straight ahead. In 280 metres ignore a dead-end road forking right. 10 metres beyond this ignore a tarmac lane left to Wood Acre and Fisher Lodge. In a further 100 metres ignore a car-wide track forking right with a footpath sign.

The road now starts to gently climb. In 150 metres, ignore a stile to the right with a Picketts Piece sign by it. 130 metres after this follow the lane as it curves right, and in 100 metres more ignore a car-wide track left, signposted as a footpath.

The road now climbs more steeply under a canopy of trees. In 250 metres, *at the top of the hill, the road turns sharp left. Go straight on here, leaving the road, through a metal fieldgate and up a car-wide track (a signposted bridleway) lined by tall trees,* your direction 300 degrees.

[!]*In 80 metres there is a metal gate and three-armed footpath sign to the left. Leave the car-wide track to go through the gate and follow the direction of the bridleway sign more or less directly uphill towards a gap in the field boundary at the top of the field,* your direction 290 degrees. (This path may be obscured by crops, but it, and NOT the track you have just left, is the bridleway).

In 130 metres pass through the gap and carry straight on in the same direction up across the next field, aiming for a large isolated tree on the hill above you (the nearest tree; not one further away to its left), your direction still 290 degrees. (This path may be obscured by crops: if

so, there is no alternative but to plough across them, as the way round the edge of the field is very circuitous.)

When you reach the tree in 150 metres keep more or less straight on, heading for a car-wide gap in the wood edge 150 metres ahead, just to the right of the brow of the ridge. (If when you get to the wood edge you do not find this clear car-wide track – marked by a blue arrow – heading into it, explore the wood edge until you find it.)

Follow this track into the woods, your direction now 260 degrees. Stay on it, ignoring all ways off. This track can be very muddy in winter.

In 250 metres there is an open field and a barbed-wire fence to your left and the track narrows. In 100 metres, *at the end of this field, follow the track as it curves right downhill,* following a blue arrow on a post, your direction 320 degrees. There is soon another field visible through the trees to the left. In 80 metres cross a car-wide track linking two fields and keep straight on, your direction now 300 degrees.

60 metres further on *you pass under electricity pylons* and there is an extensive view to your right. *250 metres after these pylons, at a three-armed footpath sign* (and before you get to a second set of pylons), *fork right off the bridleway across the open field,* your direction 340 degrees.

Head for the village of Upper Farringdon, which can be seen in the valley below, or just to the left of a mini pylon in the middle of field. There is a fine panorama ahead at this point. *Follow this path for 450 metres to the far corner of the field, where you cross a stile to the road. Turn left on the road* (in fact, more or less straight ahead) into the village of **Upper Farringdon**.

In 230 metres you come to a road T-junction where you go straight ahead down Crows Lane. Almost immediately the **Rose and Crown** pub, a possible early tea stop, is on your right.

You can now *resume the directions from point [5] in the main walk directions.*

Gibert White's House.

b) Short walk to Chawton:

[1] Exit Alton station from the main entrance on platform 1. *Turn left out of the station*, your direction 230 degrees. In 60 metres, just after a sign points left to Hangers Way, *descend steps to the road*. (Paper Mill Lane, though not named as such here). *Cross the road, and turn left.*

In 40 metres *pass under the railway bridge, and in a further 70 metres turn right up Waterside Court, a cul-de-sac. In 20 metres turn right at a T-junction, and in 15 metres, just beyond flats 28-33, turn left up a tarmac path.* In 30 metres *pass through metal barriers and turn left* on a car-wide tarmac path. **Kings Pond** is to your right.

In 80 metres curve right with the tarmac path towards a road ahead. In a further 50 metres, *20 metres before the road, turn right on a narrower tarmac path*, your direction 230 degrees initially. Kings Pond is still to your right (hidden by trees in summer, but visible after 30 metres or so).

[*] This path follows the edge of the pond right to its far end in 330 metres, where you come to a *tarmac path T-junction with the railway embankment directly ahead. Go left here*, your direction 200 degrees, to get to a road in 30 metres.

Cross the road, and go straight up concrete steps. After two flights of the steps the path continues steeply uphill. 120 metres after the road *ignore a tarmac fork to the right* and keep on uphill. *In a further 60 metres, at a T-junction, go right* along a fenced path between gardens. In 40 metres *this brings you to a residential road where you go left uphill*, your direction 130 degrees.

In 50 metres ignore a road named The Ridgeway to the right, and in 60 metres more, Crowley Drive to the left. Keep straight on and *in a further 270 metres you come to the crest of the hill*, which now identifies itself as Windmill Hill. The pedestrian pavement ends at this point.

10 metres after the crest of the hill ignore a tarmac lane forking right to keep downhill on the road. *In a further 100 metres fork right down a tarmac driveway*, just beyond a telegraph pole with the numbers 100 and 20 on it, your direction 140 degrees.

In 40 metres fork left off this onto an earth path following a rather decayed bridleway sign. In 50 metres you pass through some blue-topped wooden posts and 25 metres later you emerge from the woods to carry on between hedges.

In 180 metres cross a car-wide track and go straight ahead up an embankment, which in 10 metres brings you to the A31. [!] Cross this busy dual carriageway with great care. On the far side go straight ahead between more blue-topped posts and down the bank, your direction 120 degrees.

In 80 metres pass through more blue-topped posts and turn right on a tarmac lane following a wooden footpath sign. Another sign says 'Private No Thru Road' but this lane is a public right of way. In 30 metres pass through an open metal gate and carry straight on along the lane.

In 320 metres you pass a white house to your right and in a further 200 metres at a T-junction keep straight on, ignoring a tarmac lane that leads left uphill and a footpath to the right indicated by a three-armed footpath sign. [B1]

In 60 metres a large open field starts to the left, while to the right is a field boundary of tall trees. In 400 metres you come to a road, the B3006 (a road that is busier, with faster traffic, than it sometimes appears at first). Turn right for 30 metres along the road and then, just before white barriers on either side of the road, left over a stile following a footpath sign, your direction 240 degrees.

On the far side of the stile aim for a stile ahead, following a ditch on your right-hand side, your direction 210 degrees. In 80 metres cross another stile in a wire fence and keep straight on up a long narrow field, still to your right. (The path is indistinct from this point until point [B2] and poorly signposted, but if in doubt keep to the ditch and you will not go wrong.)

In 400 metres, at the top of the field, your way is blocked by a wire fence. Go right over the ditch on a small brick bridge, following a two-armed footpath sign. In 15 metres go left over a stile to continue in your former direction, now with the ditch to the left, your direction 190 degrees.

In 200 metres, shortly after passing under the third of sets of mini pylon cables, curve right slightly with the field edge to your right and the ditch to your left. In another 260 metres, go left over the ditch on an earth bridge sided with concrete. (A damaged yellow arrow on a post may be visible at this point.)

On the far side of the bridge go right to resume your former direction, 210 degrees, with the ditch now on your right-hand side. In 100 metres the ditch curves away right into thickets. Keep straight on to the stile 25 metres ahead (to the left of a metal fieldgate).

Cross this stile and veer half right following the direction of a yellow arrow on a stile, your direction 230 degrees, heading roughly along the right-hand side of the field. This point makes a nice **picnic** spot.

In 220 metres you meet the ditch to your right again. Here ignore a car-wide earth bridge to your right and follow the ditch for 380 metres to the far end the field, where it nearly converges with the hedge that forms the left-hand boundary of the field. [B2]

Here cross a stile to the left of a metal fieldgate and in 30 metres pass through a metal fieldgate and on along a grassy track with a hedge to your left and the ditch still to your right. In 120 metres, at a T-junction with a car-wide earth track, go left, following a two-armed footpath sign (which may be concealed by foliage in summer), your direction 140 degrees.

After 180 metres you come to a tarmac lane where you go right, your direction 200 degrees initially. In 350 metres turn left up a car-wide gravel track towards Stapley Farm, following a footpath sign, your direction 160 degrees.

In 200 metres turn right at a two-armed footpath sign just before farm buildings. Pass between a hay barn left and a shed right to reach a stile in 60 metres. Go straight on, your direction 270 degrees, and *in 50 metres, at the end of the field, cross a double stile* (it is in the far right-hand corner of the field and may not be easily visible in summer).

On the far side of this stile *turn left along the field edge,* your direction 170 degrees. In 130 metres *cross another stile and go right along the right-hand edge of a field* with a barbed-wire fence now to your right, your direction 260 degrees. *In 230 metres, at the end of this field, go left with the field boundary.*

In 70 metres, 10 metres before the field ends, turn right between a wall and a hedge to reach the road in 60 metres, where the **Rose and Crown**, the recommended lunch stop, is immediately to the right. *After lunch, to continue the walk, turn right* out of the Rose and Crown onto the road (Crows Lane).

You now *follow the main walk directions from point* [5].

Lunch & tea places

Cassandra's Cup *Winchester Road, Chawton, GU34 1SD (01420 83144).* **Open/food served** *Mar, Dec* 10.30am-4.30pm Fri, Sat, Sun; *Apr, Oct, Nov* 10.30am-4.30pm Thur-Sun; *May, Sept* 10.30am-4.30pm Wed-Sun; *June-Aug* 10.30am-4.30pm Tue-Sun. Opposite Jane Austen's House, this is the suggested tea stop on the main walk.

Gilbert White's House *The Wakes, High Street, Selborne, GU34 3JH (01420 511275).* **Open** 11am-5pm daily. **Food served** 11am-4.30pm daily. The museum tea shop is recommended. Set in an elegant 18th-century parlour, it offers cakes made to period recipes. At lunchtime, a light menu of period pies and pasties is served. You can visit the tea shop without paying for the museum: simply make known your intention at the ticket desk, and they will direct you.

Greyfriar *Winchester Road, Chawton, nr Alton, GU34 1SB (01420 83841/ www.thegreyfriar.co.uk).* **Open** noon-11pm Mon-Sat; noon-10.30pm Sun. **Food served** noon-2pm, 7-9.30pm Mon-Sat; noon-3pm Sun. Serves food at lunchtime and is open all afternoon for tea, coffee and ice-cream.

Queens Hotel *Selborne, Alton, GU34 3JJ (01420 511454/www.queens-selborne.co.uk).* **Open** 11am-11pm Mon-sat; noon-10.30pm Sun. **Food served** noon-9pm daily. Located 9.7km (6.1 miles) into the walk, this pub serves food all day from a varied menu and has a plenty of tables and a garden.

Rose and Crown *Crows Lane, Upper Farringdon, nr Alton, GU34 3ED (01420 588231).* **Open** noon-3pm, 6-11.30pm Mon-Fri; noon-11.30pm Sat; noon-10.30pm Sun. **Food served** noon-2.30pm Mon; noon-2.30pm, 7-9.30pm Tue-Sat; noon-3.30pm Sun. Situated 5.6km (3.5 miles) into the short walk to Chawton you'll come to this pub with a delightful garden and a sign welcoming walkers. This is the suggested lunch stop for the Short walk to Chawton option.

Selborne Arms *High Street, Selborne, nr Alton, GU34 3JR (01420 511247).* **Open** 11am-3pm Mon-Sat; 11am-10.30pm Sun. **Food served** noon-2pm daily. Just 60 metres down the road from the Queens Hotel, the Selborne Arms has a more upmarket menu and a garden, but it only serves food at lunchtime. This is the suggested lunch stop for the main walk.

Swan Hotel *Alton High Street, Alton, GU34 1AT (01420 83777).* **Open** 6.30am-11.30pm Mon-Fri; 9am-11.30pm Sat; 9am-10.30pm Sun. **Food served** noon-2.30pm, 6.30-9.30pm daily. Serves cream teas until 6pm, and tea and coffee until closing time.

Three Horseshoes *Cakers Lane, East Worldham, nr Alton, GU34 3AE (01420 83211/www.theshoesworldham.com).* **Open** noon-3pm, 6-11pm Mon-Sat; noon-3pm, 7-10.30pm Sun. **Food served** noon-2.30pm, 6.30pm-9pm Mon-Sat; noon-2.30pm Sun. Situated 4km (2.5 miles) into the walk, the Three Horseshoes has a garden.

Picnic: There are several fine places for a picnic on the section between East Worldham and Selborne, particularly the pasturelands around King John's Hill and the clearings in Binswood. The Long and Short Lythe valleys on the last half mile into Selborne, as well as the hill leading up to the church, are also particularly enchanting picnic spots. If you are planning a picnic later in the walk (for example, on Selborne Common), the village shop (open until 6pm Monday to Friday and 7.30pm on Saturday), has a good selection of food items. [A possible picnic spot is also indicated between point [B1] and [B2] in the short walk text.]

Petersfield to Liss

Along the Hangers Way.

Start: Petersfield station
Finish: Liss station
Length: 17.7km (11.1 miles). For a shorter walk variation, *see below* **Walk options**.
Time: 5 hours. For the whole excursion, including trains and meals, allow 9 hours.
Transport: Three trains an hour run from London Waterloo to Petersfield (journey time: 58 minutes to 1 hour 14 minutes). Trains back from Liss to Waterloo run hourly (twice an hour at peak times Monday to Saturday; journey time: 1 hour 8-14 minutes – up to 15 minutes slower on Sundays). Buy a day return to Petersfield. If driving, parking is available at Petersfield station, and Liss is just one stop up the line.
OS Landranger Map: 197 and 185
OS Explorer Map: 133
Petersfield, map reference SU743235, is in Hampshire, 25km (15.6 miles) east of Winchester.
Toughness: 7 out of 10.

Walk notes: Much of this walk follows part of the 34km (21 mile) Hangers Way, a long-distance path that lies within an area of Outstanding Natural Beauty. The name 'Hanger' derives from the old English 'Hangra', meaning a wooded slope. The majority of the landscape is unspoilt and remains as it was several hundred years ago. There are two possible ascents to the top of Shoulder of Mutton Hill, one steep and one gentle. Whichever route is taken, the view at the top is spectacular. The strenuous climb of Shoulder of Mutton Hill aside, this is a walk of gentle gradients, apart from one short steep downhill section. Please note that the steeper route up the Shoulder of Mutton Hill on this walk can become slippery in winter.

Walk options: Directions for this shorter circular walk appear at the end of the main walk text (*see p123*).

a) Shorter circular walk: Shoulder of Mutton Hill makes a fine objective in its own right. The short walk allows you to enjoy the spectacular views from its summit on a pleasant half-day stroll, returning to Petersfield station. This shorter circular walk is 8km (5 miles) long, or 3 hours walking; follow the main walk directions to point [4], then follow the shorter circular walk directions.

Saturday Walkers' Club: Take the train nearest to 9.45am (before or after) from London Waterloo to Petersfield.

Walk directions

[1] [Numbers refer to the map]
From platform 2 of **Petersfield station** *go through the ticket office and turn left.* In 30 metres turn left into Station Road and cross the railway line.

In 140 metres turn right up a tarmac footpath signposted 'The Hangers Way', adjacent to a car showroom. After 20 metres veer left following a green and white metal footpath sign, your direction 10 degrees. After 100 metres pass through some concrete posts where the path narrows.

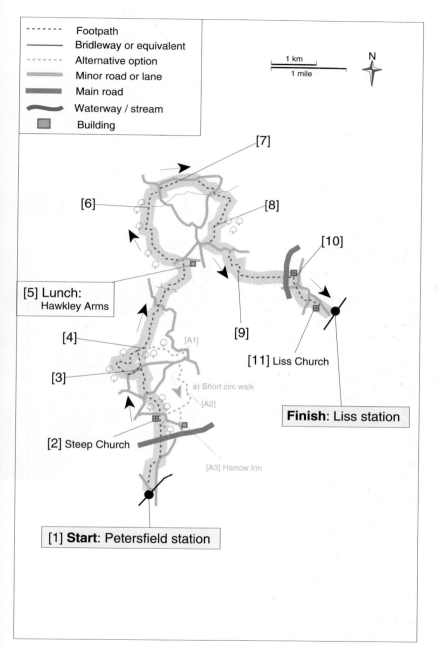

In 350 metres you reach a junction of paths marked by a four-armed wooden signpost. *Go straight on to continue on the Hangers Way,* your initial direction 40 degrees. *In 100 metres turn left onto a minor road,* your direction 30 degrees.

After 200 metres the road bends to the right at the junction with Tilmore Gardens. *At this point leave the road and follow the Hangers Way* straight on through a wooden kissing gate frame to the left of a metal fieldgate, your direction 20 degrees. The Hangers Way climbs very gently uphill. In 350 metres you cross the A3 via a footbridge. Turn right once over the footbridge.

Keep straight ahead on this enclosed footpath, ignoring any turnings off, for 500 metres (with Bedales School halfway along on your left) to reach a metre-high brick wall to a cemetery on your right. Continue straight ahead, passing **All Saints Church** in the village of **Steep** on the right.

[2] *In 100 metres you come out to a road and turn right. In 10 metres turn left to pass to the left* of a double wooden fieldgate opposite the entrance to the church. Veer slightly to the left across a recreation ground, your direction 340 degrees. In 40 metres you pass a tree with a bench surround on your left. In 5 metres you pass immediately to the right of a tree stump.

The footpath goes gently downhill through the woods. In 250 metres, at the bottom of the hill, cross over a stile next to a wooden footpath sign. In 10 metres cross a stream via a plank footbridge.

The footpath now follows the edge of a field with a stream and woodland on your left. Ahead to the right you can see the wooded slopes of Shoulder of Mutton Hill, which you will shortly be climbing. *After 300 metres go through a metal kissing gate to turn right onto a lane.*

In 100 metres you pass the driveway entrance to Mill Cottage on your left. In 20 metres, where the lane bends to the right, continue straight on up a footpath

The view from **Shoulder of Mutton Hill**.

between a waterfall and a house called Mill Corner. In 30 metres the footpath crosses a stream, goes up three steps and meets *a T-junction, where you turn left.* In 40 metres you pass a conservation viewpoint hut on your right. You are now in Little Langleys Nature Reserve.

After a further 70 metres the path veers right passing a large pond on the left. After 150 metres the path turns sharp right then, after 30 metres, sharp left. In a

further 150 metres pass to the right of
a redundant stile. In 40 metres cross a
stream via a plank bridge. *Turn right up a
car-wide track*, your direction 340 degrees.

After 180 metres you meet a road and
a Hangers Way footpath sign next to
a stile with a sign saying 'The Studio'
on the far side **[3]**. At this point you have
two choices: **(i)** Take the steep ascent
of the Shoulder of Mutton Hill, or **(ii)** take
a 1km (0.6 mile) longer but gentler ascent
of the Shoulder of Mutton Hill.

(i) For the steep ascent: *Turn right
down the lane. After 20 metres turn left*
to take a footpath that goes uphill, gently
at first, your direction 330 degrees.

After 100 metres cross a stile next to an
Ashford Hangers National Nature Reserve
sign. *Take the middle of three paths,
the one going steeply uphill.* After 30
metres there are some steps followed
by a wooden barrier bearing a no cycling
sign. The route continues steeply uphill
on a wide grassy path.

In 200 metres you reach a bench and
a stone dedicated to the memory of the
poet **Edward Thomas** (*see p121* **Poet's
rest**). Behind you are spectacular views
of the South Downs.

Continue uphill through beech trees
for a further 150 metres to reach a wooden
barrier marked on its reverse side with a
green Hangers Way sign. Continue uphill
for 30 metres passing the reverse of an
Ashford Hangers National Nature Reserve
sign. Rejoin the route at [4] below.

**(ii) For the 1km (0.6 miles) longer
but gentler ascent**: *Turn left initially
up the lane*, your direction 210 degrees. In
200 metres you pass an old timber-framed
building called Bees Cottage on your left,
as you now walk alongside a 3 metre-high
brick wall to your left.

In 80 metres, at the end of the brick
wall, you pass Old Ashford Manor, also
on the left. In 70 metres, as the road turns
to the left, *fork right onto a bridleway*
with a stream to its right and an open
field to its left. After 120 metres you pass
a Hampshire council sign indicating you

are in the Ashford Hangers National
Nature Reserve. Keep straight ahead,
your direction 290 degrees.

After 400 metres veer left steeply uphill
to follow a blue Hangers Way arrow. In a
further 80 metres follow the Hangers Way
as it turns right, doubling back steeply
uphill. A red-tipped wooden post is to
the right of the path. Continue uphill with
panoramic views of the South Downs to
the right. Ignore any paths going down.

After 1km (0.6 miles) you reach a
junction of paths, with a wooden horse-
blocking barrier on your right next
to a green Hangers Way footpath post.
Veer left uphill. In 20 metres you pass the
reverse of an Ashford Hangers National
Nature Reserve sign on your right.

[4] [At this point you can take option
a), the **Shorter circular walk** back to
Petersfield, by following the directions
at the end of this main walk text.]

Otherwise, **to carry on with the main
walk**, after passing the reverse of the
Ashford Hangers National Nature Reserve
sign, *veer left*, your direction 320 degrees.
In 30 metres pass through a wooden horse-
blocking barrier. After a further 40 metres
you reach a two-armed signpost at a T-
junction. *Turn right* following the Hangers
Way, your direction 70 degrees.

After 140 metres *turn left* over a stile
and go downhill, following the left-hand
edge of a field, your direction 340 degrees.
In 50 metres, at the corner of the field, the
footpath turns right and goes downhill
through woods, still following the fence
on your left. After 120 metres go through
a wooden gate and continue downhill with
the fence on your left. After 180 metres
cross another stile marked with a Hangers
Way green arrow. Continue downhill,
your initial direction 10 degrees.

In 40 metres cross another stile into
open fields and go steeply downhill on
a wide grassy path. The church in the
village of Hawkley can be seen ahead
in the distance. In 150 metres at the
bottom of the field go over a stile, keeping
straight down the right edge of the field.

In 180 metres at the bottom right corner of the field go over a stile and turn right down a car-wide track, your direction 30 degrees. After 200 metres you pass an ornamental pond on your left and come out to a lane. *Turn right and, after 10 metres, turn left* over a stile to continue on the Hangers Way footpath, your direction 20 degrees. After 220 metres you pass a 'Keep out Private Woods' sign on a metal fieldgate to the left.

In a further 60 metres fork left towards a stile and wooden footbridge, your direction 30 degrees, which you cross after 50 metres. In a further 40 metres cross another stile and footbridge to go up the footpath, your initial direction 20 degrees. In 80 metres the footpath veers right with woods to your left.

After 200 metres pass to the left of a redundant stile. Follow the footpath as it goes downhill and comes out into the open; it then gradually climbs uphill to pass to the left of another redundant stile after 130 metres. In 150 metres you pass a signpost on the right next to a house with a swimming pool in the garden. In 40 metres go to the left of a redundant stile to go gently up a fenced-in path.

After 300 metres, at a footpath signpost pointing back, which indicates a path to Steep and Petersfield, the path joins a tarmac lane into **Hawkley**. *Continue ahead and in 200 metres turn right at the crossroads.* The suggested lunch stop, the **Hawkley Arms [5]**, is on the left 100 metres down the road.

Come out of the pub and turn right down the road. In 100 metres at the junction next to Hawkley Place follow the Hangers Way signpost straight on to pass the village green on your right. *At a metal road signpost veer left for Oakshott/Priors Green/Wheatham. In 50 metres turn right at a wooden bridleway signpost* down a narrow concrete road. In 100 metres you pass to the right of three garages. The path now becomes a stony bridleway with a hedgerow on your right and a field on your left.

After 300 metres you enter woodland to turn right to follow the Hangers Way, as indicated by a three-armed wooden signpost. You can see Hawkley church off to your right in the distance. The footpath runs along the right-hand edge of the wood, with open fields to the right. Continue on this footpath, with fine views to your right.

In 400 metres the path joins a crossing track. *Veer right,* your direction 300 degrees. *After 600 metres, when the path forks, take the lower right fork.* In 30 metres ignore a footpath to the right. In 300 metres you emerge from woods with a fence on your left and a field beyond, now walking downhill, your direction 350 degrees.

[!] *In 100 metres, at a three-way path junction* **[6]**, *as marked by a wooden three-armed signpost, veer left down steps* across a stream and up steps. In 50 metres cross a stile to go diagonally across a field towards a stile in the far right-hand corner, your direction 10 degrees.

In 200 metres cross the stile into the next field to continue along the side of the field, with a hedgerow on the left, your direction 80 degrees. In 200 metres, *on reaching the left-hand corner of the field, cross a triple step stile to turn left up a lane passing a pond*, your direction north.

In 180 metres, and 40 metres past the brow of the lane, turn right to cross a stile. Follow the Hangers Way along the left-hand edge of the field. In 200 metres cross a stile to the left of a metal fieldgate. Continue straight ahead across the field, your direction 65 degrees.

In 200 metres cross a stile to the left of the car-wide field exit. In a further 20 metres cross another stile to reach a lane and a ford **[7]**. *Turn right, crossing the ford by a wooden bridge.* Leave the Hangers Way at this point to continue up the lane. In 250 metres you pass Quarry Farm on the right. In 50 metres *turn right up a signposted, tree-arboured byway. After 400 metres the byway meets a lane where you turn right downhill.*

Poet's rest

For more than a century the village of **Steep** has been home to **Bedales** public school. The poet **Edward Thomas** lived in the village and sent his children to the school, and his wife Helen taught there for a while. Thomas lived at 2 Yew Tree Cottages, along the lane from the largely 13th-century church of All Saints. Although his father wanted him to pursue a career in the civil service, he was determined to be a writer. He concentrated on journalism and prose writing, but found it largely unrewarding (he was paid by the word for his books). The pivotal point in Thomas's career came in 1913 when he met the American poet Robert Frost, who encouraged him to try poetry. Over the next two years he developed impressively as a poet, before enlisting in the Artists Rifles in 1915 to fight in World War I. Thomas arrived in France in 1917 and was killed soon after at Arras, on Easter Monday 1917.

During his lifetime he only published a handful of poems (under the pseudonym Edward Eastaway), but his influence on later generations of poets (such as Philip Larkin) has been considerable. Unlike most other famous 'war poets', the horrors of the Western Front played no direct part in his work, which expresses, with great beauty and subtlety, his deep love for the English countryside.

Thomas is buried in Agny Military Cemetery in France, and is commemorated in Poets' Corner in Westminster Abbey, by the windows in the south wall of the All Saints church (engraved in 1978 by Laurence Whistler in the poet's memory) and by a sarsen memorial stone on top of Shoulder of Mutton Hill overlooking the village.

[!] In 70 metres *turn left over a stile.* After 20 metres cross a footbridge over a stream. In 30 metres cross a stile to veer left. In 40 metres cross another stile next to a metal fieldgate. Continue straight ahead on a wide grassy track along the upper right side of the field, your direction 100 degrees.

In 140 metres cross a stile to the right of a metal fieldgate. In 150 metres cross a stile to the left of a metal fieldgate. Continue straight ahead, with a fence on your right. In 100 metres go over another stile in a wooded area to continue straight ahead. In 50 metres go through a kissing gate and cross a stile to emerge from the woods. *Turn immediately sharp right to follow a car-wide grass track byway along the upper right side of the field.*

In 100 metres go through a metal fieldgate. Continue up the now tree-arboured byway, ignoring any turnings off, your direction 230 degrees. After 500 metres, having emerged from the arbour, keep straight on at a junction of paths.

[!] *In 140 metres, as the lane bends to the right, fork left* **[8]**, *climbing up over tree roots to a bridleway sign* in 10 metres. Go straight ahead along the left-hand edge of the field, your initial direction south. After 400 metres *turn left through a metal fieldgate* with a pond to the right. In 20 metres *turn left down a tarmac lane.* In 80 metres you pass a house called Uplands on the left. In 200 metres you go steeply downhill.

After 280 metres pass Slip Cottage on the left. In 100 metres, *at a wooden footpath signpost, turn right up a track to a field.* Go down an enclosed footpath along the left-hand field edge. In 180 metres follow the enclosed footpath as it turns sharp left downhill. In 70 metres pass a car-wide entrance to a farm on the left. In 30 metres *turn left over a stile and turn right down a car-wide track.*

After 280 metres, at the bottom right-hand corner of the field, go through a metal fieldgate. *Turn left onto a car-wide track*, your direction 50 degrees. *In 200 metres turn right* at a one-armed footpath signpost. In 15 metres cross over a stile to continue along a fenced-in footpath. After 150 metres cross over a stile and a plank bridge to follow the path round to the right. In 30 metres turn right across another plank bridge. **[9]** *Cross a stile and turn left to follow the left side of a field*, your direction 130 degrees.

After 200 metres cross a two-plank bridge immediately followed by a three-plank bridge and then a stile. Continue up the left side of a field, your direction 100 degrees. In 40 metres, as the fence on the left veers off to the left, continue straight ahead, aiming for a stile 30 metres to the right of the left-hand corner of the field.

In 100 metres cross the stile and another stile immediately afterwards. Continue ahead along the right-hand edge of a field. In 150 metres cross a stile to the right of a metal fieldgate. Turn left and immediately right along a shingle car-wide track. After 200 metres cross over a stile into the next field, cutting off the right-hand corner of the field, your direction 80 degrees. In 180 metres cross a stile between two metal fieldgates and continue along a fenced-in car-wide earth track along the left-hand side of a field.

In 200 metres go through a wooden gate and *cross the A3 over a humpback footbridge*. Once over the bridge turn right through a wooden gate after 20 metres. *Turn left along the left-hand edge of a field.* In 100 metres, at the left-hand field corner continue straight ahead and come out onto a tarmac lane, with a church to your left. **[10]**

At the car park for Liss cemetery turn right down a car-wide shingle path with the cemetery on your right, your direction

Family fun on the **Hangers Way**.

190 degrees. In 140 metres the path narrows as it joins a fence on the right. In 40 metres ignore a stile on your right as you pass some houses on your left and come out to a road after 100 metres.

Cross the road and go straight ahead, with a car park on the right and cottages to the left. In 30 metres you come to a one-armed wooden footpath sign. *In 10 metres veer left up a car-wide track underlaid with bricks.* In 30 metres two hedges enclose the footpath and you can see the tower of Liss church ahead.

In 350 metres the footpath meets a road, which you cross. Continue straight

Passing the reverse of the Ashford Hangers National Nature Reserve sign and *turn immediately right along a broad track through woods*. In 80 metres pass a red-tipped wooden post on the left.

In 100 metres, as you approach a wooden barrier with a no cycling sign, *turn left* going gently uphill, your direction 40 degrees. After 50 metres the path curves to the right and goes downhill, your direction 120 degrees. After 250 metres you pass a wooden barrier. In 10 metres, at a T-junction, *turn right along the edge of the wood*.

In 200 metres you pass an Ashford Hangers National Nature Reserve sign. After 200 metres ignore a path that joins from the right. Keep straight on, ignoring any turnings off.

[!] In 600 metres, *as a field comes into view through the trees on the right, turn right* **[A1]** across a stile and walk straight ahead down a beech tree-lined path. After 100 metres the trees end. Keep ahead to a stile in 100 metres. Cross the stile and *turn right down the road*.

[!] In 400 metres, after a section of the road that is shaded by trees, *turn left at a footpath sign* (which in summer can be very overgrown) to walk along the left-hand edge of a field.

In 100 metres the path enters woodland and goes downhill. In another 120 metres go over a stile and straight ahead to a telegraph pole in 25 metres. *Veer right to follow the telegraph poles for 100 metres towards a stile. Go over the stile and turn left* with the field to your left and woods to your right, your direction 140 degrees.

In 80 metres *veer right* and keep straight on along the left-hand field edge, your direction 130 degrees. In 130 metres *cross another stile and turn right* down a stony car-wide track, passing farm buildings on your left. In 100 metres the path goes down a short slope into woods.

[!] *After a further 50 metres take the right-hand fork* **[A2]**, *indicated by a yellow arrow on a tree*, your direction 190 degrees. After 50 metres, with a

on through a metal kissing gate and down along the footpath leading to the church. *In 250 metres turn left in front of the church door* to leave the churchyard after 60 metres. *Turn right onto the road* **[11]**.

Liss station is 250 metres on the left. For tea options, *see p124* **Lunch & tea places**.

Walk options

a) Shorter circular walk:
Follow the main walk directions until point [4].

house on your left, *veer right* up some steps and go over a stile. Walk diagonally across the corner of the field, your direction 230 degrees.

In 50 metres cross a stile and keep straight on. In 100 metres cross a plank over a ditch. Continue through the woods for 500 metres. Cross another plank over a stream. *Turn right almost immediately over a very small brick bridge.*

Go uphill on this car-wide track. In 150 metres you reach a T-junction, passing a driveway to The Grange on the right. **If you wish to visit the Harrow Inn [A3]**, *turn left down the road* for 400 metres to meet another road where you turn left. The Harrow Inn is 50 metres on the left. **If you do not wish to stop at the pub**, *turn right* and, after 30 metres, pass the gated entrance to the Grange on the left.

In 10 metres cross a gravel drive to a fieldgate and a footpath sign. Go through the gate. *Turn left along the left-hand edge of the field.* In 100 metres veer left at a footpath sign. *In 10 metres turn right to cross a stile.* Go straight ahead over a second stile after 10 metres. Keep to the right-hand edge of the field, your direction 220 degrees. In 100 metres, at the field corner, cross a plank bridge, to go through a kissing gate and uphill through woods.

After 120 metres *turn right onto a lane.* In 100 metres *pass All Saints Church on your left* [2] *and immediately turn left* to rejoin your outward path. You are now retracing your steps back to Petersfield. Follow the narrow fenced footpath for 500 metres ignoring any turnings off. Turn left to cross the footbridge over the A3.

Continue on the fenced-in path for 400 metres to a gate next to a sign saying Steep Nursing Home. Go straight ahead down the tarmac lane. In 200 metres, *just before a stone wall starts on the left, veer right* up a stony tarmac track for 100 metres. At a junction of paths go straight on, your direction 210 degrees.

[!] *In 10 metres fork left onto the Hangers Way*, which is bordered by a wall on the right. After 400 metres pass between concrete posts and houses to reach the road. Turn left. **Petersfield station** is 100 metres on the left. To reach the town centre pass the station and turn right down Chapel Street. For the **Alley Cat** tea shop turn left off Chapel Street down Bakery Lane.

Lunch & tea places

Alley Cat *39B Bakery Lane, Chapel Street, Petersfield, GU32 3DY (01730 268427).* **Open/food served** 9am-4pm Tue, Wed; 9am-10.30pm Thur, Fri; 8.30am-10.30pm Sat. This tea shop serves home-made cakes.

Brewers *6 Chapel Street, Petersfield, GU32 3DP (01730 264400).* **Open/food served** 7.30am-5pm Mon-Fri; 9am-5pm Sat. Located next to the Waitrose car park at the end of Bakery Lane, Brewers offers specialist teas and coffees, and has a small seating area. There are also more tea shops on the High Street, some of which are open on Sundays.

Harrow Inn *Steep, Petersfield, GU32 2DA (01730 262685).* **Open** noon-2.30pm, 6-11pm Mon-Fri; 11am-3pm, 6-11pm Sat; noon-3pm, 7-10.30pm Sun. **Food served** noon-2pm, 7-9pm Mon-Fri; noon-2pm Sat, Sun. This pub with a garden has been described as 'one of the finest traditional country inns in England dating from the 17th century'. It is the suggested lunch stop for the shorter walk option.

Hawkley Arms *Pococks Lane, Hawkley, nr Liss, GU33 6NE (01730 827205).* **Open** noon-2.30pm, 6-11pm Mon-Fri; noon-3pm, 6-11pm Sat, Sun. **Food served** noon-2pm, 7-9.30pm Mon-Sat; noon-2pm Sun. Halfway into the walk, this inn has a garden and serves home-cooked food. Booking is advised. This is the suggested lunch stop for the main walk.

Whistle Stop *Hillbrow Road, Liss, GU33 7DS (01730 892202).* **Open** 11am-3pm, 5.30-11pm Mon-Sat; noon-5pm Sun. **Food served** noon-2pm, 5.30-9pm Mon-Sat; noon-3pm Sun. Serves tea and coffee, but only on Sundays (not Saturdays) at the time of writing. It may be better to go back to Petersfield for tea or head to the Crossing Gate pub (next to the level crossing) for a cold drink.

Picnic: Shoulder of Mutton Hill is a good picnic spot, with magnificent views.

Guildford to Farnham

Adventures on the Surrey Heathlands.

Start: Guildford station
Finish: Farnham station

Length: 22.2km (13.9 miles). For a shorter walk and other variations, *see below* **Walk options**.

Time: 7 hours. For the whole outing, including meals and trains, allow 10 hours 30 minutes.

Transport: Four trains an hour run between London Waterloo and Guildford (the fastest take 38 minutes). From Farnham two trains an hour run back to Waterloo (one an hour on Sundays; journey time: 51-59 minutes). If driving, you can return to Guildford from Farnham by train (changing at Woking). There are plenty of parking options in both Guildford and Farnham town centres.

OS Landranger Map: 186
OS Explorer Map: 145
Guildford, map reference SU991495, is in Surrey.

Toughness: 4 out of 10.

Walk notes: Think Surrey and you probably think of pretty villages, gentle green pastures and the country houses of retired stockbrokers. The first part of this walk conforms to that image, but the second, after lunch, takes you into the surprisingly wild and uninhabited Surrey Heathlands – a vast area of woods, sandy grassland and heather-covered moors, which at times feels more like southern Spain or Portugal than England.

The lack of habitation in this area means that it was often taken over by the army for exercises and bypassed by the railways. To visit it requires a long walk: the afternoon part of this walk is 13.9km (8.7 miles), or 4 hours 30 minutes walking time, as long in itself as some of the walks in this book. This is, therefore, a walk for a long spring or summer day. The good news, however, is that there is no rush to get to tea: the excellent Bush Hotel in Farnham serves cream teas in a lounge crammed with comfortable sofas well into the evening.

Walk options: Directions for these walk variations are given at the end of the main walk text (*see p134*).

a) Guildford circular walk: This walk does not go near the Heathlands, but it makes a pleasant afternoon or short day outing from Guildford, with the interesting Watts Gallery and Chapel or Loseley Park as its focus. This route is 12.3km (7.7 miles) or 4 hours walking time.

b) Guildford to Godalming: For this, and the two options below, you need to have the original *Time Out Book of Country Walks*. This walk option, of 12.1km (7.6 miles) or 3 hours 45 minutes walking, uses the second half of Walk 2 (Wanborough to Godalming) from that book to create a new Guildford to Godalming walk.

c) Farnham long circular walk: This walk, using directions from Walk 12 (Farnham to Godalming) in the original book, takes in two lunch stops on its way through parts of the Heathlands. It is 16.2km (10.1 miles), which is 5 hours walking time.

d) Farnham short circular walk: This option, as with option c), uses some directions from Walk 12 from the original *Time Out Book of Country Walks*. It does not include a lunch stop, but is shorter than option c) at 14.4km (9 miles), which is 4 hours 30 minutes walking.

Also, there is a very limited weekday **bus service** from a stop just next to the Good Intent in Puttenham (the lunchtime pub on the main walk) to both Guildford and Farnham, which allows you to do the morning or afternoon half of the main walk. Phone 0870 608 2608 for times and information.

Special note: This walk was created by Nicholas Albery, author of the first *Time Out Book of Country Walks* and the inspiration for this book, shortly before his untimely death in June 2001 (*see p6*). It is thus the last walk he created, and the only one in this book to have been devised by him.

Saturday Walkers' Club: Take the train nearest to 9.40am from London Waterloo to Guildford. If doing the Guildford Circular Walk, take the train nearest to 10.40am.

Walk directions

[1] [Numbers refer to the map]
Coming out of **Guildford station**, *walk down the station approach towards an office block named Bridge House.* Don't cross the road in front of Bridge House, however, but *go right down the underpass ramp,* following a sign to 'Town Centre via Riverside Walk'. *Turn left into the tunnel, and on the far side go right, up the ramp.* Follow the pavement round to the left (metal barriers make this the only choice).

Round the corner, take the left-hand (descending) ramp, signposted to the High Street. Turn right under the bridge and follow the edge of the river for 100 metres until you come to a pedestrianised stone bridge. *Do not cross the bridge, but just beyond the far wall of the bridge,* and just before the White Horse pub, *turn left on a path,* which brings you in 20 metres *to the riverside path, where you turn right,* your direction 150 degrees.

In 70 metres this path rejoins the road: keep to the river bank, following a black metal fence, for 50 metres until the pavement begins again. After 100 metres, *go left over the river on a black and white metal footbridge.*

20 metres beyond the end of the bridge, and just before a second footbridge, go right to follow a path between a canal lock to your left and the river to your right, your direction 160 degrees initially. In 120 metres the path crosses over a weir. 15 metres after this, *fork right on a tarmac path,* which crosses a park.

In 150 metres, *when this path comes to the river bank again, go right* over a green metal weir. You are now on the right hand bank of the River Wey. *Keep on the river path for 700 metres* until you see a wooden bridge over the river. *40 metres before this bridge, turn right up a tarmac path,* your direction 290 degrees. Almost immediately there is a miniature stone bridge over a tiny stream to your left.

The tarmac path becomes a tarmac lane, and climbs steeply, until in 60 metres it crosses a brick bridge over the railway line. Keep straight on, and after 80 metres you emerge onto a busy main road, the A3100. The entrance to the campus of the College of Law is straight ahead of you. *Turn right down the A3100,* following a North Downs Way sign. In 40 metres, by Ye Olde Ship Inn on your right, *go left up Sandy Lane.*

In 160 metres the North Downs Way forks right on a car-wide track **[2]**. (You can follow this route as far as the Watts Gallery if you wish – for directions, see **Guildford circular** walk at the end of the main text.) This round walk option **(a)** diverges from the main route here.

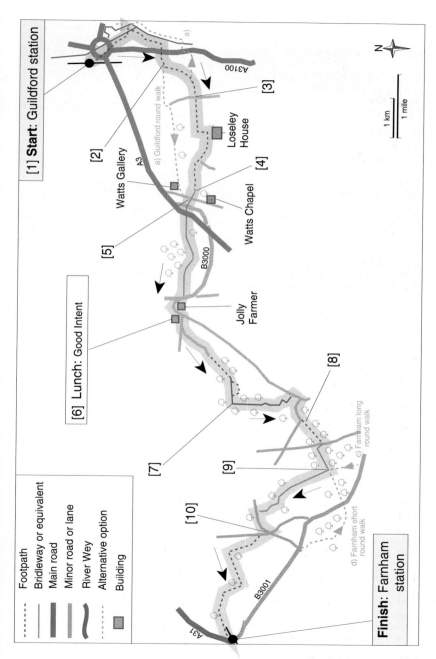

[1] **Start**: Guildford station

[2]

[3]

[4]

[5]

a) Guildford round walk

A3100

A3

Watts Gallery

Loseley House

Watts Chapel

B3000

[6] **Lunch**: Good Intent

Jolly Farmer

[7]

[8]

[9]

[10]

c) Farnham long round walk

d) Farnham short round walk

B3001

A31

Finish: Farnham station

Footpath
Bridleway or equivalent
Main road
Minor road or lane
River Wey
Alternative option
Building

N

1 km
1 mile

Canalside path near **Guildford**.

However, the recommended route is to remain on the road, keeping on the pavement on the left-hand side. *In 150 metres this pavement diverges from the road* to become a path climbing up into woods, your direction 240 degrees initially.

In 150 metres this path comes up level with a car park on your left, continuing alongside it for another 80 metres, before curving left to a road in a further 70 metres. *Cross this road and start up a* cul-de-sac marked 'The Firs 1-6'. However, *in 30 metres fork left* down a broad path into the woods, your direction 200 degrees.

In 200 metres you get a view of the valley ahead, and the path turns right. In another 250 metres it turns left for 70 metres to reach a *T-junction. Go right here*, your direction due west, with an open field soon on your right. In 150 metres the path becomes a car-wide track, with a bungalow to the left, and, in another 70 metres, a tarmac lane where a driveway joins from a large house to the left.

Follow this lane for 140 metres to a road T-junction [3], *and cross straight over to continue up a car-wide track* between the Littleton Youth House left and Pillarbox Cottage right, following a footpath sign. In 40 metres *cross a stile to the left of a fieldgate, and carry straight on across a field*, your direction due west.

In 200 metres, on the far side of the field, cross a stile to the left of a metal fieldgate into a second field, and carry on slightly to the left, aiming to the left of two trees, the first of which you pass in 100 metres. *Keep straight on, slightly downhill, aiming for the right-hand edge of a lake visible ahead*, which you reach in 140 metres.

Cross a stile to carry on in the same direction along the lake's edge, passing four wooden benches along the way. In 130 metres, just past the far end of the lake, cross another stile to carry on along the left-hand edge of a field. To the left can be seen **Loseley Park** (*see p131*).

Follow the field edge as it curves right and left, and *in 180 metres you cross a stile, with a four-armed footpath signpost marking a crossroads with a car-wide track. Keep straight on across another stile* (actually this is the only possible route: the other two arms of the footpath sign indicate that the track is private).

In 40 metres turn left with the fence, your direction now due south, and in a further 50 metres cross a stile to your left to continue in the same direction, with the fence now on your right. In 120 metres you come to a stile, and a car-wide track lined with trees leading to Loseley Park [*]. *Turn right on this track*, your direction due west.

In 250 metres this track passes a cottage on your right, and you go through a gate. *350 metres beyond this, 10 metres before the track turns left to become a tarmac road*, and just before Little Polsted House, *turn right at a two-armed footpath signpost* up a sandy path surrounded by high banks, your direction due north. (In late March, these banks are carpeted with celandines.)

[!] *In 40 metres turn left off this path, climbing steep steps up the bank*, your direction due west once more. At the top of the bank, there is an evergreen hedge to your left, and in 20 metres the footpath kinks right and then left to come out on the left-hand edge of an open field. Your direction is still due west.

Follow the left edge of this field, initially with house gardens to your left, for 250 metres to a stile. Cross this and keep straight on, now on the right-hand edge of a rough overgrown field. *In 250 metres cross a stile. Ignore a footpath to the left, and go right*, following a white footpath arrow. *In 10 metres cross another stile and go left onto a concrete track*. In 200 metres just before a barn with a corrugated iron roof, **you have a choice [4]**.

To visit the Watts Chapel – *see p138* – (a detour of a few minutes), go left for 20 metres, then right for 40 metres, and, just before another corrugated roofed barn, go through a metal fieldgate, and then left through another metal fieldgate. 15 metres beyond this, go right, following a wooden fence to your left. In 100 metres

you come to the road, where you go left. The entrance to the Watts Chapel is 60 metres along on the left.

After visiting the chapel, return to the road and turn right, retracing your steps but remaining on the road instead of veering onto the path. In 180 metres turn left down a tarmac lane, signposted 'North Downs Way', your direction 290 degrees, and resume the walk directions at point [5] below. To get to the Watts Gallery, ignore this left turn and stay on the road for another 50 metres, returning to this point after your visit.

To go direct to the Watts Gallery from point [4] **or to continue the main walk without visiting either Chapel or Gallery**, *go right over a dilapidated stile 15 metres before the barn* onto a fenced path along the edge of a wood, your direction 300 degrees once the path straightens out in 10 metres. In 150 metres cross another stile, and 50 metres beyond this, *you come to a road*.

To visit the Watts Gallery from this point, turn right on the road for 50 metres, returning to this point after your visit. (You can take option **b) Guildford to Godalming** at this point. See directions at end of main walk text.)

To continue the main walk without visiting the gallery, *go straight across the road and down the tarmac lane ahead*, signposted 'North Downs Way', your direction 290 degrees.

[5] After 150 metres on the tarmac lane, you pass under a huge arched bridge, and after a further 70 metres under a flyover (the A3). 20 metres after the flyover, and just before the entrance to a house called Monkshatch, *fork left on a car-wide gravel track*, your direction 240 degrees initially, following a blue North Downs Way arrow.

You now follow the North Downs Way, a broad sand or gravel track, for 2km (1.25 miles) all the way to Puttenham. Simply keep straight on along the main track and ignore all ways off. Initially the path is through woods, and later passes a golf course (where any deviations will lead you onto the fairway!) and a cricket field. The only potentially confusing junction is in 500 metres when there are multiple turnings left and right: but keep straight on, your direction 280 degrees, and 80 metres after this junction you pass a house – Questors – on your right.

After 2km (1.25 miles), *the path reaches a main road, the B3000*, with the **Jolly Farmer** pub straight ahead. Here, *cross the road and turn right. In 120 metres turn left down a side road into* **Puttenham** *village*. In 150 metres you pass the church on your left, and the road curves left and then right. In another 180 metres you come to the **Good Intent** pub on the right, the recommended lunch stop **[6]**.

Coming out of the pub after lunch, *turn right along the main road through the village*. Stay on this, ignoring ways off, for 350 metres until the road forks. *Take the left fork, Lascombe Lane. In 100 metres fork left again* onto Highfield Lane, leaving the North Downs Way.

Stay on this lane as it climbs up out of the village into the open countryside. In 400 metres you pass an isolated cream-coloured house to the left. *150 metres beyond the house, opposite a metal fieldgate to the right, fork left diagonally across a field* on a signposted footpath, your direction 230 degrees.

In 150 metres cross a stile, which is not obvious until you come close to it (it is to the left of the line of trees on the far side of the field). Walk diagonally across the next field and in 70 metres cross another stile.

Cross the gravel driveway of a house to continue straight on down a footpath at first between wooden fences, and later with a hedge on your left, your direction 230 degrees. In 80 metres the hedge ends and you find yourself in open woodland. Keep straight on along a clear path for a further 160 metres to a wooden kissing gate.

After the kissing gate, descend 5 metres to a three-armed footpath signpost and turn left for 15 metres to a footpath junction marked with a wooden post. Ignore the car-wide track heading uphill, and instead *go right along a smaller path*, your direction once more 230 degrees.

In 180 metres *just as you emerge from the trees into an area of open heathland* (**Puttenham Common**), *you come to a fork, where you go right. 30 metres further on, go right again onto a car-wide sandy track*, your direction 260 degrees.

You can now stay on this broad track for 600 metres to point [7], a T-junction with a fence beyond it. **But the recommended route, with better views**, is to *fork left down a sandy path in 180 metres, just before the brow of a slight hill.*

In 100 metres this brings you to an escarpment with fine onward views, and a bench (here, or anywhere in the next 300 metres, makes a fine **picnic** spot). *Follow the clear sandy path as it curves right along the escarpment*, until in 300 metres you come to a second bench. Here *follow the path as it curves right away from the escarpment edge to rejoin the main track in 80 metres at a five-way junction, where you turn left*, your direction due west.

Stay on this broad path, which in 40 metres goes downhill, and 60 metres afterwards comes to a crosspaths, where you go straight on. 60 metres after this, *you come to a T-junction in front of a wire fence* **[7]**, *where you turn left downhill*, your direction 200 degrees initially.

Follow the fence (which is on your right and is at times covered by undergrowth) on a clear path downhill, ignoring ways off. *In 500 metres you pass a small lake screened by trees to your left* (**General's Pond**). At the end of the lake, keep straight on along the fence, your direction 220 degrees.

In 300 metres follow the main path as it curves left away from the fence, ignoring a minor path that goes straight on (there is a big oak tree to the right by the fence at this junction). 25 metres later you pass a footpath post with green,

Park life

In 1562, on the request of Queen Elizabeth I, Sir William More started to build a grand manor house using stone from the ruins of Waverley Abbey in Farnham. The result, **Loseley Park**, is one of the finest examples of Elizabethan architecture in the south-east.

The house can be visited on guided tours that focus on the splendid Great Hall; among the interior's riches are tapestries and panelling from Henry VIII's now-vanished Nonesuch Palace.

Outside, within 1,400 acres of grounds and countryside, are five themed gardens that make up a Walled Garden based on a Gertrude Jekyll design. One of these, the award-winning Rose Garden, contains over 1,000 old-fashioned rose bushes.

Loseley Park remains within the More family today, and the current owner, Michael More-Molyneux, has cannily expoited a range of revenue streams from his inheritance. It's a popular venue for weddings, banquets and other events, as well as appearing in a number of film and TV productions, including *Blackadder* and *Jonathan Creek*. Most famously, the house gives its name to a brand of ice-cream that was traditionally made from the milk of the Loseley Jersey Herd. It, and other Loseley food products, can be bought from the estate shop.

(The official entrance to the house is 600 metres south along the lane crossed at point [3] in the walk. However, the information staff at the house say that walkers can stroll up to the house from the lake, or go through the gate marked 'PRIVATE' at the point marked [*] in the text, provided that the gardens are open to the public that day, and provided that your intention is to visit the house, gardens or tea room. Once inside the grounds, to get to the tearoom, follow the signs through a gateway in the wall to the left-hand (eastern) end of the main façade of the house. The shop and ticket kiosk for the house and walled garden are also through this gateway.)

Loseley Park

Guildford, GU3 1HS (01483 304440/24hr info line 01483 505501/www.loseley-park.com). **Open** *House (guided tours)* early June-late Aug 1-5pm Wed-Sun & bank hols in May, Aug. *Walled garden, shop & tearoom* early May-late Sept & bank hols in May, Aug 11am-5pm Wed-Sun. *Restaurant* May-Sept noon-2.30pm Sat, Sun. **Admission** *House, garden & grounds* £6; £3-£5 concessions. *Garden & grounds only* £3; £1.50-£2.50 concessions. **Credit** MC, V (over £10).

purple and colourless bands on it, your direction now 160 degrees.

80 metres further on, ignore a path to the right at a post with white, green and purple bands on it. *In a further 30 metres at the bottom of the dip you cross a stream* (which may be dry in summer), your direction now 130 degrees. *Just beyond the stream, at another three-banded footpath post, turn right*, your direction due south, following the edge of a marsh to your right *to reach the shore of a large lake 50 metres later. Turn left along its shore*, your direction 140 degrees.

Keep to the edge of the lake for 180 metres until *you come to a road, where you go right.* The road passes between two lakes, both concealed by trees, until in 200 metres *you come to a crossroads, and go right*, following a sign to 'Sands'. Follow this road past a parking area on your right. In 100 metres you pass the entrance to the parking area, which has a wooden height barrier to stop vans. 80 metres later, follow the road as it curves left, ignoring a road to the right and 50 metres further on another one.

In 300 metres, *as the road curves right and opposite Whitefield Cottages, turn left along a car-wide track (leading to a parking area) and immediately turn right onto a signposted footpath to the right of a 'NO MOTORCYCLES' sign*, your direction 230 degrees.

[!] *In 200 metres, 30 metres beyond the end of the garden of a house just visible through the trees to the right, fork right off the main track on a broad but less well-defined path*, your direction 250 degrees. (In summer, this path can be indistinct: in this case, turn right at a crosspaths 50 metres beyond the end of the garden, along a narrow earth path, your direction 290 degrees initially). **[8]**

In 35 metres (25 metres if you are coming via the crosspaths), *ignore a track forking right to a wooden barrier. 5 metres further on, keep to the left-hand side of a small island of trees.*

[!] *20 metres further on, as the path you are on curves right, keep straight on along an initially indistinct path*, your direction 240 degrees. This develops into a clearer sandy footpath, which in 50 metres starts to climb a hill. In 80 metres it comes to a crossroads. Go straight on, up a broad forest track into a pine forest, your direction 260 degrees.

(If you are confused just after point [8], *fork right to the wooden barrier and carry on past it for 100 metres to another low wooden barrier. Turn left just before it up a car-wide forest track. In 70 metres you come to a crossroads, where you turn right uphill onto a car-wide track, and resume the directions below).*

Keep straight on the broad track for 500 metres, ignoring ways off, first climbing uphill and then downhill, *until you come to a tarmac road. Cross the road, and go half right down a signposted public bridleway*, your direction 330 degrees. *In 80 metres this merges with a car-wide gravel track*, your direction now 310 degrees.

50 metres further on, just before a wooden barrier and a Forestry Commission sign for Crooksbury Wood, turn left uphill on a sandy path, marked by a footpath post, your direction 250 degrees. In 30 metres ignore a path to the right to carry on uphill. In 60 metres you emerge onto the open heath of **Crooksbury Common**, a large area of heather and gorse.

Keep on this path, which passes over the brow of the hill in 180 metres, and is later paralleled by a broader track on the right-hand side. 300 metres beyond the brow of the hill, *after a section under pine trees, you come to a house on your left behind a wooden fence. When the fence ends, you find yourself at a crossroads*, with houses to either side of the car-wide track to your left.

Turn right at this crossroads onto a car-wide sandy track, through wooden barriers, passing another Forestry

Commission sign for Crooksbury Wood (Crooksbury Common on the OS map), your direction 330 degrees **[9]**.

Keep on this broad path as it gently climbs upwards across the common. *In 800 metres you pass a gated drive to Woodland Cottage to your left, and a house named Gairnshiel to your right.* The track is now gravelled. *50 metres beyond these houses, and just before other houses on the right, fork left off the track through a wooden fieldgate on a signposted bridleway,* a car-wide track, your direction 300 degrees.

In 450 metres you come to a road, which you cross over, following a signposted bridleway, your direction 300 degrees. In 20 metres ignore a path up off to the left with a wooden barrier. Keep on the bridleway, heading downhill, your direction 350 degrees initially.

15 metres after this you pass a blue-tipped post to the left of the path with the number 577 on it. In 70 metres at a crosspaths keep straight on uphill passing another blue-tipped 577 post, and in 50 metres another. *At the next post, in 50 metres, just before a wooden barrier, turn left downhill,* your direction 290 degrees initially.

In 100 metres, at a blue-tipped post with 341 on it, and with a wooden barrier to your left, *go right,* your bearing due north. *In 110 metres,* 10 metres after the second of two more 341 posts, *the path forks. Go left for 30 metres to reach a road.*

Turn left on the road (take care here as there are no verges or pavement and the traffic is sometimes quite fast). *In 450 metres you come to a staggered crossroads* **[10]** *and go right* on Crooksbury Road, another potentially busy road. *In 120 metres, just beyond the Compton Way on your left, take a signposted bridleway that forks half left,* your direction 320 degrees.

Stay on this path, which runs along the back of suburban gardens. In 450 metres ignore a footpath to the left (marked by an almost illegible footpath sign), and 200 metres beyond this, as a green wire fence around a garden on your right-hand side ends, ignore a broad path to the right and carry straight on downhill.

You have now re-joined the North Downs Way, which you follow all the way into Farnham.

But in more detail: *140 metres after the junction, turn left, initially up three wooden steps, following a yellow arrow and white acorn symbol on a footpath post,* your direction 250 degrees. There is a 'No Horse Riding' sign to the right of this path.

In 70 metres ignore a path to the left to continue straight on, with a field now on your right. In 220 metres pass through a wooden kissing gate and into an open field. Carry straight on along the right-hand edge of the field, your direction 250 degrees.

In 200 metres ignore a metal kissing gate to the right by a three-armed footpath sign to continue along the field edge. In another 120 metres exit the field through a wooden kissing gate and keep straight on along a path between barbed wire fences. 50 metres further on, *cross a gravel track and keep on downhill on a road,* your direction 250 degrees.

In 130 metres you pass the entrance to Moor Park House on your left and a car-wide track on your right: keep straight on along the road, crossing the River Wey in 120 metres (a mere trickle compared to the river you walked along out of Guildford this morning).

In 100 metres *ignore a road to the left to curve right* on a road named Moor Park Way. *In 120 metres, as the road curves left, fork right through a kissing gate,* following the North Downs Way sign.

In 300 metres you come to a curious wooden seat (shaped like a bee orchid), which marks the start of the 245km- (153 mile-) long North Downs Way, which stretches all the way from Farnham to Dover. *Just beyond the seat, you pass through a kissing gate and turn left on a broad track between wire fences,*

following a North Downs Way arrow,
your direction 240 degrees.

*In 50 metres, where the path forks, go
right,* following the North Downs Way
sign, your direction now 300 degrees.
Stay on this main track, ignoring a
footpath to the left in 280 metres, and
passing in 100 metres through a tunnel
through the railway embankment. 40
metres beyond the railway embankment
curve left with the track along the river.

Stay on this track, ignoring all ways off
(which are all driveways). *In 600 metres
you come to a large petrol station, after
which the path curves right* around a
picnic area and heads towards a dual
carriageway, the A31. *30 metres before
the dual carriageway go left up a car-wide
tarmac drive,* following the North Downs
Way sign. In 200 metres *this brings you
out onto the A31, where you turn left for
120 metres to the traffic lights.*

To go direct to Farnham station,
turn left here: the station is in 100 metres,
uphill on the right.

For tea, *turn right at the traffic lights,
crossing the A31,* down a road into the
town centre of Farnham. In 60 metres
you cross a bridge over the River Wey. In
150 metres you pass the United Reform
Church on your left and in 50 metres
more, Sainsbury's on your right.

Opposite Sainsbury's, on the left-hand
side of the road, you can see the **Bush
Hotel**, the recommended tea stop.
When you enter the hotel, turn left by
the reception desk and walk towards
the restaurant: the armchair-filled
lounge where tea is served is just on
your right. You may need to alert hotel
staff to your presence.

*After tea, turn right out of the hotel
entrance,* and walk back down past
Sainsbury's and the church. In 200
metres you cross the bridge over the
Wey, and in 60 metres you come to traffic
lights and the junction with the A31 dual
carriageway. Cross straight over the A31
and **Farnham station** is 100 metres
uphill on the right.

Walk options

a) Guildford circular walk:
[Follow the main walk directions to point
[2] but *fork right off the road onto the
North Downs Way,* your direction 290
degrees, instead of remaining on the road.]

*You now follow the North Downs
Way for 4km (2.5 miles) all the way
to the Watts Gallery.* The way is clear
throughout – a car-wide track for the
most part – and well signposted.

But in more detail: Almost immediately
on leaving the road ignore a driveway
to Piccards Manor right. In 60 metres
follow the track as it curves left and a
field opens up on the right. In 200 metres
you enter the edge of a wood, and in a
further 350 metres a private track curves
in from the left.

70 metres beyond this, you come to
a metal gate marked 'Private Road –
Piccards Farm Only'. Despite this
warning, the public footpath is actually
straight on through the gate. In 50 metres
you pass the farm buildings on your left
and right and carry on along what soon
becomes a tarmac lane. *350 metres
after the farm, curve left with the road,
ignoring tracks straight ahead and to
the right.*

In 80 metres *as you approach the end
of the field to your left, leave the road
and take the sandy car-wide track right,*
following the yellow arrow and white
acorn symbol on a post, your direction
due west. In 30 metres ignore turnings
to the left to keep straight on. In 150
metres the sandy track becomes a gravel
one, with a field fence to your right and
a fine view across the valley. There are
woods to your left.

In a further 450 metres, *at the bottom
of a long hill, where the track turns right,
go left on a broad path, following a white
arrow on a post. In 10 metres curve right
with this path* following a blue arrow
and ignoring a minor path to the left, to
resume your former direction, due west.

In 50 metres ignore a track to the left

that goes to a gate (which is in any case private). Keep straight on along the sandy track, which now narrows and climbs a hill. At the top of the hill, ignore any minor paths off to the right and keep on the main track. In 500 metres, at a major path crosspaths, keep straight on, following a blue arrow on a post, your direction still due west.

In 25 metres you start to descend, with an open field to your left. The path descends deeper and deeper into a cutting, emerging in 200 metres by some farm buildings. Keep straight on, along what is now a gravel car-wide track with a hedge to your right that climbs gently uphill.

In 450 metres you come over the crest of a hill and descend. In another 200 metres, just before you get to a tarmac road, the **Watts Gallery** (*see p138* **Say Watts**) and its tearoom, the recommended lunch stop, are on your right.

Coming out of the tearoom or gallery, *walk down its driveway to the road, and go left. In 50 metres ignore a tarmac lane to the right.* Keep on along the road, in 80 metres passing the drive to Coneycroft Cottages on your left.

70 metres further on, past the end of Coneycroft Farm, turn left along the wooden fence, your direction 80 degrees. (However, for the recommended visit **Watts Chapel** – *see p138* **Say Watts** – which can be seen on the hill straight ahead, stay on the road for 60 metres to find its entrance gate on your left. After visiting the chapel, return to Coneycroft Farm and turn right just before its buildings, with the wooden fence to your right.)

Carry on with the wooden fence to your right and barns to your left. *In 80 metres as you come to the end of an open-sided barn on your left, turn left with the fence,* following a white arrow. In 15 metres go through a metal field gate with a white barn ahead, and *turn right* through another metal fieldgate. In 40 metres at the end of the barn *turn left* following an arrow on a fence, and in 20 metres *turn*

right onto a concrete car-wide track, your direction now 110 degrees [4].

In 180 metres, just before the track ends at a rusted metal fieldgate, turn right across a stile, following a yellow arrow, and *in 5 metres go immediately left over another stile*, ignoring the path straight on. You are now on a path along the left-hand edge of an overgrown field, your direction 100 degrees. *In 280 metres cross a stile to follow a path between fences*, now with an open field on your left.

In 280 metres, at the top of the hill, you pass the garden of a house on your right, and soon after *the path kinks right and then left. 20 metres later it descends steep steps into a gully, at the bottom of which you go right*, your direction due south. (The steep banks here are a delight in late March and April when they are covered with yellow celandines).

In 40 metres, *at a junction with a car-wide earth and gravel track, go left*, following a footpath sign, your direction 110 degrees initially. In 350 metres you pass a house – Polsted Lodge – on the left and go through wooden gates to carry straight on along the track, now under an avenue of trees.

In 250 metres *you get to a wooden fieldgate* **[*]**, a private way into the grounds of **Loseley Park**. For directions to the possible tea option here, *see p131*. Otherwise, *just before the fieldgate, go left over a stile* at a three-armed footpath sign, your direction 10 degrees.

The path follows a line of trees for 120 metres, and then goes left over a stile to resume its former direction (due north), now on the right-hand edge of a field. *In a further 50 metres turn right with the field boundary, and in another 40 metres you come to a stile* and a four-armed footpath sign.

Keep straight on across the track and over the stile on the far side to follow the right-hand edge of a large open field, your direction due east. Loseley Park can be seen to the right. In 50 metres follow the fence as it bends right slightly. *Keep along the field edge* for another 120 metres *to a stile. Cross this stile to walk along the left edge of a lake.*

At the far end of the lake, in 130 metres, *cross another stile into an open field, heading just to the right of two big trees* (the first of which is 70 metres ahead), your direction 80 degrees. Beyond the trees, it is 100 metres to the end of the field, where you cross a second stile and head straight on towards the gap between two houses on the far side. In 200 metres *cross a stile between the two houses*, and walk down a driveway for 40 metres to a road [3].

Cross the road and go straight on down a tarmac lane, your direction 80 degrees. In 130 metres, when this tarmac lane veers off right over a cattle grid, keep straight on along an earth car-wide track, which narrows to a path in 70 metres. In 130 metres, *just over the top of the hill, ignore a footpath to the left, to carry straight on downhill between fences.* The grounds of the Surrey Police Headquarters and training school are on your left.

In 500 metres you come to a suburban road, where you carry straight on for 130 metres to the main road, the A3100. *Go left on the A3100 for 70 metres*, passing a bus stop on the right, and then *turn right through a metal barrier down a car-wide track*, signposted as a public footpath, your direction 120 degrees initially.

In 100 metres pass through a brick arch under the railway line. 130 metres after this you come to the River Wey, with a black-and-white metal bridge over a lock ahead. Do not cross this bridge, but turn left along the riverside path, your direction due north initially.

Follow the river bank for 650 metres until you come to the footbridge which marks the junction with the North Downs Way and brings you full circle on your route. You can continue on the same side of the river into Guildford, but, for variety, *cross the bridge, and turn left along the river on the far side.* In 40

metres ignore a path signposted to the right, and go straight ahead through a wooden kissing gate. In 120 metres you pass through another kissing gate into the Shalford Water Meadows.

Keep along the river, and in 500 metres you come to a kissing gate. Pass through this and up a path between fences. *In 70 metres at a T-junction, turn left*, and in 20 metres pass the entrance to Guildford Rowing Club. In another 30 metres *turn left over the River Wey on a footbridge. On the far side of the river, turn right*, with the river now on your right-hand side. In 300 metres you come to Millmead Lock.

For tea, *turn right* at this point over a footbridge. In 70 metres you come out to the entrance of the **Yvonne Arnaud**

A cutting in the **Surrey Heathlands**.

Theatre, whose café has a riverside terrace. After tea, retrace your steps to Millmead Lock and follow the directions below to Guildford station.

To go straight to Guildford station, *turn left at Millmead Lock, crossing a footbridge. On the far side, turn right along a road.* In 100 metres the pavement ends and you follow the black metal fence for another 50 metres, before *forking off the road onto a gravel path along the riverside. In 70 metres just before the bridge, and just after the White Horse Inn, turn left for 20 metres to the road, where you go right.*

Ignore the pedestrianised Town Bridge immediately to the right. Beyond the bridge, *follow the river's edge for 100 metres until you come to the next bridge*, a road bridge. *Pass under this and on the other side turn left*, not up the steps immediately to your left, but the steps just ahead of them, signposted to the station.

In 50 metres *bend right with the road* (a metal barrier gives you no choice) and the station sign and approach can now be seen ahead. To get to it *cross the road using the underpass*, which starts in 50 metres, *turning right at the far end of the underpass* to climb a ramp, at the top of which you will find **Guildford station** directly in front of you.

b) Guildford to Godalming:

[Follow the short walk route above from Guildford to the Watts Gallery.]

At this point, pick up the directions in Walk 2 (Wanborough to Godalming) in the original *Time Out Book of Country Walks*. This creates a Guildford to Godalming walk of 12.1km (7.6 miles), which is about 3 hours 45 minutes walking time.

c) Farnham long circular walk:

[Follow the directions for walk 12 (Farnham to Godalming) in the original Time Out Book of Country Walks *as far as the* **Donkey**, *that walk's recommended lunch stop in Charleshill.]*

Coming out of the Donkey, turn right (or, if coming from Tilford and not stopping at the Donkey, keep straight on past it down the road). *In 50 metres you come to the main road, which you cross.* On the far side, ignore the gated driveway marked 'Private Road leading only to Foxhill' that goes uphill directly ahead of you, but instead *take the car-wide track* (initially tarmac, but later earth) *to its left, signposted as a public bridleway*, your initial direction 340 degrees.

In 40 metres ignore a signposted public bridleway to the right to keep straight on along the main track.

You now follow this track uphill, at first through rhododendron-filled woods, and then past several large houses for 700 metres. At the top of the hill, about 60 metres after the slope finally levels out, *the track ends at a wooden car barrier with a Forestry Commission sign next to it announcing* **Crooksbury Wood**. *Pass through the barrier* and go straight on, taking up the main walk directions above after point [9] to get back into Farnham.

d) Farnham short circular walk:

[Follow the directions for walk 12 (Farnham to Godalming) in the original Time Out Book of Country Walks *as far as point [3] in those directions.* You will emerge from the Moor Park Estate and pass Stella Lodge to come out onto Camp Hill road.]*

Go right on Camp Hill Road, downhill for 20 metres, and then left on a road signposted to Godalming, Milford and Elstead, your direction 145 degrees.

In 180 metres, as the road curves left, fork right downhill on a car-wide track, your direction 185 degrees initially. *In 300 metres the track curves left, and in 200 metres more comes to a T-junction.* Ignore a byway signposted to the right to continue straight on, your direction 140 degrees, passing two wooden posts in 15 metres.

In 80 metres the path is bounded by wire fences, and in another 60 metres the garden of an idyllic house in a forest

Say Watts

Much celebrated in his day, painter and sculptor **George Frederick Watts** (1817-1904) occupied an unusual niche in belonging to no school but his own (though he had links with the Pre-Raphaelites and the Symbolists).

Watts wished to do good through art – a very Victorian notion – and his insistence upon message is the primary reason why many of his works seem so dated today; but the best of them remain fascinating. His oeuvre includes landscapes, social comment pieces, allegories, portraits, drawings and sculptures. Watts' painting *Hope* was for many years one of the most reproduced pictures in the world.

Examples of all these genres can be found in the delightful **Watts Gallery**. The purpose-built gallery opened just two months before Watts' death in 1904, and has an Arts and Crafts homeliness that is instantly endearing. As Nicholas Albery, creator of the original *Time Out Book of Country Walks* commented: 'This is how all galleries should be: wonderfully intimate, eccentric and on a human scale.'

Watts' life was devoted to art. He was not rich until the last decades of his life, but he lived in comfort thanks to a series of wealthy patrons. After an unconsummated marriage to the actress Ellen Terry in 1864 (he was 47, she was just 17), he met his ideal match in Mary Fraser-Tytler (1849-1938), whom he married in 1886. Also an artist, and a believer in good works, she was responsible for the other reason to visit Compton – the extraordinary **Watts Chapel**.

In building the chapel Mary Watts saw a way to combine the glories of art with her philanthropic instincts – it was the ideal Arts and Crafts project. Compton villagers attended evening classes under her guidance and learned to work in clay so as to decorate the chapel. So successful was the training that they soon turned professional, becoming the Compton Potters' Arts Guild.

The chapel was consecrated in 1898 (the interior took another six years to complete) and is a riot of symbolism, inside and out. The building is a blend of styles, but is most strongly Byzantine – seeing it incongruously perched on a low Surrey hill, surrounded by grazing livestock, is a thrill that doesn't diminish with repeated visits.

The exterior is adorned with Christian Celtic geometric patterns mutated by art nouveau forms. The attention to detail is amazing – everything, right down to the iron hinges on the main doors, is representative of an idea or a thing (and often both). The stunning, colourful interior is decorated with images depicting the Tree of Life. The graveyard contains the Watts Memorial Cloister (1911), designed by Mary in memory of her husband.

Watts Gallery
Down Lane, Compton, GU3 1DQ (01483 810235/www.watts gallery.org.uk). **Open** *Apr-Sept* 2-6pm Mon, Tue, Fri, Sun; 11am-1pm, 2-6pm Wed, Sat. *Oct-Mar* 2-4pm Mon, Tue, Fri, Sun; 11am-1pm, 2-4pm Wed, Sat. **Admission** free. A £5 million renovation may mean the gallery is closed for part of 2005.

Watts Chapel
Off Down Lane, Compton (no phone). **Open** 9am-dusk daily. **Admission** free.

clearing (a bit like a woodcutter's cottage in a fairytale) starts to your right. Keep straight on along the left-hand edge of this garden.

In 110 metres you come level with the house, which is screened from view by a high wooden fence. In another 120 metres *you come to a wooden garden gate. This looks like the entrance to someone's private garden, but the public right of way is straight ahead through the gate* and along a wooden fence to the right of the garden. In 50 metres you pass a brick bungalow, Friars Way Cottage, and start up its gravel drive. In 100 metres *you come to a road, where you go left*, your direction 80 degrees.

In 35 metres *you come to a T-junction, where you go right*. Take care on this road as traffic comes quite fast around the corner. In 70 metres *turn left along a lane signposted Elstead and Milford*, your direction 80 degrees. This road is also prone to speeding cars, so once again take care.

In 600 metres *the road comes to a T-junction with the busy B3001. Go straight across up a car-wide bridleway* to the right of Uplands Cottage, your direction 40 degrees. The track takes you into pine forest. *In 250 metres ignore a track diverging left to keep straight on*, your direction now 50 degrees, still on a car-wide track. In 150 metres you cross over a crosspaths, with tracks marked 'Private: No Trespassing' right and left.

120 metres after this, *a green mesh fence starts on the right*, and on the left is an area where at time of writing the trees had all been felled (but may be replanted). Keep straight on along the green fence, which *in 200 metres gives way to a brick wall. 100 metres after this you come to a major track crossroads.*

To the right are houses, but you *turn left here, passing a wooden barrier for cars, and a Forestry Commission sign for* **Crooksbury Wood**. You can now resume the main walk directions above after point [8].

Lunch & tea places

Bush Hotel *1 The Borough, Farnham, GU9 7NN (01252 715237/www.macdonald hotels.co.uk).* **Open/food served** 6.30-9.45am, noon-2pm, 7-9.45pm daily. A fine old coaching inn that welcomes non-residents into its comfortable, sofa-filled lounge, and serves generously proportioned cream teas, as well as sandwiches and light meals until around 10pm. This is the suggested tea stop for the main walk.

Good Intent *The Street, Puttenham, GU3 1AR (01483 810387).* **Open** 11am-2.30pm, 6-11pm Mon-Fri; 11am-11pm Sat; noon-10.30pm Sun. **Food served** noon-2pm Mon, Sun; noon-2pm, 7-9.30pm Tue, Thur; 6-9.30pm Wed, Fri, Sat. Located 8.3km (5.2 miles) into the walk, this pub serves a short, wholesome menu that includes the likes bangers and mash and curries. It has a small garden. This is the suggested lunch stop on the main walk.

Loseley Park courtyard tearoom *Loseley Park, GU3 1HS (01483 304440/www.loseley-park.com).* **Open** *May-late Sept & bank hols in May, Aug* 11am-5pm Wed-Sun. **Restaurant** *May, Sept* noon-2.30pm Sat, Sun. The tearoom is lovely but only open from May to September (*see p131* **Park life**).

The Tea Shop *Down Lane, Compton, GU3 1DQ (01483 811030).* **Open** 10.30am-5.30pm daily. Located 5.5km (3.4 miles) into the walk (and very close to the Watts Gallery), it serves excellent fry-ups, as well as cakes and sandwiches. This is a possible early lunch stop on the main walk.

Yvonne Arnaud Theatre café *Millbrook, Guildford, GU1 3UX (01483 569334/www.yvonne-arnaud.co.uk).* **Open** 10am-9.30pm Mon-Sat. **Food served** noon-2pm, 6-7.45pm Mon-Sat. Has a riverside terrace. There are many other refreshment possibilities in Guildford town centre.

Picnic: On the main walk, the best place is on Puttenham Common at the place indicated between points [5] and [6] in the walk directions. Loseley Park, early in the main walk, also has a picnic area by its lake. On either of the Farnham circular walks, possible picnic spots include by the river just beyond Moor Park House, or (on the longer version only) the green of the village of Tilsbury.

Guildford
to Gomshall

Follow the pilgrims through the pristine North Downs.

Start: Guildford station
Finish: Gomshall station

Length: 13.7km (8.6 miles). For a shorter walk and other variations, *see below* **Walk options**.

Time: 4 hours. For the whole excursion, including trains and meals, allow 7 hours 30 minutes.

Transport: Four trains an hour run between London Waterloo and Guildford (the fastest take 38 minutes). Trains back from Gomshall to Guildford run every hour Monday to Friday and every two hours at weekends (journey time: 15 minutes). If you miss the train at Gomshall, buses go fairly regularly to Guildford from the main road just outside the Compasses Inn (0870 608 2608 for info). If driving, park at Guildford station, and make your way back by train or bus.

OS Landranger Maps: 186 and 187
OS Explorer Map: 145
Guildford, map reference SU991495, is in Surrey.

Toughness: 5 out of 10.

Walk notes: The section of the North Downs that runs eastwards from Guildford is one of its most unspoiled stretches. The North Downs Way runs along its crest, but this walk takes a more varied route, introducing not just the high grassy ridges with their fine views, but also hidden valleys, ancient woodlands, and the pretty farmland just below the Downs. It starts with a short, steep climb out of Guildford that leads straight to the dramatic viewpoint of Pewley Down. Then it joins the North Downs Way to climb to the hilltop church of St Martha-on-the-Hill. From here the route passes through undulating farmland beneath the North Downs escarpment, following the ancient Pilgrim's Way, to lunch in the cute village of Shere. The afternoon gives a contrasting view of the Downs, involving a stiff climb up into ancient woodlands – carpeted with bluebells at the end of April/early May – before a descent to tea at a remote farmhouse.

Walk options: Directions for the following walk options are given at the end of the main walk text. See p146.

a) Shortcut via Shere: You can take the 1.8km (1.1 mile) shortcut from Shere (point [5] in the main walk text) to Gomshall, and cut out the entire afternoon section. This reduces the walk to 10.9km (6.8 miles), or 3 hours 15 minutes walking time.

b) Guildford to Chilworth: For an even shorter walk from Guildford, you can walk as far as St Martha-on-the-Hill church, and then take the shortcut from St Martha's to Chilworth (from point [4] in the main walk text) for a train or bus back to your starting point: Chilworth is served a few minutes after Gomshall by the return trains and buses described in the Transport section above. This route is 6.4km (4 miles) and makes an invigorating two-hour walk.

c) Guildford to Boxhill/Dorking:
On a long summer's day, it is quite possible to walk from Shere all the way to either Boxhill & Westhumble or Dorking stations, adding 7.2km (4.5 miles) to the walk. This largely wooded walk is particularly stunning in the bluebell season (late April/early May).

Saturday Walkers' Club: Take the train nearest to 9.30am, before or after, from Waterloo to Guildford. Buy a day return to Gomshall.

Walk directions

[1] [Numbers refer to the map]
Coming out of the station, walk down the station approach towards an office block named Bridge House. Do not cross the road in front of Bridge House, however, but *go right down the underpass ramp,* following a sign to 'Town Centre via Riverside Walk'.

Turn left into the tunnel and on the far side go right, up the ramp. Follow the pavement round to the left (metal barriers make this the only choice). *Round the corner, take the left-hand, descending, ramp, signposted to High Street. Turn*

right under the bridge and follow the edge of the river for 100 metres.

Turn left over a pedestrianised stone bridge, and cross the main road. Walk up the High Street ahead of you for 60 metres, and then *turn right down Quarry Street, the first turning right,* your direction 160 degrees. In 150 metres, after passing a church on your right, *turn left up Castle Street.* In 50 metres ignore a turning to the left, and in 20 metres ignore another left turn (Chapel Street).

Curve right up Castle Street and in another 40 metres, opposite Tunsgate Square shopping centre, is the entrance to **Guildford Castle**. This is worth a brief visit: you can climb the tower and get a fine view over the town and Wey river valley. Coming out of the castle, resume your former direction up Castle Street and in 50 metres, *you come to a staggered crossroads.*

Go right along South Hill and in 20 metres turn half left up Pewley Hill, your direction 110 degrees. Climb this steep hill for 400 metres all the way to the top, ignoring side roads. On the way up be sure to turn round to get a fine view of Guildford and its modern cathedral.

At the top of the hill, you come to a small crossroads: High Pewley Road is to the right, and Semaphore Road to the left. Carry straight on, along a now level road until it comes to a dead end in 350

Countryside around **Shere**.

metres. An opening with wooden posts leads out onto **Pewley Down**, which is named on a sign.

Walk about 20 metres ahead, and a concrete plinth that looks like a trigonometry point comes into view on the hill half left (the plinth commemorates the purchase of Pewley Down in 1920 as a memorial to those who died in World War I): make a beeline for this, though you may like to walk closer to the escarpment first to enjoy the fine view over the Wey Valley. Though it is really too early for a rest, some benches immediately below the trigonometry point make a fine point to stop and stare, or even to have a **picnic [2]**.

From the trigonometry point, walk onwards along the ridge for 80 metres, your direction 80 degrees, and then fork right on a path that slants diagonally downhill to the right of a line of bushes, your direction 140 degrees. Almost immediately you pass on your right a green metal bench inscribed to 'Brion David Jago, a free spirit'.

In 230 metres, the path enters a wood and levels off. **[!]** *In 200 metres two paths fork left: take either of these two paths and in 5 metres turn right onto a parallel path to the one you have just left.* In 10 metres ignore a path to the left at a footpath post, to continue straight on. You soon emerge onto a long path between hedges, bearing 120 degrees, that slants downwards into the valley bottom.

No turning is possible on this path for 600 metres, by which time it is at the edge of the wood. At this point, you *cross a car-wide track to carry straight on, initially bearing 140 degrees, up a path which climbs gently uphill just inside the left-hand edge of a wood of pine trees.*

In 50 metres you can use the less muddy 'WALKERS ONLY' path to the left of the main path if you wish. In another 150 metres the path curves half right to climb more directly up the hill into the wood, with a wooden fence to the left of the path. *Where this ends in 70*

metres, go left at a T-junction, your direction 110 degrees.

In 90 metres you come to a metal barrier, beyond which is a road. A two-armed footpath sign confirms that you are now on the North Downs Way, which you now follow all the way to the church of St Martha-on-the-Hill.

But in more detail: *go left along the road. In 30 metres, just past Southernway Cottage on your right, turn right* up a track, following a North Downs Way sign, your direction 100 degrees.

In 70 metres, after a short climb, you *cross a tarmac driveway and go straight on through a wooden barrier* to continue on a car-wide sandy track, with a grassy space soon opening out to your left. When the space narrows to an end in 180 metres carry straight on along a broad track into a wood, with a wooden fence to your right.

In 100 metres the fence ends and the path starts to climb more steeply and, in a further 75 metres, a bridleway for horses and cyclists forks right. Stay on the wide footpath, however, and continue to climb for 225 metres more until you reach the church of **St Martha-on-the-Hill** at the very summit of the ridge. **[3]** (This church, formerly a stop on the Pilgrim's Way to Canterbury, was restored in the 19th century.)

Pass through the gate into the churchyard and past the church door to the far side of the church, where you will find a series of benches that face the noonday sun. This is another good place for a **picnic**, but can be rather popular on a fine day: an alternative place, with better views, can be found in the next paragraph.

After resting on the benches, *turn left (that is, resuming the same direction as before)* and walk along the line of the ridge and out through the churchyard gate. You are now on a broad sandy path that follows the top of the hill, with a wooden fence to the right (to the right is another possible **picnic** spot).

In 80 metres a fence begins to the left of the path and it starts to descend sharply.

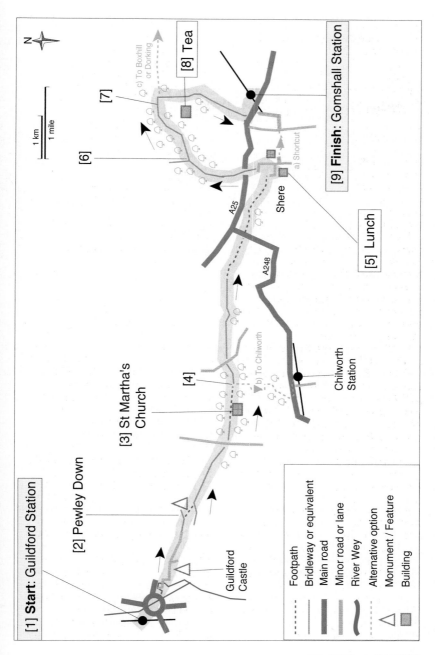

[1] **Start**: Guildford Station

[2] Pewley Down

Guildford Castle

[3] St Martha's Church

[4]

b) To Chilworth

Chilworth Station

A248

A25

Shere

a) Shortcut

[5] Lunch

[6]

[7]

[8] Tea

c) To Boxhill or Dorking

[9] **Finish**: Gomshall Station

N

1 km
1 mile

Footpath
Bridleway or equivalent
Main road
Minor road or lane
River Wey
Alternative option
△ Monument / Feature
▦ Building

Castle in the air

After the Battle of Hastings the conquering Normans hastily constructed a rash of simple motte and bailey castles across southern England. Their aim was to intimidate the locals and provide a base from which troops could sally forth to pacify the neighbourhood. Many grew into major fortifications over the centuries; Guildford's did not.

Built a few years after 1066, Guildford Castle's prime lasted little more than a century. Its original wooden defences were replaced by stone in the 12th century, but its military importance soon waned. However, as the only royal castle in Surrey, it became the local administrative and judicial centre, and Henry III had plush royal apartments fitted out in a palace in the bailey.

However, after Henry's death in 1272 the castle fell into terminal decline. In the early 17th century its crumbling remains were converted into a private house by local worthy Francis Carter, and it stayed in the hands of his family until the 18th century, but rapidly fell into disrepair.

Eventually, in 1885, the ruins were bought by Guildford Borough Council, and the picturesque ruined keep now forms the centrepiece of a beautiful park. From the top of the keep there is a fine view of the Wey river valley. The castle park is open the hours of daylight.

In 250 metres, as the surroundings get more wooded, an acorn on a post marks the point at which the bridleway merges from the right.

100 metres beyond this the North Downs Way forks left following a blue arrow on a post, but keep straight on for another 30 metres to a signpost and large information board describing the Downs Link route. **[4]**

(At this point, you can take the **shortcut** from St Martha's to end the walk in **Chilworth**; see option **b)** directions at the end of the main walk text).

To carry on with the main walk, *go straight on*, your direction 90 degrees, passing a World War II pillbox on your left. In 130 metres the path curves left and then right, and 70 metres after this *you come to a three-way fork* (the centre path may be concealed by a tree in summer). *Take the middle of the three paths, your direction 70 degrees, and in 40 metres stay right at another fork.*

In 30 metres, just before a car park, ignore a path sharp right, but 5 metres further on turn right on a footpath, which in 75 metres brings you to a road. You can see open fields ahead, rising to a ridge, with another World War II gun emplacement about 100 metres away.

Cross over this road and go straight ahead down a signposted bridleway between wooden fences (this section of the path is part of the **Pilgrim's Way**). A short post with a pink cow's head symbol on top also marks the start of this path. *You now follow this path, straight on at every junction, all the way into Shere. Note the points marked* **[*]** *below, however.*

In more detail: In 400 metres you skirt a wood on your right (a good bluebell wood in spring). In 200 metres, *at the end of the wood, cross an earth path and go through a wooden gate to follow a bridleway sign half right across a field,* your direction 100 degrees

At the top of the hill the path exits the field by a wooden gate and turns left to follow the edge of a wood along the field edge, descending gently after a short distance. 160 metres later it starts to descend much more steeply, and *70 metres after that you come out on a tarmac lane between high banks.*

[*] *Turn left onto this, and almost immediately, in 10 metres, turn right,* following a blue arrow and a pink cow symbol, to resume your former direction on a car-wide track. Stay on this track for 600 metres, until you come to a house and a three-armed footpath sign, where you go straight on, still on a car-wide track, following a sign to Silent Pool (a name belied by the noise of the A25 ahead), your direction 115 degrees.

In 30 metres cross a stile to the right of a green metal gate and keep straight on. *In 100 metres fork right off the track up a path, following a wooden footpath sign and a pink cow's head symbol.* In 200 metres this track passes a black wooden shed, and in 90 metres crosses a concrete road, the entrance to a quarry.

Keep straight on into what at the time of writing was a wood of largely newly planted trees, veering right with the path in 20 metres. In 70 metres the path curves left, and in 40 metres you cross a stile to the left of a metal fieldgate to enter an open field, with the A25 to your left and a church ahead.

Keep on the left-hand edge of the field and in 230 metres you cross two stiles beside metal fieldgates to emerge onto a road. *Be careful crossing this road: though it may look like a quiet country lane at times, it is in fact a main road, the A248.*

Cross straight over the road (note the rare Victorian postbox to your left: VR stands for Victoria Regina) *to carry straight on up a car-wide track.* In 70 metres cross a stile to the right of a rusted metal fieldgate and keep straight on up the grass slope beyond. In 120 metres you pick up the line of a wire fence to your right, around an area of newly planted saplings, and you follow this for another 130 metres to a stile to the right of a metal fieldgate.

Keep straight on, now on a path flanked by a wire fence and an earth bank, into a wood. In 370 metres this emerges from the wood to cross an open field (though again, at time of writing, the right-hand side of the path here has been planted with saplings). In 150 metres cross a car-wide earth track and in another 80 metres enter a pine wood through a metal kissing gate.

In 50 metres you come to a narrow road, which you cross to carry on up a path alongside a high brick wall. [*] *In 140 metres you come to another road, where you go right downhill, your direction 120 degrees.* In 120 metres (not 200 yards as the road sign would have it) the road comes to a ford, which you cross on a footbridge.

Beyond this, *turn left along a road,* with a walled vegetable garden to your left. Ignore ways off and in 260 metres you come to a crossroads, which is the centre of **Shere**.

Up the road ahead is the **Church of St James**. (At this point you can take the **Shortcut via Shere** option; option **a)** – directions at end of main walk text.) Immediately to the right is the **White Horse** pub, the recommended lunch stop **[5]**, with the **Prince of Wales** another 40 metres further up the road. Alternatively, turn left up Middle Street for the **Lucky Duck** tearoom and restaurant, 20 metres beyond the stream on the left. For picnic items, the post office, open daily until 10pm, is just beyond the Lucky Duck on the right.

After lunch, *come out of either pub or restaurant and turn left.* Walk up Middle Street to a T-junction. On the left-hand side of the road in an alcove is a drinking fountain given to the village by 'two maiden ladies' who wanted to save it from the evils of the alcohol served at the White Horse.

Turn left into Upper Street. In 30 metres turn right up a concrete drive. Shere Recreation Ground is ahead to the right. Pass to the left of this on a car-wide track with a public byway sign. In

100 metres ignore a track forking left to go straight through an underpass under the main road.

Beyond this the track starts to climb and in 180 metres it curves right, still rising steadily. In 300 metres ignore a fork to the right and remain on the main track, in 30 metres passing a World War II gun emplacement overgrown by trees. In 20 metres ignore another fork to the right, and in 60 metres another.

280 metres later you reach the top of the ridge, and come to a footpath crossroads. **[6]** *Turn right here* onto a car-wide track, your direction due east, which is the North Downs Way (marked by an acorn on a post).

You now stay on the North Downs Way for just over a kilometre until you come to point **[7]**, *which can be recognised by a stone pond-like structure to the left of the path.*

In more detail: in 400 metres you pass a bridleway sign on a post where there are paths left and right. 250 metres further on, at a junction marked by a striped footpath post, ignore a gravel track left and a less distinct path to the right. In 160 metres a mud track merges from the left, and 50 metres after this is a wooden barrier to the left. In 80 metres a track to the right is marked 'PRIVATE, NO ENTRY'.

In 210 metres you come to a five-way junction, with two tracks left, and a stone structure to the left (a debris-filled pond). Ahead is a wooden bench inscribed 'Gravelhill Gate'. **[7]**

Go right here on a minor footpath, which soon starts to descend steeply. There may be a handwritten sign here for the Ramblers Rest tearoom. In 330 metres there is an open field to the right, and in 200 metres the same on the right.

In 80 metres pass through a broken down gate, and 50 metres further on you see a white house on the right with a teapot on it. This is the **Ramblers Rest** tearoom. **[8]** Coming out of the Ramblers Rest, return to your former path and turn right along what almost immediately becomes a tarmac lane: *follow this lane*

for just over a kilometre, ignoring all ways off, down to the main road, the A25.

Turn left onto the A25. In 70 metres you come to the **Compasses Inn**, an alternative tea stop, on your right. Note that buses to Guildford go from the stop just by the inn (and on the same side of the road).

For **Gomshall station**, follow the main road for about 250 metres until it is crossed by a railway bridge. Just before the bridge turn left up the entrance road to the station. **[9]** Once you get to the platforms, cross the lines for trains back to Guildford.

Walk options

a) Shortcut via Shere:
Follow the main walk directions until point [5].

[5] *From the White Horse pub, go straight ahead,* your direction due east, across the square towards the Church of St James. *Take the road to the right of the churchyard* – Church Lane.

At the end *take the signposted path half right through a wooden gate,* your direction 130 degrees, ignoring a drive straight ahead to High House, and a road – Church Hill – to the right. In 120 metres *go through a wooden gate. Ignore a wooden fieldgate immediately to your left but after 3 metres turn left to walk along the left-hand edge of an open field.* At the end of the field pass through a metal gate and onto a wide path between fences, your direction 120 degrees.

In 250 metres by a red bin, ignore an opening to the left leading to garages and carry straight on a further 90 metres *to emerge onto a gravel drive and turn left,* your direction 40 degrees, by houses named The Old Barn and Highlands. In 60 metres stay on the track, ignoring a turning to the left to curve right with the track to a road.

Cross this road and walk up the short slip road ahead to turn left onto another road. A sign announces 'Arch Bridge Ahead'. When you get to this bridge

Shere calm

Sitting on the edge of the North Downs, astride the River Tillingbourne, is **Shere**. Often cited as Surrey's prettiest village, it's a fine spot for a wander and contains a couple of interesting diversions.

The church of St James, dating from 1190, is a rare example of a church constructed entirely in the Early English Transitional Style. Its most devoted attendee was the anchoress Christine Carpenter (an anchoress was a kind of halfway house between a lay woman and a nun). In 1329 she had herself enclosed in a cell in the north wall of the church, receiving food through a grating on the outside wall. After three years she returned to the world, but then petitioned to be re-enclosed; the bishop consented. You can still see where her cell was situated to the left of the altar.

Shere also has a local museum in Shere Lane (01483 203245; open

Easter Sunday-end Sept 1-5.30pm Mon, Tue, Thur, Fri, Sun).

If you visit the village, note that a shortcut to Gomshall station takes no more than half an hour: see 'Shortcut via Shere' at the end of the main text.

---

do not go underneath, but *turn left along Goose Green*. In 300 metres this brings you to the A25 and the centre of Gomshall.

Blubeckers restaurant in Gomshall Mill is to your right on this corner and the **Compasses Inn** is just down the A25 to your left. Buses to Guildford go from outside the Compasses Inn.

For **Gomshall station***, however, turn right on the main road* for 180 metres (passing the **post office** on your left) until you reach the railway bridge, just before which you turn left up the entrance road to the station. **[9]** Once you get to the platforms cross the lines for trains back to Guildford.

b) Guildford to Chilworth:
Follow the main walk directions until point [4].

From point **[4]** *turn sharply right onto the Downs Link*, your direction 240 degrees. This sandy path descends gently through a wood at first, then after 170 metres more steeply between fields in a cutting. In 180 metres it curves right, and in another 90 metres it emerges from the cutting and levels out, now running parallel to the ridge of the Downs. In another 80 metres it turns left downhill on a broad track.

In 270 metres you approach a thicket of trees and *a T-junction marked by a two-armed footpath sign. Follow the Downs Link left*, your direction due east. After 120 metres *you cross a stream, and 15 metres beyond this turn right through a gate* to the left of a fieldgate to walk along a permissive path, your direction 200 degrees, with a small stream to your left after 20 metres.

60 metres further on the path crosses this stream, so that it is now on your right, and 15 metres later the stream forks off to the right. Continue straight on for 40 metres to *a T-junction, where you turn right, your direction due west.* After 100 metres you cross another stream, and 50 metres after this *you come to picnic tables on the right in a small open space. Turn half left here,* your direction 200 degrees, and in 25 metres cross a footbridge.

Beyond the bridge keep straight on for 10 metres, then curving right with the path to pass between two fields, your direction 220 degrees. After 200 metres *you come to the A248, where you turn left,* your direction due east.

In 120 metres you come to the **Percy Arms** pub on your left. **Chilworth station** is a further 40 metres along the road to the right. You can then catch a train or a bus back to Guildford (buses are more frequent).

c) Guildford to Boxhill/Dorking:
Follow the main walk directions until point [5].

Now follow the directions in the main walk text from the White Horse to the North Downs Way, and then remain on this well-marked route. After about 6km (3.75 miles) you come to Steers Field (marked as such by a National Trust sign), a major clearing, with Ranmore church visible ahead, and Dorking in the valley below ahead right. Here you can join up with the walk in the chapter that follows (Effingham to Westhumble); pick up the directions at point [8] in that walk. That chapter explains the tea options on this route, and how to reach the station for the return journey.

Lunch & tea places

Blubeckers *52 Station Road, Gomshall Mill, GU5 9LB (01483 203060).* **Open** noon-2.30pm, 5.30-10pm Mon-Thur; noon-2.30pm, 5.30-10.30pm Fri; noon-3pm, 5.30-10.30pm Sat; noon-4pm, 5.30-9.30pm Sun. A possible lunch option.

Compasses Inn *50 Station Road, Gomshall, GU5 9LA (01483 202506).* **Open** 11am-11pm Mon-Sat; noon-10.30pm Sun. **Food served** noon-9pm Mon-Sat; noon-8pm Sun. A riverside garden and all-day snacks and meals.

Lucky Duck *Middle Street, Shere, Guildford, GU5 9HF (01483 202445).* **Open** 9am-5pm daily; hot food served noon-3pm daily. Sandwiches, cakes and drinks are available all day at this tea room and restaurant, though hot dishes are only served at lunch. In season, it has tables indoors and outdoors.

Percy Arms *75 Dorking Road, Chilworth, GU4 8NP (01483 561765).* **Open** noon-11pm daily. **Food served** noon-3pm, 6-10pm Mon-Sat; noon-3pm, 6-9.30pm Sun. On the main road not far from the station, this is a possible lunch option should you be ending the walk here.

Prince of Wales *Shere Lane, Shere, GU5 9HS (01483 202313/www.sherepub.com).* **Open** 11am-11pm Mon-Sat; noon-10.30pm Sun. **Food served** noon-2.30pm Tue, Sun; noon-2.30pm, 7-9pm Wed-Sat. This pub has a more traditional menu (roasts and the like) than the White Horse.

Ramblers Rest *Colekitchen Farm, Colekitchen Lane, Gomshall, GU5 9QB (01483 203845).* **Open** 10am-5pm Sat, Sun. The friendly owners of this idyllic farm, set in a hidden fold of the Downs, offer own-made cakes, tea and coffee, which you can eat either inside or out. Highly recommended. The tearoom might open at other times or days for groups that book in advance. [Note: it is about 25 minutes' walk from the Ramblers Rest to Gomshall station, but all on tarmac roads and car-free as far as the main road, so as long as you have a torch there is no trouble walking it in the dark in winter.]

White Horse *Shire Lane, Shere, GU5 9HS (01483 202518).* **Open** 11am-11pm Mon-Sat; noon-10.30pm Sun. **Food served** 11am-10pm Mon-Sat; noon-9pm Sun. Located 9.2km (5.75 miles) into the walk, this rambling ancient inn has a small but charming garden out the back. Though busy at weekends, it is well run and efficient at serving meals from its long menu. In theory, food is served all afternoon, but, if busy, the pub sometimes closes to new orders at 3pm. This is the suggested lunch stop for the main walk.

Picnic: Possible picnic spots are highlighted at points [2] and [3] in the main walk text.

Effingham to Westhumble

Polesden Lacey and England's largest vineyard.

Start: Effingham Junction station
Finish: Boxhill & Westhumble station

Length: 16km (10 miles)

Time: 5 hours walking time. For the whole excursion, including trains and meals, allow 8 hours 30 minutes.

Transport: Four trains an hour (one an hour on Sundays) run from London Waterloo to Effingham Junction (fastest journey time: 38 minutes). Two or three hourly trains return from Boxhill & Westhumble to Victoria (journey time: 50-56 minutes; or you can change at Dorking for Waterloo). If driving, the shorter round walk may be a more convenient option, parking at Boxhill & Westhumble station. Otherwise, Effingham Junction has a large station car park (free at weekends), and you can get from Boxhill & Westhumble back to Effingham Junction, by changing at Leatherhead (though this is not possible on Sundays).

OS Landranger Map: 187
OS Explorer Map: 146
Effingham, map reference TQ102558, is in Surrey, 7km (4.5 miles) north-east of Guildford.

Toughness: 5 out of 10.

Walk notes: The idyllic estate of Polesden Lacey, a fine country house nestling just behind the North Downs escarpment, is the highlight of this walk – a landscape of hidden valleys, pretty woodland and gentle pasture that seems lost in a golden yesterday. The walk has something to offer at almost any time of the year. In spring, it passes through a number of lovely bluebell woods, in autumn there is plenty of golden colour in the woodlands, while in winter the bare branches open up new views and vistas. In summer, the walk offers several fine spots for a picnic, and, despite being relatively close to London, a deep rural tranquillity. The long evenings also make this the best time to come if you want to also make a thorough afternoon visit to the house and grounds at Polesden Lacey.

Walk options: Directions for these variations are given at the end of the main walk text (*see p157*).

a) Short cut avoiding Effingham Village: If you are not planning to have lunch at the Sir Douglas Haig in Effingham Village, you can save 0.8km (0.5 miles) off the main walk by using this short cut (point [2] in the main walk text).

b) Shorter circular walk from Westhumble: If your aim is to spend some time at Polesden Lacey, this option described gets you to the house in just 5.2km (3.2 miles) from Boxhill & Westhumble. The walk then rejoins the main route to get back to Westhumble, making a total circular walk of 12km (7.5 miles), or 3 hours 45 minutes walking time.

c) Alternative ending at Dorking:
From the visitor centre on the Denbies Wine Estate (point [10] in the main walk text), it is easy to finish the walk at Dorking station, if you prefer, adding 1km (0.6 miles) to the walk. Trains from Dorking back to London go roughly twice as frequently as those from Boxhill & Westhumble. This option also offers a late tea option in the shape of the Lincoln Arms (*see p161*).

Also, on Saturdays, Sundays and bank holidays, there are five buses a day from Dorking station to Polesden Lacey. The first bus from Dorking is around 10am and the last bus from Polesden Lacey just after 5pm. To get up-to-date times for this National Trust-sponsored service, call Polesden Lacey house on 01372 452048.

Saturday Walkers' Club: Take the train nearest to 10am from London Waterloo direct to Effingham Junction. For the shorter circular walk, take the train nearest to 10.30am to Boxhill & Westhumble.

Walk directions

[1] [Numbers refer to the map]
Leaving platform 2 at **Effingham Junction station**, climb the stairs to the road. *Turn right*, your direction 140 degrees.

In 50 metres ignore a road to the right (the entrance to the car park, which is also signposted as a public bridleway) and keep straight on along the road. In 50 metres more, *where the pavement on the right-hand side of the road ends, fork right through the trees*, emerging in 10 metres into the open space of **Effingham Common**.

Veer right along the edge of the common, with a line of trees to your right, your direction 230 degrees. *In 250 metres, where the tree boundary starts to turn right towards some bungalows, continue straight ahead for 20 metres to a telegraph pole, where you turn left across the open common*, away from the bungalows, following a well-defined grassy path, your direction 150 degrees.

After 100 metres *the path converges with the wooded edge of the common to your right*. Carry on along this boundary, ignoring all turnings off, up a narrowing neck of the common. *In 200 metres follow the path as it diverges slightly from the trees to your right towards a gap in the trees ahead*, your direction 220 degrees. 100 metres later *pass through this gap in the trees into a large open field. Here you go right*, your direction due west initially, with the field boundary to your right.

Follow this field edge for 150 metres to a *T-junction in front of some houses. Go left here up the edge of the field*, your direction 190 degrees, passing a half-timbered house on your right in 80 metres. Keep on gently uphill, with the field edge to your right. *In 400 metres, where the field narrows to a point*, and where your onward way is blocked by a wire fence with farm sheds beyond it, *curve right to a tarmac and concrete road*, with bungalows to your right and blue double fieldgates to your left.

Go left here for 5 metres and then just before the blue fieldgates *turn right up a signposted public bridleway* past four wooden car-blocking posts, your direction 200 degrees, ignoring a signposted footpath that forks off immediately to its right. Remain on this car-wide bridleway (which is known as **Old London Road**) into **Great Ridings Wood**. Ignore all ways off. *In 700 metres there is a mossy stone wall along the right-hand edge of the bridleway*, which veers slightly to the left along it.

Continue along the bridleway, keeping the wall to your right. In 200 metres, at the top of a small rise, *you come to a T-junction of car-wide bridleways* (actually a crossroads, if the way through locked wooden gates to the right, marked by a Private Property sign, is counted). **[2]**

[At this point, to follow the **Short cut avoiding Effingham Village**, option a), keep straight on, and follow the directions at the end of the main walk text. *See p157.*]

Effingham to Westhumble

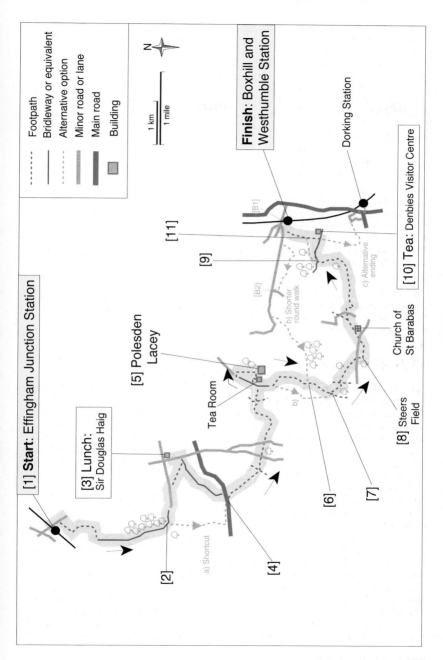

[1] **Start:** Effingham Junction Station

[3] Lunch: Sir Douglas Haig

[2]

a) Shortcut

[4]

[5] Polesden Lacey

Tea Room

[6]

[7]

[8] Steers Field

Church of St Barabas

b)

b) Shorter round walk

[B2]

[9]

[11]

[B1]

Finish: Boxhill and Westhumble Station

Dorking Station

c) Alternative ending

[10] **Tea:** Denbies Visitor Centre

N

1 km
1 mile

To continue to Effingham village, *turn left at the T-junction,* your direction 70 degrees, following a car-wide bridleway away from the gates marked private. This soon starts to go downhill. In 250 metres it emerges from a wood onto a gravel car-wide track with an open field to the left and in 80 metres *comes to a tarmac road, where you go straight on,* your direction due east.

You can follow this road all the way to the Sir Douglas Haig pub in Effingham, but a prettier route is to look out for a *footpath signposted to the right in 280 metres at the top of a rise in the road.* This initially goes up the driveway to a house, but in 15 metres turns left, following a yellow footpath arrow into an alley between two garden fences. Follow this for 200 metres between gardens until it comes to *a metal barrier. Go round the barrier and continue on a path between fields,* with a barbed wire fence either side.

In 70 metres *it emerges into a larger open field, which you cross diagonally,* your direction 110 degrees. If the path is not clear, head towards a large red house with two chimneys, which is to the right of more modern houses.

In 220 metres, *in the far corner of this field, cross a stile and go left along a car-wide grass path* with a brick wall to your right, your direction 60 degrees. In 30 metres this becomes a gravel driveway and in 70 metres brings you to a road, with a parade of shops to the right (including a convenience store, open all day, seven days a week, in case you need to stock up on picnic items). This is the village of **Effingham**.

Turn left along the road, passing Chapel Hill on your right in 100 metres. 120 metres further on, on the right, is the **Sir Douglas Haig**, the lunchtime pub **[3]**. Coming out of the pub, *turn left to retrace your steps uphill,* passing Chapel Hill in 120 metres. 100 metres further on, *just before the parade of shops on the right, go right up a driveway that*

is also a signposted public footpath (the same one you came into the village on).

In 40 metres ignore a fork in the driveway to the left. 30 metres further on, keep to the right of a brick wall up a car-wide grass path. In 30 metres ignore a footpath over a stile to the right (the one you used to enter the village) and keep straight on, still with the brick wall to your left.

50 metres after this the brick wall ends. Keep straight on along a narrow path between hedges and open fields. *In 500 metres the path ends at an open field, where you turn left along the field edge,* your direction 150 degrees. *In 40 metres you pass through a gap in the field corner and go right,* with a wooden fence to your left. This soon becomes a car-wide grass track between trees and wooden fences, your direction 240 degrees.

In 100 metres you pass a bungalow to your left and the track turns to earth and gravel. Keep straight on and in 350 metres, *just before you come to the main road, the A246, turn right up a signposted public bridleway, running parallel to the main road.*

In 90 metres you emerge onto the A246 next to a house called the Beeches. Cross the road with care and go through a wooden gate to the right of a driveway with metal fieldgates leading to some stables, a signposted public footpath. **[4]**

Keep on the left-hand edge of the field. In 50 metres *pass through a gate to the left of a concrete block building.* **[!]** This path can be overgrown in summer and looks somewhat unlikely at first, but it is the correct route. In 30 metres, just beyond the end of the building, you are forced to *turn right by a wooden fence* and emerge through a defunct gateway into an open field (actually a golf course).

Go straight ahead across this golf course fairway, your direction 150 degrees, *aiming for a wooden footpath signpost* in 140 metres. (Watch out for flying golf balls from the left!) At the signpost keep straight on across a plank bridge. In another 60

Rooms with a view

Though a Regency House, built in 1821, it wasn't until the Edwardian period that Polesden Lacey really came into its own. Between 1906 and 1909 it was taken over and extensively rebuilt by Mrs Ronald Greville, a society hostess, and was the scene of many glamorous house parties. King George VI and Queen Elizabeth, the late mother of the present queen, spent part of their honeymoon here in 1923. Mrs Greville's collections of silver and porcelain, paintings and furniture are displayed in its rooms and galleries, but the real appeal of the house today is its stunning location on the crest of a hidden North Downs valley, and the pastoral tranquillity of the 560-hectare (1,400-acre) estate, which includes a walled rose garden, lawns, landscaped walks, the Home Farm, cut-flower nursery and Edwardian frame yard.

Polesden Lacey

Great Bookham, nr Dorking, RH5 6BD (01372 452048/ www.nationaltrust.org.uk). **Open** *Garden* 11am-6pm daily. *House Late Mar-early Nov* 11am-5pm Wed-Sun. *Shop Late Mar-early Nov* 11am-5pm daily; *early Nov-late Nov, mid Jan-late Mar* 11am-3pm Wed-Sun; *Dec* 11-3pm daily. **Admission** *House & grounds* £8; £4 children; £20 family. *Grounds only* £5; £2.50 children; £12.50 family. **No credit cards**.

metres *pass through a gap between two tall trees at the far end of the field.*

There is another two-armed footpath sign here. Follow the direction it indicates, veering left *across the corner of the next field*, your direction 140 degrees. In 130 metres, at the far edge of this field, *follow a yellow arrow on a post left through a gap in the hedge*, descending a small bank to the next field.

Your onward way is now half right across this field, *heading for a footpath sign to the right of a clump of bushes* at the top of the hill, a direction indicated by the footpath sign on your right as you emerge through the gap, your direction 130 degrees. When you reach the footpath sign by the clump of bushes in 120 metres, *carry straight on across another golf course fairway*, bearing slightly right, your direction 140 degrees.

In 50 metres you pass into the rough (uncut grass) and in 100 metres *you come to the corner of a hedge and a footpath post with two yellow arrows. Turn left*

here on a gravel golf course path for 5 metres, passing a drinking water tap, until you come to an old footpath sign on the left and another two-arrowed footpath post on the right, the latter next to a tree boundary on your right-hand side.

Go straight ahead following this tree boundary on your right-hand side, passing a golf course hole to your left, your direction 80 degrees. In 35 metres ignore a turning into the woods to the right and keep on into another area of rough. In 30 metres more *you come to another fairway* and a footpath post with a yellow arrow on it (hidden in the bushes to the right in summer).

Cross this fairway, going slightly right, heading just to the right of a house that can be seen ahead, and keeping about 40 metres to the right of the sand traps, your direction 110 degrees. This brings you in 90 metres to *a pathway whose start is marked by two wooden posts.* [!] In summer this is concealed by bushes until you are almost upon it.

You are now on an enclosed pathway, with a green mesh fence to your left, heading due east. In 40 metres this becomes a car-wide earth track and in 80 metres comes to a road. *Cross straight over this road, up a path through undergrowth,* signposted as a public footpath by a sign hidden in the bushes to the right, your direction still due east.

In 20 metres fork left to a stile 10 metres further on (there is a 'Please keep out: newly planted area' sign at the fork – redundant, as this area is now all overgrown). *Cross this stile,* ignoring a footpath to the left just before it, and *follow the top or right-hand edge of a large field,* with a wire fence and trees to your right. (There are extensive views to your left, which on a very clear day include the towers of central London on a bearing of about 30 degrees).

In 300 metres, at the far end of this field, *cross a stile to the right of a metal fieldgate onto a road. Turn right on this road for 5 metres, and then left up a driveway marked 'High Barn'.* **[!]** *Do NOT go through the black fence posts, but keep to the right of them* up a car-wide track between the wooden fence right and a hedge and wire fence left, your direction 100 degrees.

In 40 metres this track enters into woods. In a further 40 metres, where the wire fence ends to the left, ignore a turning to the left and keep straight on. In 150 metres ignore a stile into a paddock to the left. In 50 metres more, at the end of this paddock, *you pass a National Trust sign marking the boundary of the Polesden Lacey estate.*

120 metres after this, at a footpath crossroads, go left through a kissing gate to the right of a wooden barrier, your direction 30 degrees initially. Keep on this path, just inside the woods. **[!]** *In 250 metres you see a stile to the right. Cross this* to emerge onto an open hillside and *turn immediately left along the boundary with the woods you have just left,* with a wire fence to your left.

Follow this boundary and *in 200 metres you come to another stile, which you cross. Beyond it, turn right onto a broad well-defined path,* with the wire fence now to your right, your direction initially 130 degrees. *In 140 metres you come to a crosspaths, where you go straight on through a metal barrier, onto a car-wide track.* Follow this at it curves right almost immediately and then left again in 30 metres around the corner of a field, heading towards a white house ahead.

In 150 metres this brings you to a tarmac lane, with Garden Cottage ahead, one of the outbuildings of the main house of **Polesden Lacey. [5]**

If you are not planning to visit the house you can turn right on this lane, towards a covered bridge with a thatched roof. Resume the walk directions at **[*]** below.

To visit Polesden Lacey, *turn left on the tarmac lane.* In 60 metres, just after the tarmac lane becomes a gravel track, there is a footpath signposted with a National Trust arrow through a wooden gate to the right. *If you are already a National Trust member* you can use this as a short cut to Polesden Lacey's courtyard tearoom. Follow the right-hand edge of the field, your direction east, curving round to the right to another wooden gate in 180 metres. Once through the gate, the courtyard (the former stable yard) with the tearoom is through the towered gateway to your right.

If you are NOT a National Trust member you should pay the entrance fee to the Polesden Lacey grounds to visit the tearoom or at least go to the gatehouse to ask permission (sometimes granted) to visit the tearoom without paying. To do this, *remain on the gravel lane for 350 metres* until you come to a junction with a byway and another gravel track to the left. Just beyond this *there is a small parking area to the right. Go right over the logs at the back of the parking space* for 60 metres and then through a staggered gap in a wooden fence.

Summer walking in **Surrey**.

10 metres beyond this you come to the entrance road to Polesden Lacey and *North Lodge, the ticket office*, on your right.

After lunch or tea, *come out of the courtyard through the tower gateway.* In 20 metres ignore a tarmac drive to the left to the Regional Office and car park, but 10 metres further on, just before the start of car parking spaces ahead, *turn left through a wooden gate* to emerge into open parkland.

Follow the path as it curves round to the left in 30 metres along the edge of this parkland, your direction ultimately due west, for 220 metres *until you reach another gate and emerge through this onto a gravel lane. Turn left onto this lane*, which soon becomes tarmac, passing Garden Cottage on your left in 60 metres.

[*] Beyond Garden Cottage the tarmac lane starts to go steeply downhill, passing in 140 metres *under a thatched bridge* (built to join two halves of the garden: the lane was apparently sunk below ground level to hide passing tradesmen from the house) and in 120 metres *under a modern wooden bridge*.

20 metres beyond this second bridge turn left with the lane, signposted to Prospect Lodge and Polesden Farm, ignoring paths that go straight on and right. (The road from this point is a private estate road, but also a permissive walkers' route.) In 280 metres, *at the bottom of the hill, curve right with the lane*, passing Polesden Farm on your left. Here the tarmac lane becomes a concrete track, your direction due south.

50 metres beyond Polesden Farm, *where the concrete track curves right, go straight ahead through a fieldgate* on a permissive footpath uphill, following a sign to Prospect Lodge and a green YHA arrow, your direction due south. Beyond the gate, *follow a car-wide track uphill*, with a wire fence to your left, for 400 metres.

At the top of the hill go through another fieldgate. Your onward way is straight ahead, but take a moment to walk 30 metres to the right to the wooden benches, from where you get a fine view of Polesden Lacey house across the valley. This is also a good **picnic** spot. [6]

Returning to the track, turn right to resume your former direction, 160 degrees. In 20 metres ignore a signposted footpath downhill to the left and pass a house, Prospect Lodge, on your right. Keep on past the Lodge and on up a path, which soon becomes a car-wide track, into the woods.

In 400 metres ignore a signposted National Trust path to the right and keep straight on around a wooden barrier, your direction 210 degrees. (Note the huge 200-year-old beech tree on the right here. This marks the boundary between the Polesden Lacey estate and wooded **Ranmore Common**.)

[7] You are now on a car-wide grassy path. *Carry on along this for 70 metres to a wooden fence that seems to block the path. Pass through the staggered gap in this fence and go left at a horseshoe-shaped T-junction on a car-wide bridleway,* your direction 120 degrees initially.

In 150 metres this path starts to descend and in another 200 metres *it comes to a crossroads with another bridleway in a dip. Go straight ahead* up the bank ahead, following a white arrow on a post and passing a wooden barrier in 10 metres, your direction now 100 degrees. Keep on this path, ignoring ways off. In 250 metres your route is confirmed by an arrow on a post, and in a further 300 metres you come to *a wooden barrier and the end of the woods.*

Turn right here onto a car-wide gravel track, which in 30 metres brings you to a road. Cross this road and turn left along its grassy verge. *In 50 metres fork right up a gravel track for 5 metres and then turn right off this heading towards a yellow arrow on a post* (barely visible in summer) *20 metres ahead,* your direction due south.

Beyond the post *carry straight on down a path under trees,* with an open field beyond the hedge to your right at first, then later on your left as well. In 100 metres you pass round a decaying fieldgate and in 10 metres more *you come to a T-junction with a car-wide*

track (the North Downs Way), *where you go left,* your direction due east.

In 20 metres *you come to a gate and beyond it emerge into a big open field,* with a fabulous vista of Dorking and the Weald to your right. A National Trust sign announces this as **Steers Field. [8]** At the National Trust sign the path forks. *Take the right fork, straight ahead along the crest of the hill.*

In 150 metres there are two benches on your left. This is a good spot for a **picnic tea**. It is also worth stopping here to look back over your right shoulder for a fine view up the valley towards Gomshall. *50 metres beyond the benches go left at a three-armed footpath sign,* just before a wire fence, following the North Downs Way through a fieldgate.

In 50 metres *pass through a kissing gate* and turn half right, your direction 50 degrees, to a road T-junction in another 40 metres. *Go straight ahead down the road signposted to Bookham, West Humble (sic) and Parish Church.* (This is also still the North Downs Way.) In 80 metres you pass a wood on the left that is carpeted with bluebells in season. In another 100 metres you pass the church of **St Barnabas, Ranmore**, on the right.

650 metres further on, where the road curves left and you pass the entrance to Denbies house right (note: this is NOT the vineyard visitor centre), *keep straight on down a concrete track, following the North Downs Way sign. In 40 metres go right on a gravel car-wide track,* still following the North Downs Way, your direction 170 degrees.

In 180 metres, *at a crossroads, go left along a gravel track,* still following the North Downs Way, your direction 70 degrees. In 110 metres *pass through a high metal gate,* the entrance to **Denbies Wine Estate**, and on down the track. There is an extensive view of the vineyard and Dorking to your right. *In 500 metres pass through an identical gate.* 80 metres after this the track curves round the left. You can now see Box Hill ahead and the Denbies Wine Estate Visitor Centre in the middle of the vineyard below.

In 370 metres there is a crossroads with gravel tracks left and right. **[9]**

At this point, **if you are NOT having tea at the Denbies Wine Estate tearoom,** you can *go straight on,* remaining on the North Downs Way. Curve right and left with the track and **[!]** *in 140 metres, where a concrete track starts and curves right, go straight on along a car-wide gravel path, following a yellow arrow on a post* to remain on the North Downs Way. 30 metres after this you come to a three-armed footpath post and keep straight on. **[!]** *In 400 metres, at a four-armed footpath sign, easily missed in summer, go left through a kissing gate* on a public footpath signposted to West Humble, your direction 10 degrees. From here, follow the directions from point [11] below.

Otherwise, to have tea in the Denbies Wine Estate Visitor Centre (and also to end the walk at Dorking) *go right at the crossroads, downhill into the vineyard,* your direction 70 degrees.

In 150 metres *merge with a concrete track and 20 metres later you come to a four-armed footpath sign by an electricity pylon. Keep straight on down the concrete track* towards the buildings of Denbies Wine Estate, which you reach in 350 metres.

Keep to the right of the buildings, passing the Farmhouse Bed and Breakfast on your left. *100 metres further on turn left along the front of the Visitor Centre,* with its car park to your right. The entrance to the **Denbies Wine Estate Visitor Centre** is the arched doorway 80 metres along on the left. Once inside, turn immediately right, passing through the shop to the glass-roofed courtyard and the self-service restaurant. **[10]**

[After tea, if you want to **end the walk at Dorking station**, option c), follow the directions at end of main walk text. See p161.]

Otherwise, for Boxhill & Westhumble station, come out of the Denbies Wine Estate Visitor Centre, *turn right for 80*

metres through the car park to a road. Turn right on this road, following a signpost to 'Farmyard B&B and Vineyard Trail', with the buildings of Denbies Wine Estate now on your right. In 120 metres you come to a three-armed footpath sign.

Turn right here onto a car-wide grass path between vines, your direction due north. (Note: NOT the gravel track sharp right, which leads back to the vineyard buildings).

In 280 metres *leave the vineyard by a wooden gate and 15 metres later keep straight on across the North Downs Way to a kissing gate.* **[11]** *Beyond this gate keep straight ahead across a field for 40 metres to another kissing gate. Carry on up a path between garden fences.* In 200 metres *cross a road and carry on up a path to the right of the wooden fence ahead and to the left of a driveway.* This path, which is soon bounded on both sides by garden fences, is at times very narrow and a bit overgrown.

In 150 metres *you come to a road and turn right.* Take care on this road, which is not over-busy but very narrow. In 30 metres, just after a private road turns off to the right, you can escape from the road by taking the path between two wooden fences, passing to the left of 'Beware Children' and '15mph' signs.

In 110 metres this path rejoins the road and there is now a pavement on its right-hand side. In 60 metres this brings you to a brick railway bridge. **Boxhill & Westhumble station** is to the right on the far side, through the white wooden gate. Cross the footbridge to platform 1 for trains to London.

Walk options

a) Short cut avoiding Effingham Village:

Follow the main walk directions until point [2]*.*

Keep straight on along a car-wide bridleway. In 700 metres, after a gentle descent and a long gentle climb, *this comes to a residential road, Calvert Road. Turn*

Vin Anglais

Denbies Wine Estate is a remarkable sight – a huge vineyard that looks like a slice of France that has been airlifted into southern England. Billing itself as the 'largest wine estate England has ever seen', it produces 400,000 bottles of wine a year, or around 10 per cent of total UK production. Two reds, five whites, a rosé and a couple of sparkling wines are produced, and if you want to learn more about them, there's a visitor centre, plus tours and tastings and, between April and October, a 'Vineyard Train' that tootles around the estate with a commentary. And you can buy a bottle or two to take home from the shop.

Denbies Wine Estate
London Road, Dorking, RH5 6AA (01306 876616/www.denbies vineyard.co.uk). **Open** *Tours & tastings Jan-Mar* 11am, noon, 2pm, 3pm Mon-Fri; 11am, noon, 2pm, 3pm, 4pm Sat; noon, 1pm, 2pm, 3pm, 4pm Sun. *Apr-Dec* 11am, noon, 2pm, 3pm, 4pm Mon-Sat; noon, 1pm, 2pm, 3pm, 4pm Sun. *Wine & gift shop* 10am-5pm Mon-Fri; 10am-5.30pm Sat; 11.30am-5.30pm Sun. *Refreshment areas* phone to check. **Admission** *Indoor tour* £7.25; £6.50 concessions; £3 children 6-17; under 5's free. *Outdoor tour* £4; £3.50 concessions; £3 6-16s; under-5s free. **Credit** AmEx, DC, MC, V.

right on this, your direction south, for another 300 metres to the main road, the A246. *Turn left along the A246*, following the pavement on its left-hand side.

In 300 metres, at the top of a hill, you pass a house called the Spinney to the left and just beyond that a telegraph pole. 10 metres beyond the telegraph pole, by the entrance to a house named the Beeches, ignore a signposted

bridleway to the left, but instead *cross the road and go through a wooden gate to the right of a metal fieldgate*, resuming the main walk directions at point [4].

b) Shorter circular walk from Westhumble:

[B1] Leave platform 2 on Boxhill & Westhumble station (called just Boxhill on most of its platform signs). *Do NOT go up the metal footbridge over the railway lines, but instead up the concrete steps to the right of it*, following a white wooden fence 20 metres to the road. *Turn left onto the road, over a brick bridge*, your direction west.

In 50 metres, ignore two driveways forking right, one through an ornamental arch, and keep on uphill along the road. 30 metres later, *where the pavement on the left-hand side of the road ends, veer left onto a tarmac path* parallel to the road. In 120 metres, *where this comes to an end, rejoin the road*, ignoring a private road turning to the left called Pilgrims Way. Keep straight on, taking care on what is in places a very narrow road.

In 100 metres you pass another private road, Burney Road, on the left, and in 150 metres two more private roads left and right (the left-hand one again being Burney Road). *50 metres beyond these fork left off the road up a signposted footpath* past a National Trust sign for Chapel Farm Fields. This crosses open fields between wire fences, your direction 260 degrees.

In 200 metres *you come to a tarmac road, where you go left uphill*, your direction 220 degrees. In 280 metres, just after you pass under a line of electricity pylons, and 20 metres before the road curves sharp left, *fork right up a signposted public footpath*, your direction due west. In 25 metres *go right over a stile into an open field*. Keep straight on across it, following a line of mini pylons, your direction 330 degrees. (Turn around at this point for a fine view of Box Hill.)

In 150 metres *curve left under the mini pylons to a stile* to the left of a metal fieldgate, 60 metres away to your left. Cross this and carry on along a path with a barbed wire fence to the right and trees to the left, your direction west. In 180 metres *cross another stile and keep on along the right-hand edge of a field*, your direction 280 degrees initially. In 250 metres *cross a stile and turn right, downhill, onto a tarmac road*, your direction 20 degrees.

In 120 metres you come to a road T-junction **[B2]**, where you go left, following a sign to Polesden Lacey. Take care on this road, which though quiet sometimes has quite fast traffic. Stay on this road, ignoring ways off.

In 500 metres, just before a signposted bridleway to the right, turn left up a car-wide track leading to Badgen Farm. In 20 metres this curves right and in 20 metres more you pass a National Trust sign for Polesden Lacey. 40 metres later *you pass a house on your right and in a further 40 metres you turn right at a footpath post with two blue arrows on it*, also signposted to 'Youth Hostel', your direction 240 degrees.

In 50 metres pass through a wooden gate to *emerge into an open field. Follow the earth bank on your right-hand side* across this field as it gently curves to the right. In 380 metres, *at the far end of the field, pass through a wooden gate and go left up a car-wide earth track*, following a blue arrow on a post, your direction 210 degrees.

This climbs steadily uphill and *in 500 metres passes* **Tanners Hatch Youth Hostel** *on the right. 40 metres beyond this, where the track veers left uphill, go straight on along a forest path*, with a wooden fence to your right for the first 20 metres, your direction west. In 200 metres the trees end to the right and you have a view of Polesden Lacey house across the valley. In 120 metres the path goes back into the woods and starts to climb steeply.

In 380 metres more it *comes to a footpath T-junction*. To the left is signposted Yew Tree Farm, but *your route is right, following Prospect Lodge Walk*, your direction due north. *In 20 metres you come to a gate*, but before you go through it, go left for 20 metres to two benches for a magnificent view of Polesden Lacey directly across the valley. This is a fine **picnic spot. [6]**

After enjoying the view *pass through the gate and carry on downhill on a car-wide track*. In 400 metres *pass through another gate, merging on the far side* with a concrete track to carry on downhill. In 50 metres you pass Polesden Farm on your right and keep on up a tarmac lane, which curves left uphill.

In 280 metres ignore paths left and ahead and curve right uphill with the lane under a wooden footbridge. In 120 metres pass under a thatched footbridge (built to enable the mistress of Polesden Lacey to pass from one part of her gardens to the other without seeing the tradesmen passing on the lane below) and keep on uphill. At the top of the hill, in another 140 metres, ignore a bridleway to the left opposite Garden Cottage to the right **[5]** and keep straight on.

In 60 metres more, just after the tarmac lane becomes a gravel track, there is a footpath signposted with a National Trust arrow through a wooden gate to the right. *If you are already a National Trust member,* you can use this as a short cut to **Polesden Lacey**'s courtyard tearoom. Follow the right-hand edge of the field, your direction east, curving round to the right to another wooden gate in 180 metres. Once through the gate, the courtyard (the former stable yard) with the tearoom is through the towered gateway to your right.

If you are NOT a National Trust member, you should pay the entrance fee to the Polesden Lacey grounds to visit the tearoom, or at least go to the entrance gate to ask permission (sometimes granted, but don't rely on it) to visit the tearoom without paying. To do this, *remain on the gravel lane for 350 metres* until you come to a junction with a byway and another gravel track to the left. Just beyond this *there is a small parking area to the right. Go right over the logs at the back of the parking space* for 60 metres and then through a staggered gap in a wooden fence. 10 metres beyond this you come to the entrance road to Polesden Lacey and *North Lodge, the ticket office,* on your right.

After lunch or tea *come out of the yard through the tower gateway.* In 20 metres ignore a tarmac drive to the left to the Regional Office and car park, but 10 metres further on, just before the start of car parking spaces ahead, *turn left through a wooden gate* to emerge into open parkland.

In 30 metres *follow the path as it curves round to the left* along the edge of this parkland, your direction ultimately due west. In 220 metres *you reach another gate and emerge through this onto a gravel lane. Turn left onto this lane,* which soon becomes tarmac, passing Garden Cottage on your left in 60 metres. **[5]**

Beyond Garden Cottage the tarmac lane starts to go steeply downhill, passing in 140 metres *under the thatched bridge,* and in 120 metres *under a modern wooden bridge. 20 metres beyond this second bridge,* do not go left with the road (the way you came up) but instead *keep straight on downhill on a car-wide bridleway under tree.*

In 150 metres this gets to the bottom of the valley and starts to climb. In 170 metres *it comes to a T-junction with a gravel track, where you go right uphill,* your direction 230 degrees. In 130 metres, *at Yew Tree Farm, curve right with the track, 5 metres later, take the left fork, a broad car-wide track,* your direction here 240 degrees initially.

100 metres beyond this you pass a bench on your right with a wonderfully tranquil view of the valley – another good **picnic spot**. In 70 metres ignore a footpath forking right through a fieldgate and stay on the main track. In another 130 metres, where the open field ends to the left, there is another bench and another fine view backwards to Polesden Lacey. Keep on up the track, now with an easier gradient.

[!] In 300 metres, *30 metres before a metal barrier across the track* (which may however be open), *turn left down a footpath to the left through staggered wooden barriers.*

You are now on a path with the edge of the wood to your left, your direction east. *In 100 metres you come to a huge beech tree* (its trunk more than a metre in diameter), which used to mark the formal boundary between the Polesden Lacey estate (left) and Ranmore Common (right). Just beyond it is a T-junction. *Turn right here through wooden barriers, onto a car-wide grassy path*, your direction 210 degrees.

You now follow the main walk directions from point **[7]**.

c) Alternative ending at Dorking: *Follow the main walk directions to point* [10], *the Denbies Wine Estate Visitor Centre.* Coming out of the Centre, *turn right for 80 metres through the car park to a road. Turn right on this road*, following a signpost to 'Farmyard B&B and Vineyard Trail', with the buildings of Denbies Wine Estate now on your right. In 120 metres you come to a three-armed footpath sign. *Turn left here onto a car-wide gravel track*, your direction 210 degrees. After 430 metres on this track *you come to a two-armed footpath sign, where a path merges from the right.*

Keep straight on here, still on a car-wide track, towards the trees ahead, your direction 190 degrees. *In 150 metres, at the edge of the trees, go through a metal fieldgate* and on uphill into a wood on a clear path, your direction due south. In 70 metres, *at the top of the hill, turn left at a three-armed footpath sign* (hidden by a tree, but you can fork left before the tree), following the sign to Dorking station, your direction 70 degrees.

In 400 metres this path comes to a gate and a two-armed footpath sign. Do not go down the gravel drive ahead but *turn left just before the gate* along the left-hand side of a driveway to a house named Kelvin Lodge, following a sign to Dorking station and a yellow arrow on a post, your direction 70 degrees.

In 20 metres *keep to the left of the house and its garden on a grassy path*, heading directly towards Box Hill ahead and with the vineyard to your left. In 130 metres *this brings you to a kissing gate and 10 metres beyond this to a road. Keep straight on down this road*, your direction still 70 degrees and still with the vineyard to your left.

In 100 metres, 50 metres before the road comes to a dead end, turn right at a T-junction down a suburban road. In 200 metres this brings you to the main road, the A24.

Turn right onto the A24. In 70 metres you come to a set of traffic lights, where you go straight ahead and, 70 metres after this, the sign to **Dorking station** can be seen on the left-hand side of the road (you can cross by the pedestrian subway under the A24), with the **Lincoln Arms**, a possible late tea stop, on the corner.

Lunch & tea places

Denbies Wine Estate Conservatory Restaurant *London Road, Dorking, RH5 6AA (01306 876616).* **Open/food served** *Jan-Mar* 10am-5pm Mon-Fri; 10am-5.30pm Sat; 11.30am-5.30pm Sun. *Apr-Sept* 10am-5.30pm Mon-Sat; 11.30am-5.30pm Sun. There's a spectacular glass roof over the self-service restaurant. This is the recommended tea stop for the main walk.

Lincoln Arms *Station Approach, Dorking, RH4 1TF (01306 882820).* **Open** 7am-11pm Mon-Sat; 9am-10.30pm Sun. **Food served** noon-2.30pm, 6-9pm Mon-Sat; noon-3pm Sun. At the start of the station approach, this pub serves tea and coffee all evening.

Polesden Lacey tearoom *Great Bookham, RH5 6BD (01372 456190).* **Open/food served** *late Mar-early Nov* 11am-5pm daily. *Nov-late Dec* 11am-4pm Wed-Sun. *Mid Jan-late mar* 11am-4pm Wed-Sun. The best place to have lunch, romantically set in the old stable yard, and ideally situated about half-way through both the walks described here.

Sir Douglas Haig *The Street, Effingham, KT24 7LU (01372 456886).* **Open** 11am-11pm Mon-Sat; noon-10.30pm Sun. **Food served** noon-2.30pm, 6-9pm Mon-Sat; noon-3pm Sun. About 5km into the walk, this is a modernised pub that has more of a suburban than a village feel, but there's a small garden front and back and basic meals served at lunch. It also does tea and coffee all afternoon.

Picnic: There are several good places for a picnic in the environs of Polesden Lacey, which are marked as such in the main walk directions. The escarpment on Ranmore Common is also a wonderful place to stop and have a picnic tea.

9.53 Victoria ~~London Bridge~~ *Dick 14,146 pst:*

Coulsdon South Circular

Happy Valley and Farthing Down.

Start and finish: Coulsdon South station

Length: 14.2km (8.9 miles). For a shorter walk and other variations, *see below* **Walk options**.

Time: 4 hours 30 minutes. For the whole excursion, including trains and meals, allow 6 hours 30 minutes.

Transport: Two trains an hour (more at peak times; one an hour on Sunday) run from London Bridge and London Victoria to Coulsdon South (most involving a change at East Croydon; journey time: 23-39 minutes). Coulsdon South is within London Transport zone 6, so a one-day travelcard is an option. There is very limited parking at Coulsdon, and the station is well served by trains and buses, so this is one walk where travelling by public transport is by far the better option.

OS Landranger Map: 187
OS Explorer Map: 146 (and 161 for part of Riddlesdown start). Coulsdon, map reference TQ298590, is in Surrey, 8km (5 miles) north of Redhill.

Toughness: 4 out of 10.

Walk notes: Considering that it starts in the suburbs of London (and within the boundaries of London Transport Travelcard zone six), this walk passes through some remarkably unspoilt countryside. Farthing Down, Kenley Common, Riddlesdown and Coulsdon Commons are all ancient grazing lands, lovingly preserved as part of the London Greenbelt, and offering a delightful series of woods and open spaces. In spring the area is famous for its wild flowers, including several bluebell woods, while in autumn it is a riot of gold. This is also a fine walk for a brisk winter's day, and in summer offers numerous idyllic spots for a picnic.

Walk options: Directions for the alternative start and the short cut are given at the end of the main walk text (*see p168*).

a) Shortening the walk: By using the short cut to Chaldon Church at the point indicated in the text 1.7km (1.1 mile) after the Fox pub (at point [4]), you can cut 4.3km (2.7 miles) off either the main walk, or the option below.

b) Alternative start from Riddlesdown: By starting in Riddlesdown, also within the LT zone 6, you can make the walk slightly longer to 16.8km (10.5 miles). Trains to Riddlesdown also go from Victoria, with a similar journey time of 30 minutes.

You can also end the walk at the Fox pub (point [3]) and catch the 466 bus from the end of Fox Lane to East Croydon station (phone 020 8673 6109 for bus times), or the 404 bus from the pub itself to Coulsdon South station (call 020 7222 1234 for bus times).

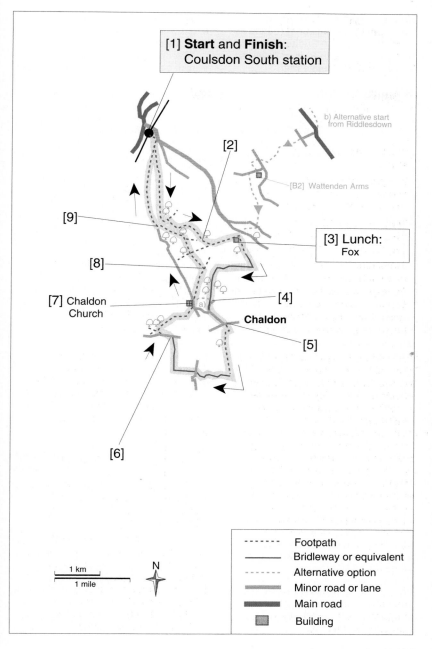

[1] **Start** and **Finish**:
Coulsdon South station

[2]

b) Alternative start
from Riddlesdown

[B2] Wattenden Arms

[9]

[3] Lunch:
Fox

[8]

[7] Chaldon
Church

[4]

Chaldon

[5]

[6]

	Footpath
-------	Footpath
————	Bridleway or equivalent
- - - -	Alternative option
▓▓▓▓	Minor road or lane
▓▓▓▓	Main road
▧	Building

1 km

1 mile

N

Walk directions

[1] Numbers refer to the map.
From platform 2 of **Coulsdon South** station, *go down concrete steps and along a tarmac path.* After 50 metres *go up steps to meet a minor road and turn left,* marked by a metal signpost indicating the London Loop.

In 40 metres ignore the junction with Fairdene Road up to the right. In a further 60 metres *turn right up a main road.* In 25 metres *fork right up a road with a sign 'Weak bridge one mile ahead'.* In 30 metres pass a large Corporation of London sign on your left for **Farthing Downs**.

In 40 metres the road forks. Take the right fork along the pavement. After 80 metres, *where the road curves to the right, fork left to cross the road and pass between two short wooden posts* next to a London Loop footpath post (which may be obscured by foliage in summer). *Go directly across the road* to a post with 'Corporation of London Permissive Ride' on it. *Turn right towards a wooden gate to the left of a cattle grid.*

In 20 metres *go through the gate* (marked no.26) and *continue up the grass parallel to the road on your right.* In 80 metres ignore a wooden gate (no.22) on your right. *In 120 metres turn left through a wooden gate* (no.21 on the reverse side), *and then turn right.*

Continue up the footpath in the same direction, with a wood to the left and a wire fence to the right, ignoring all turnings off, passing gates numbered 20, 19, 18, 17, 16 and 15 on the right. *After 1km (0.6 miles), at gate 14, continue straight ahead,* ignoring a path to the right forking along the fence. In another 180 metres, *immediately after passing through two white-topped wooden posts,*

with a view of common land straight ahead, *bear left down a stony track to enter a wood.*

After 30 metres, *at a crosspaths* next to a small black Corporation of London sign for Farthing Downs, *turn left down a steep stony track.* After 80 metres you *emerge from the wood and turn right along a wide permissive bridleway along the bottom of the valley,* your direction 160 degrees. After 120 metres ignore a wide path up to the right. In a further 20 metres *turn left up through a wooden kissing gate* next to a sign saying 'Pedestrians Give Way to Horses'.

Bear right immediately. In 8 metres you pass a concrete stone with the number 14 on it on your right. Continue uphill, your direction 110 degrees. In 30 metres *fork left uphill,* your direction 70 degrees. In 100 metres *by a bench at the top, veer right to go through a kissing gate* and turn right down a path with a fence on your right.

In 150 metres, *where the fence on your right ends at a crosspaths, continue straight on for 15 metres and turn sharp left up some wooden steps. In 20 metres turn right to leave the steps,* climbing gently uphill alongside a wood on your left with fine views of **Happy Valley** to your right. In 250 metres go straight across a track. In 40 metres ignore some steps up to your left leading up into the wood. *Continue along the crest of the escarpment,* ignoring any paths up or down.

[!] In 80 metres *immediately before the path enters a wood* with a concrete marker to your left with a (not very legible) number 14 inscribed on it, *bear right downhill keeping to the left edge of the field,* following the line of scrub. In 40 metres, *as you pass a wooden bench on the left, bear left to continue steeply downhill towards a concrete marker* to the right of the path, your direction 160 degrees.

In 35 metres, when you get to the marker (which has a more legible 13 on it), continue downhill to cross a wide wood-chip bridleway after a further 60 metres. Keep straight ahead uphill through scrub.

In 70 metres *you reach a wooden table and benches next to a three-armed wooden footpath signpost.* **[2]**

Turn left uphill, following a London Loop arrow and the footpath sign to Coulsdon Common, into a wooded area, your direction 140 degrees. *In 15 metres take the right-hand fork.* In a further 25 metres you emerge from the wooded area to fine views of the valley to the right.

Continue up this path. In 200 metres, *at a three-armed wooden footpath, continue straight on towards* **Coulsdon Common** up into a wooded area. In 80 metres, as you emerge from the wooded area and pass a London Loop footpath post, the path levels off and becomes a car-wide tarmac track. Further on you pass a fitness trail on your right.

In 300 metres pass round a wooden fieldgate with a car park on your right. Continue straight ahead, passing a van-blocking metal height barrier after 50 metres. In a further 120 metres you reach the **Fox** pub on your right, the recommended lunch stop. **[3]**

Coming out of the main entrance to the Fox pub, *turn immediately right along a footpath* on the right edge of a field bordering the pub garden, your direction 140 degrees. In 80 metres *go through a wooden gate and continue straight on* through a lightly wooded area, ignoring all ways off. In 150 metres *go through another wooden gate and cross a tarmac road.* Continue straight ahead down a car-wide track passing to the left of a car-blocking metal barrier in 80 metres. Continue on the track with a housing estate on the left.

In 350 metres, at a three-armed wooden bridleway signpost, *turn right along a bridleway* lined by trees, your direction 280 degrees. In 350 metres, this path starts to descend gradually, and in a further 200 metres more steeply as the trees thin out. In another 180 metres, *at the bottom of the hill, turn left at a four-armed wooden signpost,* following the arm to Leazes Avenue, your direction 240 degrees.

Follow the path uphill through woods with a wire-mesh fence on your right. After 150 metres, where the wire-mesh fence ends, continue straight ahead up the path. In 300 metres *you pass a two-armed signpost on your right and merge with a gravel lane.* Continue up the lane, your direction south. After 300 metres you reach a three-armed wooden signpost. **[4]**

[At this point, you can take option **a)**, **Shortening the walk,** to cut 4.3km (2.7 miles) off the walk. See directions at end of main walk text.]

Otherwise, **to continue on the main walk,** continue straight ahead following the sign to Leazes Avenue. In 30 metres the lane becomes tarmac and you pass a green on your left.

In 200 metres, *at a road T-junction, turn left.* After 200 metres you pass the white-fenced entrance to Chaldon Cottage on your right. In a further 300 metres *you reach a T-junction with a main road* opposite Rook Farm. **[5]**

Cross the road with care and turn left for 5 metres. Turn right to cross a stile and pick up a footpath signposted 'Pilgrims Lane', your direction 150 degrees. (The signpost may be obscured by foliage in summer.) After 180 metres the fenced-in footpath turns to the right up the edge of a wood. After a further 70 metres turn left over a stile into the wood, still following the sign to Pilgrims Lane. In 40 metres the footpath passes a fenced-off field on your left to continue along the edge of the wood.

In 300 metres *pass to the right of a redundant stile to reach a crosspaths marked by a wooden five-armed signpost* with 'Fiveways' inscribed on it. *Continue straight on* following the signpost to the North Downs Way, your direction due south. *In 700 metres* pass to the right of a redundant stile and in 10 metres *turn right up a car-wide track* signposted 'North Downs Way'.

In 150 metres ignore a signposted path to the right and continue up along the North Downs Way. In 100 metres *you*

The people's playgrounds

England was once patchworked with **commons** – common grazing lands for a particular village. Many were lost to private landowners as a result of the enclosure movement in the 18th century, and others have reverted to woodland for lack of management, or become farmland.

The preservation of **Farthing Down**, **Kenley Common**, **Coulsdon Common** (*above*) and **Riddlesdown** on this walk is due to the forward thinking of the Corporation of London (the local authority for the City of London), which, in the 1880s, started to acquire rural land in and around London to give city folk green places of recreation and to promote good health. These particular commons were purchased in 1883, and the decision was a popular one. In the 1900s thousands of day-trippers would

come to picnic on the commons on summer weekends and visit Gardner's fairground on Riddlesdown.

All four commons are particularly rich in wild flowers in spring, and are the habitat for many birds and insects. The Corporation still owns around 10,000 acres of land, which is all managed for the public good at no cost to the taxpayer.

Happy Valley is different from the other commons in that it was only turned into an open space in 1937-38, when various local farms were bought by Coulsdon Council as part of the London Greenbelt scheme, which sought to limit the spread of the capital by preserving a ring of open countryside around its periphery. It is a Site of Special Scientific Interest for its flora and as a habitat for ground-nesting birds such as larks.

pass a sign for Park Ham on your left. 10 metres further on bear left, passing a hollow on your right. In 120 metres there are fine views to your left of the High Weald.

In 450 metres, towards the end of the gravel lane, *take the left-hand fork to meet a road after 20 metres. Cross the road and continue straight ahead,* following the wooden North Downs Way signpost.

After 400 metres, *at a wooden signpost, continue straight on* in the direction of Rook Lane. *In 80 metres turn right,* signposted to Tollsworth Manor, down a car-wide track on the left edge of a field. In 200 metres, *at the bottom corner of the field, follow the track left at a wooden footpath sign to meet a T-junction* after 15 metres. *Turn right* down a concrete car-wide track for 500 metres to a road. **[6]**

Cross the road with care to go through a wooden kissing gate and turn immediately left along the left edge of a field. *After 300 metres,* at the left field corner, *cross a stile* marked with a Tandridge Border path sign to enter a wood. *In 50 metres veer right onto a concrete car-wide track. In 20 metres turn right along another concrete track,* your direction 20 degrees initially.

[!] *In 150 metres,* where a further concrete car-wide track joins from the left, *turn right to cross a stile* after 15 metres to emerge from the wood. (The stile is next to a very old coppiced beech tree and is marked 'Tandridge Border Path'.)

Bear left to follow the left edge of the wood for 40 metres to reach a corner post of the wood. *Continue straight on to go diagonally down across the field,* your direction 60 degrees, heading for the left end of some farm buildings ahead.

In 180 metres go over a stile at the bottom and continue in the same direction (40 degrees) going gently uphill. **[!]** *60 metres after this* the footpath originally turned right along a field boundary, but this has been ploughed up: instead, *aim for a gap in the hedge about 100 metres to the right of the barns,* your direction 100 degrees.

In 250 metres *pass to the left of a redundant stile and bear left* and downhill, diagonally across a field towards a metal fieldgate, your direction 30 degrees. *In 200 metres go over a stile* to the left of the metal fieldgate, *and turn right down a tarmac road.* **Chaldon Church** is on your left after 30 metres and is worth a visit. **[7]**

After visiting the church come out of the entrance to the churchyard and turn left. In 10 metres take the left fork downhill. In 50 metres *turn left at a T-junction. In 30 metres turn right to follow a signposted footpath diagonally across a field,* your direction 20 degrees. After 500 metres, *the footpath veers slightly right and down across the next field,* your direction now 40 degrees.

In 200 metres *pass a footpath signpost to go down through a small wood.* In 30 metres emerge from the wood at the top corner of a field, with a fine view of **Happy Valley** in front of you. **[8]**

Turn left along the upper left edge of the field. In 300 metres, *at the upper left hand corner of the field, go straight ahead into the wood,* ignoring a path up to the left, your direction 310 initially. In 50 metres, at a wooden footpath signpost, *veer right into the next field. Turn left* down along the top left edge of the field, your direction 320 degrees.

In 180 metres, at the corner of this field, pass a footpath signpost on your left to enter a wood, your direction 310 degrees initially. In 200 metres you pass a two-armed wooden footpath signpost and a track merges from the left. *Keep straight on, ignoring ways off. In 300 metres pass to the left of a car-blocking metal barrier,* and emerge from the wood.

In 20 metres turn left uphill past a Corporation of London sign for **Farthing Downs** on your right and with houses on your left. In 60 metres *cross a tarmac lane to reach the car park* where you can buy hot drinks at the refreshment trailer on your left (parked in front of the public toilets). **[9]**

If not stopping for refreshments, *turn right and walk along the top of the ridge.* In 50 metres you exit the tarmac part of the car park and in 90 metres a grassy part. In 600 metres you pass a concrete sundial view pointer (which is worth a look) 15 metres to your right.

In a further 70 metres, at a four-armed wooden signpost under three large trees, *continue straight ahead downhill.* Keep to the main path, ignoring ways off, and in 700 metres at the bottom of the hill you rejoin the road to your right at a cattle grid.

Go through a wooden gate to the left of a cattle grid and carry straight on down the road, following the residential slip road for the first 100 metres, which then merges with the Farthing Downs road for another 100 metres to reach the main road.

Turn left here. In 25 metres the entrance to the Coulsdon Memorial Ground, whose café is a possible tea stop, is to your right: go through the entrance and then turn left for 60 metres to reach the café.

If not stopping for tea, *turn left up Reddown Road,* opposite the Memorial Ground entrance. In 70 metres ignore Fairdene Road on the left and in another 30 metres *turn right down steps* onto a footpath between houses, following a metal signpost to Coulsdon South station. Cross the footbridge over the railway line to the opposite platform for trains back to London.

Walk options

a) Shortening the walk:
Follow main walk directions until point [4].

Turn right here to follow the arm for 'Chaldon Church ¼ mile', along a footpath with the wood on your right and a field on your left, your direction 280 degrees. *After 200 metres* you reach the corner of the wood and *veer left, still following the field boundary* but now with fields either side.

In 200 metres you reach a lane and turn right. In 10 metres take the lane forking up to the left to reach the entrance to Chaldon Church after 60 metres. You now *resume the walk directions at point [7]* in the main walk directions above.

b) Alternative start from Riddlesdown:
[B1] From the exit of platform 2 of Riddlesdown station, *turn sharp right up a tarmac path immediately after the station exit,* your direction 120 degrees.

In 15 metres ignore a tarmac footpath down to the left. After 280 metres *the tarmac footpath leads out onto a road. Turn right up the road* (Mitchley Avenue). In 150 metres you pass Ingleboro Drive on your left. There is a view of Croydon and the City of London to the right here. After a further 100 metres, *turn left up Riddlesdown Road,* your direction 150 degrees. In 120 metres go through a wooden gate and straight ahead past a Corporation of London sign onto **Riddlesdown**.

Continue along the tarmac lane. After 140 metres you pass a small car park on your left-hand side. After a further 50 metres, *at end of the car park,* pass through some bollards and *continue along a fine gravel track,* your direction 120 degrees. There is a fine view of the valley down to your right

In 200 metres ignore a tarmac track forking off to the left. *After a further 300 metres go through a wooden gate to the left of a wooden fieldgate.* Continue gently downhill.

After 500 metres go through another wooden gate to the left of a wooden fieldgate, now with a wooden fence on your left-hand side. In 60 metres ignore a wooden fieldgate on your left-hand side and a three-armed footpath signpost on your right. The path now descends slightly more steeply.

After 100 metres cross a bridge over a railway line. After 300 metres you pass a Corporation of London board on your left. Go to the left of a metal car-blocking barrier *to come out onto a main road. Cross the road* directly in front of the Rose and Crown pub *and turn left. In 35*

metres turn right onto Old Barn Lane,
your direction 250 degrees.

*After 80 metres cross a concrete
footbridge over the railway line to
continue up New Barn Lane,* passing
Kenley Primary School on your right.
After 120 metres go over a crossroads
to reach the top of New Barn Lane
after 80 metres.

Go up some steps marked by a wooden
footpath signpost on your left. **[!]** *After
30 metres* (or two turns of the path) *turn
right up some earth steps,* your direction
250 degrees. *In 50 metres,* at the top of the
steps, *you emerge into the bottom corner
of a field* with a wooden footpath post on
your right. On your left is a Corporation of
London noticeboard for **Kenley Common**.

*Follow the direction of the London Loop
arrow on the post up the right edge of the
field,* your direction 220 degrees initially.
After 120 metres a*t the corner of the field
you enter a wood.*

Follow a wooden footpath post on your
right to *continue straight ahead along a
car-wide earth track* through the wood,
your direction 260 degrees. In 150 metres
ignore an unmarked footpath leading off
to the left. In 60 metres, *where the path
forks, fork left, as indicated by a public
footpath arm marked 'no.35 Hayes
Lane'.* After 80 metres ignore unmarked
footpaths to the left and right to continue
straight ahead.

In a further 10 metres *you emerge from
the wood* passing a wooden footpath post
on your left. *Follow the footpath arrow
diagonally across a field,* your direction
210 degrees. *In 160 metres,* on the far side
of the field, *pass a four-armed wooden
footpath post on your right and an oak
tree with a bench at its foot on your left, to
enter a wood,* your direction 210 degrees.

*In 70 metres emerge from the wood
and turn right onto a car-wide track,*
following a signposted path to Hayes
Lane, your direction 250 degrees. In 15
metres *go through some wooden posts*
with a missing gate and *continue along
a shingle car-wide track.*

A rare plant, the **Greater Yellow-rattle**
and a male **Chalkhill Blue** butterfly,
both found on this walk.

*In 250 metres, at a T-junction with a
road, turn right* following a London Loop
footpath signpost. *In 100 metres turn
left along a footpath following the London
Loop signpost,* initially with a garden
on the right and woods on left. *In 100
metres, at an unmarked path T-junction,
turn right.* After 50 metres *you come out
to a corner of a field. Turn left and left
again to re-enter the woods,* your direction
170 degrees.

In 60 metres, at a path T-junction
marked by a three-armed footpath
signpost, *continue straight ahead, now*

with a wooden fence on your right. After 40 metres cross a sand shingle driveway. In 25 metres *you come out onto a lane* with the **Wattenden Arms** pub, a possible lunch stop, directly in front of you. **[B2]**

Turn right along the road, passing a thatched house on your left after 30 metres. In another 50 metres, *where the lane curves to the right, fork left* onto a car-wide shingle track, signposted 'Access to The Haven'. In 5 metres turn left across a stile, following a footpath signpost to Waterhouse Lane.

Follow the footpath along the left side of the field, your direction 170 degrees initially. In 30 metres the path curves to the right *aiming for a small white observatory bubble. In 230 metres go over a stile to the left of the observatory. Continue straight ahead,* merging with a tarmac driveway. *In 80 metres pass to the left of a metal fieldgate to enter a wood.*

In 15 metres fork right down a narrow footpath, following a London Loop arrow on a post. *In 40 metres, at a staggered footpath junction, go left and then immediately right at a three-armed footpath sign,* following a car-wide public bridleway downhill to Caterham Drive, your direction 210 degrees.

In 160 metres *the bridleway comes out to a road where you turn left.* After 180 metres you pass Rydons Wood Close and a Corporation of London sign for **Coulsdon Common** to your right. *30 metres further on take the unmarked footpath forking off to the right* into a wood, your direction 200 degrees initially.

The path curves to the left to roughly parallel the road. *In 150 metres, at a path T-junction, turn right onto a car-wide earth track,* passing a small Coulsdon Common sign on the left, your direction 170 degrees. After 20 metres you go through a 15 metre clearing to then re-enter the wood.

In 200 metres cross a road. Ignore a path forking up to the right to continue straight ahead uphill on a footpath, your direction 250 degrees. *In 20 metres take*

the right-hand fork, continuing uphill more obliquely, your direction now 290 degrees. In 150 metres a path merges from the left. After another 30 metres you pass a pond on your right.

In 150 metres *you emerge from the woods and pass a cottage and then a metal car-blocking barrier on your left. In 25 metres take an unmarked left fork,* your direction 240 degrees. *In 80 metres veer left to join the main path.*

In 70 metres pass to the right of a wooden fieldgate and **cross over the main road**. Continue straight ahead to reach the **Fox** pub, the recommended lunch stop, in 120 metres.

You now *resume the main walk directions at point* [3].

Lunch & tea places

Fox *Coulsdon Common, Caterham, CR3 5QS (01883 330401).* **Open** 11am-11pm Mon-Sat; noon-10.30pm Sun. **Food served** noon-10pm Mon-Sat; noon-9.30pm Sun. Located 3.7km (2.3 miles) into the walk, the Fox serves food all day and has a large seating capacity, both inside and in the garden. This is the suggested lunch option for the main walk.

Wattenden Arms *Old Lodge Lane, Kenley, CR8 5EU (8763 9131).* **Open** noon-11pm Mon-Sat; noon-10.30pm Sun. **Food served** noon-2.30pm, 6-9pm Mon-Sat; noon-2.30pm Sun. Just past Kenley Common, this pub serves a moderately inventive menu. It's smaller than the Fox but has a cosy charm. This is a suggested earlier lunch alternative, but only if starting from Riddlesdown.

Options for tea are somewhat limited: this is perhaps a good walk to bring a thermos flask, as Farthing Down and Happy Valley both have benches with fine views for a picnic tea. Otherwise, in Farthing Down car park there is a refreshment trailer on weekends and fine summer days, though it shuts at around 4pm. If you call Carol, the manager, (07815 314846) in advance she will usually stay open for groups, however. Alternatively, try the café in Coulsdon Memorial Ground, which is opposite Reddown Road and a 5-minute walk to Coulsdon South station. Once again this is seasonal, open on fair days in summer until about 5pm.

Hurst Green to Chiddingstone Causeway

The Greensand Way, the High Chart and Ide Hill.

Start: Hurst Green station
Finish: Penshurst station

Length: 21km (13 miles). For a shorter walk, *see below* **Walk options**.

Time: 6 hours 30 minutes. For the whole outing, including trains, sights and meals, allow 10 hours.

Transport: Two trains an hour (one on Sunday) run from London Victoria to Hurst Green (journey time: 39 minutes/49 minutes on Sunday). Between two and four trains an hour run back from Penshurst to Victoria, requiring a change at Redhill or Tonbridge (journey time: 57 minutes

to 1 hour 20 minutes). This main walk is probably the most car-unfriendly in this book, as it is tricky to get back from Penshurst to Hurst Green (you can do so via Edenbridge/Edenbridge Town stations). A better option is the short walk: you can park your car at Hurst Green, one stop down the line from Oxted.

OS Landranger Maps: 187 and 188
OS Explorer Maps: 147 and 146 (for the short walk)
Hurst Green, map reference TQ400514, is in Surrey, 12km (7.5 miles) east of Redhill.

Toughness: 6 out of 10.

Walk notes: This is a long but rewarding walk along the hills of northern Kent, much of it passing through woodland along the Greensand Way. In the afternoon you can enjoy views over the countryside to the south. This is a walk recommended in late April and early May, when it offers a series of bluebell woods, and also in the autumn with a beautiful show of colours. The walk also passes Chartwell (the former home of Winston Churchill) and through the secluded upland village of Ide Hill.

Walk options:

a) Shorter walk to Oxted: You may reduce the length of the main walk by

12km to 9km (5.6 miles) by following the main walk directions as given until [3]. Then follow the directions at the end of the main walk text to finish at Oxted. Trains go back to Victoria from Oxted.

Further to the above, you can also trim a 1-km (0.6-mile) descent and ascent section off the main and short walks by using the short cut at [2] indicated in the main walk text (*see p179*).

Saturday Walkers' Club: Take the train nearest to 9.10am (before or after) from London Victoria. For the shorter walk option, take the train nearest to 10.30am.

Walk directions

[1] [Numbers refer to the map]
Coming off the London train from
platform 2 at **Hurst Green station**,
exit and *turn right*. In 25 metres *go up the
steps leading to the road bridge and turn
left* to cross Greenhurst Lane. Continue
along Hurstlands, your direction 60
degrees. *Ignore the road turning off to the
right after 70 metres*, cross over the road
and continue up in the same direction on
the other side.

In 120 metres cross Wolfs Wood and,
after a further 130 metres, cross Home
Park and continue up Wolfs Hill. **[!]** In
30 metres *turn right along an unmarked
tarmac footpath* between wooden fences.

In 80 metres cross a brick road and
continue along the tarmac footpath. After
100 metres this becomes an earth footpath
and curves to the right to go *round the
edge of a playing field*. In 15 metres follow
the field round and down to the left and
then, after 50 metres, follow the field round
to the left, your direction 20 degrees.

In 100 metres, at the end of the playing
field, the footpath goes uphill and veers
to the right between wooden fences. In
180 metres go over a stile to *cross over
a road and a stile to continue down
in the same direction*. After 100 metres
the footpath goes up an incline, with
a metal fence on your left and woods
on your right. In 200 metres *go through
a wooden gate to go up a tarmac lane,
passing a house on your right.*

After 300 metres, *at the end of the
lane, go over a crossroads to continue up
Pastens Road*, your direction 110 degrees.

After 170 metres, as the road curves
to the right, ignore a footpath sign to
the left. In another 300 metres, *where the
road ends at Arden Lodge, turn left up
a tarmac lane by a four-armed footpath
signpost*. Almost immediately you pass
a white cottage (Pastens Cottage) on
your right, with an inscription to Sergey
Kravehinsky Stepniak (1852-95) on its
side, your direction 60 degrees.

In 35 metres you pass the entrance to
Chartfield Cottage on your left and after
a further 20 metres *you reach an easily
missed three-armed footpath signpost on
your right, hidden in a clump of reeds*. **[2]**
Now there are two alternatives. **(i)** Take
the short cut, reducing the main and short
walks by 1km, or **(ii)** continue with the
recommended walk.

(i) Short cut: Ignore the right double
back turn and *continue up the car-wide
track*. After 60 metres, the footpath
becomes a narrow path. In 60 metres
go through a wooden gate to right of a
wooden fieldgate. Pass by a house on your
right (The Hollies), and continue up the
path, which now enters a lightly wooded
area. In 160 metres cross over a car-wide
track and keep to the right-hand path with
wooden pole fencing to the right, your
direction east. In 120 metres *cross over the
B269 and turn right* down a tarmac path,
your direction 100 degrees. In 50 metres
the path runs between trees on your right
(screening you from the road) and garden
fencing on your left. Follow this path
which subsequently diverges to the left
away from the B269. In 220 metres you
emerge from the wooded area to cross a
quiet road. Continue along a sandy car-
wide track. After 80 metres follow the
track round to the right to reach the
Carpenters Arms on your left, the
lunchtime stop for the short walk. Rejoin
the route at the asterisk [*] below.

(ii) Main walk route: **[!]** *Turn sharp
right to double back, down a footpath*
through a slight cutting, your initial
direction 240 degrees. Follow this footpath
for 350 metres as it curves to the left, latterly
through a wooded area, to then *cross over
a stile into a field. Continue down the
right-hand side of the field*, your direction
160 degrees. In 300 metres, at the bottom
of the field, go through a metal fieldgate
and continue with a ditch stream on your
right and a fence on your left and Tenchleys
Manor ahead and slightly to the left.

In 140 metres the official route is actually
through the garden of Tenchleys Manor,

Hurst Green to Chiddingstone Causeway

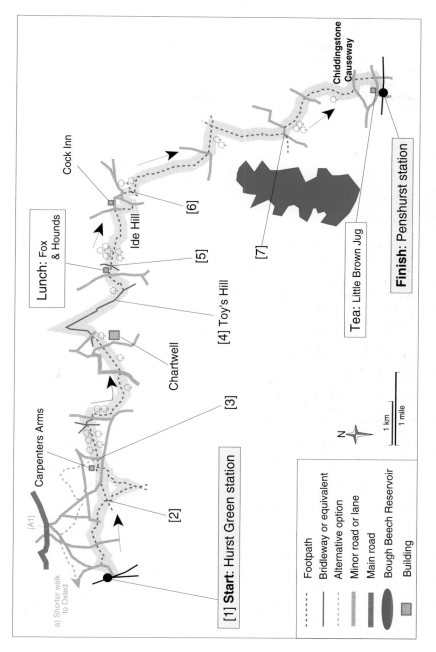

Cock Inn

Lunch: Fox & Hounds

Carpenters Arms

[A1]

a) Shorter walk to Oxted

Ide Hill

[6]

[5]

[4] Toy's Hill

Chartwell

[3]

[2]

Chiddingstone Causeway

[7]

Finish: Penshurst station

Tea: Little Brown Jug

[1] **Start**: Hurst Green station

N

1 km
1 mile

Footpath
Bridleway or equivalent
Alternative option
Minor road or lane
Main road
Bough Beech Reservoir
Building

however the owners have provided a *preferred alternative route marked 'Alternative Path' to the right. Turn right to cross a footbridge,* your direction 200 degrees. In 40 metres *follow the path round to the left to cross over another footbridge after 40 metres and then come out onto a car-wide earth track and turn left,* your direction 20 degrees.

In 70 metres you come out into a field and continue in the same direction, up the left-hand edge of the field along a farm track. After 160 metres, at the field corner, cross over into the next field and continue up the track. In 200 metres go through a metal fieldgate and continue up the track, which curves gradually to the right.

In 160 metres *go through a metal fieldgate to continue up a car-wide earth track passing a house on your right after 40 metres.* **[!]** *In 50 metres, next to an electricity substation enclosed by wooden fencing on your left, turn sharp left uphill* following a blue bridleway arrow on a post, your direction 330 degrees.

At the top, after 150 metres, you pass a footpath post on your right to come out to a lane junction. Ignore the downhill lane to the right and *turn half right along the lane to Quince House and Champions Cottage,* your direction 130 degrees.

In 60 metres, *just before Quince House, turn up to the left,* your direction 20 degrees. After 40 metres you pass Champions Cottage on your right and continue straight up an earth footpath. In 50 metres you *come out onto a tarmac lane. Continue along the lane* in the direction of the yellow footpath arrow on a post *to reach a road junction* after 180 metres. *Cross over the B269 to continue through a wooded area. In 80 metres* you reach a lane with a footpath signpost on your right. *Turn right along Tally Road* to arrive outside the **Carpenters Arms** in Limpsfield Chart, the lunchtime stop for the short walk.

[*] Emerging from the Carpenters Arms turn left along Tally Road for 130 metres *to reach a road junction.* **[3]**

[At this point you can take option **a)**, the **Shorter walk to Oxted,** by following the directions at the end of this main walk text.]

Otherwise, for the main walk, *you now follow the* **Greensand Way** *all the way to Toys Hill* [4] and for the most part it is clearly signposted.

In more detail: Cross over the road, passing a footpath signpost on your left with a footpath arrow indicating 'Limpsfield walk NT'. Continue in the same direction as you latterly enter a wooded area. (This area is known as the **High Chart.**) After 80 metres the path curves slightly round to the right by a small National Trust (NT) notice on your right with a public bridleway blue arrow and a notice for horseriders. In a further 160 metres, at a footpath post with a 'Greensand Way' (GW) arrow, fork left off the main bridleway, your initial direction 60 degrees.

After 140 metres go straight over a crosspaths indicated by a GW arrow on a footpath post, your direction 70 degrees.

In a further 40 metres cross a car-wide track and continue along in the same direction, marked by a yellow GW arrow on a post. In 350 metres you pass a post with a GW arrow, just before crossing another car-wide track to continue straight ahead, your direction 50 degrees. After 250 metres, at a footpath junction, turn half left along a car-wide track, following a GW arrow on a post, your direction 40 degrees.

In 140 metres you reach a footpath junction with a yellow GW footpath arrow on a post. Continue straight ahead, passing another post with a GW blue bridleway arrow after 20 metres. The bridleway now becomes fenced-in between gardens. After 300 metres you come out onto a road.

Cross the road and cross over a stile to the left of a wooden fieldgate. *Go along a car-wide track into a wood,* your direction east. In 80 metres, *at a footpath junction* marked by a footpath post with GW arrows to the right and to the left, *turn right*, your direction 170 degrees.

In 200 metres cross a stile to the right of a metal gate to continue along a path, which soon becomes a car-wide track, your direction 210 degrees. After 100 metres, at a footpath junction, turn left to follow a GW arrow on a post, your direction 150 degrees. In 70 metres you pass a footpath post with a GW arrow on your right to continue straight on, your direction now south.

After 100 metres cross a car-wide track and continue straight on, following a GW arrow on a post, your direction 170 degrees. In 30 metres, where the footpath forks, take the left fork.

Continue straight ahead on the Greensand Way for the next 400 metres, following the footpath arrows on posts, to come out into an opening and onto a lane. In 25 metres you pass a bench and a footpath post on your left with a GW arrow pointing half left. 20 metres further on follow a GW arrow on a post to the left of a small green up a car-wide track, your direction 100 degrees.

In 250 metres you pass a post with a GW yellow footpath arrow, your direction now 50 degrees. In 50 metres you pass a house (The Warren) on your right. Veer right past the house, ignoring a footpath to the left, and in 30 metres you pass a footpath post with a GW blue bridleway arrow, your direction now 80 degrees.

In 15 metres *veer left downhill*. After 100 metres go over a crosspaths marked by a post with a blue GW bridleway arrow, your direction 60 degrees, to descend more steeply to *reach the bottom of the hill* after 180 metres. Veer right to follow a blue bridleway arrow on a post past the entrance to April Cottage on your right to go up a lane and reach a road junction after 80 metres.

Cross over the road and take the GW bridleway uphill, marked by a metal signpost, your direction 80 degrees. In 120 metres, at a footpath junction at the top of the hill (20 metres after a

wooden fence starts on the right), turn left, indicated by a GW arrow on a post, your direction 10 degrees.

Follow the Greensand Way arrows on footpath posts, ignoring all ways off for the next 600 metres. *Eventually the path descends steeply down to a road. Cross the road and go over a stile to the left of the entrance to* **Chartwell** (*see p176* **Churchill's finest hours**), and walk along a footpath, initially between fences.

In 400 metres you come out onto a road. Cross the road to pass round to the right of a car-blocking barrier, passing a metal footpath signpost with bridleway/GW signs, your initial direction 40 degrees. In 150 metres you pass a post on your left with a blue GW arrow and continue straight on, your direction 40 degrees. After 350 metres *the footpath forks; take the right fork* and 40 metres further on you pass a post with a GW arrow to veer round to the right down a car-wide track, your initial direction 50 degrees.

In 80 metres the track joins a driveway and after a further 30 metres you *come to a road junction, where you turn right down a lane* following a Greensand Way signpost. *In 70 metres fork left to follow a sign 'Private Road – French Street Farm'.*

Go down this winding lane to pass through French Street Farm at the bottom after 160 metres and continue up the lane. In 600 metres you *come to a fork with a dilapidated footpath post on your right. Take the right fork along a car-wide shingle track*, marked by a sign 'Bridleway to Toys Hill', your direction 160 degrees. After 250 metres, at the end of the track, *pass to the left of a metal fieldgate to go uphill with a green mesh fence on your right initially* to **Toys Hill**. In 150 metres you reach a 'Toys Hill – National Trust' sign. **[4]**

In 25 metres ignore a track to the left and continue straight ahead, indicated by a blue GW bridleway arrow on a post to *climb a steep hill*, your direction 140 degrees. In 130 metres continue straight on at a footpath junction marked by a blue

Churchill's finest hours

Not only was Winston Churchill the pre-eminent British political figure of the 20th century, but he was also a Nobel Prize-winning author and a talented amateur painter. Much of his writing and painting took place at his beloved country home, **Chartwell** (where he lived from 1924 until his death in 1965). Inspiration was provided by its glorious views over the Weald, and by its lovely gardens. Visitors can stroll around its terraces and see the lakes Churchill created, the water garden where he fed his fish, Lady Churchill's rose garden and the Golden Rose Walk (a Golden Wedding anniversary present from their children). Inside, the house has been left much as it was in Churchill's day, filled with the great man's books, maps, pictures and personal effects.

Chartwell

Mapleton Road, Westerham, TN16 1PS (01732 868381/infoline 01732 866368/restaurant 01732 863087). **Open** *House late Mar-June, Sept-early Nov* 11am-5pm Wed-Sun; *July, Aug* 11am-5pm Tue-Sun. *Restaurant/shop early-late Mar* 11am-4pm Wed-Sun; *late Mar-June, Sept-early Nov* 11am-5.30pm Wed-Sun; *July, Aug* 11am-5.30pm Tue-Sun; *early Nov-mid Dec* 10.30am-4pm Wed-Sun. **Admission** £7; concessions £3.50; family £17.50. **Credit** AmEx, MC, V.

GW bridleway arrow on a post. Again, after a further 160 metres, continue straight ahead and downhill at a path junction marked by a blue GW bridleway arrow on a post, your direction 110 degrees.

After 220 metres, *at a path junction, turn left and up, as marked by a GW arrow on a post*, your direction 10 degrees. After 300 metres *go down some steps taking you into a car park*, with an NT information board about Toys Hill on the right.

Turn left at the bottom of the steps to leave the Greensand Way and follow the NT red footpath arrow, your direction west. In 120 metres you *reach a car-wide track with a footpath post ahead with red, green and orange footpath arrows to the left. Turn right* along the car-wide earth track, your direction 50 degrees. After 160 metres you *reach a footpath junction* with a footpath post on your left. *Cross over the junction to continue along a car-wide earth track,* your direction now 30 degrees.

After 120 metres you *reach a T-junction, where you turn right*, your direction east, *to come out after 40 metres to a road which you cross*.

In a further 40 metres you reach an unmarked crosspaths. [5] *For the recommended lunch stop turn left* (if not stopping at the recommended lunch stop, turn right, your direction 200 degrees, and pick up the directions at the double asterisk [**] below) along an unmarked footpath (with an NT 'No horses allowed beyond this point' notice on the right), your initial direction north. Walk for 80 metres along this twisty footpath to emerge into the garden of the **Fox and Hounds**.

After lunch come out of the pub and cross the pub garden to retrace your steps back along the twisty footpath to the unmarked crosspaths, where you cross straight over. [**] After 20 metres you reach a footpath post where you *turn left down a footpath*, your direction 120 degrees.

In 120 metres, *at a five-way footpath junction* with a footpath post with various arrows, *you rejoin the Greensand Way*, indicated by a GW arrow, *and continue*

straight on, your direction 110 degrees. You now continue straight ahead on the Greensand Way for the next 500 metres, *following arrows on footpath posts all the way downhill until you emerge from the wood at the bottom of the hill and cross over a stile into a field* (a possible **picnic** spot).

Turn left down the upper left edge of the field, your direction 70 degrees. After 90 metres *cross a stile and turn half right down across the field* towards a gap in the trees ahead, your direction 120 degrees. In 100 metres cross over a stile into the next field and continue straight ahead, *heading down towards the bottom right-hand corner of the field*, your direction 120 degrees.

In 160 metres, *at the field corner, cross a footbridge and follow the direction of the GW arrow on a footpath post* up the left-hand edge of a field, with a wood on your left, your direction east. In 200 metres, at the top corner of the field, cross a stile to continue uphill along the right-hand edge of the next field, your direction east.

After 200 metres, at the top right-hand corner of this field, cross a stile into the next field. Continue up **Ide Hill** on a car-wide track along the right-hand edge of the field. After 250 metres, at the top corner of the field, cross a stile and continue along a tarmac lane. In 50 metres turn right at a road junction to arrive at the **Elan Arts Centre**, Ide Hill, the early tea stop, on your right.

Coming out of the Elan Arts Centre turn right *to then pass a mini roundabout* on your left after 20 metres. If you are opting for the late pub lunch stop, then turn left here for the **Cock Inn**, 80 metres further on. Otherwise *continue straight on, with the village green to your left*, your direction 170 degrees.

In 60 metres *go through the white gates that lead in to the National Trust (NT) entrance to Ide Hill* with a sign 'No access for cars, footpath only'. Go along the tarmac lane with Ide church on your left, your direction 200 degrees.

In 70 metres *leave the tarmac lane to fork right along a shingle track*. You pass an NT Ide Hill sign on the left and *continue alongside a wooden fence on your right*. After 120 metres the wooden fence ends and, 10 metres further on, you turn half left, following a footpath post with a Greensand Way arrow, *to go downhill through a wood*, your direction 150 degrees.

In 110 metres *turn left at a footpath junction following a GW arrow*, your initial direction east. In 15 metres *veer left at a stone bench* with an inscription commemorating Octavia Hill *and 5 metres further on go straight downhill* following a GW arrow on a footpath post. After 300 metres, *at a footpath junction, turn half right downhill*, following a yellow GW arrow, your direction 70 degrees.

In 25 metres you come down to a slip road, just off the main B2042 road on your right. *Cross over the slip road to the grass verge on the other side.* There are public conveniences to your left. Take care as you *cross over the main road onto the grass verge* on the opposite side, with a view of Bough Beech water directly ahead. *Turn left* along this grass verge.

In 100 metres turn right down a lane. After 15 metres fork left up a car-wide shingle track marked by a Greensand Way bridleway signpost, your direction 160 degrees. In 180 metres you *reach a small open area with a green island with a footpath post on the left.* **[6]**

Continue straight on, passing the gates to Quarry Cottage on your right after 10 metres, your direction 150 degrees. In 10 metres you pass a stone public bridleway marker on your right to go downhill with a wire fence on your right.

After 200 metres you *come out onto a lane and turn left*. In 100 metres *follow the lane round and down to the right*, your direction 160 degrees.

After 150 metres, *at the bottom of the lane, turn left down a car-wide earth track. In 20 metres turn right* as indicated by a footpath arrow on a post to go down the right-hand edge of a field bordered

by a wood, your direction 150 degrees. In 180 metres, at the right-hand field corner, cross a plank footbridge into the next field and veer left across this field, marked by a footpath arrow, your direction 145 degrees.

In 300 metres go through a small wooded area field boundary to emerge into the next field after 30 metres and continue down across this field, your direction 150 degrees. In 120 metres go through a gap in the trees and follow the footpath down the left-hand edge of this (initially narrow) field in a southerly direction.

After 350 metres, at the left-hand field corner, cross into the next field and follow the footpath arrow down across this field, aiming for the bottom left-hand corner, your direction 130 degrees.

In 280 metres go over a stile to enter a small wooded area to cross a footbridge after 10 metres. Continue up the footpath, passing a redundant stile, to emerge from the wooded area after 60 metres. Turn left to go through a car-wide entrance after 10 metres and follow the path up and round to the right, with a hedgerow on your right-hand side.

In 60 metres, having crossed a stile, *go through a wooden fieldgate* and follow the path round *to the left to come out onto a lane after 20 metres. Turn left* along the lane and *in 30 metres turn right over a stile*. Go up the right-hand edge of a field bordered by a small wooded area, your initial direction 70 degrees. In 120 metres, at the top where the wooded area ends, continue down the right-hand side of the field towards the bottom right-hand corner.

In 140 metres *cross a stile followed by another and turn half right* to follow an arrow on the second stile diagonally across the field, with a wooded area off to your right, your direction 100 degrees.

The field subsequently narrows and descends and, *after 400 metres* at the field corner, go through a metal fieldgate to *cross a stream into the next field*. Go up the right-hand edge of this field and, *in 50 metres, turn right across a stile* along a footpath with a fenced-in wood on your left, your direction 200 degrees. In 50 metres, at the corner of the wood, continue across the field, passing just to the left of a mini pylon pole in the middle of the field, aiming for a stile in the far right-hand field corner.

After 400 metres cross over the stile and a footbridge into the next field to continue in the same direction along the right-hand side of the field.

In 180 metres (just before a mini pylon pole to your left) *turn right to cross a stile* to the right of a metal fieldgate and, after 10 metres, *turn left down a car-wide earth track* between hedgerows, your direction south.

In 160 metres the farm track becomes a concrete driveway. Continue ahead to subsequently pass by farm buildings and workshops. In 300 metres the driveway swings to the left to *join a tarmac lane, where you turn right, passing a small car park on your left-hand side*, your direction 190 degrees.

[7] In 500 metres, *at a T-junction, turn left* along a lane, your direction 70 degrees. After 20 metres the lane crosses a stream. In 160 metres, *just before the lane swings to the left, turn right up a driveway* to go through the white post entrance to Little Sidcup Farm.

[!] *In 200 metres* (and 80 metres before a white house ahead) *turn right along a car-wide track*, marked by a yellow footpath arrow on a telegraph pole, your direction 190 degrees. In 25 metres go over a stile to the right of a metal fieldgate and *veer left up the left side of a narrow field* to pass a fenced-in narrow pond on your left after 70 metres. In a further 80 metres, *at the top of the narrow field, turn left over a plank bridge to follow a path through a lightly wooded area*.

In 60 metres you go through a wooden gate, your direction 130 degrees. After 200 metres go over a stile to *emerge*

from the wooded area to go down the left-hand edge of a field, your direction 80 degrees.

In 140 metres, where the left-hand edge of the field curves sharply to the left (marked by a tree with a right footpath arrow), *turn right across the field*, passing between a small pond on your left and a tree on your right in the middle of the field, your direction 120 degrees.

In 160 metres go over a stile (to the right of a metal fieldgate) to cross a lane and a stile. Veer right across the field, your direction 130 degrees. After 200 metres go through a gap in the hedgerow field boundary and veer right across the next field, towards the right-hand field corner, your direction 160 degrees.

After 200 metres cross a stile to enter a wooded area and continue along a track passing a pond on your left. In 60 metres cross a stile (to the left of a metal field-gate) to emerge from the wooded area into a field to go along the right-hand edge of the field. After 130 metres, at the right-hand field corner go over a stile to cross the next field, your direction south.

After 200 metres cross over a stile into the next field and head towards its left-hand corner. In 150 metres cross a stile and *veer left along a footpath aiming to the left of the farm buildings*, your direction 160 degrees.

After 250 metres *cross a stile and turn left along a car-wide track towards a road*. In 50 metres, *at the junction with the road, turn left* along the grass verge on the left-hand side of the road. *After 100 metres turn right* to cross the road to go along a tarmac footpath, your direction 170 degrees.

In 400 metres turn right down the B2027 to pass on your left after 50 metres the church of St Luke, Chiddingstone Causeway. In 120 metres you reach the **Little Brown Jug** on your right, the recommended tea place. **Penshurst station** is on the left opposite the pub.

Walk options

a) Shorter walk to Oxted:

Follow the main walk directions until point [3].

At the road junction turn left, your direction north, and *then, after 10 metres, fork left* along Stoneleigh Road, your direction 340 degrees. In 200 metres, *as the road curves round to the left, keep straight on*, indicated by a wooden public bridleway sign, along a shingle car-wide track, which narrows to a footpath after 100 metres.

In 70 metres *cross over a road and continue down a car-wide shingle track. After 15 metres fork right off this onto a signposted bridleway,* your direction 340 degrees. In 130 metres ignore a path forking right and in 35 metres, at a post with a blue bridleway arrow, ignore a path merging from the right to continue downhill. In 70 metres, *at the blue bridleway signpost, ignore the minor path to the left and curve right. In a further 5 metres fork left downhill* to resume your former direction, 340 degrees, with the wood edge 10 metres away on your left.

In 200 metres, *at a path junction* marked by a post, *go left following a blue bridleway arrow,* your initial direction 290 degrees.

Continue along the near edge of the woods on a meandering path to *reach a footpath T-junction after 300 metres. Turn left and after 5 metres turn half left,* marked by a yellow arrow on a post. In 20 metres *cross a plank footbridge and stile and continue straight on across a narrow field,* your direction 250 degrees.

In 30 metres, *continue straight ahead up into a wood.* After 180 metres you *emerge from the wood to continue straight ahead,* marked by an arrow on a post, your direction 300 degrees.

In 35 metres, *at a derelict stile with arrows pointing ahead on the fieldgate posts, turn left* along a permissive path, your direction 200 degrees. After 180 metres *cross over a stile to enter the corner of a wood, where you turn right,*

with the edge of the woods on your right-hand side, your direction 250 degrees.

Ignore all ways off until, in 150 metres, you emerge from the wood to pass a golf course on your left. In 150 metres, and *40 metres before the road, you reach a footpath crosspaths* in a slight dip, marked by a wooden footpath post to the left. Imagining this dip as a roundabout, *take the second left,* your direction 150 degrees.

After 120 metres take care as you exit a small wooded area as there is a golf tee just to your right. Carrying straight on you reach a footpath crosspaths with a blue bridleway arrow on a post pointing ahead. However, *turn right, towards the main road,* your direction 220 degrees. In 50 metres *cross over* the road and continue along the footpath. *In 40 metres, at a footpath junction,* with a golf course in front of you, *turn right,* your direction 290 degrees.

Go straight along this path, which soon enters a wood. In 450 metres *you reach a triangular road junction. Cross over and ignore the public footpath forking immediately right and instead, 5 metres further on, take the signposted bridleway forking right (the Greensand Way),* your direction 270 degrees.

In 225 metres you pass a crosspaths and descend towards a dip. 75 metres further on, at the bottom of this dip, continue straight on across another crosspaths (marked by a wooden post with multiple arrows), following the blue GW arrow, your direction 310 degrees.

After 30 metres, *where the path forks, take the right fork uphill and continue straight on, marked by a GW arrow. Continue straight ahead along the Greensand Way for the next 180 metres to reach a road.* **[A1]**

Cross over the road and continue in the same direction. *In 40 metres fork left,* following a GW arrow on a post, your direction 280 degrees. *After 200 metres cross over a road and continue along the Greensand Way* (also signposted

'Public Bridleway') up a lane, your direction 240 degrees. In 170 metres you pass the entrance to Little St Michael's on your right.

In a further 300 metres, *where the tarmac lane comes to an end, continue straight on*, indicated by a GW arrow on a post, your direction 250 degrees. *In 90 metres fork left following a blue GW arrow.* After 160 metres you come out of the woods to continue straight on along a car-wide shingle track between houses. In 120 metres you reach a road.

Turn right and, in 80 metres, ignore a no through road on your left but immediately after fork left downhill along a signposted bridleway, your direction 310 degrees.

In 250 metres you cross over a drive to continue in the same direction. In 400 metres you *come out to the A25. The onward way is up the alleyway directly across the road.* However, to cross this busy road safely, use the traffic lights 70 metres to the left.

Go up the alleyway, *which leads out into a residential road* after 20 metres. Continue straight ahead *to reach a small green* after 50 metres, then *go to the right of the green down the road to reach, after 120 metres, the main road, where you turn left.*

Go up Station Road East. *In 280 metres turn left* for 40 metres to the Station Road East entrance to Oxted station. For tea go straight through the station subway towards 'Shops and Station Road West'. If taking tea at the alternative **Oxted Inn**, turn left for 30 metres to the Oxted Inn; otherwise, for the preferred tea stop, turn right out onto Station Road West, where you turn left and go down for 40 metres to **Robertson's**.

Lunch & tea places

Carpenters Arms *12 Tally Road, Limpsfield Chart, RH8 0TG (01883 722209).* **Open** 11am-3pm, 5.30-11pm Mon-Fri; 11am-4pm, 5.30-11pm Sat; noon-4pm, 7-10.30pm Sun. **Food served** 11.30am-2pm Mon-Sat; noon-3pm Sun. Located 4km (2.5 miles) from the start of the walk, the Carpenters offers good food at lunchtimes. This is the suggested lunch stop if taking the shorter walk option.

Chartwell Restaurant *Mapleton Road, Westerham, TN16 1PS (01732 863087).* **Open/food served** *Mar-June, Sept-Nov* 10.30am-5pm Wed-Sun. *July, Aug* 10.30am-5pm Tue-Sun. *Dec-Feb* 11am-4pm Wed-Sun. Located 7.5km (4.7 miles) from the start of the walk, the restaurant at Churchill's house serves good food, though you'll have to pay the entrance fee to access it (though ask at the gatehouse: staff don't always insist on payment if you are only visiting the restaurant).

Cock Inn *Ide Hill, Sevenoaks, TN14 6JN (01732 750310).* **Open** 11.30am-2.30pm, 6-11pm Mon-Sat; noon-3pm, 7-10.30pm Sun. **Food served** noon-2pm Mon, Sun; noon-2pm, 6-8.30pm Tue-Sat. This pub is located 13km (8.1 miles) from the start of the walk and is a possibility for a late lunch, though all that's on offer are sandwiches and rolls.

Fox & Hounds *Toys Hill, Westerham, TN16 1QG (01732 750328).* **Open** 11.30am-3pm, 6-11pm Mon-Sat; noon-10.30pm Sun. **Food served** noon-2pm Mon; noon-2pm, 6-9pm Tue-Fri; noon-2.30pm, 6-9.30pm Sat; noon-2.30pm Sun. Situated 11km (6.9 miles) from the start of the walk, this pub serves good enough food and is the suggested lunch stop on the main walk.

Little Brown Jug *Chiddingstone Causeway, Tonbridge, TN11 8JJ (01892 870318/www.thelittlebrownjug.co.uk).* **Open** noon-11pm Mon-Sat; noon-10.30pm Sun. **Food served** noon-3pm, 7-9pm Tue-Sat; noon-5pm Sun. This pub offers tea and coffee. It is the suggested tea stop for the main walk.

Oxted Inn *1-4 Station Road West, Hoskins Walk, Oxted, RH8 9HR (01883 723440).* **Open** 10am-11pm Mon-Sat; 10am-10.30pm Sun. **Food served** 10am-10pm Mon-Sat; 10am-9.30pm Sun. An alternative for those doing the shorter walk.

Robertson's *42 Station Road West, Oxted, RH8 9EU (01883 712777).* **Open** 8.30am-5pm Mon-Sat. Provides coffee, light meals and teas. This is the suggested tea option for those doing the shorter walk ending in Oxted.

Picnic: Recommended spots are between Toys Hill and Ide Hill, and after Ide Hill, looking south towards Bough Beech water.

Snodland to Sole Street

The North Downs and Kent's Weald Way.

Start: Snodland station
Finish: Sole Street station

Length: 13.1km (8.1 miles).

Time: 4 hours. For the whole outing, including trains, sights and meals, allow at least 7 hours.

Transport: To reach Snodland by train from London Charing Cross you'll need either to change at Rochester and again at Strood or change at Maidstone East, walk to Maidstone Barracks station and continue to Snodland from there. There are three trains hourly Monday to Saturday and two hourly on Sundays (journey time: about 1 hour 30 minutes – on Sundays the Maidstone route is around 20 minutes quicker than the Rochester/Strood route). Trains from Sole Street run direct to London Victoria (two per hour Monday to Saturday, one per hour Sunday – journey time: 49-53 minutes).

Trains go from London Charing Cross to Snodland. You will have to change at Strood (on the Gillingham line), and the journey time is 1 hour 11 minutes. Trains back from Sole Street to Victoria run twice an hour. Journey time 57 minutes. Buy a day return to Snodland. (Check on whether a combined Travelcard and train ticket would be your cheapest option.) For those driving, it is recommended that you leave your car at Strood station and catch the train to Snodland. For the return train from Sole Street to Strood change at Rochester.

OS Landranger Map: 178
OS Explorer Map: 148
Snodland, map reference TQ 706618 is in Kent, 7.5km (4.7 miles) north-west of Maidstone.

Toughness: 5 out of 10.

Walk notes: Don't be put off by the rather industrial nature of the train ride to the start of this walk. As soon as you leave Snodland, the landscape becomes rural and peaceful with good views and a surprisingly away-from-it-all feel. The majority of the walk is over the North Downs, mostly through wooded areas and across open fields, and is hilly at times. Some of the paths may be overgrown with nettles in summer, so shorts aren't recommended.

Soon after lunch at Harvel, the views open out before you descend into tranquil Luddesdown, with its historic church and what may be the oldest continually inhabited house in the country. In summer you're likely to encounter Kent's favourite sport, cricket, both on the green behind the lunchtime pub stop (which comes half-way through the walk) and in Luddesdown behind the Victorian school. Real-ale lovers will appreciate the tea stop, the Cock Inn at Luddesdown.

Luddesdown village sign.

Walk options: At the suggested lunch stop in Harvel (point [4]), you could ring for a taxi to Meopham Station (about five miles away), in order to shorten the walk.

Saturday Walkers' Club: Take the train nearest to 10am (before or after) from Charing Cross.

Walk directions

[1] [Numbers refer to the map.]
At **Snodland station** (*see p184* **Paper tiger**), *cross the railway footbridge and descend the left-hand set of steps. Turn right* and follow the red sign to the town centre, your direction 300 degrees. In 70 metres the road bends to the left. After another 50 metres turn right over a bridge across the A288. *Immediately over the bridge turn right along a concrete path* with metal railings on your right. *After 60 metres turn left* just past the Red Lion pub on your left, your direction west.

Go straight along the road, which becomes the High Street. You pass a church then a playing field on your left

and after a while you can see the North Downs ahead in the distance. *After 230 metres you reach a crossroads.*

Turn right along Holborough Road, your direction 20 degrees. *After 70 metres turn left down Lee Road, then in 150 metres turn right down Covey Hall Road. After 120 metres, just before house no.121, turn left down a concrete road between houses and a row of garages*, your direction 290 degrees. (If you reach a small green on the left you have gone too far.) *After 70 metres the road narrows to a path.*

Continue along the path and, after 50 metres, you reach an open space on your left. Keep straight along the right-hand edge of the open space. At the far end continue along a path, now unpaved, slightly to your right. After 300 metres *the path leads out onto a lane. Turn right* and follow the lane, as it becomes a car-wide track. *Follow the path for 1.2km until you reach a large wood* ahead. **[2]**

In more detail: after 50 metres the path swings round to the left, with a cemetery on your left, your direction now 280 degrees. The path goes slightly uphill and past a disused quarry on your right. After 200 metres ignore a path leading off to the left.

After 80 metres the hedgerow on your left gives way to a low bank and open fields. The path enters a tree arbour as you continue uphill, your direction 280 degrees. After 160 metres the trees on your left give way to open fields. The path bends right then left. After 600 metres you reach a crosspaths with a dense wood ahead and double metal fieldgate on your left.

Cross the track and *cross a stile into the wood*, following a yellow arrow on the stile, your direction 310 degrees. Follow the path as it ascends through the wood. After 30 metres cross a car-wide earth track and keep straight on uphill, passing a house on your right.

After 800 metres along this twisty, narrow but well-defined path, *you emerge into a grassy opening. Cross a car-wide earth track 20 metres ahead and, following the dilapidated public footpath sign, keep straight on a diverging car-wide track ahead, going slightly downhill through a wood,* your direction 300 degrees.

In 180 metres, just before a metal fieldgate ahead and a 'Private' sign on a tree, *you reach a crosspaths. Turn left,* following a public footpath sign on a tree on your left, along what may at first be a poorly defined path, your direction 280 degrees. Ignore a fork to the left after 30 metres. Carry on along the path through the wood, steadily ascending. After 400

metres *you come out into a field.* You see two fields ahead. *Go into the left-hand field and walk uphill with the hedge on your right,* your direction 300 degrees.

After 280 metres, at the top of the field, the path levels off. Continue straight ahead along a car-wide track between trees, your direction 280 degrees. In 20 metres cross a tarmac driveway and keep ahead. After 80 metres **[3]** follow the public footpath sign on your right, cross a lane and keep straight ahead along the path across a field following a telegraph wire, your direction 290 degrees.

After 120 metres you pass a mini pylon, where the path begins to descend more steeply. Continue downhill along the path, following the line of the telegraph wire. There is now a wood on your right and an open field on your left. As you reach the edge of the wood keep straight on downhill, ignoring a track off to the right.

In 100 metres the hedge to your right ends. Keep straight on downhill with a hedge now on your left. In 80 metres, at the bottom of the hill, cross a car-wide dirt track. Continue in the same direction slightly uphill along the left-hand edge of the next field following a grassy car-wide track, your direction 280 degrees. Continue until you reach the corner of the field, ignoring the entrance to the field to your left.

After 400 metres, *at the top-left corner of the field, follow the main track left* of a

Paper tiger

Snodland was once proud to boast that it was the largest village in England. In 1988, however, its status changed and it's now just another small town. Founded by the Saxons (Snod himself may be buried on the hill nearby), it wasn't until the 19th century that this fairly insignificant little agricultural settlement hit its stride. The growth of paper and cement-making brought prosperity to Snodland (the current population is around 9,000). The town's most famous landmark is the Snodland Clock Tower, built in 1877 by the Hook sisters in memory of their brother Charles. The Hook family were the owners of the Townsend Hook Papermill that borders the Medway.

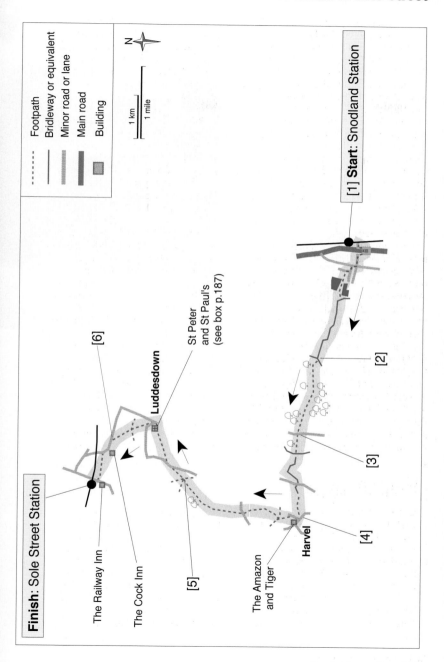

post with a yellow arrow, your direction 250 degrees, under an avenue of trees. In 100 metres the path passes an open field on the left. After 200 metres, *as the path swings round to the right, keep straight ahead past a wooden horse-blocking barrier* and a yellow arrow on the left-hand post. Cross a tarmac road and go through a kissing gate. Keep straight ahead following the yellow arrow, your direction 280 degrees.

After 50 metres, on the far side of the field, cross a wooden stile and a tarmac lane and follow the public bridleway sign ahead, your direction 300 degrees. In 80 metres, just after you pass some metal buildings on the left, the path starts to descend. In 100 metres you pass a yellow post on your right and reach track junctions. Keep straight ahead; you are now going downhill in a wood with a wire fence to your right. Ignore paths off. In 130 metres the path curves between two open fields.

In 30 metres, at the end of the fields, *keep straight on uphill, ignoring a broad path to your left*, your direction 280 degrees. After 50 metres cross a stile taking you into a field. Follow the yellow arrow straight ahead across the field following a path. Aim for a timber-frame house ahead of you to your left, your direction 290 degrees.

After 240 metres *leave the field at double metal fieldgates and a stile and turn left onto a tarmac lane to Harvel.* There is a public bridleway arrow on your right. *In 20 metres fork right diagonally across a grassy open space* (a suitable picnic spot), heading towards the bench on the opposite side, your direction due west. There is a thatched house and oast house on your right.

In 80 metres **[4]**, *when you reach the lane, turn right* following the signpost to Harvel and Meopham. Pass a duck pond on your right. In 180 metres you reach the **Amazon and Tiger** pub, the suggested lunch stop.

After lunch *turn left out of the pub and* backtrack *to the duck pond. Turn left down*

St Peter and Paul, Luddesdown.

Dean Lane, signposted to Luddesdown, with open space on your right, your direction 40 degrees. *In 250 metres*, at a green footpath sign, *cross a stile on your left*. Follow the sign half right across the field, your direction 340 degrees.

In 150 metres, *in the far corner of the field, cross a stile* with a yellow arrow. In 30 metres you come out into a field. Continue downhill on the right-hand edge of the field along a possibly overgrown path, with woodland on your right, your direction due north. In 80 metres, when you reach a wire fence ahead, turn left and follow the fence downhill, your direction 320 degrees.

In 80 metres, *at the bottom of the field, turn right over a stile with three yellow arrows and continue straight on downhill, along the left-hand edge of the next field*, your direction 70 degrees. Keep to the edge of the wood on your left along the top of the field (not the bottom of the valley that develops to its right). After 300 metres, at the corner of the field, cross a stile into the next field, continue with the wood on your left-hand side, your direction north.

Ignore a wide path off into the field on the left. After 180 metres, at the corner of this field, go through a gap between holly and hawthorn trees into the next field. Continue across the upper (left-hand) edge of this field in the same direction, north. After 120 metres cross a stile slightly to your left and *enter a wood. In 150 metres cross a tarmac lane and carry on uphill, following a green byway sign, your initial* direction 340 degrees.

After 100 metres the byway swings round to the left but you turn right following the old stone footpath sign to Luddesdown, your direction 70 degrees. This path soon narrows and may be over-grown in summer. In 120 metres the path plunges into a dense wood. Keep straight ahead along the path, now clearly defined. After 600 metres you *come out alongside a field on the left, with a wooden fence and a house on the hill. Where the fence ends, ignore the path to the left and go right downhill*, your initial direction 60 degrees.

After 140 metres go through a wooden kissing gate into a small field. Keep straight ahead, your direction 40 degrees. After 50 metres go through a wooden gate

back into woodland and keep straight on. After 200 metres ignore a fork off to the right and keep straight ahead, your direction 50 degrees. After 80 metres go through another kissing gate. In 30 metres the track becomes grassy. In 60 metres pass the gates of a house on your left and continue straight along a car-wide track.

After 250 metres, *where the car-wide track swings round to the left, keep straight ahead*, across a stile **[5]** with information about four possible walks on it. You are now in a large field. *Go straight on* in the same direction along a faint path, your direction 40 degrees. Head *towards the right-hand corner of the field*, descending slightly. When you reach the corner of the field cross a possibly concealed stile onto a lane.

Turn left onto the lane. After 140 metres turn right across a stile in a gap in the hedge. *Turn left along the upper left-hand edge of the field.* In 160 metres, about 80 metres before a pylon, cross a wooden stile in the fence on the left. Keep to the right-hand edge of the next field, your direction 60 degrees. In 150 metres cross some metal steps into the next field; you can see Luddesdown church straight-ahead. Keep to the right-hand edge of the field.

Thanks but no tanks

Luddesdown is a remote, peaceful village nestling in a picturesque valley and surrounded by wooded hills and organic farmland. It could have been so different. In 1983 the Ministry of Defence planned to take over 500 acres of prime farmland for year-round training for army minelaying and tactical exercises. A tank was brought into the valley to demonstrate its low noise levels, but this – literally – backfired and, after fierce opposition from local people, the plan was scrapped in 1984.

Luddesdown can trace its origins back to the Iron Age, and with such an ancient heritage it seems appropriate that the modern village lays claim to containing the oldest continually inhabited house in England. Beside the Norman tower of St Peter and Paul church stands Luddesdown Court (not open to the public). It dates from 1100 and incorporates features from Saxon, Norman, Tudor and Jacobean eras. Past residents have included various Earls of Pembroke and Owen Glendower, the 14th-century Welsh national leader.

In 250 metres, *at the far edge of the field, turn left* following a yellow arrow and wire fence, with a wood on your right.

In 60 metres turn right at the wood edge, again following the field edge and a yellow arrow, your direction 70 degrees. After 160 metres *in the corner of the field cross a stile and descend some steps. Turn right along a lane* towards the church. Turn right into the church-yard to visit the church of **St Peter and Paul, Luddesdown**.

Coming out of the main door of the church, note the house behind the wall on your right, **Luddesdown Court** (*see p187* **Thanks but no tanks**). *Go through the small wooden gate ahead and turn left.*

In 30 metres *turn left at the millstone* onto a cobbled road. In 80 metres go through large wooden gates and keep straight on. (You may like to turn right at the footpath sign to look at the village noticeboard, which is targeted at walkers and has information about Luddesdown Organic Farm.)

After 30 metres *turn left at the road fork* with the green space sporting the Luddesdown village sign on your right. *In 30 metres cross the road and go through a kissing gate* following the direction of a yellow arrow. *Keep straight on*, your direction 350 degrees, passing a Victorian school and house on your right. Beyond the school keep on along the field edge following a wooden fence that encircles a cricket pitch.

At the bottom of the dip, where the fence curves, keep on straight uphill, your direction 350 degrees. In 300 metres, at the top edge of the field, after possibly pausing on the bench to catch your breath and enjoy the view, go through the gap in the hedge and, following the direction of the yellow arrow, take the path through an area of undergrowth.

Keep straight ahead through the next field, your direction 330 degrees. Once over the brow of the hill head for the field corner ahead. After 350 metres go through

a small wooden gate and follow the path, which descends through a small wooded area. In 20 metres cross a stile into a field. Keep straight across this field, your direction 340 degrees.

In 120 metres cross a stile **[6]** and *turn left onto a lane* into Henley Street. After 250 metres you come to the **Cock Inn** on your left for refreshments.

Coming out of the pub turn left. In 140 metres turn left down a path between street signs for Henley Street and Gold Street. *In 60 metres cross a fence by a tree into a large field*. Keep straight ahead across this, your direction 300 degrees. *Once a white house becomes visible ahead, aim slightly to the left of it.*

In 600 metres, when you reach the field edge, cross a stile 30 metres to the left of the white house. Go straight along a narrow, enclosed path. After 100 metres go through a kissing gate. Cross the road, the Railway Inn on the left. **Sole Street station** is straight ahead.

Lunch & tea places

Amazon and Tiger *Harvel Street, Harvel Village, nr Meopham, DA13 0DE (01474 814705).* **Open** noon-11pm Mon, Fri-Sun; noon-3pm, 6-11pm Tue-Thur. **Food served** noon-2.30pm Mon-Sat; noon-4pm Sun. The terrace garden at the rear of the pub overlooks the cricket pitch. Groups of more than eight should phone in advance. This is the suggested lunch stop for the walk.

Cock Inn *Henley Street, Luddesdown, DA13 0XB (01474 814208).* **Open** noon-11pm Mon-Sat; noon-10.30pm Sun. **Food served** noon-2.30pm Mon-Sat. Known for its real ales, this pub also serves tea and coffee and has a seafood bar at weekends, serving until 8pm. This is the suggested tea stop for the walk. (Note: allow 15 minutes to walk to Sole Street station from the pub.)

Railway Inn *Sole Street, DA13 0XY (01474 814375).* **Open** 11am-2.30pm, 6.30-11pm daily. This pub beside Sole Street station serves food at lunch and also in the evenings from 6.30pm.

Sole Street Post Office, 50 metres from the Railway Inn, sells drinks and snacks (closed Sunday afternoon).

Wadhurst Circular

The stunning High Weald, Mayfield and Wadhurst Park.

Start and finish: Wadhurst station

Length: 19km (12 miles). For a shorter walk and other variations, *see below* **Walk options**.

Time: 5 hours 50 minutes. For the whole outing including trains, sights and meals, allow 8 hours.

Transport: Two trains an hour (one an hour on Sundays) run from London Charing Cross to Wadhurst (journey time: 1 hour). For those driving, parking in Wadhurst station car park costs £2 a day on weekdays and is free at weekends.

OS Landranger Maps: 188
OS Explorer Map: 136
Wadhurst (station), reference TQ621330 is in East Sussex, 7km (4.4 miles) south-east of Tunbridge Wells.

Toughness: 4 out of 10.

Walk notes: The prime attraction of this walk is the pleasure of strolling through the unspoiled countryside of the High Weald, a region classed as an area of outstanding natural beauty. In August and September the hedgerows are rich with blackberries. The route at the outset follows the Sussex Border Path, but soon diverts south to Tidebrook, and continues south to Mayfield. It is worth spending some time in Mayfield as it has many attractive old buildings, and the 14th-century church is now a grade I-listed building. The route after lunch heads north-east before continuing north to Wadhurst village for tea.

Walk options: Directions for these variations appear at the end of the main walk text. See p200.

a) Shorter walk: You may reduce the length of the main walk by 9km (5.6 miles) to a total of 10km (6.25 miles) by following the main walk directions as given until [3]. Then follow the directions at the end of the main walk text, before picking up the main walk directions at [10].

b) Alternative ending at Stonegate: If you are happy to go without tea, then you may vary the end of this walk and finish at Stonegate. This reduces the length of the main walk by 3km (1.9 miles) to 16km (10 miles). Follow the main walk directions to [7], then follow the directions at the end of the main walk text to link up with the end of the long Stonegate directions (see next walk, walk 19). Buy a return rail ticket to Stonegate if doing this option. You cannot do this ending if you take the shorter walk option above.

Saturday Walkers' Club: Take the train nearest to 9.20am (before or after) from Charing Cross.

Walk directions

[1] [Numbers refer to the map]
Coming off the London train from platform 2 at **Wadhurst station** go through the exit into the station car park. Turn right for 70 metres to leave the car park and cross over the main road. *Turn left down the driveway in front of the closed-down Rock Robin pub* on your right.

After 50 metres *turn right onto an unmarked footpath immediately to the left*

Wads upon a time

Over the last century or so Wadhurst Hall, known as **Wadhurst Park** since 1928, has been home to some of Britain's richest men. The multi-millionaire founder of the Home and Colonial Stores, Julius Drewe, bought the house at the end of the 19th century. He lived here until moving to the eccentric, forbidding Castle Drogo, which Sir Edwin Lutyens built for him on the edge of Dartmoor between 1910 and 1930.

During World War II Wadhurst Park served as a barracks for Canadian soldiers and, later, as a prisoner of war camp, but fell into such a state of disrepair that it was demolished in 1948.

In 1976 the packaging millionaire Hans Rausing (who is a fixture at the top of lists of Britain's wealthiest people) bought the estate and had an unusual single-storey house constructed as his home. He preserved remaining fragments of the old house as features in the extensive gardens, which are today roamed by a herd of deer.

---

of the Rock Robin pub, your direction 70 degrees. *In 40 metres at a path T-junction turn right* to go up the Sussex Border Path, your direction south.

After 100 metres the footpath leads out to a driveway. Go down the driveway to join the main road after 70 metres. *Turn left and after 20 metres cross the main road to take the footpath leading down to the railway*, your direction 160 degrees. After 100 metres cross over the railway and in 30 metres cross over a stile to go up across a field towards a wood, your direction south.

In 120 metres continue straight ahead to enter the wood, indicated by a yellow arrow on a footpath post. After 140 metres cross over a stile as you pass a corrugated metal barn to the left, your direction 220 degrees.

In 40 metres you come out onto car-wide shingle track. Continue straight ahead and after 100 metres you come to *a T-junction with a lane. Turn right here and in 20 metres* [!] *turn left onto an easily missed unmarked footpath*, which after 15 metres straightens out, your direction 220 degrees.

After 200 metres *where the footpath meets a road you turn left*, your direction south. *In 140 metres turn right onto a footpath leading down a shingle lane*,

marked by a yellow arrow on a footpath post, your direction 300 degrees. After 350 metres follow the footpath along the lane as it curves to the left (marked by a yellow footpath arrow on a telegraph pole on the corner), your direction now 200 degrees.

In 160 metres the lane ends and the footpath continues up on a narrow track, marked by a yellow arrow on a post. After 400 metres the narrow path comes out to a car-wide shingle track. Continue up the track, your direction 200 degrees.

In 200 metres *at a junction* **[2]** *turn right along the B2100*, your direction 270 degrees. In 140 metres you pass the entrance to Pennybridge House on your left. After a further 100 metres *turn left following a signpost for Pennybridge Farm*, your direction 140 degrees. Go down a driveway immediately passing the driveway entrance to Three Trees house on your right.

Follow the driveway for 300 metres to reach Pennybridge Farm to go through a wooden gate to the left of a wooden fieldgate, your direction 170 degrees.

In 20 metres you pass three garages on your right and stables to your left. After 40 metres ignore a car-wide entrance on the right and continue along the car-wide track, with a pond to your right, your direction 200 degrees. In 40

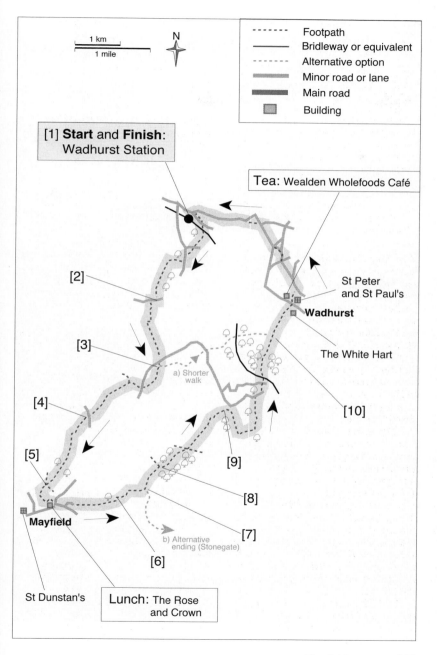

1 km
1 mile

N

- - - - - - Footpath
———— Bridleway or equivalent
- - - - - Alternative option
——— Minor road or lane
——— Main road
☐ Building

[1] **Start** and **Finish**:
Wadhurst Station

Tea: Wealden Wholefoods Café

[2]

St Peter
and St Paul's

Wadhurst

[3]

a) Shorter
walk

The White Hart

[4]

[10]

[5]

[9]

[8]

Mayfield

[7]

[6]

b) Alternative
ending (Stonegate)

St Dunstan's

Lunch: The Rose
and Crown

High Weald woodland.

metres *turn right off the driveway to go through a wooden gate*, your direction 170 degrees.

Go down, along the right-hand edge of a field. After 20 metres *turn right through a double metal fieldgate*, marked by a signpost, to go down a car-wide track, your direction 260 degrees. In 40 metres, at the corner of a fenced-in gully on your left, continue straight ahead up to the gate on the upper side of the field, your direction west. In 90 metres go through the gate and *turn left along a concrete car-wide track between fields*, your direction 160 degrees.

In 220 metres the concrete track becomes an earth track and after a further 50 metres starts to narrow and goes downhill between fields. In 400 metres on reaching a wooden gate follow a yellow footpath arrow pointing half right, your direction 160 degrees. Go down across the field towards a not-too-visible footpath post, 150 metres distant, at the base of a large oak tree, 15 metres to the right of two dead trees. (Ignore the sheep track veering off to the right, direction 180 degrees).

On reaching the footpath post follow the footpath down through a lightly wooded area to cross a stile and a footbridge after 60 metres. Continue up the footpath for 40 metres to then *turn right onto a B road* opposite a house 'Long Meadows', your direction 230 degrees.

In 90 metres *turn left up a driveway that curves to the right*. After 80 metres (and before the wooden fieldgate up ahead) you reach a stile to your left and a stile on your right **[3]**. [If you are intending to take the short walk refer to the **Shorter walk directions** at the end of this main walk text.]

Otherwise, for the main walk, cross the stile on your right and turn left along the top edge of a slope with a wooden fence on your left, your initial direction 210 degrees.

After 60 metres continue straight ahead past a three-armed footpath signpost. In 30 metres *turn left along a fenced-in footpath*, your direction 140 degrees. In 25 metres **[!]** *turn right, indicated by a yellow public footpath arrow, and go through a wooden gate* to come out onto a tarmac driveway, your direction 200 degrees. Ensure that you bolt the gate.

Iron in the soul

You'd never believe it to look at it now, but the attractive village of **Wadhurst** was once at the heart of the thriving Wealden iron-smelting industry. From modest beginnings in the second century AD, the growth of iron-smelting in the area slowly propelled Sussex to the position of England's foremost industrial county by the middle of the 16th century, and made Wadhurst a wealthy, handsome settlement. However, by the 17th century competition from Swedish iron imports led to a gradual decline in the industry, resulting in its eventual extinction at the start of the 19th century.

Today, the ridgetop village, with its many distinguished weatherboarded and tiled houses, has regained its air of prosperity. Its main point of interest is the church of St Peter and St Paul, which dates from the 11th century. The graveyard reflects Wadhurst's industrial past, with its 31 iron tomb slabs (dating from 1617 to 1799), more than can be found at any other church in England. The church has a Norman tower with a pretty needle spire, and the west window in its south aisle was designed by Burne-Jones and made by William Morris.

Go down the driveway passing a house and garden on your left. In 140 metres, as the garden on the left ends, follow the driveway round to the right and down more steeply through a wooded area.

In 100 metres *at a T-junction turn left,* your direction 190 degrees, and *in 10 metres turn right to go through a wooden fieldgate* with a yellow footpath arrow indicating half left. Go diagonally across the field heading 30 metres to the left of the bottom field corner so that you pass 60 metres to the left of a mini pylon pole on the far side of the field, your direction 220 degrees. (After 50 metres you start to reach the brow of the field and a footpath post with a yellow arrow becomes visible.)

In 180 metres continue straight ahead, marked by the yellow arrow on the footpath post, to cross over a stile into the next field, cutting off the corner of this field, your direction 240 degrees. (There is a clear footpath after 50 metres or so.)

After 130 metres at the bottom edge of the field cross over a (partially obscured) stile to go down some steps through a wooded area. In 20 metres *cross a B road and turn left. After 5 metres turn right along a shingle lane,* your direction 290 degrees. In 15 metres you pass a house called 'The Fountain' on your left and cottages on your right.

In 300 metres the shingle lane becomes tarmac; follow it round to the left to *go over a bridge. Continue on the lane as it veers to the left and goes uphill* with a field to your left. After 180 metres you pass the field corner on your left, adjacent to a pylon pole, and continue along the lane as the tarmac ends after 40 metres, your direction 255 degrees.

In 100 metres you pass a converted oast house on your left. In 50 metres you go through a wooden fieldgate to continue along a car-wide grassy path. In 80 metres, having passed some farm buildings on your right, you go through another wooden fieldgate. Continue on the track down through a wooded area to cross a small stream after 90 metres.

Continue up an earth car-wide track, your direction 220 degrees.

After 60 metres you go through a fieldgate entrance to turn half left, marked by a yellow footpath arrow. Head up across the field towards the right of the gap between the trees, your direction 200 degrees, aiming for a stile (which only becomes visible once you are over the brow of the field). In 160 metres go over the stile. In 10 metres veer right at the arable edge of the field.

Continue up along the top right-hand edge of the field, your direction 220 degrees. In 220 metres at the right-hand field corner cross a stile to enter a wood, and continue along the right-hand edge of the wood. After 130 metres, having come out of the wood, you pass through some distinctive white brick gateposts (entrance to Harewood Lodge) and reach a road **[4]**. Cross the road and then a stile into parkland.

Go straight downhill, heading towards the gap between the fencing on your right and the trees on your left, your direction 240 degrees. After 300 metres at the bottom you go through a dilapidated wooden kissing gate and then after 15 metres cross a dilapidated stile to then go over a small stream. In 25 metres you pass through a wooden gate to come out into a field.

Turn left to go down the bottom left-hand edge of the field, your direction 220 degrees. In 220 metres, on reaching the bottom field corner, continue along the footpath to cross a stream and enter a lightly wooded area. After 25 metres *cross over a stile to the left,* your direction 190 degrees. *In 50 metres* at a footpath signpost *turn right,* marked by a yellow footpath arrow, your direction west.

After 15 metres you cross a plank footbridge to turn right, your initial direction 330 degrees. Go up following footpath posts and signposts for the next 80 metres (including a sharp left turn) to cross over a dilapidated stile into a field. Go along the bottom edge of the field, with a wood to your left, your direction 190 degrees.

After 220 metres at the corner of the field go through a squeeze stile. In 40 metres, at the corner of the wood on your left, veer slightly to the right along a well-defined footpath across the field, your direction 200 degrees.

In 200 metres go through a gap in the hedgerow into the next field to continue down in the same direction. After 250 metres, having crossed the field, go through a small wooden gate to descend more steeply with woods to your right.

After 120 metres *cross a dilapidated piece of wooden fence (once a stile) to enter a wood and turn left to cross a concrete footbridge.* Go uphill for 30 metres and *where the footpath forks, marked by a wooden footpath post, fork right,* your initial direction 230 degrees. *After 40 metres fork left at an unmarked footpath fork* to continue uphill, your direction 190 degrees. In 110 metres go over a stile to emerge from the wood into a field.

Continue straight ahead along the bottom left-hand edge of the field, your direction 230 degrees. In 180 metres cross a stile into the next field and continue up the bottom left-hand side of this field along a shrubbery alleyway.

After 180 metres cross a stile and continue uphill in the same direction along the left-hand side of the field towards a four-armed wooden footpath signpost with a yellow painted top, 180 metres ahead. On reaching the four-armed footpath signpost **[5]** continue along a car-wide track. In 70 metres cross a stile to go along the top left-hand edge of a field, your direction 220 degrees.

In 140 metres *cross a stile at the top corner of the field and then cross a car-wide track to go up some steps* and continue along with a football pitch on your left-hand side, your direction 200 degrees. In 100 metres *you reach Mayfield Jubilee Skateboard Facility on your right.* At the corner of the football pitch *turn left,* your direction 130 degrees, to continue between the football pitch

on your left and a basketball court 30 metres up to your right.

After 110 metres at the end of the football pitch you start going downhill *to reach the bottom corner of the parkland area.* After 140 metres *turn left* onto a tarmac footpath to go along an alleyway, your direction 70 degrees. In 140 metres you come out to a shingle driveway. You are now in **Mayfield**. *Turn right* down the pavement for 25 metres to a *T-junction where you turn right* to reach the **Rose & Crown**, the lunchtime stop.

(To visit the church of **St Dunstan**, a detour of a few minutes: from the front of the Rose & Crown turn right up Fletching Street. The church is 500 metres further up on the right.)

After lunch walk to the *bottom of the small green and turn left* along East Street, your direction east. In 200 metres *turn left up Southmead Close.* Follow the road round to the right and *after 220 metres, just past house number 18, turn left,* along a car-wide track, your direction 30 degrees. *After 30 metres fork right* along the footpath marked by a wooden footpath post, your direction east.

In 70 metres you come out to a field to continue in the same direction. In 200 metres go over a stile to enter a small wooded area between fields. In 15 metres cross over a stile (ignore a stile immediately to your right) and continue in the same direction east along the upper right-hand edge of the field. After 220 metres you pass under some mini-pylon cables. After a further 30 metres you cut off the corner of the field and then continue down the right-hand edge of the field.

After 100 metres, at the bottom corner of the field, you *enter Hole Wood and go down the right-hand edge of the wood,* your direction 50 degrees. In 30 metres ignore an unmarked footpath forking off to the left to continue along the right edge of the wood.

[6] *After 140 metres you reach a staggered footpath crosspaths marked by*

a four-armed footpath signpost on the right. Turn right and after 5 metres turn left, your initial direction 40 degrees, to continue down the footpath. In 50 metres the footpath curves to the right with a stream to your left.

After 120 metres *cross over a footbridge and continue up ahead,* passing a small South East Water brick building on the left after 40 metres, your direction 60 degrees. In 20 metres go over a stile and continue up a concrete car-wide track along the left-hand side of a field, your direction 40 degrees.

After 180 metres *at the top corner of the field cross a stile and turn right* onto a concrete car-wide track, your direction 110 degrees. In 70 metres at a path junction marked by a wooden signpost on your right with just two arms (the arm pointing ahead is missing) continue straight ahead down the car-wide track.

After 200 metres you pass a derelict barn on your right. In 50 metres *follow a blue bridleway arrow on a post at the corner of a small brick building on your left.* After 10 metres you pass a stone building on your left with a wooden bridleway indicator plus horseshoe pointing ahead, your direction 80 degrees.

[7] In 50 metres you *reach a path T-junction.*

[If you are intending to finish the walk at Stonegate refer to the directions at the end of this main walk text under **Alternative ending at Stonegate**.]

Otherwise, *to finish the walk at Wadhurst, turn left,* as marked by a yellow footpath arrow, to go up a car-wide track, your direction 30 degrees.

After 60 metres cross over a stile to continue along the left-hand edge of a narrow field. In 250 metres cross another stile to go up across this long narrow field towards a stile in the top corner (which becomes visible after 100 metres), your direction 40 degrees. 300 metres further on *you cross over the stile to enter a lightly*

The town of **Mayfield**.

wooded area, and then cross another stile after 15 metres to arrive at a footpath junction marked by a three-armed footpath signpost. **[8]**

Veer to the right, uphill along the left-hand edge of the wood, your direction 110 degrees. In 40 metres, by a white footpath sign on a tree trunk to the left and a two-armed footpath signpost to the right, turn half left across a field initially between fenced-in nursery trees (the path is marked by occasional white footpath signs), your direction 70 degrees.

After 140 metres you cross a stile to the left of a metal fieldgate to enter Combe Wood to go down a wide track, your direction 40 degrees. In 600 metres, at the bottom of Combe Wood, cross a stile to veer slightly right following a footpath signpost, your direction 70 degrees. In 90 metres step over an 80 centimetre-high wire fence (between two yellow taped posts; stile requested). In 5 metres you cross a footbridge. (Note that steps up

are missing; the bridge is best tackled from the left using the trunk as a step and passing under the footbridge rail.)

Go uphill through a wooded footpath field separator, your direction 20 degrees. In 120 metres you cross a stile to reach a crosspaths and cross over the stile ahead. Continue up in the same direction along the wooded footpath field separator, crossing two more stiles along the way. After 350 metres you pass a mini pylon pole with a yellow footpath arrow pointing ahead and come out to a lane. Continue up the lane, your direction 40 degrees.

After 200 metres you pass Lodge Hill farm, a creosote clapboard building, on your right. In 550 metres, at a lane junction **[9]** marked by a footpath post on the left, turn right to pass Octagon Lodge on your right, your initial direction 140 degrees.

In 10 metres the tarmac car-wide track becomes sand shingle. Follow the car-wide track round to the left passing through two brick gateposts after 50 metres; the track now becomes earth.

After 500 metres *at a T-junction turn left*, your direction 30 degrees. *In 80 metres at another T-junction continue straight across to go through a 2 metre-high (deer protective) kissing gate* to enter **Wadhurst Park** (*see p190* **Wads upon a time**). *Go down the right upper edge of Wadhurst Park*, your direction 70 degrees. (You may well see deer in the Park; they are very nervous and easily disturbed.)

After 300 metres, *by a three-armed footpath signpost, turn left down a car-wide earth track*, your direction north. After 120 metres you cross a stream to continue uphill through a wooded area, your direction 340 degrees. In 140 metres you emerge from the wooded area to follow a yellow arrow on a footpath post across a field, heading towards a gap in the trees in the corner of the field, your direction 10 degrees.

In 250 metres, when you reach the corner of the wood on your left, go into the next field (there is no hedge at this point) and continue in the same direction down the left-hand edge of the field, with the wood on your left.

After 120 metres at the bottom of the field you pass through missing 2 metre-high fieldgates to the right of a 2 metre-high kissing gate to go up the left-hand edge of the field. In 100 metres, *at the top corner of the field, go through a 2 metre-high kissing gate to go along a car-wide track*, passing a pond on your left after 30 metres, your direction 20 degrees.

In 80 metres you go through a wooden gate to the left of a metal fieldgate to *come out to a driveway. Turn left* along it, your direction 340 degrees, and follow it downhill.

After 100 metres *at a T-junction turn right down the lane*, your direction 60 degrees. In 150 metres **[!]** *turn left into a driveway* along a public footpath indicated by a concrete public footpath marker on the left bank of the driveway entrance, your direction 340 degrees.

In 15 metres you pass a house on the right to continue straight ahead and *cross a footbridge* after 30 metres. Continue uphill and cross a stile after 20 metres to go up a narrow footpath, your direction 350 degrees.

In 60 metres *go up some steps to cross a lane* and continue up the footpath, your direction 10 degrees. After 80 metres you climb over a stile to *cross the railway line* and then cross another stile. *In 8 metres continue straight across an unmarked crosspaths.* **[!]** *Then in 15 metres follow the footpath forking up off to the left through woods*, marked by a yellow arrow on a footpath post, your direction 350 degrees.

In 110 metres ignore an unmarked footpath turning to the left to continue uphill in the same direction north. In 60 metres the path levels out and shortly after the path descends. After 350 metres *go over a crosspaths* (shingle car-wide track) marked by a footpath post, and after 40 metres *cross a plank footbridge to then cross a stile* and go along the top left edge of the field, your direction 20 degrees.

In 150 metres, on reaching the top field corner, cross a stile to go through a lightly wooded area. After 40 metres cross over a stile to go up the right edge of a small field, your direction 10 degrees. After 50 metres at the top corner of this small field cross a stile to continue along the right-hand edge of the adjacent field, your direction 20 degrees. Directly ahead of you, about 1km in the distance, you can see the spire of St Peter and St Paul, which we will be passing later.

Follow the right-hand edge of the field round as it curves slightly to the left. After 180 metres, on reaching the field corner, continue on a short path through blackberry bushes and after 10 metres *cross over a stile onto a lane. Cross the lane and the stile immediately opposite you* (ignoring two stiles to your left) to

Devil in disguise

Mayfield is a delightful village of Saxon origin situated at the end of an almost detached ridge above the headwaters of the River Rother. Along with other settlements in the area, such as Wadhurst (*see p193* **Iron in the soul**), Mayfield prospered in medieval times thanks to the thriving Wealden iron industry. Its High Street, with its raised red-brick pavements, is lined by attractive old buildings.

Set back from the street is the church of St Dunstan, which was destroyed and rebuilt (along with most of the village) after a fire in 1389 (look out for two cast-iron tomb slabs within the church). The Dunstan in question served as Archbishop of Canterbury between 960 and 988, and founded Mayfield Palace, one of the great

residences of the medieval archbishops of Canterbury. The building survives today as a Roman Catholic boarding school.

St Dunstan is primarily famous in these parts, however, for his part in a often-declaimed legend. The saint was formerly a blacksmith and was casting a horseshoe one day when a beautiful woman approached him at his forge. The wily saint spotted a cloven hoof protruding from under her dress, and, realising that this was the Devil come in disguise to tempt him, he grabbed Beelzebub's nose with his red-hot pincers, causing the evil one to make a mighty leap to Tunbridge Wells to bathe his nose in a stream. Thereafter, the devil vowed never to enter any building with a horseshoe over the door.

reach the corner of a field. **[10]** Head across the field towards Wadhurst, your direction 20 degrees.

Having walked 300 metres over the field, cross over a stile to the right of a wooden fieldgate and *turn left to go up Washwell Lane.*

After 450 metres you pass Courthope Avenue on your left to continue uphill into **Wadhurst** (*see p193* **Iron in the soul**) to arrive after 180 metres at the T-junction with the High Street, with the **White Hart** on the right-hand corner. This is the recommended lunch stop for the short walk and the alternative tea place for the main walk. (If you are pressed for time, turn left here along the B road for the 2km/1.25 mile direct route back to Wadhurst station.)

From the White Hart *cross over the High Street and turn left. In 10 metres you arrive at Church Street on your right.* For the recommended tea place for the

main walk continue ahead to reach the **Wealden Wholefoods Gallery Café** on the right after 30 metres. Otherwise *turn right onto Church Street.* In 50 metres *turn left along the brick path into the churchyard of* **St Peter and St Paul**.

After visiting the church *turn right out of its entrance to go round the church on the brick footpath* along the building's west side, your direction north. In 60 metres go through a metal kissing gate and continue along an earth footpath with the graveyard on your right.

After 250 metres you pass through a squeeze stile and follow the footpath downhill. In 170 metres *you pass a wooden bench on your left to go down some steps and turn left down a lane,* your direction 310 degrees.

After 150 metres *cross Pell Bridge and soon after, where the lane forks, take the left fork uphill,* your direction 320 degrees. *In 400 metres you reach a crossroads.*

Cross the B road to go up Turners Green Road. In 150 metres *follow Turners Green Road as it forks left*, your direction 310 degrees, and after 70 metres *go over the crossroads at Turners Green to continue along Turners Green Road*.

In 180 metres, *as a lane comes in from the right, turn left to cross a stile*, heading towards the left side of a house on the far side of the field, your direction west.

After 200 metres, having crossed the field, cross over a stile to go down the right-hand edge of the field and skirt round the garden of the house to your right. In 120 metres you go through a metal fieldgate to come out onto a lane. *Turn left down the lane*, your direction 240 degrees. After 180 metres *turn right at a T-junction*, your direction 310 degrees.

After 250 metres ignore a public footpath off to your right; after a further 400 metres down the lane you pass by a driveway on the right leading up to Quarry Cottages to then pass a fieldgate entrance to a small car parking area.

A further 20 metres on the left, ignore a public footpath leading up through the driveway entrance to Briers (marked by a concrete public footpath marker on the left bank) and continue down the lane. **[!]** In 140 metres *turn left onto a footpath marked by a concrete public footpath marker, and cross a plank bridge to go up some steps to join the Sussex Border Path*, your direction 220 degrees.

In 30 metres you reach the summit and continue downhill for 60 metres to *reach a path T-junction to turn left*, your direction south. *After 40 metres turn right* along an unmarked footpath, your direction 260 degrees, to emerge by the Rock Robin opposite Wadhurst station.

Walk options

a) Shorter walk:
Follow the main walk directions to [3].

Turn left off the driveway up towards a stile, your direction east. After 5 metres cross over the stile built into a wooden

fence with a yellow arrow on the top bar of the fence. Cross a small field heading up towards the corner of the field, your direction east. After 70 metres pass through a metal fieldgate to head diagonally up across the field towards the upper left corner, your direction 80 degrees.

In 200 metres on reaching the corner of the field go through a metal fieldgate. After 15 metres *go through a metal gate to follow a yellow footpath arrow up across the field towards a stile (initially hidden by the brow of the field) 100 metres to the right of the left field corner*, your direction 120 degrees.

After 150 metres *cross the stile and turn left* along the left-hand edge of the field, your direction 50 degrees. After 100 metres at the corner of the left adjacent field meeting the corner of a wood, *cross a stile and turn right onto a car-wide earth track*. Follow the track, passing the wood on your left.

In 300 metres go over a stile to the left of a double metal fieldgate to *cross a lane*. Cross over a stile to the right of a metal fieldgate and follow the yellow footpath arrow down a car-wide track along the left edge of the field, your initial direction 60 degrees.

After 300 metres, at the bottom left-hand corner of the field, cross a stile to the right of a metal fieldgate to continue down the left-hand edge of the next field. After 200 metres, at the left-hand corner of the field, cross a stile. Continue down the left edge of this small field, your direction 50 degrees. After 100 metres, *at the bottom corner of the field, pass round to the left of a redundant stile to enter some woods*.

In 35 metres cross over a two-plank footbridge to immediately cross a stile and turn left up some steps that bring you out to the railway line after 40 metres. *Cross the railway line with care to go up some steps for 10 metres and then cross a stile and go up a footpath through the woods*.

After 250 metres *at a path junction turn left*, indicated by a yellow footpath arrow on a footpath post to your right, your direction 20 degrees. After 15 metres you pass another footpath post on your right. Follow the arrow *to reach a path T-junction* after a few metres. *Turn left*, as marked by a footpath arrow on a post directly ahead, *to go up a car-wide earth track with a densely wooded area on your right and a sparsely wooded area to your left*, your initial direction north. The track curves to the right.

In 220 metres the footpath forks, marked by a footpath post at a junction. *Take the left fork*, your initial direction 10 degrees. *After 120 metres turn half left*, indicated by a yellow footpath arrow on a post. *In 15 metres go over a stile to emerge from the woods. Turn right* along the right-hand edge of a field, your direction east. In 120 metres, at the right-hand field corner, cross a stile and continue down in the same direction along a footpath along the right fenced-in edge of the field with trees to your right.

In 400 metres you reach a wooden stile with two yellow arrows on the top bar. *Cross over the stile and cross over another stile immediately on your left to reach the corner of a field.*

To continue the walk, refer to the main walk directions from [10].

b) Alternative ending at Stonegate:
Follow the main walk directions to [7].

Turn right along the path marked by a bridleway arrow, your direction 190 degrees. In 280 metres you pass a large wooden post on your left with a bridleway arrow to enter a lightly wooded area. After 50 metres the path forks. Fork left down a sunken bridleway, following an arrow on a post at the fork junction, your initial direction 150 degrees. (In muddy conditions you may prefer to fork right along the parallel path.)

In 70 metres both paths link up. Continue down through the lightly wooded area. After 30 metres go through some fieldgate posts. In 30 metres you *pass a footbridge on your right and veer left to cross a stile after 7 metres into a field.*

Continue along a footpath through the narrow field, your direction 120 degrees. After 250 metres cross over into the next field, with a stream immediately to your right, towards a stile to the left of a metal fieldgate. In 120 metres go over the stile. After 30 metres *cross a car-wide bridge over the stream* and pass a concrete three-car garage on your left, your direction 130 degrees. *After 30 metres you reach a two-armed footpath post. Continue straight ahead*, your direction 120 degrees.

In 300 metres cross over into the next field and *turn left to follow the left arm of a two-armed footpath signpost*, your direction 30 degrees. After 50 metres you *reach a path junction marked by a three-armed footpath signpost.*

You now follow the Stonegate long walk directions from [7]. (For details, *see* **Walk 19**.)

Lunch & tea places

Rose & Crown *Fletching Street, Mayfield, TN20 6TE (01435 872200).* **Open** 11am-11pm Mon-Sat; noon-10.30pm Sun. **Food served** noon-2.30pm, 6-9pm daily. 8km (5 miles) from the start of the walk, this pub serves inventive food. (No bar snacks on Sundays.) This is the suggested lunch stop for the main walk.

Wealden Wholefoods Gallery Café *High Street, Wadhurst, TN5 6AA (01892 783065/www.wealdenwhole foods.co.uk).* **Open** 9am-5.15pm Mon-Sat. **Food served** 9.30am-4.45pm Mon-Sat. Just along the road from the White Hart, this café is the suggested tea place for the main walk.

White Hart *High Street, Wadhurst, TN5 6AP (01892 782878).* **Open** 11am-11pm Mon-Sat; noon-10.30pm Sun. **Food served** noon-2pm Mon-Fri; noon-2.30pm Sat, Sun. Located 7km (4.4 miles) from the start of the walk, the White Hart has decent pub food and is the suggested lunch stop for the shorter walk option. It also serves tea and coffee.

For options in Stonegate (if doing the alternative ending), *see p217* **Walk 19: Lunch & tea places**.

Stonegate Circular

The peaceful Burwash Weald and Kipling's retreat.

Start and finish: Stonegate station

Length: 15.5km (9.7 miles). For a shorter walk and other variations, *see below* **Walk options**.

Time: 4 hours 45 minutes. For the whole outing, including trains, sights and meals, allow 9 hours 15 minutes.

Transport: Trains between London Charing Cross and Stonegate run hourly (journey time: 1 hour 10 minutes; 15 minutes longer on Sundays). For those driving, Stonegate station car park costs £2 a day on weekdays, but is free at weekends.

OS Landranger Map: 199
OS Explorer Map: 136 and 124 (for part of the long walk). Stonegate station, reference TQ659272, is in East Sussex, 14km (8.75 miles) south-east of Tunbridge Wells.

Toughness: 3 out of 10.

Walk notes: This walk is a good introduction to the Sussex Weald, an area that isn't well known to most walkers; its relative quietness is one of its attractions. Passing over gentle hills and into tranquil valleys, through classic English wood- and pastureland, the Weald's attractions include the unspoiled village of Burwash for lunch, and Bateman's, the one-time rural retreat of Rudyard Kipling. In summer, one stretch before lunch through Upper Collingtons Wood can become quite overgrown with nettles and brambles, so wear long trousers and select a suitable stick on entering the wood. For those venturing on the long walk section after lunch at Burwash Common, this could with some justification be described as a wilderness walk.

Walk options: Directions for the following options are given at the end of the main walk text (*see p208*).

a) Shorter walk: You may reduce the length of the walk by over 5km (3 miles) to 10km (6.25 miles) by following the main route directions given until [5]. Then follow the shortened route directions at the end of the main text, before picking up the main route directions at [8].

b) Longer walk: You may increase the length of the walk by 14km (8.75 miles) to 29.5km (18.4 miles) by following the main route directions given until [6]. Then follow the lengthened route directions at the end of the main text, before picking up the main route directions at [9].

c) Alternative ending at Wadhurst (Longer walk): You may also vary the end of the longer walk and finish in Wadhurst for tea. This increases the length of the long walk by 3km (1.9 miles) to 32.5km (20.3 miles). Follow the longer walk directions to [B5], then follow the alternative ending directions at the end of the main text, before linking up with the main Wadhurst directions at [8] (the previous walk, walk 18).

Alternatively, to shorten the main walk you can catch the 318 bus (hourly until 6pm Mon-Fri, every other hour until 4pm Sat) from Burwash High Street to

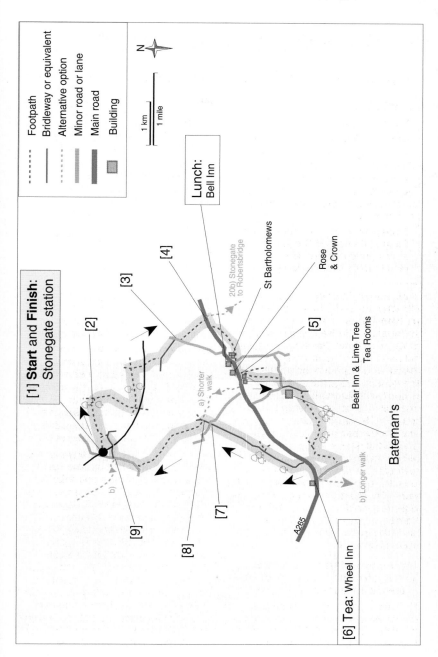

[1] **Start** and **Finish**: Stonegate station

[2]

[3]

[4]

Lunch: Bell Inn

20b) Stonegate to Robertsbridge

St Bartholomews

Rose & Crown

[5]

Bear Inn & Lime Tree Tea Rooms

Bateman's

a) Shorter walk

b)

[9]

[7]

[8]

b) Longer walk

A265

[6] Tea: Wheel Inn

N

1 km
1 mile

Footpath
Bridleway or equivalent
Alternative option
Minor road or lane
Main road
Building

Etchingham station (one stop down the line from Stonegate). For information, phone 0870 608 2608. Note: buy a return rail ticket to Etchingham.

Saturday Walkers' Club: Take the train nearest to 10.15am (before or after) from Charing Cross.

Walk directions

[1] [Numbers refer to the map]
Coming off the London train from platform 2 at **Stonegate station** go through the exit into the station car park and *turn half right up a car-wide concrete track between fences*, your direction 85 degrees. In 150 metres the track surface becomes shingle. After 45 metres go through a metal fieldgate with a house directly ahead.

In 35 metres the track curves to the right with a pond on your right. After 45 metres *turn left up a car-wide shingle track*, passing through a metal fieldgate, your direction 30 degrees. In 200 metres you reach two metal fieldgates. Go through the fieldgate on your right into a field and go diagonally across the field, aiming for a metal fieldgate to the left of a border of trees, your direction 70 degrees.

In 280 metres go through the metal fieldgate and continue in the same direction diagonally across the next field. After 200 metres go over a stile 20 metres east of the bottom corner of the field to enter a wood. Follow the footpath down through the wood. In 100 metres cross a plank footbridge and continue up the footpath. In 60 metres you *emerge from the wood into a field*. **[2]**

Turn right along the lower right-hand edge of the field, your initial direction south. In 80 metres, at the field corner, follow the edge of the field round and up to the left, your direction 100 degrees. In 80 metres, at a footpath signpost, *turn right through a lightly wooded area between ponds*, your direction 200 degrees.

In 50 metres, *on emerging from the lightly wooded area, turn left* to go along the left-hand edge of a field, your direction 120 degrees. In 50 metres you reach a wooden footpath post on your right at the border to the next field.

Burwash village, the best place to stop for lunch.

Follow the footpath signpost half right, diagonally down across this next field, following a faint path, your direction 170 degrees. After 220 metres, in the corner of the field, go over a shallow ditch and *turn right onto a car-wide shingle track,* your direction 220 degrees.

In 500 metres, with an oast-house just ahead of you, go through a wooden fieldgate to reach a footpath signpost 15 metres further on. Follow the direction of the signpost half left. The path curves round to the right passing a pond (which is often dried up in summer) on your right, followed by a derelict house on your left. Continue down with a hedge and trees on your right, your direction now 210 degrees. After 100 metres *cross over a ditch. In a further 12 metres turn left* (ignoring a footpath ahead that leads to the railway), your initial direction 120 degrees.

After 50 metres you pass the decorative stone windows of a ruined church 20 metres to your left. In 50 metres you enter a small wood and in a further 50 metres emerge into a field. Continue up the right-hand edge of the field. In 80 metres follow the field corner round and up to the left, your direction 35 degrees. [!] In 120 metres *turn right onto an easy-to-miss unmarked footpath into Upper Collingtons Wood,* your initial direction 150 degrees.

Follow this footpath as it meanders through the wood. In 140 metres go over a stile; there is now a fence on the left of the path. In 130 metres, at the end of the fence, fork right, as indicated by a yellow footpath arrow on a tree ahead, your initial direction 100 degrees.

After 140 metres you emerge into a small opening to continue in an easterly direction. In 50 metres you cross a stream (often dried up in summer). The path curves to the right between blackberry bushes up a gentle incline. In 150 metres you reach the top of the gentle incline and cross a stile into a field.

Continue along the top left-hand edge of the field, your direction east. In 100 metres, at the field corner, *ignore a stile* to the left and walk down to the right for 20 metres. Go through a metal fieldgate to cross into the next field, then turn right to go down the right-hand edge of the field, your direction south.

After 150 metres cross over into the next field and continue down its right-hand edge. In 60 metres, at the corner of the field, follow the path along the edge of the field to the left. In 35 metres turn right and *cross the railway line,* which is flanked by two stiles. Once across, *veer left diagonally across the field ahead of you,* aiming for a gap in the left-hand field boundary hedgerow some 280 metres distant, your direction 140 degrees.

On reaching the hedgerow gap, *cross into the next field and turn right.* Continue along the edge of this field, with the hedgerow on your right, your direction south. After 50 metres cross into the next field and continue in the same direction, this time along the left-hand edge of the field. There is a stream on the left.

In 70 metres *turn left to cross a bridge flanked by two gates. Turn half right* across the next field, in the direction shown by a blue bridleway arrow on the second gate, your direction 130 degrees. Aim for a metal fieldgate with a bridleway signpost next to it. In 140 metres go through the fieldgate and continue diagonally up across the next field, heading towards the top left-hand corner to the left of some farm buildings, your direction 130 degrees.

After 200 metres, at the top of the field, go over a stile to the left of a metal fieldgate and bridleway post. Continue up a farmyard track, passing a pond on your right. In 60 metres go through a fieldgate and on past a bungalow on your left. In 50 metres *go through a wooden gate and turn right onto a road* [3].

In 120 metres *take the footpath on the left-hand side of the road, crossing a stile to the right of a metal fieldgate.* In 10 metres follow the fenced-in footpath as it turns left away from the road gently downhill between two fields. In 200 metres the path curves to the right through a lightly wooded area. Carry on over a footbridge and a stile. In 30 metres you emerge from the lightly wooded area; continue straight ahead up through a field, your direction 140 degrees. In 200 metres, as the field gets narrower, continue on the left-hand side of the field.

In 200 metres, at the top left-hand corner of the field, *cross a stile to the right of a metal fieldgate onto a road* (the A265). **[4]** (Note: To exit via the metal fieldgate at the top right-hand corner of the field would slightly shorten the subsequent walk along the A265 by 100 metres, but this route is not the legal right of way).

Turn right along the road. After 100 metres you pass a metal fieldgate on your right. In 70 metres you pass the entrance to a house called Capstone on your left, and 20 metres further on your left there is a gate marked Little Totts. After another 15 metres *turn left to cross the road and head through some stone brick gateposts*, the entrance to Glebe Farm.

After 25 metres ignore a car-wide track forking off to the right leading to a metal fieldgate. After a further 10 metres *turn right to go over a stile to the right of a metal fieldgate* into a field. Head along the top of the field along the line of a ridge with a fence on your right, your direction 210 degrees.

In 300 metres you pass a corrugated metal barn on your right. Carry on into the next field in the same direction. After 150 metres go through a wooden kissing gate. In a further 100 metres go through a wooden gate into the churchyard of the church of **St Bartholomew, Burwash**.

Go through the churchyard past the church entrance and leave through the main churchyard entrance gate onto the High Street. The suggested lunch stop, the **Bell Inn**, is directly opposite across the High Street.

From the Bell Inn, cross over the road again and turn right along the pavement. (Or if you visit the church, come out of the main churchyard entrance, opposite the Bell Inn, and turn left along the High Street), your direction west.

In 140 metres you pass the Burwash Map on your left and then, 25 metres further on, the **Rose and Crown** pub sign on your right with the Rose and Crown 30 metres off to the right. In 60 metres you reach a public footpath sign on your left (immediately after a terrace of cottages Nos.1-5 and *just before the* **Lime Tree Tea Rooms**) **[5]**.

[If you are intending to take the **Shorter walk** option, follow the directions given at the end of this main walk text.]

Otherwise, for the main walk, *turn left down this footpath*. In 60 metres go over a stile and *turn half right diagonally down across a field*, your direction 210 degrees.

In 200 metres cross a wooden plank bridge and go over a stile into the next field. Continue down in the same direction. In 150 metres cross another wooden plank bridge flanked by two stiles, and continue in the same direction, now with a hedgerow on your right. In 160 metres cross a stile to continue gently downhill in the same direction, diagonally across a field with clumps of trees on your left and a partly fenced-off group of trees to your right.

After 250 metres, and *100 metres further on from the clumps of trees on your right, go through a fieldgate entrance* passing a redundant stile on your right. *Turn left downhill* with a hedgerow and stream on your left, your direction due south. After 180 metres cross over a stile and *turn right onto a lane*, heading towards **Bateman's** (*see p209* **Mr Kipling's sanctuary**), which you reach after 240 metres.

If you wish to visit Bateman's turn right for 80 metres to the entrance gate on the left. Otherwise, at the lane junction in front of Bateman's, *turn left* and follow the lane as it curves to the right. After 140 metres cross over a stream. In 200 metres you reach Corner Cottage on your right. *Turn right immediately after Corner Cottage*, marked by a wooden footpath signpost with a waymark arrow to the right.

After 20 metres you reach a pond. *Follow the footpath round to the right of the pond* to then pass a bench and a wooden slat bridge on your left, then a bench on the right. Follow the path, with a stream on your left, your direction 260 degrees. In 160 metres go over a stream and through a gate, now with a larger stream on your right. After 70 metres ignore a bridge on the right to continue on the path.

In 120 metres go through a wooden kissing gate into a field. Follow the path through the field, your direction 250 degrees. Ignore an old farmyard crossing after 25 metres on your left. After 200 metres *turn left through a metal fieldgate to cross a car-wide plank bridge over a stream into the next field. Turn right* and continue in the same westerly direction with a hedge on your right.

In 150 metres go through a metal fieldgate into the next field. Continue straight ahead, following the westerly arm of a three-armed footpath signpost. In 130 metres *turn right through a metal fieldgate next to a three-armed footpath signpost, and cross a car-wide bridge back over the stream. Turn left and follow the left-hand edge of the field.* In 100 metres go through a wooden kissing gate and follow the footpath up through Bog Wood.

In 300 metres go through a wooden kissing gate to emerge from the wood, into a field. Continue up the right-hand side of the field, your direction 290 degrees. In 260 metres, at the top right-hand corner of the field, follow the field edge round to the left and continue along the upper right-hand field border, your direction 230 degrees.

In 120 metres, *at the top left-hand corner of the field*, go through a wooden kissing gate to the right of a metal fieldgate. *Turn half right*, your direction 290 degrees. *In 50 metres* go through another wooden kissing gate to the left of a wooden and metal fieldgate. *Turn left and follow the path diagonally across the field, aiming for the upper corner of the field*, your direction 200 degrees.

In 150 metres go through a metal gate into the next field. Go diagonally across this field, your direction still 200 degrees. (There is still a faint path.) In 80 metres you pass the corner of a field on your left. Continue downhill aiming to pass 30 metres to the right of a large sycamore tree in the middle of the field; then after 140 metres go through a wooden kissing gate into the next field.

Go along the top right-hand side of the next field, your direction 230 degrees. In 120 metres, at the field corner, *go through a wooden kissing gate and turn right onto a lane.* Go up the lane for 450 metres until you reach a T-junction with the A265, at the centre of Burwash Weald. Cross over to the **Wheel Inn [6]**, the suggested lunch stop for the long walk and the tea stop for the main walk.

[Coming out of the Wheel Inn, if you are intending to take the **Longer walk** option, refer to the directions at the end of the main walk text.]

Otherwise, for the main walk, *turn left along the pavement*, your direction east. After 350 metres, *where the pavement comes to an end, cross the road and continue along the right-hand side. After 80 metres cross back over the road, and onto a shingle driveway on the other side.* The entrance to Green Farm and Pine Oast is on your immediate right, and there is a footpath post with an arrow on your left.

Ignore the track to the left with a sign for Lower Bough Farm on a gate. Go along the car-wide shingle track to the right, following the bridleway arrow, your direction north-west. After 80 metres you pass an oast-house on your right, and continue on the now car-wide earth track down through a cutting.

After 170 metres *follow the bridleway round to the right*, your initial direction 30 degrees. *Keep on this bridleway for the next 2km (1.25 miles) until it reaches Spring Lane* by a bridleway signpost. The path gradually becomes narrower and can be muddy. *When you reach Spring Lane, turn left.* After 60 metres, at a small junction, turn right onto a minor lane with a sign for Honeybrook Organics, [7] your direction 30 degrees.

After 150 metres you pass a memorial plaque marked 'F/Lt. R.F. Rimmer, Aged 21, Killed in action September 27th 1940'. In 80 metres turn left at a crosspaths, your direction 310 degrees.

Cross over a stile to the right of a double wooden fieldgate. In 30 metres you go up some steps.[8] Go down the edge of the field with a wooden fence on your right (possibly having to cross over an electric fence with protective covering en route). In 280 metres cross over a stile and then another one after 10 metres. Bear slightly left through an orchard and cross a third stile after 30 metres, which takes you into a field.

Go along the right-hand edge of the field, noting the lake ahead to the right, your direction 340 degrees. At the corner of the field, continue in the same direction between two fences to cross over a stile (to the right of a wooden fieldgate) into the corner of the next field.

Go diagonally across this field, heading towards a not-too-visible footbridge 30 metres to the left of the right-hand corner of the field, your direction 340 degrees. (You may prefer in muddy conditions to go around the left edge of the field.)

In 350 metres cross over the double-plank footbridge and go straight across the field ahead of you, your direction 300 degrees, and through the gap in the hedge opposite. This takes you into the corner of a hop field. Go along the left-hand edge of the hop field and then several further fields, your direction 310 degrees.

After 550 metres, at the end of the hop fields, cross a stile and turn half right to head towards a metal fieldgate, your direction 340 degrees. In 180 metres go through the metal fieldgate and continue, bearing slightly left towards a metal fieldgate, your direction 310 degrees. When you reach the gate turn right onto a road.

Go along the grass verge of the road, which crosses a bridge after 70 metres.

Continue for another 330 metres until you pass a house on the right called Martlets, with a car-wide track immediately after it.[9] Turn right down the track. (If pressed for time continue straight ahead along the road to reach a farm shop on your right after 180 metres. After 80 metres cross a bridge and turn right for Stonegate station).

Go through a metal fieldgate, indicated by a bridleway arrow on the left post, and go down a car-wide earth track with a fence to the left, your initial direction 90 degrees. The track goes slightly downhill. At the bottom go through a metal fieldgate and follow the bridleway arrow uphill towards a metal gate, your direction 100 degrees.

In 300 metres go through the gate to cross a car-wide bridge over the railway line and then through a second metal gate. Continue along the bridleway across a field towards a metal fieldgate, your direction 70 degrees. You pass some corrugated metal farm buildings and later a pond on your left.

Go through the metal fieldgate and turn left onto a car-wide shingle track, your direction 340 degrees. After 50 metres you pass a car-wide earth track on your right. Continue along the shingle track with the pond to your left and veer to the left (retracing your initial route up from Stonegate station) down the car-wide track back to Stonegate station.

Walk options

a) **Shorter walk directions**:
Follow the main walk directions until point [5].

From [5] ignore the footpath sign on the left to continue along the High Street in the same direction. After 80 metres you pass the Bear Inn on your left.

After a further 160 metres, when you reach Burwash Village Hall on your left, cross the road. Christ the King Catholic Church is straight ahead. Immediately turn half left down a shingle car-wide track, your direction 300 degrees. Go

Mr Kipling's sanctuary

In 1899, Josephine, the six-year-old daughter of the most famous writer in the English-speaking world of the time, died of pneumonia. Her father, Rudyard Kipling, was poleaxed by grief, and, according to his younger daughter Elsie, 'his life was never the same after her death.'

He, and his American wife Carrie, longed to retreat from the world to a haven deep in the countryside. They found it in the Sussex Weald; the Kiplings bought **Bateman's** in 1902 (together with its outbuildings, a mill and 33 acres of land) for £9,300.

The rambling sandstone house, built around 1634 for (according to tradition) a Wealden ironmaster, had no electricity, no running water upstairs and no bathroom, but Kipling was captivated by it – he wrote, 'it is a good and peaceable place... we have loved it ever since our first sight of it.'

He had found his sanctuary, and was to need its consolations even more when his son John was killed in action at the Battle of Loos in 1915.

Kipling died in 1936. His widow continued to live at Bateman's, bequeathing the house to the National Trust on her death in 1939. It has been left as it was in the author's time, and is filled with mementoes and memories of his life.

Outside is the Rose Garden, which Kipling designed himself and paid for from the £7,700 he received on winning the 1907 Nobel Prize for Literature. Visitors can also see the mill, into which he fitted a water turbine that generated enough electricity to light ten 60-watt bulbs for four hours each evening.

Kipling was a pioneering motorist and loved cars (though their capriciousness often infuriated him); his Rolls Royce Phantom I can be admired in his garage.

Bateman's
Burwash, Etchingham, TN19 7DS (01435 882302/www.national trust.org.uk/places/batemans).
Open *House & garden Apr-late Oct* 11am-5pm Mon-Wed, Sat, Sun. *Shop & Tearoom 1 Apr-late Mar* 11am-4pm Sat, Sun; *late Mar-early Nov* 11am-5pm (shop until 5.30pm) Mon-Wed, Sat, Sun; *early Nov-21 Dec* 11am-4pm Wed-Sun. **Admission** £5.50; £2.70 concessions; £13 family. **Credit** AmEx, MC, V.

through a wooden kissing gate to the left of a wooden gate with a notice saying Dawes Farm on it.

After 60 metres ignore the footpath to the left-hand side, and follow the path as it curves to the right more steeply down the car-wide track. In 120 metres pass Dawes Farm on your left and a two-armed footpath signpost on your right. In 30 metres at the bottom of the track go over a stile to the right of a metal fieldgate.

Go along the right-hand edge of the field, your direction 330 degrees. In 80 metres you pass under some mini pylon cables. Continue in the same direction, keeping to the right-hand edge of the field. In 220 metres, at the corner of the field, *you cross a footbridge flanked by two stiles. Turn left* and go down the left-hand side of the field, your initial direction 290 degrees.

In 140 metres, at the bottom field corner, go through a wooden fieldgate and then after 30 metres through a metal fieldgate and cross a bridge. Go uphill along the right-hand edge of the next field. After 200 metres, at the upper right-hand field corner, go through a metal fieldgate. In 25 metres, *turn right down a lane*, your initial direction 300 degrees.

[!] In 100 metres and *20 metres before a house and garage, turn left up an easily missed footpath*, as indicated by a footpath post (2 metres off the lane to the left).

After 25 metres *cross over a stile. Turn right* and go up the right-hand edge of an orchard, your initial direction 310 degrees. In 180 metres, at the top right-hand corner of the orchard, go through a wooden fieldgate onto a lane. Continue straight ahead and across a stile to the right of a double wooden fieldgate. In 30 metres you go up some steps.

You now follow the main walk directions from [8].

b) Longer walk directions:

Follow the main walk directions to [6].

Coming out of the Wheel Inn, cross straight over the A265 to go down a lane. *After 20 metres fork right down a footpath leading off the lane* through a lightly wooded area, your direction 200 degrees.

In 250 metres go over a stile and turn right to then cross a footbridge after 7 metres. Continue up through woods with a barbed-wire fence to your left, your initial direction 200 degrees. In 150 metres go over a stile to emerge from the woods into a field; go up the left-hand edge of the field. In 100 metres, *at the top left corner of the field, cross a stile and veer left up a tarmac lane.*

In 70 metres you pass a corrugated metal barn on your left, your direction now 220 degrees. After a further 90 metres ignore a footpath leading off to the right to continue along the now shingle lane between hedgerows. In 120 metres the hedgerows give way and you come out to an open space with a house up to your right.

Continue straight ahead along a shingle car-wide track. In 20 metres ignore a stile on the left. In 60 metres *where the shingle track ends, continue in same direction, across grass.* In 25 metres *go up a narrow grass path.* In 50 metres where the path merges with a car-wide track from the right veer left. The footpath now starts to descend through a wooded area, your direction 220 degrees.

After 150 metres *cross a stile to emerge from the wooded area, to go down the right-hand side of a field*, your direction 200 degrees.

In 120 metres on approaching the right-hand field corner ignore a stile to the right, and cross over a stile after a further 50 metres in the field corner. Continue down in the same direction across the field aiming, for the gap in the lower hedgerow of the field. In 180 metres go through the gap into the next field and continue down in the same direction to reach a footbridge at the bottom after 300 metres.

Cross the footbridge and cross a stile to continue straight on up the right-hand edge of a field, with a wooded area to your right, your direction 110 degrees. *After*

100 metres veer right to go through a gap into the next field to head downhill, your direction 150 degrees. In 70 metres *go through a car-wide opening into the next field.*

Follow a yellow footpath arrow on the left post and veer left, aiming for a tree 30 metres to the left of a derelict farm building, your direction 100 degrees. In 200 metres *go over a stile to veer right, passing the derelict farm building on your right* after 20 metres. Continue down in the direction of an oast-house, your direction 160 degrees.

After 130 metres *cross over a stile* **[B1]** by a wooden footpath signpost with just one arm pointing back (the other two arms pointing left and right are missing). *Turn right to go up a wide earth bridleway,* your direction now west. In 250 metres at a staggered crosspaths marked by a two-armed bridleway signpost continue up the car-wide earth track through a wooded area, your direction 220 degrees.

After 600 metres, the car-wide earth track having levelled out, you pass by a two-armed bridleway signpost, where the track veers to the right, your direction 280 degrees. After 200 metres *the car-wide earth track forks,* marked by a two-armed bridleway signpost back and in the direction of the left fork. *Fork left* to follow the bridleway arm, your direction 250 degrees. In 350 metres *turn left onto a lane.* After 20 metres the lane curves to the right, your direction now 280 degrees.

In 400 metres you *pass some corrugated metal barns on your left. 30 metres beyond the barns you pass some double metal fieldgates on your left* (leading to a van parking area). *After 50 metres you reach a telegraph pole on the left. 15 metres beyond, at a four-way footpath junction* **[B2]** marked on the left by a hidden four-armed wooden signpost with the right arm broken off, **[!]** *turn right along a driveway.* (This is immediately to the left and parallel to the concrete driveway to Watkins Farmhouse.) You

will have *a wooden fence on your right and a hedge on your left; you pass a house immediately on your left,* your direction north. You may have to go over an aluminium sheep-pen barrier between the wall of the house on your left and the wooden fence on your right.

In 50 metres cross a stile built into the right-hand side of a rusted metal fieldgate, with a yellow public footpath arrow on the right post of the fieldgate. Continue straight ahead with the wooden fence on your right. In 35 metres pass a telegraph pole with a yellow footpath arrow. After 45 metres *cross a stile next to a two-armed footpath signpost to go across a field, walking to the left of mini pylon cables* towards the left-hand corner of the field, your direction north.

In 100 metres, *at the corner of the field, cross over a metal sheep-pen barrier. Continue diagonally across this next field,* towards a footpath post in the bottom left-hand corner, your direction 320 degrees. After 120 metres at the corner of the field pass round a redundant stile next to a two-armed footpath signpost, *to enter a wood.* In 10 metres veer right to follow a yellow footpath arrow on a tree, your direction north. After 30 metres continue along the footpath through a slight cutting, your direction 20 degrees.

In 120 metres *the footpath curves to the left and in 30 metres, at a footpath junction, with a footpath off to the right. Turn right* to follow a yellow footpath arrow on a tree (5 metres ahead), down through a slight cutting, your direction 30 degrees. In 80 metres *follow a yellow public footpath arrow on the corner post of a wire fence to your left, to now continue down with the wire fence on your left,* your direction 60 degrees.

[!] In 70 metres, *at the corner post of the wire fence on your left, turn left* to follow the fence round to pass a yellow public footpath arrow on a tree on your right, your direction 10 degrees.

After 120 metres *cross a stile to emerge from the wood into a field and turn half left*. Slice the corner of this field to then *after 50 metres cross a stile into the next field*. Cross this field and *aim for a stile 40 metres down from the top left-hand corner* of the field, your direction west. In 140 metres *cross the stile and turn right* to then cross another stile after 10 metres to go down a field boundary cutting between hedgerows, your direction 340 degrees.

After 120 metres *cross over a stile into a field with a three-armed footpath signpost to the left marking a footpath junction. Follow the left fork downhill aiming just to the right of a clump of trees*, your direction still 340 degrees. After 140 metres you pass a yellow arrow on a footpath post and the clump of trees on your left. Continue downhill in the same direction.

In 120 metres *go over a stile and go down into a wood*. In 30 metres go down some steps to *cross over a footbridge* over the river Dudwell to *continue up through the wood*.

After 50 metres you pass through a normally open metal fieldgate to continue up through the wood. In 10 metres *follow a footpath arrow on a post to fork right*, your direction 330 degrees. After 170 metres *follow a footpath arrow on a post to fork left*, your direction west. In 50 metres *follow a footpath arrow on a post to turn right*, your direction 350 degrees.

After 25 metres go over a stile to your right and continue along a fenced-in footpath, your direction 350 degrees. In 80 metres *go over a stile to emerge from the wood into a field, to go up the top right-hand edge of the field*, your direction 340 degrees.

After 300 metres, *at the top corner of the field, go over a stile to continue straight ahead up through a lightly wooded area*. After 350 metres the footpath leads out to a car-wide track, your direction 350 degrees. In 500 metres go through a metal fieldgate to *reach a T-junction with the A265*. [B3]

Cross over this main road to *follow a bridleway signpost along a car-wide*

shingle track, your direction 340 degrees. After 100 metres *the car-wide track curves down to the right* (with a telegraph pole on the right-hand side). *Fork left off the track along a footpath, with a hedge on your right and a hedgerow on your left*, your direction 330 degrees. In 100 metres *go through a metal gate to turn left, and after 10 metres turn right down a footpath* with a mesh wire fence on your left, your direction 330 degrees.

After 50 metres the footpath comes out to *join a shingle car-wide track downhill*. In 180 metres you go through a metal fieldgate as the shingle track now becomes a tarmac lane. After 80 metres you *come down to a T-junction and turn right down a lane*, your direction 20 degrees.

After 100 metres *at a triangular lane junction fork left*, your direction north. In 80 metres you pass the entrance to Prospect Farm on your left, and continue down the lane, your direction now 350 degrees. In 300 metres *at a crossroads turn left*, passing the wooden gate entrance to Corner Farm on your left, your direction 310 degrees. In 120 metres, and *immediately after a corrugated metal farm building to your right,* [!] *turn right* along a shingle driveway between a house on your left and the corrugated metal farm building on your right *towards a wooden fieldgate to the left of a metal fieldgate*.

After 15 metres *go through the wooden fieldgate and turn half left* (ignore a yellow public footpath arrow on the fieldgate pointing erroneously ahead) *to go diagonally down across a field, towards the bottom left-hand corner*, your direction 300 degrees. *In 160 metres, at the bottom left-hand corner of the field, you reach a stile with a yellow public footpath arrow to the right of the stile pointing misleadingly ahead. Having crossed the stile, do not continue straight ahead as indicated by the footpath arrow, but* [!] *turn right to go down to the bottom corner of this narrow field*, your direction 320 degrees.

Classic **East Sussex**: gently rolling countryside, hedgerows and hidden villages.

In 150 metres, at the bottom corner of the field, *cross a plank bridge flanked by two stiles* to continue down through a narrow field in the same direction (320 degrees). *In 100 metres ignore the left-hand fork to a fieldgate and bear slightly right to enter a wooded area*, passing a fenced-in pond (which is often dried up in summer) on your left. After 80 metres go over a dilapidated stile to emerge from the wooded area and go down across a field towards a gap in the hedgerow, your direction 320 degrees.

In 160 metres, at the field edge, cross over a metal-barred stile (80 metres to the left of the right field corner; in summer this stile can become very overgrown) and continue down across the next field in the same direction (320 degrees) towards a footbridge (20 metres to the left of a large oak tree). After 180 metres *cross over the footbridge to go up for 15 metres and then fork right, along the right-hand edge of a field*, your initial direction 40 degrees.

In 180 metres pass through a metal fieldgate and continue along a car-wide earth track, your direction 330 degrees.

After 80 metres go through another metal fieldgate. In 90 metres *turn right through a wooden fieldgate marked by a three-armed footpath signpost* (which is often hidden by foliage in summer) to continue along the right-hand side of a field, your direction 10 degrees.

After 150 metres *at the right-hand corner of the field cross a stile* (to the left of a wooden fieldgate) next to a three-armed footpath signpost. **[B4]** *Follow the left fork arm of the signpost towards the left-hand corner of the field*, your direction 350 degrees.

In 250 metres *at the left field corner, go over a stile to go along the left-hand edge of a field*, your direction north. **[!]** *After 100 metres, and 40 metres before reaching the field corner, turn left to cross an easily missed corrugated metal footbridge* flanked by two stiles. *Follow a yellow arrow on the second stile half right towards the corner of the field*, your direction 300 degrees.

In 150 metres, *at the corner of the field, cross a footbridge to go up towards the gap in the woods ahead*, your direction

340 degrees. In 100 metres cross a two-plank bridge to then *cross a wooden barrier to enter Little Calem Wood*, your direction 350 degrees. After 50 metres just past a crater on your left the footpath becomes less distinct and forks. Take the left fork, your initial direction 300 degrees. (The left and right forks in fact link up 40 metres further on, where the footpath becomes more distinct).

In 350 metres *cross a stile to emerge from Little Calem Wood* and *turn left up along the left-hand edge of a field* with Little Calem Wood on your left, your direction 310 degrees. In 180 metres, at the top left-hand corner of the field, *go through a metal fieldgate to go up a concrete farm driveway*. In 80 metres go through another metal fieldgate to reach a T-junction.

Turn left along a lane, your direction 280 degrees. In 400 metres, *just past the crest of the lane, you reach a 2-metre high metal gate* entrance to a Transco plant station on your left. *Continue on for 35 metres to turn right to cross a dilapidated stile* (opposite to a second set of gates to the Transco plant). Cross a farm track and *go down the right-hand edge of a field*, your direction 30 degrees. In 180 metres, *at the right-hand corner of the field, cross a dilapidated stile and turn right along the top right-hand edge of a field*, your direction 110 degrees.

After 120 metres, *at the right-hand corner of the field, go through a metal fieldgate and turn left down a tarmac driveway*, your direction 20 degrees. In 140 metres go through a metal fieldgate with a red-brick house to your left. In 60 metres pass by some stables on your left and after 20 metres *cross a stile to the right of a metal fieldgate into a field*. Continue down the left-hand edge of the field to cross over a stile in the left-hand field corner after 180 metres. Go down across the next field. After 50 metres you *pass to the right of a fenced-in pond, aiming for a wooden gate*, which you reach after 150 metres. **[B5]**

[If you are intending to finish the walk at Wadhurst refer to the **Alternative ending directions** at the end of this section.]

Otherwise, *to finish the walk at Stonegate, go through the gate and turn right down a car-wide track* lined with concrete slats, your direction 120 degrees. In 70 metres you cross over a ditch stream and continue uphill, now on a car-wide shingle track.

In 120 metres you *reach a junction. Turn left down a lane*, your direction 40 degrees. In 60 metres pass round to the left of a wooden fieldgate and *cross over a bridge*. After 30 metres, at a path junction marked by a two-armed signpost **[B6]**, *turn right* along the left-hand edge of a narrow field, your direction 120 degrees.

In 300 metres cross over into the next field and *turn left to follow the left arm of a two-armed footpath signpost*, your direction 30 degrees. After 50 metres you *reach a path junction marked by a three-armed footpath signpost.* **[B7]**

At this point you have the choice of two routes for the 2km (1.25 miles) route to Batt's Wood. The preferred route is north and then east, the alternative route is east and then north.

If taking the alternative route east and then north pick up the directions at the double asterisk [**] below.

Otherwise, *for the preferred route, continue straight ahead up a car-wide track*. In 7 metres go through a (normally open) metal fieldgate (or go over the stile to the left) into a field. Go up the left-hand edge of the field, your direction 10 degrees. *In 400 metres you cross a stile to veer left and down*, your initial direction 350 degrees. Continue along the left-hand edge of the field, with a wood to your left and nursery trees to your right. In 150 metres *close to the field corner curve round to the right to go up a car-wide grass track* between the nursery trees, your initial direction 120 degrees.

After 180 metres *at the top of the field* you cross a farm track to then *cross over a stile into the next field* with the corner of a wood to your right. *Go along the lower right-hand edge of the field with the wood on your right,* your direction east.

In 200 metres you *pass a metal fieldgate on your right. In 40 metres turn right over a stile, to go down through the wood,* your initial direction 160 degrees. *After 20 metres turn left and follow an arrow on a wooden post,* your direction east. In 25 metres you pass a two-plank bridge 15 metres to your right. After a further 25 metres *cross a two-plank bridge to turn right* and follow an arrow on a wooden post, your direction 120 degrees.

After 30 metres you *come down to a river bank to veer left,* indicated by an arrow on a wooden post, with the river to your right, your direction 40 degrees. In 30 metres *turn right across a footbridge and in 25 metres cross a stile to emerge from the wood; go along the top left-hand edge of a field,* with woods to your left, your direction 170 degrees.

After 180 metres at the corner of the field cross a stile into the next field to continue down the left-hand edge of the field, your direction 120 degrees. After 150 metres at the corner of the field *cross a stile to turn half left towards the corner of the field to slice the squiggly left field boundary,* your direction 50 degrees.

In 200 metres, at the corner of the field, cross a stile to immediately cross a two-plank footbridge; then go up for 40 metres to enter a small field with nursery trees. Continue straight ahead, marked by a wooden T-post, your direction 60 degrees. In 70 metres continue straight ahead following an arrow on a footpath post through a wooded field boundary. In 20 metres follow an arrow on a wooden post, along the right-hand edge of a nursery tree field, your direction 110 degrees.

After 80 metres, *at a footpath junction indicated by a three-armed footpath signpost, continue straight ahead up to the corner of the nursery field,* your direction east. In 40 metres *at the corner go through a wooded field boundary to turn left after 20 metres up the left-hand edge of a field,* your direction 30 degrees.

After 150 metres follow an arrow on a footpath post to continue straight on, your direction 30 degrees. In 50 metres, just past a house on your left, you *reach the edge of Batt's Wood. You now follow the walk directions from* [B8] *below.*

[**] *Turn right along a car-wide concrete track,* which after 30 metres becomes slat concrete, your direction 110 degrees. In 300 metres, where the track dips, you pass a pond on your left bordered by a wooden fence. In 120 metres go over a stile to the right of a metal fieldgate and pass a white clapboard house on your left.

In 70 metres you *reach a metal fieldgate ahead and a metal fieldgate to your right marked by a two-armed footpath signpost. Turn right* through the metal fieldgate to follow the right arm of the footpath signpost *to enter a wood.* Go down through the wood, your direction 150 degrees. After 120 metres *cross a stile to turn left to emerge from the wood,* your direction 130 degrees.

In 200 metres *cross a stile to the right of a metal fieldgate* and continue straight ahead to enter the right-hand edge of a wood, your direction 140 degrees. *After 50 metres ignore a car-wide bridge to the right and veer left,* your direction 120 degrees. In 80 metres you pass a three-armed footpath post on your left. In 40 metres the footpath comes out to a tarmac drive; continue straight ahead, your direction east.

In 30 metres you pass a tennis court on your right, and then after 80 metres pass an oast-house on your right. After 80 metres you pass some garages on your left to continue along the left-hand edge of a field. In 100 metres, at the top corner of the field, go through a wooden fieldgate and continue along a tree arbour car-wide earth path. In 140 metres at a *three-way path junction, turn left up a car-wide earth track marked by a wooden post with a yellow arrow and 'Batt's Wood',* your initial direction 350 degrees.

After 200 metres you reach the brow of the hill to continue downhill. In 100 metres where the track comes to a dip you cross a stile on your left; then turn right to continue up in the same direction along the right-hand edge of a field, your direction north.

After 50 metres you cross a stile on your right, and turn left to continue up in the same direction (10 degrees), along the car-wide earth track. (This short detour off the track is to avoid an occasional muddy track). After 200 metres *the car-wide track reaches the bottom corner of a field. Follow the arrow on a footpath post to veer left diagonally up across the field*, towards a house, your direction 350 degrees.

In 300 metres, *having crossed the field, follow the arrow on a footpath post, to turn half right*, your direction 30 degrees. In 50 metres, just past a house on your left, you *reach the edge of Batt's Wood*.

[B8] Continue up the footpath to *enter Batt's Wood. In 40 metres, at a footpath junction* marked by a wooden post on your right, *follow the arrow straight ahead up the footpath to pass a 'Welcome to Batt's Wood' noticeboard on your left*, your direction 70 degrees.

In 150 metres, the footpath having levelled out, *turn left at a footpath T-junction* marked by a yellow arrow on a post, your direction 60 degrees. *After 50 metres, where the footpath merges with a car-wide grass track, turn half left* down a gradual descent, marked by a yellow arrow on a post, your direction 20 degrees.

In 100 metres go straight across a crosspaths, marked by a post on your left, as the path starts to descend more steeply. After 300 metres *the car-wide track curves round to the right*. In 20 metres the car-wide path now runs *alongside a 2-metre high deer protective fence to the left* with Wadhurst Park Lake beyond, your direction 110 degrees.

After 550 metres the path forks. Take the left downhill fork marked by a yellow arrow on a post at the fork junction, with the 2-metre high deer protective fence still to your left, your direction 80 degrees.

In 120 metres you go over a plank bridge over a stream. After 250 metres *the footpath forks. Turn left* to follow the left yellow arrow on a post ahead, your direction 40 degrees.

After 60 metres you pass a redundant stile on your left to cross a stream. In 20 metres, where the footpath forks, take the right fork to go to the right of a redundant stile after 7 metres, to emerge from the wood into a field. Go along the left-hand edge of the field, with a wood to the left, your direction 80 degrees.

After 70 metres turn left to enter a wood, your direction 20 degrees. In 10 metres you pass a footpath post *and continue up the right-hand edge of the wood*. After 200 metres you *emerge from the wood and turn left downhill* along the left-hand edge of a field, marked by a yellow arrow on a post, your direction 30 degrees. In 200 metres *at the bottom left-hand corner of the field, cross over a stream* and continue along a car-wide earth track, your direction 60 degrees.

In 100 metres you reach a three-armed footpath signpost on your left. **[B9]** *Turn right to go through a metal fieldgate*; then go along the bottom right-hand edge of a field, your direction 150 degrees. After 200 metres, *where the right-hand edge of the field curves to the right, continue straight ahead aiming for a metal fieldgate*. In 100 metres go through the fieldgate and continue along the right-hand edge of the next field with a wooden fence on your right, your direction 160 degrees.

In 70 metres *cross a car-wide plank bridge and turn half right. Go diagonally across a field aiming for a stile 40 metres to the right of the left field corner*, your direction south. After 200 metres *cross the stile to go diagonally across a field, aiming for a not clearly visible stile on the far side* (look for the gap in the hedgerow), 100 metres to the right of the far left corner of the field, your direction 160 degrees.

After 300 metres *cross over a plank bridge and the stile. Veer slightly left in the direction of a stile* 70 metres to the right of the left corner of the field (look for the gap in the hedgerow 5 metres to the right of a tree), your direction 150 degrees. In 300 metres at the field edge, cross a plank bridge to immediately cross the dilapidated stile. Continue straight on across the field, passing under mini pylon cables after 100 metres. 20 metres further on you *reach a stile with a four-armed footpath signpost to its right. Do not cross this stile but turn left up the right-hand edge of the field,* your direction east.

In 100 metres, *at the corner of the field, go through double metal fieldgates and follow the earth farm track up through the farm.* In 150 metres the now-concrete car-wide track curves round to the right and you pass a house on your left, your direction 130 degrees.

In 180 metres you *reach a T-junction. Turn left* along the right grass verge of the B road. In 60 metres *you pass a house on the right; turn right* here.

You now follow the main walk directions from [9].

c) Alternative ending at Wadhurst (longer walk)
Follow the long walk directions to [B5].

Go through the gate and turn left to go down a car-wide track lined with concrete slats, your direction 300 degrees. In 150 metres go over a plank bridge as the bridleway narrows down to a metre-wide shingle path. In 140 metres, *at a footpath junction marked by a post, turn right,* your direction 70 degrees.

In 40 metres cross over a footbridge and turn left into a lightly wooded area, your direction 350 degrees. In 30 metres go through some fieldgate posts. In 30 metres the path forks. Fork right up along a sunken bridleway marked by an arrow on the wooden post at the fork junction. (In muddy conditions you may prefer to fork left along the parallel path.)

In 70 metres both paths link up. After 50 metres you emerge from the lightly wooded

area. In 280 metres you reach a bridleway junction. Continue straight ahead up a car-wide track, your direction 30 degrees.

After 60 metres cross over a stile to go along the left edge of a narrow field. In 250 metres cross another stile and head across this rather larger long, narrow field towards a stile in the top corner, which becomes visible after 100 metres, your direction 40 degrees. 300 metres further on *you cross over the stile to enter a lightly wooded area, and then cross another stile after 15 metres to arrive at a footpath junction marked by a three-armed footpath signpost.*

You now follow the main Wadhurst walk directions from [8]. (*See p197.*)

Lunch & tea places

Bateman's (*see p209* **Mr Kipling's sanctuary**) has a tearoom.

Bear Inn & Burwash Motel *The High Street, Burwash, TN19 7ET (01435 882260).* **Open** 8am-midnight daily. **Food served** noon-2.30pm, 6.30-9.30pm Mon-Fri; noon-3.30pm Sat, Sun. An alternative lunch stop, 90m west of the Rose & Crown.

Bell Inn *High Street, Burwash, TN19 7EH (01435 882304).* **Open** noon-3.30pm, 5.30-11pm Mon-Fri; noon-11pm Sat; noon-10.30pm Sun. **Food served** noon-2pm, 7-9pm daily. Located 6km (3.75 miles) from the start of the walk, this is the suggested lunch stop for the main walk.

Lime Tree Tea Rooms *Chaunt House, High Street, Burwash, TN19 7ES (01435 882221).* **Open** 10am-5pm Wed-Sat; 11am-5pm Sun. Serves morning coffee, tea, light (hot) snacks and cakes.

Rose & Crown *Ham Lane, Burwash, TN19 7ER (01435 882600).* **Open** noon-11pm daily. **Food served** noon-2.30pm, 6-9pm Tue-Fri, noon-2.30pm Sat. This pub is 160m west down the High Street from the Bell Inn.

Wheel Inn *Heathfield Road, Burwash, TN19 7LA (01435 882758).* **Open** 11am-11pm Mon-Sat; noon-10.30pm Sun. **Food served** noon-2.30pm, 6.30-9.30pm Tue-Sat; 12.30-3pm Sun. Situated 10km (6.25 miles) from the start of the walk, this pub serves inventive lunchtime food. It is the suggested tea stop for the main walk.

Robertsbridge Circular

Classic High Weald, plus a castle and a steam railway.

Start and finish: Robertsbridge station

Length: 18.5km (11.6 miles). For a shorter walk and other variations, *see below* **Walk options**.

Time: 5 hours 45 minutes. For the whole outing, including trains, sights and meals, allow 11 hours.

Transport: Hourly trains run between London Charing Cross and Robertsbridge (journey time: 1 hour 18 minutes). For those driving, Robertsbridge station car park currently costs £2 on weekdays and is free at weekends.

OS Landranger Map: 199
OS Explorer Map: 136
Robertsbridge, map reference TQ733235, is in East Sussex, 22km (13.8 miles) south-east of Tunbridge Wells.

Toughness: 4 out of 10.

Walk notes: This High Weald walk passes through rolling hills, woods, hop fields and orchards. A highlight of this walk is arriving for tea at picture-perfect Bodiam Castle, nestling in the Rother Valley, with the hooting of the steam trains of the Rother Valley Railway nearby. From here the route continues on a gently undulating course to Salehurst, before a leisurely final stretch back into Robertsbridge.

Walk options: Directions for the following options are given at the end of the main walk text (*see p225*).

a) Shorter walk: You may reduce the length of the main walk by over 4km (2.5 miles) to 14km (8.8 miles) by following the directions for this option at the end of the main walk text (it still starts at Robertsbridge station, but is different thereon), before picking up the main walk directions from [6].

b) Stonegate to Robertsbridge long walk: You may increase the length of the walk by over 8km (5 miles) to 27km (16.9 miles) by following the main route directions for the **Stonegate circular walk** (walk 19 in this book) as given until [4]. Then follow the directions at the end of the main walk text, before picking up the main walk directions at [2].

c) Alternative ending along the river Rother: If you would prefer to end the walk with a flat, easy walk back into Robertsbridge from Bodiam Castle, then follow the directions for this option at the end of the main walk text back to Robertsbridge from [6]. This applies to all three walks – main, short and long – and reduces the length of each walk by 500 metres. [Note that between mid May and mid September the 700-metre footpath along the embankment of the river Rother can become extremely overgrown. It is thus advisable not to take this alternative walk ending from Bodiam Castle in summertime.]

As a further option for shortening the walk, you may catch the 254 bus

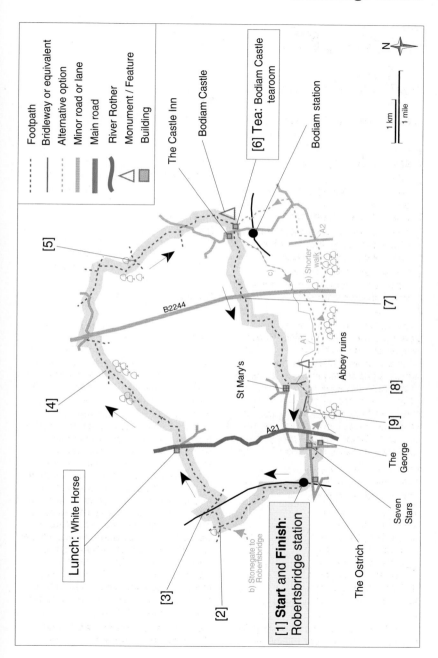

Robertsbridge Circular

Legend:
- Footpath
- Bridleway or equivalent
- Alternative option
- Minor road or lane
- Main road
- River Rother
- Monument / Feature
- Building

N

1 km
1 mile

The Castle Inn

Bodiam Castle

[6] Tea: Bodiam Castle tearoom

Bodiam station

A2

[5]

B2244

[7]

a) Shorter walk

c)

A1

Abbey ruins

[4]

St Mary's

[8]

Lunch: White Horse

A21

[9]

The George

[3]

Seven Stars

[2]

[1] Start and Finish: Robertsbridge station

b) Stonegate to Robertsbridge

The Ostrich

(hourly service until 5.20pm Mon-Sat) from outside the road entrance to Bodiam Castle (west side – Castle Inn pub side of the road) to Wadhurst and Tunbridge Wells railway stations. Call Traveline 0870 608 2608 for information.

Saturday Walkers' Club : Take the train nearest to 9.50am (before or after) from Charing Cross station to Robertsbridge.

Walk directions

[1] [Numbers refer to the map] Coming off the London train from platform 2 at **Robertsbridge station** *cross over the footbridge to platform 1* to the exit adjacent to the level crossing. *Turn right onto the pavement* and, after 15 metres, *turn right and take the initially tarmac footpath* marked by a stone footpath marker, your direction north. After 80 metres ignore a tarmac path left and continue straight ahead for a further 180 metres on an earth path. Cross over a stile into a field.

Continue straight ahead along the bottom right-hand edge of the field. When you reach the bottom corner of the field cross over two stiles separated by a plank bridge into the next field. Continue along the bottom right-hand edge of this field.

In the far corner of the field ignore a stile on your right; cross over the stile ahead and then a plank bridge. *Turn left and up a narrow field*, your direction 260 degrees.

In 200 metres, *at the top of this field* beyond a gap in the hedgerow, *turn sharp right uphill, aiming towards a stile 100 metres distant*, your direction 330 degrees. (Note: not the stile that you may be able to see right ahead in the direction of some oast-houses.) On reaching the stile *go over and veer to the right*, your direction 340 degrees. In 90 metres *cross over another stile and turn left*, your direction 310 degrees.

Go down the left-hand edge of the field to cross over a stile after 100 metres. **[!]**

Keep straight ahead and to the left down a footpath between fences. In 100 metres go over a plank footbridge and cross a stream.

Just beyond the stream *cross a stile into the corner of a field. Go uphill diagonally across the field*, your direction 290 degrees, to latterly descend towards a car-wide bridge with brick walls. (However, depending on the time of year and the state of the field, you may prefer to walk along the right-hand edge of the field and then turn left at the corner and walk along the field edge to the car-wide brick bridge.)

In 300 metres cross the bridge and continue straight ahead along the left-hand edge of a field. In 90 metres you reach a stile and a precarious wood plank footbridge. In fact, you are advised to pass round this footbridge on the path to the left to circumvent it. *Continue up the left-hand edge of the next field*, your direction 340 degrees.

After 140 metres *go through a car-wide entrance to cross over into an adjoining field to continue along the top left-hand edge of the field*. In 150 metres, at the top corner of the field, you go through a metal fieldgate. In 80 metres go through a second metal fieldgate. After 40 metres you *arrive at a footpath crosspaths at the centre of Squibs Farm*, with a four-armed footpath signpost ahead. **[2]**

Veer to the right down a car-wide earth track. In 50 metres ignore a car-wide track off to the right and continue downhill through a cutting, marked by a yellow footpath arrow on a post, your direction 70 degrees. In 250 metres you come out of the cutting in front of a stream. *Bear right and continue along the edge of the stream for 70 metres to then turn left and go over a car-wide bridge over the stream*.

Turn right and continue along the edge of the field and stream. On reaching the corner of the field follow the field round to the left along its right-hand edge, with the railway to your right.

In 250 metres *turn right* and cross a stile to cross the railway line and to cross another stile. **[3]** *Turn right*, your direction 140 degrees. After 180 metres, at the end of this narrow strip of land (which may be thick with nettles in the summer), cross a stile and continue along the left-hand side of a field bordering a stream.

In 200 metres, at the end of the field, *turn left and cross over a stile and a car-wide brick bridge* over the stream. Go up a car-wide track, your direction 70 degrees. In 60 metres ignore a track leading off to your right into a field and continue uphill on a path between trees through a cutting. In 150 metres fork left through a trench uphill.

After 30 metres you come out of the trench into an open space. Bear right along the right-hand side of the open space. In 100 metres you pass the private entrance to Ockham House on your right. 10 metres beyond this the footpath veers right uphill into a light wooded area and comes out to a driveway after 80 metres.

Continue up the driveway. (After 20 metres there is a footpath forking off to the left, which runs parallel to the lane, leading through a wooded area to the left of the lane, which eventually peters out.) After 800 metres the driveway reaches the main road. *70 metres before the driveway meets the A21, and as the driveway veers to the right, continue straight ahead on a footpath across the left-hand edge of a grassy open space.* In 60 metres pass through an opening to the left of a metal fieldgate and cross over a stile, which brings you out to the A21.

Cross over the A21, turn left and continue for 120 metres along the grass verge, before crossing back over the A21 *to arrive at the* **White Horse Inn**, the recommended lunch stop.

After lunch, *coming out of the pub*, cross over the main road and *turn right to go along the slip road* (leading off the main road), signposted to Bodiam and Staplecross. *In 30 metres turn left onto*

a lane, your direction 70 degrees. *Follow the lane*, which after 350 metres curves round to the left, your direction north. *In a further 400 metres, just before a collection of houses*, the lane forks to the left and to the right.

[!] Do not take either fork but *leave the lane and go straight ahead on a path with a garden hedge on your right, along the official footpath* through the garden of a detached house on your left. In 40 metres go through a gap in a hedge and, in a further 40 metres, cross a tarmac drive and go through a wooden gate. Continue straight ahead, passing a slate-roofed building on your right. After 30 metres you come to two adjacent gates. Go through the left-hand gate and, after 40 metres, cross a shingle car turning. Go straight ahead along a shingle footpath for 40 metres and then go through a wooden gate to cross a field, your direction 40 degrees.

In 600 metres, at the far end of the field, veer slightly to the right and take the footpath through a wood, your direction 70 degrees. In 100 metres *you come out of the wood into a field. Veer left* along the edge of Mill Wood, your direction 20 degrees.

After 340 metres, at the corner of Mill Wood, continue straight on across the field, your direction now 50 degrees. In 260 metres, at the far side of this field, continue through a gap and follow a car-wide track for 100 metres into the next field. **[4]** Remain on the track along the bottom left-hand edge of this field. In 400 metres, on reaching the corner of this field, at a path junction, *turn left along a car-wide earth track between hedgerows*, your direction 10 degrees.

In 200 metres you pass to the right of a metal fieldgate and *come out onto a lane. Turn right* and cross a bridge after 35 metres, just before you reach the crossroads with the main B road.

Cross over and go up Conghurst Lane. After 450 metres the lane curves to the left and you pass Carpenters Cottage on your right. In a further 300 metres, as the lane curves to the right, you pass Coach Hill Cottages on your left and, 100 metres further on where the lane curves sharply to the left, *turn right onto the drive marked 'Conghurst Farm – Private drive'*, your direction 130 degrees.

In 100 metres you pass Conghurst Barn and Ragstone Barn on your right. Continue down this drive past farm buildings, ignoring ways off. In 220 metres you pass a small pond on your right and come out to a field. Continue down a car-wide earth track along the left-hand edge of the field.

In 250 metres ignore a footpath off to your left and continue down. **[!]** In 70 metres *turn right, as indicated by a post on your right, with a yellow footpath arrow pointing to the right, and go gently downhill along the bottom edge of the field, with a hedgerow on your left*, your direction 190 degrees.

In 340 metres, at the bottom corner of the field, *cross over into the next field and go along an embankment*, your direction 230 degrees. In 60 metres cross a footbridge (and a low fence on the other side) and go up the right-hand edge of a field, your direction 210 degrees.

In 250 metres follow the corner of the field round to the left and continue uphill with a wooden fence on your right, your direction 110 degrees. After 400 metres, *just before some farm buildings, turn left onto a farm drive*, your direction 70 degrees. *In 100 metres* **[5]** *turn right down a car-wide track*, initially with a wooden fence on your right, your direction 170 degrees.

In 320 metres you reach the bottom corner of the field and cross over a stream. In 15 metres go over a stile and uphill along a car-wide earth track. After 150 metres you pass under some mini pylon cables. In 100 metres the earth track comes out to a shingle track as you pass a stile on your right after 10 metres and continue downhill.

In 80 metres you pass a farm building on your left and a small pond on your

right and go through a wooden gate. After 10 metres you come out onto a lane with a house on the right. Continue down the lane.

In 130 metres you pass a house on your left with a hop field behind it. Continue along this winding lane for 400 metres to then pass the entrance to Kitchenham House on your left. *Follow the lane* as it swings sharply round to the left and continue along the lane for a further 100 metres *until it reaches a T-junction*.

Turn right, your direction 190 degrees, and cross the road. *After 20 metres turn half left diagonally up across a field* towards a stile to the right of a large oak tree, your direction 160 degrees. In 200 metres, at the top of the field, *cross the stile and turn left* as indicated by a wooden footpath signpost.

Continue along the bottom edge of a small field. In 120 metres, having crossed into the adjacent small field, *turn half right and go uphill*, your direction 170 degrees. In 40 metres cross a stile and continue across a concrete driveway straight ahead to the top of the hill for 50 metres. *Cross a stile at the top and turn right*, your direction 190 degrees.

Go down the right-hand edge of the field, with a wooden fence on your right. In 140 metres the footpath veers to the right as you leave the immediate field edge; continue in the same direction on the footpath between a wire fence on your right and bushes on your left. In 200 metres *cross over a stile and enter the grounds of* **Bodiam Castle** (*see p228* **Castle in the air**). *Turn half right* to reach the entrance to the castle after 70 metres.

If not visiting Bodiam, at the entrance of the castle, follow the shingle path to the right of the fortress, with the moat and castle on your left. After 220 metres, where the footpath forks, take the right-hand fork away from the castle towards the tearoom and main exit. In 180 metres you go through a wooden kissing gate and arrive at **Bodiam Castle tearoom**.

The vineyard at **Bodiam Castle**.

[At this point you have the option of taking option **c)**, the **Alternative ending along the river Rother**. To do so, follow the directions at the end of this main walk text. Please note: this is NOT advised in summertime.]

Otherwise, to continue with the main walk route, *come out of the main exit* **[6]** next to the tearoom and toilets, *cross over the road and turn right to go past the Castle Inn. Turn left along the lane*, with a green on your right, your direction west. In 70 metres, at the end of the green, continue straight ahead along the lane.

In 450 metres, when the tarmac lane comes to an end, you pass to the right of a metal fieldgate. Continue straight ahead along a decayed tarmac car-wide track for 700 metres *to reach some light industrial buildings.* (Ignore a car-wide track off up to the right.) Go round a metal fieldgate and continue along a service road through a small rural industrial estate.

In 200 metres you pass the entrance to Ruskin House on your right, where you *fork left. After 10 metres cross over a footbridge. Veer right along the edge of a pond. After 70 metres, at a path T-junction, turn left*, your direction 190 degrees. *In 40 metres cross over a stile and turn right across a field* towards a wooden stile to the left of a wooden fieldgate, your direction 260 degrees.

In 200 metres go over the stile **[7]** *and cross the B road and a stile on the other side taking you into a field. Turn left* and up the left-hand edge of the field. In 60 metres, at the field corner, follow it round to the right, your direction now 260 degrees.

In 100 metres, at the far corner of the field, you go over a stile and a plank bridge. *Go across the next field, heading towards a clump of trees* 250 metres distant, your direction 260 degrees. In 150 metres you pass a wooden footpath post on your left. Continue straight ahead in the same direction, aiming to pass to the right of the clump of trees.

In 100 metres, *on reaching the clump of trees on your left*, you pass a wooden footpath post *and continue straight ahead*, your direction west, *towards a stile on the far side of the field*, with a three-armed footpath signpost, 150 metres distant. **[!]** *Do not cross the stile, but turn left down the right-hand edge of the field.*

In 250 metres you pass a wooden footpath post on your right and continue straight ahead, with Six Acre Wood on your right. In a further 80 metres you pass another wooden footpath post on your right. **[!]** After 140 metres, *at the corner of the cultivated field, continue straight ahead, with the field boundary on your right, onto an uncultivated section curving right and down to a footbridge* after 50 metres.

Having crossed the footbridge follow the footpath through a wooded area, your direction west. In 200 metres turn left as indicated by a post with a yellow arrow. In 25 metres cross over a stile and continue along the lower left-hand edge of a field, your direction 240 degrees.

In 180 metres, at the bottom corner of the field, cross over a stile and turn left and then right through an orchard, your direction 260 degrees. *In 150 metres, at the end of the orchard field, turn right and follow the white post diversion*, your direction 10 degrees. *In 50 metres turn left and cross over a stream into the next orchard field.* Go uphill and continue to follow the white post diversion, your direction west.

In 150 metres, *at the far side of the orchard and just before the mini pylon cables, turn left*, your direction south, following white posts *downhill for 60 metres where you* **[!]** *turn right*, marked by an easily missed footpath post with yellow waymark arrow.

In 25 metres go over a stile and continue straight ahead to cross a field, your direction 280 degrees. In a further 200 metres go over a stile and continue straight on, your direction west. Ahead of you, 650 metres distant, you can see the tower of the church of St Mary's, Salehurst, which we will be visiting. Cross the field for 200 metres and then go along the right-hand edge of the field for another 150 metres, with a hedgerow on your right.

On reaching the field corner, turn right for 10 metres along the lane and then left to continue in the same direction as before into the next field. Continue up the right-hand edge of the field for 120 metres and on into the next field. In 180 metres, on

approaching the top right-hand field corner, ignore the track straight ahead and fork left along the edge of the field for 60 metres and enter the churchyard between two large oak trees.

Having visited **St Mary's, Salehurst**, *go down the steps from the main entrance and turn left, and then left again after 15 metres to go down a car-wide drive. In 30 metres, as the drive curves to the right, continue straight ahead*, along the bridleway, your direction 70 degrees. In 50 metres the bridleway curves to the right before straightening out. Continue downhill with a metal pole fence alongside.

In 120 metres, at the end of this fence *at a path junction, continue straight ahead*, passing a pillbox on your right, your direction 150 degrees. In 120 metres *go over a footbridge across the river Rother. On the other side cross a stile on your right and go diagonally across a field* towards a metal fieldgate in the opposite corner of the field and passing to the right of a mini pylon pole, your direction 240 degrees. (Depending on the time of year and the state of the field, rather than crossing the stile and walking diagonally across the field, you may prefer to continue south along the bridleway and then, at the junction with the lane, turn right and walk along to the fieldgate.)

In 250 metres, at the opposite corner of the field, *go through the metal fieldgate* **[8]** and *turn right along a lane*, your direction west. In 300 metres ignore a lane off to the left at a lane junction **[9]** and continue straight ahead along this lane for 400 metres, heading towards the A21, your direction still west. *Just before the A21, take the tarmac path that forks left off the lane*. After 80 metres *turn right across the footbridge* over the A21.

Continue straight ahead down Fair Lane, your direction west. In 250 metres you reach a T-junction with the Seven Stars pub on your left. *Turn left up the High Street*, passing the entrance to the Seven Stars on the your left.

In 40 metres you pass Station Road on your right. Continue on for 90 metres and *cross over the road and go down a tarmac footpath* between the Robertsbridge town sign on your right and the clock war memorial on your left, with the George pub beyond.

Continue along this footpath between houses and back gardens. In 200 metres you cross over a car-wide bridge and, in 20 metres, turn right onto Willowbank. In 35 metres turn left along Station Road.

In 180 metres you reach the **Ostrich** pub on your left and, 25 metres further on the right-hand side of the road, Robertsbridge station.

Walk options

a) Shorter walk:

Coming off the London train from platform 2 at **Robertsbridge station** go through the exit into the station car park and *turn right for 40 metres to then cross over the road and turn left*. After 200 metres *turn right along Willowbank*, your direction 150 degrees.

After 35 metres, *just before a brick bridge, fork left*, your direction east, along a car-wide footpath, crossing over a stream after 15 metres. Continue along the footpath between houses and gardens. In 200 metres the footpath leads out to a road between the clock war memorial on your right and the Robertsbridge town sign on your left.

Cross over the road to go up a gravel footpath (to the right of a bookshop). After 40 metres cross over a stile. Follow this fenced-in footpath, ignoring a left turn off after 120 metres. After a further 30 metres *turn left down a short driveway for 5 metres to a lane and then turn right*, your direction 100 degrees.

In 100 metres *leave the lane to fork right along a tarmac path to cross the A21 via a footbridge. On the other side of the footbridge, turn right*, initially parallel to the A21 on your right.

Follow the footpath as it curves to the left. In 200 metres you come out into a field and continue down along the right-hand edge of the field, your direction 140 degrees. In 50 metres, where the edge of the field kinks round to the right, continue straight ahead down to the bottom of the field.

In 90 metres pass through a gap in the hedgerow boundary and cross a stream to go uphill between wire-mesh fencing. In 50 metres *ignore a wooden stile ahead to turn half left along a footpath through woods*, your direction 80 degrees. *In 80 metres you pass over a not too clearly defined crosspaths. 15 metres further on you reach a clearly defined crosspaths, where you turn half left*, down a wide earth track, your direction 40 degrees.

In 140 metres, *at the corner of the woods, go to the left and cross over a stile to leave the woods* and keep straight on down the right-hand side of a field, your direction 340 degrees.

In 100 metres go through a metal fieldgate and *turn half right onto a concrete driveway*. After 20 metres go through a wooden fieldgate, your direction 20 degrees. After 150 metres, *at a T-junction, turn left*, your direction 330 degrees. **[9]** *After 120 metres you reach another T-junction and turn right*, your direction east.

Continue along this lane for 1km (0.6 miles) to reach a converted oast-house on your right, a house on your left and double gates ahead leading to (the remains of) Robertsbridge Abbey (closed). Follow the lane as it curves to the right and, after 100 metres, curves to the left. In 140 metres you *pass a three-armed footpath signpost and continue straight ahead along the lane*, your direction 80 degrees. *In 60 metres, as the lane curves to the right, go straight ahead across a stile* to the right of a wooden fieldgate, following a wooden signpost.

Go along the left-hand edge of the field to the field corner to *cross over a stile after 120 metres and turn right along a footpath between fences*. In 100 metres *you come out into a field. Turn left and continue along the left-hand edge of the field*, your direction 80 degrees. In 150 metres, just before the corner of the field **[A1]**, keep straight on past a three-armed wooden footpath signpost and *cross over into the next field. Turn right*, as indicated by a yellow arrow on an old wooden fieldgate post, your direction 170 degrees.

In 100 metres, on reaching the right-hand corner of the field, follow the field boundary round to the left, your direction 70 degrees. In 270 metres ignore a car-wide track entrance into woods on your right and continue straight on along the right-hand edge of the field. After 250 metres *cross over into the next field and continue along its right-hand edge*, with woods on your right, heading towards some large corrugated metal buildings.

After 280 metres, *at the corner of this field, turn left* along a wire fence *to bypass some earthworks*, your direction north. (The official footpath marked on the OS map runs along the north side of the large corrugated metal buildings, but it is currently blocked.)

Where the fence and earthworks (earth bank) end after 70 metres *keep along the right-hand edge of the field for 80 metres to the corner. Here turn right for 10 metres into the next field*, crossing a ditch and *turn right again* **[!]**, *doubling back towards the corrugated metal buildings*, with the ditch now on your right, your direction 160 degrees. *In 80 metres turn left along the wire fence*, with the corrugated buildings now on your right, your direction 100 degrees.

In 80 metres follow the fence round to the right and then to the left, now with a tree nursery on your left. After 160 metres *cross over a footbridge* and follow the footpath through a lightly wooded area for 40 metres *to cross over a stile out onto a B road*.

Cross this busy road with care and continue straight ahead, going up the footpath through woods. In 30 metres you cross over a car-wide track, with a wooden fieldgate on your right, and continue straight on gradually uphill, your direction east, along the right edge of the woods, with a fence 10 metres off to your right.

In 100 metres you emerge from the woods into the bottom of an orchard. *Cross a car-wide track to go uphill along a 10 metre-wide path through the orchard*, your direction 110 degrees. In 140 metres, *at the top edge of the orchard, turn left*, as indicated by a yellow direction arrow on a footpath post. Follow the orchard edge as it curves to the right and uphill.

In 120 metres, *at the top right-hand corner of the orchard, cross a stile* to go up a footpath through woods, your initial direction 150 degrees. In 100 metres the footpath merges with a wide path from the right. After 150 metres you emerge from the woods and *pass a three-armed wooden footpath signpost. Continue straight on* up through a slight cutting between two fields, your direction 80 degrees.

In 350 metres, *at a footpath junction marked by a three-armed wooden footpath signpost, ignore a stile to the right and follow the footpath half left uphill through a cutting*, your initial direction 100 degrees. In 160 metres this path merges with a car-wide track from the right. In 50 metres you *come out onto a road. Cross this road to go up Shoreham Lane*, signposted 'Ewhurst Green ¼'. *In 50 metres turn left across a stile.* **[A2]**

Go down across the field passing to the left of a tree 30 metres ahead, aiming for a mini pylon pole with a transformer box mounted on it (which is often hidden by foliage in summer, but the cable run into the trees gives it away), your direction 10 degrees.

In 250 metres *you reach the corner of the adjacent land (which juts onto this field) with the mini pylon pole just over the field boundary. Cross over a stile* next to the pylon pole to come out onto a shingle drive after 20 metres, your direction 20 degrees.

Go down an initially sand shingle car-wide track. In 130 metres *as the track turns to the left, turn right* at a four-armed footpath signpost, to go through Bramley organic orchard, your direction 80 degrees. In 250 metres cross a footbridge and leave the orchard to go up a footpath through woods. In 200 metres cross a stile to emerge from the woods and continue across a field, heading towards a wooden fieldgate, your direction 80 degrees. In 120 metres *cross a stile to the left of the wooden fieldgate and continue straight on, along a lane,* towards Ewhurst Green.

In 220 metres turn left, as marked by a wooden footpath signpost, just before the driveway leading down to Romney Lodge (a house with a large pond in its front garden), your direction 340 degrees.

Go down a car-wide earth track for 100 metres to *cross a stile to the left of a metal fieldgate. Continue straight down the middle of the field,* your direction 330 degrees, with a hedgerow approximately 30 metres up to your right. Where the hedgerow turns *right in 220 metres, curve slightly left downhill towards a stile 150 metres distant.* (The stile is to the right of a metal fieldgate and 15 metres before a mini pylon pole.)

Cross the stile and turn right. In 50 metres cross over a footbridge with a stile on it and go along the left-hand edge of a field, your direction 350 degrees. *In 300 metres, at the corner of the field, cross over a footbridge flanked by two stiles* and continue in the same direction, passing a corrugated metal barn on your right.

In 50 metres turn left to cross a stile to then, after 2 metres, go over a stile on your right. Cross the **Rother Valley Steam Railway** *track, climb over a stile and turn right* to go along the right-hand edge of the field parallel to the railway.

In 150 metres, *on reaching the field corner, follow it round to the left,* as indicated by a wooden footpath post, and continue along the right-hand edge of the field, your direction 340 degrees.

In 240 metres, at the next field corner, go up onto the flood protection embankment and turn left with the river Rother on your right. After 280 metres, as you approach Bodiam Road Bridge, *drop down to the left to cross over a stile to the right of a metal fieldgate* (50 metres to the left of Bodiam Bridge).

Having crossed over the stile, *turn right to go along the pavement to cross over Bodiam Bridge* and, after a further 80 metres, you reach the **Castle Inn** on your left for lunch. (Alternatively, 10 metres after Bodiam Bridge, turn right through the gate for the Bodiam Castle tearoom for lunch.)

To continue the walk refer to the main walk directions from [6].

b) Stonegate to Robertsbridge long walk:

Follow the main walk directions of the **Stonegate Circular** *walk (walk 19 in this book) until* [4].

Having crossed over the stile, *cross the road (A265) and turn left. In 30 metres turn right as marked by a bridleway signpost.*

Go down a car-wide track as it veers to the right. **[!]** After 180 metres, and *15 metres before reaching a bungalow, fork right away from the bungalow* down a car-wide earth track, indicated by a bridleway arrow on a post to your right (which is often hidden by foliage in summer), your initial direction 190 degrees. In 100 metres, at the bottom of this car-wide track, go through a metal fieldgate into a field. Continue straight ahead, marked by a bridleway arrow, down across the field, aiming for the right-hand corner of a wood, your direction 140 degrees.

In 120 metres at the fenced in corner of the wood continue down with the wood on your left as the path veers to the right. In 100 metres go through a wooden gate into the wood and continue down a cutting through the wood.

After 200 metres go through a wooden gate to emerge from the wood to continue

Castle in the air

Picture the platonic ideal of a medieval fortress and, guaranteed, you'll come up with somewhere that looks very similar to **Bodiam Castle**. With its bucolic parkland setting, its turrets and towers and wide spring-fed moat, all Bodiam needs to complete the fairytale picture is a troop of knights clattering over its drawbridge and a keening damsel gazing from its walls.

The castle was built by the splendidly named Sir Edward Dalyngrygge on his estate in 1385 as a defence against the increasingly threatening French (who had sacked nearby Rye and Winchelsea in 1377). However, by the end of the century the danger of invasion has reduced considerably and Bodiam became more of a family home for Dalyngrygge.

The only military action that the castle saw was during the Civil War (1642-51), when the interior was more or less gutted. It was then left to deteriorate until a local squire, John 'Mad Jack' Fuller, bought it for £3,000 in 1828 to save it from destruction. It wasn't until 1916, however, when it was bought by Lord Curzon, that an extensive restoration was carried out, though today it remains essentially a shell.

Bodiam Castle

Bodiam, nr Robertsbridge, TN32 5UA (01580 830436/tearoom 01580 830074/www.nationaltrust.org.uk). **Open** *Castle Early Feb-Oct* 10am-6pm daily; *early Nov-early Feb* 10am-4pm Sat, Sun. *Tearoom/shop Early Feb-Oct* 10am-5pm daily. *Nov-23 Dec* 10am-4pm Wed-Sun. *Jan-early Feb* 10am-4pm Sat, Sun. **Admission** £4.20; £2.10 concessions; £10.50 family. **Credit** AmEx, MC, V.

---

down the left-hand edge of a field, with a hedgerow on your left. In 100 metres, *at the corner of the adjacent field on your left, turn half left* to go diagonally across the field towards a metal fieldgate, your direction east.

In 200 metres go through the metal fieldgate and continue along the right edge of a field, with a stream on your right, your direction 60 degrees. In 180 metres, *at a car-wide bridge on your right with a three-armed footpath signpost next to it* **[B1]**, *turn left towards a metal fieldgate* (5 metres to the right of a large oak tree) 70 metres distant, your direction 350 degrees.

Go through the metal fieldgate to turn half right into the next field, your direction 45 degrees. Go up a gentle incline, passing by a shrub hill fenced in on your left, heading towards a car-

wide field entrance just to the left of a mini pylon pole.

In 140 metres go through the car-wide field entrance. Continue up, in the direction marked by a footpath arrow, towards two adjacent electricity wooden poles with a grey transformer box mounted half way up, your direction 50 degrees.

In 220 metres cross a stile just to the right of the transformer box poles to then cross a four-plank footbridge and then go along the left-hand edge of a field. In 70 metres go through a fieldgate to go along the left-hand edge of a small open space, with an oast-house ahead to your right, your direction 10 degrees.

In 80 metres *turn left onto a lane*, your direction 290 degrees. In 50 metres go through a metal fieldgate into Borders Farm. Bear round to the right to pass

a cowshed on your left and then a red-brick house. After 100 metres, *on reaching a T-junction, turn right* up a lane. In 70 metres you pass the cattle grid entrance to Borders Farm on your right.

35 metres further on *turn right over a stile* **[B2]** to go down the left-hand edge of a field, your direction 160 degrees. *In 120 metres turn left to cross a stile and footbridge to then turn right* and continue in the same direction along the right-hand edge of a field.

After 50 metres veer right to go through a metal fieldgate to cross back over the stream and continue in the same direction along the left-hand edge of a field. In 60 metres, *where the left-hand field hedgerow curves to the left, go diagonally across the field towards a metal fieldgate on the far side*, passing under mini electricity pylon cables, your direction 100 degrees.

In 150 metres *go through a car-wide gap to the left of the fieldgate*. Continue along with a stream on your right. *In 35 metres turn right to go through a metal gate* and over a footbridge. Continue up the left-hand edge of a field, your direction 150 degrees.

[!] *In 100 metres* (60 metres before the top left-hand corner of the field) *turn half left through a dilapidated wooden fieldgate* to go diagonally across the next field towards a car-wide exit with a footpath arrow on the right post, your direction 80 degrees. *In 60 metres cross a car-wide bridge* and go through a wooden fieldgate *into the next field. Turn right up a slight incline* towards the top right-hand corner of the field, your direction 120 degrees.

In 100 metres, at the right-hand field corner, go through a metal fieldgate and continue up the right-hand edge of the

next field, with a wood on your right.
In 180 metres, near the top right-hand corner of the field, ignore a metal fieldgate on the right and follow the right-hand edge of the field round. In 30 metres (with a cattle trough 10 metres to your left) turn right through a metal fieldgate up into the next field. Go up this field initially, with a fenced-in wood on your left, your direction south-east, towards a metal fieldgate at the top left-hand corner of the field.

In 180 metres go through the fieldgate to *continue up a lane* passing a red-brick house on your right and cowsheds on your left. In 100 metres the lane curves to the right and, after 80 metres, to the left by a two-armed footpath signpost. In 50 metres you pass the entrance to Fontridge Manor on your right and, after 80 metres, reach a lane junction with a small postbox on your right.

Continue down the lane and, after 100 metres as the lane curves to the right, **[!]** *fork left along an unmarked footpath,* your initial direction 130 degrees.

In 40 metres cross a stile to follow the footpath arrow diagonally down across the field, heading towards a fieldgate with a small wood to the left of the fieldgate, your direction 100 degrees. In 200 metres, *having crossed the field, do not go through the fieldgate, but veer right* to go down the left edge of the field, your direction 140 degrees.

In 70 metres, at the left-hand corner of the field, *cross a footbridge flanked by two stiles to immediately cross a third stile. Turn left* to follow the arrow on the third stile to go *along the left-hand edge of a field,* with mini pylon poles on your right, your direction 60 degrees. In 140 metres, as you approach the second wooden pylon pole on your right, turn half right up a slight incline between the second and third wooden pylon poles.

After 200 metres, *at the rise of the hill,* go through a narrowing to *cross into the next field.* Continue along the upper ridge

of this field, passing Willard's Hill Farm buildings on your right, *to reach the upper right corner of the field.* In 200 metres go through a metal gate **[B3]** to *cross a lane and continue along the footpath,* bearing round initially to the left, with a wooden fence on your right, *to then emerge into a field* after 30 metres.

In 20 metres turn right onto a shingle track, with mini pylon cables on your left, your direction east. In 140 metres *follow the track round to the right to cross a stile* to the left of a metal fieldgate. *Turn left* to go down the left-hand edge of a field. *After 200 metres,* at the left-hand corner of the field, *cross a footbridge* flanked by two stiles.

Go diagonally up across a field, with mini pylon cables away to your right, and head *towards a stile,* your direction 80 degrees. In 180 metres, at the field edge, go through a car-wide gap into the next field, passing the (redundant) stile on your right. *Continue in the same direction up towards a wooden telegraph pole to the left of a partly obscured red-brick house.*

After 150 metres you reach the brow of the hill at the right-hand edge of the field, with the red-brick house on your right, to continue down the upper right-hand edge of the field. In 50 metres, *at the corner of the field, go through a wooded field boundary,* passing a dilapidated stile on your right. *In 15 metres emerge into a field and turn left* to go down the left-hand edge of the field. After 180 metres, at the bottom of the field, *cross over a car-wide concrete bridge,* your direction 30 degrees.

[!] *On the other side of the bridge continue straight ahead to go along the left-hand edge of a field,* with the hedgerow on your left. (The footpath post straight after the bridge indicates that you should cross over into the next field to walk with the hedgerow on your right – this is erroneous.)

After 130 metres, at the left-hand corner of the field, go through a metal fieldgate into the next field. Head uphill along the right-hand edge of the field. In 150 metres, at the top right-hand corner of the field, pass through a metal fieldgate to come out onto a concrete car-wide track leading to Squibs Farm. After 20 metres you pass a footpath arrow on a post on your right. In 50 metres you reach a farm track crossroads, with a four-armed wooden footpath signpost 15 metres ahead.

You now follow the main walk directions from [2].

c) Alternative ending along the river Rother:

Follow the main walk directions to [6].

Come out of the main exit next to Bodiam Castle tearoom and toilets [6] to *cross the road and turn left.* In 30 metres, *immediately before Bodiam Bridge, turn right to go through a gap between a hedge and the bridge.* Follow the path along the river in a south-west direction.

In 1.5km (0.9 miles) you come *out onto a busy B road* [C1] (**take care** on this road – it has no verges or pavement and traffic sometimes comes quite fast). *Cross over to turn left* and immediately cross a road bridge, your direction south. *In 150 metres turn right across a stile just before a narrow bridge*, following a footpath signpost, your direction 240 degrees, to go along the left-hand edge of a field with a ditch on your left.

In 400 metres, *at the corner of this field, continue straight on, passing a pillbox on your right. In 20 metres you go up onto an embankment*, with the river Rother on your right and a stream on your left.

After 700 metres follow the footpath left down some steps into a field, with a three-armed footpath signpost [C2] at the bottom of the steps. *Turn right along the right-hand edge of the field*, your direction 250 degrees. In 150 metres, at the field boundary, ignore the footpath to the right to *continue straight ahead along a fenced-in footpath between fields.* (Note:

if there has been recent heavy rainfall this may be flooded, in which case take the footpath to the right, which will link up after 150 metres.)

In 200 metres follow the footpath to the left to come out onto a concrete car-wide track after 15 metres. Continue along the track, your direction 190 degrees. After 40 metres *turn right, as marked by a bridleway post, and follow the bridleway round, with the house on your right. In 180 metres turn left onto a lane*, your direction west. In 140 metres the lane curves to the right and, after 100 metres, curves to the left as you pass the double gates on your right leading to (remains of) Robertsbridge Abbey (closed). Continue along this lane for 1km (0.6 miles) to reach a lane junction with a lane off to left (Redlands) [9] to join up with the main walk route.

Lunch & tea places

Bodiam Castle tearoom *Bodiam, nr Robertsbridge, TN23 5UA (01580 830436).* **Open** *Early Feb-Oct* 10am-5pm daily; *early Nov-23 Dec* 10am-4pm Wed-Sun; *Jan-early Feb* 10am-4pm Sat, Sun. This is the suggested tea stop for the main walk.

Castle Inn *Main Street, Bodiam, TN32 5UB (01580 830330).* **Open** 10am-3pm, 5-11pm Mon-Thur; 11am-11pm Fri, Sat; noon-10.30pm Sun. **Food served** noon-2pm, 7-9pm daily. Located 8km (5 miles) from the start of the walk, the Castle serves moderately inventive food and has a west-facing garden. This is the suggested lunch stop for the shorter walk option.

Ostrich *Station Road, Robertsbridge, TN32 5DG (01580 881737).* **Open** 11am-11pm Mon-Sat; noon-10.30pm Sun. This pub serves tea and coffee.

White Horse Inn *Hurst Green, Etchingham, Silver Hill, TN19 7PU (01580 860235).* **Open** noon-11pm Mon-Sat; noon-10.30pm Sun. **Food served** noon-9.30pm daily. Situated 5km (3 miles) from the start of the walk, the White Horse serves imaginative food and has a large west-facing garden. This is the suggested lunch stop for the main (or long) walk.

Pluckley Circular

The Low Weald of Kent and the *Darling Buds of May*.

Start and finish: Pluckley station
Length: 11km (6.8 miles)
Time: 3 hours 30 minutes. For the whole outing, including trains and meals, allow 7 hours.

Transport: Two trains an hour (one an hour on Sunday) go from London Charing Cross to Pluckley (journey time: 1 hour 12-26 minutes). Trains back from Pluckley are once an hour. For those driving, the car park at Pluckley station costs £2 a day on weekdays, but is free at weekends.

OS Landranger Map: 189
OS Explorer Map: 137
Pluckley, map reference TQ922433, is in Kent, 9km (5.6 miles) west of Ashford.

Toughness: 1 out of 10.

Walk notes: There's a remote, away-from-it-all feeling to this short, gentle, peaceful, quintessentially English walk in rural Kent. Passing small farms, oast-houses, timber-framed houses, lush pastures, apple orchards and ancient oaks, it's easy to see why HE Bates, whose house is passed in the idyllic hamlet of Little Chart Forstal, was inspired to create the country-loving Pop Larkin and family in the classic *The Darling Buds Of May*. The walk is almost entirely flat or with gentle gradients, but later gives you a surprising view out across the plains of the Low Weald. It is at its most 'perfick', as Pop Larkin would say, in the first two weeks in May, when the apple blossom is out. However, in summer there's an abundance of wild flowers and gardens in full bloom, and in early autumn the orchards are heavy with fruit.

Walk options: To shorten the walk, you can stop at Little Chart, and catch a bus from the Swan Inn (point [5] in the text) to Ashford. From Monday to Friday there are two afternoon buses, at about 1pm and 5pm, from the Swan Inn to Ashford (phone 0345 696996 for details), and there are trains every half hour from Ashford to London.

Saturday Walkers' Club: Take the train nearest to 9.30am (before or after) from Charing Cross to Pluckley.

Walk directions

[1] [Numbers refer to the map]
Coming from London, exit the platform at **Pluckley station** through a yellow gate to *cross the small car park and follow the path straight ahead to the right of a lamp-post*, your direction 30 degrees.

In 70 metres, at the end of the path, turn right down a gravel track. In 40 metres go through a gate beside a house to your left, and then *cross a small field*, your direction 100 degrees. In 25 metres *cross a dilapidated stile and follow the path slightly left across an open field, aiming for a tall oak tree* to the right-hand end of a line of lower trees, your direction 70 degrees.

In 150 metres *cross a hidden stile to the left of the oak tree*, then go across two wooden planks over a ditch. Turn right and in 5 metres *head out across a large open field*, your direction still 70 degrees. In 150 metres pass under mini pylons. In a further 400 metres go through a

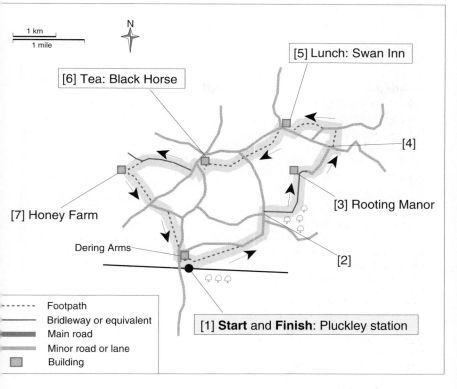

1 km
1 mile

N

[5] Lunch: Swan Inn

[6] Tea: Black Horse

[4]

[3] Rooting Manor

[7] Honey Farm

[2]

Dering Arms

- - - - - Footpath
———— Bridleway or equivalent
━━━━ Main road
━━━━ Minor road or lane
⬛ Building

[1] **Start** and **Finish**: Pluckley station

hedge in the middle of a field via an obscured wooden bridge and a stile.

Continue in the same direction across the corner of the next field towards a gap in the hedge to your left, which is roughly at the left end of a clump of trees. *In 150 metres go over a stile and turn right along a tarmac lane*, your direction initially east. Continue along the lane as it veers to the left, ignoring all turnings off.

In 400 metres ignore two roads off to the right. In another 320 metres ignore a road to Hothfield on your right. 140 metres after this *as you come level with a tall hedge on the left-hand side of the road, turn right down a bridleway* beside a house called Saracens. **[2]**

Follow the track past the house on your left and pass to the left of wooden stables,

with a wood on your left. In 70 metres *go through a wooden gate* and continue straight ahead. In a further 60 metres *go through another wooden gate and continue along the fence to your right*, your direction initially east.

In 80 metres the fence veers left. In another 80 metres, where it turns sharply to the right, follow the car-wide track half left across the field, your direction east. In 140 metres ignore a yellow arrow pointing right along the edge of a wood. In a further 100 metres *pass through into the next field and turn left onto a car-wide track*, with woodland to your left and the open field to your right, your direction north.

In 150 metres ignore a path off to the left and keep straight on, now with a crumbling brick wall to your left. Follow

The church of **St Nicholas**, **Pluckley**. *See p237.*

this for 350 metres until you pass through a fieldgate. In a further 70 metres you pass houses, including an oast-house and the half-timbered **Rooting Manor [3]** on your left; *the lane becomes tarmac. Continue on this tarmac lane ignoring ways off.*

In 450 metres pass houses on both sides, and in 100 metres *you come to a T-junction with a road*, with a view of the North Downs ahead **[4]**.

Cross the road and turn right. In 60 metres, 10 metres after Rooting Street Farm Riding Centre on the opposite side of the road, turn left across a stile, your direction 20 degrees. Walk down the edge of the field, keeping the hedge on your right. I*n 150 metres, at the end of the field, cross a high stile in the hedge on your right, and then turn left*, your direction 160 degrees initially, to follow the edge of a fenced garden surrounding an oast-house.

In 60 metres follow the fence as it veers to the left. In a further 60 metres cross another high stile behind an oak tree *leading to a quiet road. Turn left*, your direction west, into the attractive village

of **Little Chart Forstal**, passing the oast-house on your left, and with the village green on your right. In 130 metres on your left, just past a slit-windowed barn, is the house where **HE Bates** lived (*see p236* **It's got to be perfick**).

In another 50 metres, *just beyond the end of the green, take the signposted footpath to your right*, your direction 320 degrees, with a delightfully lopsided timber-framed house on your left. In 30 metres pass a pond on your right, then another one in 20 metres on your left, and then pass Thatch House. Keep straight on through the house's parking area, and then on with a garden hedge to your left.

In 30 metres *turn left with the hedge*. In 60 metres *cross a stile to the right of a large oak tree*, and a small dilapidated plank bridge immediately afterwards. Keep straight ahead along the left edge of a field, your direction west. *In 70 metres, cross a stile on your left and follow the Greensand Way (GW) arrow half right across a large field*, keeping 10 metres to the left of a tree immediately ahead, your direction west initially.

Keep straight on. *Once you reach the brow of the hill aim for a house in the corner of the field below.* There are likely to be electric fences crossing the path; the way to safely cross these is to unhook the orange handles to pass through.

Having passed through the fences continue towards the house in the far corner of the field. When you reach this, in about 200 metres, *cross a stile to the left of a metal fieldgate, and turn right onto a road* that has faster traffic than it may at first appear into the village of **Little Chart**.

To avoid walking along the road, in 40 metres cross over to the churchyard and follow the grass verge parallel to the road. On your left is the brick church of **St Mary the Virgin**. In 70 metres descend steps to get back onto the road. The suggested lunch stop, the **Swan Inn**, is now on your right **[5]**.

After lunch, come out of the pub and *from the car park cross back over the road and go up steps and into a grassy field, with the church on your left. Veer slightly to your right across the field,* your direction 220 degrees, following the direction of the middle of the GW signs.

In 110 metres *cross over a car-wide track and enter an orchard through the gap in the corner of a line of tall trees* (these are planted to protect the apple trees from the wind), following a yellow GW arrow.

Turn right immediately, with the line of trees to your right, **[!]** *but in 15 metres veer left at another yellow arrow on a post, to cross diagonally through the orchard on a narrow track,* your direction 230 degrees.

In 70 metres *pass through another line of tall protective trees,* with another yellow arrow on your right. Continue straight on and in another 150 metres *pass through a gap in another line of trees into an open space* with three large chestnut trees in it. *Turn right* along the edge of the open space, your direction initially 310 degrees.

In 50 metres turn left with the line of trees, and in another 100 metres **[!]** *cross a low stile on your right,* marked with a yellow arrow. *Veer half left along a wide grassy track* through more fruit trees, your direction 260 degrees, passing under a line of mini pylons.

The **Black Horse, Pluckley**, reputedly the most haunted pub in Britain. *See p238.*

It's got to be perfick

Pluckley has two claims to fame: as the setting for the TV series of **HE Bates'** *The Darling Buds of May* and as the most haunted village in England.

Herbert Ernest Bates was born in Northamptonshire in 1905. He honed his literary skills as a provincial journalist, and published a series of highly praised novels, short stories and essays, largely concerning rural life, in the 1920s and '30s. It was World War II, though, that made HE Bates famous. He was commissioned as a writer for the Royal Air Force in 1941 and produced a number of much-lauded collections of stories and novels on wartime themes (such as *How Sleep the Brave*). He continued to develop as a writer after the war, and wrote his most popular novel *The Darling Buds of May* in 1958. In the early 1990s the book was adapted as a TV series, starring David Jason and Catherine Zeta Jones, and filmed in Pluckley. Bates lived in nearby Little Chart Forstal, and died in 1974.

As to Pluckley's other boast, it is difficult to find a local who'll admit to ever having seen one of the many **ghosts** (at least 12) that are reputed to haunt the village. (This could have much to do with weariness at the endless procession of ghost-hunters who pass through.) If you are very lucky, and possessed of a highly active imagination, though, you could stumble across the discerning poltergeist that haunts the Blacksmiths' Arms and is supposed to prey only on teetotallers, or the Red Lady who frequents nearby St Nicholas' churchyard, sobbing as she searches for the unmarked grave of her stillborn baby.

The land on which this walk takes place was owned for almost 900 years by the **Dering family**, who only sold it in 1928. One reminder of this is the distinctive double-arched Dering windows on all the houses that you pass on this walk. The Dering family crest of a black horse is also visible on the cowls of the oast-houses, and in the south chapel of the church of St Nicholas in Pluckley, as well as on the sign of the Black Horse pub in Pluckley.

In 140 metres, at an arrow on a post, go down a short slope through a copse, your direction 240 degrees. In 10 metres *go through a wooden swing gate*, your direction initially 250 degrees. *Carry on along a fenced path*, with a vineyard on your right. In 100 metres *cross two stiles* and continue straight along the right-hand edge of a meadow, with a wire fence and a line of trees on your right.

In 120 metres *cross a stile between brick walls* and keep straight on, with a garden on your left and a brick wall to your right. In 50 metres *go left onto a tarmac road* and [!] *in 5 metres go through an unsignposted*

opening to your right to resume your former direction, 250 degrees. Continue straight ahead through the orchard. In 100 metres pass a house with a pretty cottage garden on your right. Continue straight on, with a tall hedge now on your right.

70 metres later cross a tarmac track, noting on your right a barn with an unusual glass tower on its roof. Carry straight on with a hedge on your right, in 60 metres passing an impressive Dering-style (*see p236* **It's got to be perfick**) house with a formal garden on your right. In another 120 metres go over a faint car-wide track, and keep straight on with

a line of protective trees now on your left and fruit trees on your right.

In 400 metres *go through a gap between tall trees and emerge onto a cricket pitch. Veer half left across the pitch, passing a skateboard area on your left. In 30 metres turn left to go through a wooden gate and in 30 metres pass through a lych-gate to enter the churchyard of* **St Nicholas**.

Follow the path to the right of the church, and after visiting it exit the churchyard by the black hooped gate, then continue for 25 metres down a gravel track and *turn right on the road* into **Pluckley** (*see p236* **It's got**

to be perfick) to the suggested tea place, the **Black Horse [6]**.

Coming out of the pub, turn right. In 40 metres at a T-junction cross the road and turn left down Forge Hill, your direction 240 degrees. *After 40 metres turn right on the signposted bridleway*, initially a part tarmac driveway. In 100 metres go through a small metal gate to the left of a fieldgate.

In 80 metres cross a stile to the left of a fieldgate. In 10 metres turn left through a metal gate into a field with fine views of the Low Weald to the south. *Cross the field diagonally*, heading towards a farm with an oast-house in the distance in the valley below, your direction 310 degrees. In 150 metres go through a metal gate and continue across the next field, your direction 290 degrees.

In a further 250 metres pass a GW arrow on a post on your left and in 40 metres *go through a concealed fieldgate tucked away to the left in the far corner of a field. Turn right, following the field edge,* your direction initially west. *In 100 metres ignore a path to the right and veer left with the field edge,* keeping the ditch to your right and heading for a house ahead (Honey Farm), your direction 240 degrees.

In 300 metres you reach the edge of the garden of Honey Farm and a yellow arrow footpath signpost. **[7]** *Turn left here, heading out across the centre of a large arable field,* aiming for the left corner of the wood and a house on the low ridge in the distance, your direction 140 degrees. In 500 metres at the far side of the field, continue in the same direction uphill along the right edge of the next field.

In 200 metres turn right onto a suburban road. In 25 metres pass the **Blacksmith's Arms** on your right. In 60 metres more *turn left down Lambden Road.* In 80 metres ignore a now redundant stone marker for a footpath sign on your right. In 200 metres pass a green arrow footpath sign to your left. 20 metres after this, just past Spens Cottage on your right, *turn right through a metal fieldgate with an overgrown stile to its right,* your direction 210 degrees.

In 60 metres *emerge into an open field and veer left across it* in the direction of a GW arrow on a pole, your direction due south. In 140 metres *cross a wooden bridge and a stile in the corner of the field and continue uphill half right across a field,* heading towards two small trees whose tops are just visible on the horizon (NOT the two more fully visible trees more to the right), your direction 200 degrees.

Cross the field for 300 metres. As you climb the two small tree tops become a clump of trees: head towards a stile to the left end of these. (As you get closer still,

you see the trees are in fact aligned along a field boundary stretching away from you.) *When you get to the stile cross it* and beware of the electric fence immediately past it. Lift an orange handle to cross this.

Continue diagonally downhill across the next field, your direction 170 degrees, heading towards a house partly hidden by trees, and later an arched gap in the trees/ hedge. In 300 metres, when you get to the gap, pass through another electric fence to cross a stile. *Turn right onto the road.*

In 300 metres you come to the **Dering Arms** on your left-hand side, with hump bridge and slippery road hazard signs on the road ahead of you. *Turn left on the road beside the inn,* and in 80 metres you come to **Pluckley station**. Cross the footbridge to the opposite platform for trains to London.

Lunch & tea places

Black Horse *The Street, Pluckley, TN27 0QS (01233 840256).* **Open/food served** 11am-11pm daily. Located 8.2km (5.1 miles) into the walk, this pub serves fairly basic food all day. It has a cosy old-fashioned charm and a pleasant walled garden, and also serves tea, coffee and desserts. This is the suggested tea stop for the main walk.

Dering Arms *Station Road, Pluckley, TN27 0RR (01233 840371).* **Open/food served** 11.30am-3pm, 6-11pm Mon-Sat; noon-3pm, 7-11pm Sun. Beside Pluckley station, this former hunting lodge is now an award-winning pub specialising in seafood. Be sure to book. Note that only a snack menu is available on Sunday evenings.

Swan Inn *The Street, Little Chart, TN27 0QB (01233 840702).* **Open** *May-Oct* noon-11pm daily. **Food served** noon-3pm daily. Located 5.8km (3.6 miles) into the walk, the Swan has a riverside garden and serves good, home-cooked food at lunchtimes. This is the suggested lunch place for the main walk.

St Nicholas Church in Pluckley, serves cream teas with home-made jam from the end of May until the end of August.

Picnic: Across the road from the Swan Inn in Little Chart, the grassy field beside the church makes a good picnic spot, as does the churchyard at St Nicholas in Pluckley.

Amberley to Arundel

The Downs, the river Arun and a riot of wildflowers.

Start: Amberley station
Finish: Arundel station
Length: 14.5km (9 miles)
Time: 4 hours 30 minutes. For the whole outing, including trains, sights and meals, allow at least 9 hours 30 minutes.
Transport: Hourly trains run from London Victoria to Amberley (journey time: 1 hour 20 minutes). Arundel is one stop up the line, so buy a day return to Arundel. Return trains from

Arundel to Victoria run twice an hour (hourly on Sunday; journey time: 1 hour 22-26 minutes). For those driving, park at the station car park at Amberley. Trains back from Arundel only take 5 minutes, but are hourly.
OS Landranger Map: 197
OS Explorer Map: 121 Amberley, map reference TQ026118, is in West Sussex, 9km (5.6 miles) north of Littlehampton.
Toughness: 5 out of 10.

Walk notes: This is a very beautiful and not too strenuous Downs walk, which starts with a gradual climb among a luxuriance of wild flowers throughout the summer months. It takes in the pretty village of Burpham for lunch. After lunch it meanders along the River Arun to Arundel, allowing a visit to the castle for those who arrive before 4pm. Arundel is also remarkable for the fact that it contains five branches of Peglers, the specialist walking and expedition outfitters.

Walk options: It is possible to shorten the walk by calling a taxi from the lunchtime pub in Burpham back to Amberley or on to Arundel.

Saturday Walkers' Club: Take the train nearest to 9.20am (before or after) from Victoria to Amberley.

Walk directions

[1] [Numbers refer to the map]
On arrival at **Amberley station**, coming out of the exit from platform 2, turn left down the road. *In 50 metres cross the main road and turn right. Continue along*

the pavement. After 200 metres, just after Boundary Cottage, the footpath runs behind a 3 metre-high hedge. In 180 metres *turn right up a lane called High Titten*. Climb this lane steadily, avoiding all signposted paths or turn-offs for the South Downs Way, *until you reach some 5 metre-high round grain silos after 1.1km (0.7 miles)*. (En route the tarmac lane curves to the right past a house called Highdown.)

Just before the grain silos turn left at a two-armed footpath sign. **[2]** (Looking back from this point there is a wonderful view down the valley.) Follow the sign up a car-wide farm track. In 60 metres go through a metal fieldgate with a sign to the right prohibiting 'Access to Cars and Motor Bikes (Except for Access)'. The track here goes past two sets of farmyard barns. In 250 metres, at a three-armed footpath signpost, bear right, continuing on the car-wide farm track.

In 50 metres *at a metal fieldgate with a stile on its left bear right along the lower farm track*, your initial direction 120 degrees. (On this walk it is important not to be tempted to take signs for the South Downs Way.) Keep climbing up and

Arundel Castle from the river.

round to the left, ignoring ways off on the right-hand side. *Follow this white unmade road*, its borders alive with red poppies and white wild daisies and a myriad of other wildflowers in late July, *for 1.5km (0.9 miles) always climbing gently.*

Carry on upwards *towards a large wooded area on the brow of a hill. Just before the wooded area turn left off the track through a gate* by a two-armed signpost and take the path beyond to the right. Keep going up this bridleway with woods on your left. *In 250 metres, at a field, bear right.* (Another track joins from the left.) *In 350 metres you come to a very obvious junction* with a three-armed footpath signpost. **[3]** *Go right for 20 metres and immediately left* at another three-armed signpost. Your way is now straight on down this bridleway, with lovely views to your right *for 1.8km (1.1 miles).* After 1.5km (0.9 miles) you come to a three-armed sign on your left and a sign announcing 'Angmering Park Estate Walkers and Riders Welcome'. Go straight on past the sign, continuing in the same direction as before.

In 300 metres, *at a bridleway post* **[4]** *on your left, just before a fieldgate*

opening and a wooden fieldgate beyond, turn right down a car-wide track (turning back slightly on yourself across a field), your direction 290 degrees. *After 500 metres, at the bottom* by a wooden bridleway post, *turn left*, your direction 200 degrees. Follow a car-wide bridleway *towards some farm buildings*, which can be seen ahead 900 metres distant.

After passing the farm buildings on your left you continue along the car-wide farm track. *A kilometre past the farm buildings you come to a main road. Go straight across and on into* **Burpham**. Going along this road with pretty cottages and houses to left and right you ignore one turning to the left and come after 500 metres to the **George and Dragon** on the left (opposite **St Mary the Virgin Church**), the suggested lunchtime stop in Burpham.

After lunch *go left out of the pub.* In 40 metres follow a signpost in foliage to your right to go *past a cricket pavilion on your left and along the left side of the cricket pitch.* (Please give respect to the game: pausing when balls are being bowled, etc.) In 120 metres take a path to the left of a children's play area. In 50 metres go straight through a gate and continue

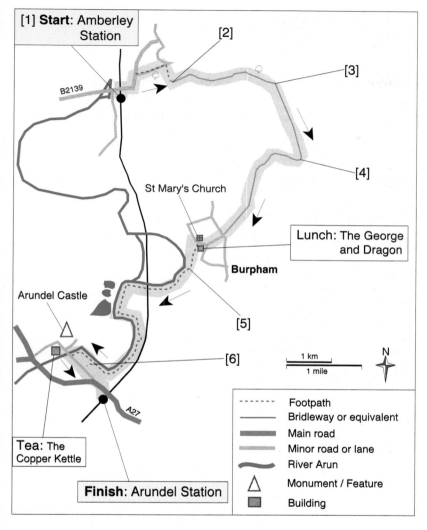

[1] **Start**: Amberley Station

B2139

[2]

[3]

[4]

St Mary's Church

Lunch: The George and Dragon

Burpham

[5]

Arundel Castle

[6]

1 km
1 mile

N

Tea: The Copper Kettle

Finish: Arundel Station

- - - - - - Footpath
———— Bridleway or equivalent
━━━━ Main road
▬▬▬▬ Minor road or lane
〜〜〜 River Arun
△ Monument / Feature
▣ Building

straight ahead. In 160 metres *go down some steps leading down to the valley below.*

In 40 metres, at the bottom of the steps, go over a stile **[5]**, your direction 260 degrees. **Arundel Castle** is visible in the distance. *You now follow the river into Arundel* for the next 4km (2.5 miles) until **[6]** below.

In more detail: In 250 metres go over another stile. In 70 metres cross a footbridge flanked by two stiles. Turn right along an embankment. Continue onwards for 300 metres to go over a pair of stiles, still following the embankment.

In 250 metres you come to a railway line and turn left towards a pedestrian railway

Cottage industries

Located next to Amberley station, **Amberley Working Museum** lives up to its name. Not only does the 36-acre open-air site provide a fascinating retrospective on the industrial heritage of South-east England, but it also provides a home for a range of craftspeople working in traditional ways and aims to preserve and promote such skills for future generations. The museum's collection ranges from transport-based exhibits (such as vintage buses and a narrow-gauge railway) to industry-based displays (including the Print Workshop and Wheelwrights).

Amberley Working Museum
Amberley, Arundel, BN18 9LT (01798 831370/www.amberley museum.co.uk). **Open** *Mid Mar-end Oct* 10am-5.30pm Wed-Sun. **Admisson** £7.50; £4.30-£6.50 concessions; free under-5s. **Credit** MC, V.

crossing. Go right over the crossing, looking and listening carefully for trains. Climb over the stile on the other side and head towards a rock face with an attractive pub underneath called the Black Rabbit (which can only be reached by crossing the bridge at Arundel or South Stoke).

Continue on the embankment, crossing four more stiles. In 2km (1.25 miles) cross the fourth stile with a railway crossing ahead. Don't go over the railway crossing; instead, go to the right with the river on your right. Cross over another stile, with the river on your right-hand side. Arundel Castle now looms ahead again about 1.5km (0.9 miles) away.

In 1km (0.6 miles) you go through a kissing gate frame. Boats and craft are moored to your right. In 70 metres you reach a two-arrow footpath post. **[6]**

[If you don't want to take tea, turn left here. At the road you turn left to the roundabout after 80 metres. Continue straight on to reach the station on your right after 300 metres.]

Otherwise continue straight on. In 350 metres follow the footpath round to the left away from the river to continue straight ahead through two concrete posts. In 40 metres you come *out onto a road* (Queen Street). *Turn right to cross the road bridge.* In 60 metres *continue ahead across a mini roundabout* up the

High Street. *In 90 metres (25 metres past the war memorial) turn left onto Tarrant Street.* In 60 metres you reach the *recommended tea stop, the* **Copper Kettle**, *on your left.*

After tea, retrace your steps back to the High Street. Turn right at the High Street to go back down towards the river. *Cross the bridge and proceed for 400 metres to a roundabout.* At this roundabout *bear left to* **Arundel station***, which is located on your right-hand side,* 300 metres along this busy road.

Lunch & tea places

Copper Kettle *Tarrant Street, Arundel, BN18 9DG (01903 883679).* **Open/food served** 9.30am-5.30pm Mon, Tue, Sun; 9.30am-5.30pm, 7-9.30pm Wed-Sat. This pleasant tea shop is the suggested tea stop for the main walk. There are plenty of other tea places in Arundel.

George and Dragon *Burpham, BN18 9RR (01903 883131).* **Open** 11am-2.30pm, 6-11pm Mon-Sat; noon-3pm, 7-10.30pm Sun. **Food served** noon-2pm, 7-9.30pm Mon-Sat; noon-2.30pm Sun. Serves good if somewhat pricey food. This is the suggested lunch place for this walk.

Swan *27-29 High Street, Arundel, BN18 9AG (01903 882314).* **Open** 11am-11.30pm Mon-Sat; noon-10.30pm Sun. **Food served** noon-2.30, 6-9pm Mon-Fri; noon-9pm Sat, Sun. Probably the best of Arundel's many pubs.

Hassocks to Upper Beeding

Devil's Dyke and the South Downs escarpment.

Start: Hassocks station
Finish: Upper Beeding (bus to Shoreham-by-Sea station)

Length: 16.1km (10 miles). For a shorter walk and other variations, *see below* **Walk options**.

Time: 6 hours. For the whole excursion, including meals and trains, allow 10 hours 30 minutes.

Transport: Two direct trains an hour (one an hour on Sunday) go from London Bridge to Hassocks (journey time: 55 minutes). Buy a day return to Shoreham-by-Sea, however (not Shoreham in Kent). To return from Upper Beeding, take bus 2A or 20X from the opposite side of the road to the Kings Head pub. Buses to Rottingdean and Old Steine both go to Shoreham station (half-hourly Monday to Saturday, hourly on Sunday, until around 10pm; for info call 01273 886200 or see www.buses.co.uk). Hourly direct trains run from Shoreham to London Victoria (two an hour at peak times; journey time: 1 hour 12-20 minutes); there are also trains to London Bridge if you change at Brighton.

For those driving, it is best to park in Hassocks, returning at the end of the day from Shoreham, changing at Brighton station. Or, on Sundays, you can park at Brighton and use buses to do just the afternoon section of the walk.

OS Landranger Map: 198
OS Explorer Map: 122
Hassocks, map reference TQ304155, is in West Sussex, 9km (5.6 miles) north of Brighton.

Toughness: 8 out of 10.

Walk notes: It is a matter of opinion as to which is the finest view in South-east England, but the amazing panorama from Devil's Dyke on the South Downs escarpment is a strong contender. Such beauty comes at a price, though, and the area around the viewpoint can be exceedingly busy on a fine weekend. However, the South Downs also afford numerous other less-frequented viewpoints; this walk introduces you to several of them, including tranquil Wolstonbury Hill and Edburton Hill.

The morning in particular is a delightful series of climbs and descents on slopes covered by rare chalk grassland. Note, however, that this section is quite strenuous, with around 500 metres of ascent and 300 of descent before the lunch pub. In the afternoon – which is somewhat easier on the leg muscles, though still with a couple of short uphill sections – you follow the South Downs Way for a while across Fulking Escarpment, before descending into the riverside village of Upper Beeding for tea.

Walk options: Directions for the following variations are given at the end of the main walk text (*see p251*).

a) Alternative ending via the valley:
This is a longer optional ending that
avoids all civilisation all the way into
Upper Beeding. It takes you on a
dramatic route right down the front of
the Downs, and then across the flat
plains, through tranquil water meadows
and pasture to Upper Beeding. However,
this way can be **flooded or very wet
in winter**. From November to February,
therefore, the route as per the main text
is probably best. Directions for this are
given at the end of the main walk text.

b) Ending at a railway station: You can
take a different, if slightly longer, route
from point [6] or [7] respectively in the
text to finish at either **i)** Fishersgate or
ii) Shoreham station. See the directions
at the end of the main walk text.

On Sundays only, bus No.77 goes
hourly from Brighton's main railway
station to Devil's Dyke, which enables
you to do either the morning or
afternoon of this walk as a separate
section. The morning section (8km
/5 miles: 3 hours walking time) is
particularly recommended for this
treatment. The afternoon section is
also 8km (5 miles), or slightly longer
via the alternative ending above. From
Brighton the first bus is at around
10.40am: the bus stop can be found
on the right-hand side of the left-hand
of the two roads leading away from the
front of the station. The last bus back
from Devil's Dyke is 5.25pm (possibly
later in summer): the stop is right next
to the pub. To check times call 01273
886200 or look on www.buses.co.uk.

Saturday Walkers' Club: Take the
nearest train to 8.50am from London
Bridge to Hassocks (note that trains
also serve Kings Cross Thameslink
16 minutes earlier).

Walk directions

[1] [Numbers refer to the map]
Leave **Hassocks station** *by the exit
on platform 2* (the platform you arrive

at from London), passing out into the
station car park.

*In 40 metres, opposite the Hassocks
Pub, turn right down a path between
houses* signposted 'South Downs'. *At the
main road turn right.* In 40 metres *cross
the road to turn left* up a wide earth path,
following a South Downs signpost.

In 150 metres *cross a road to go half
right* following a footpath sign. In 100
metres go left at a T-junction in front of
the stone wall of the railway embankment,
your direction 200 degrees. The path
comes up level with the railway line in
due course and you carry straight on with
a wood on your left.

Ignore various stiles to the left. In
370 metres, where the wood ends, keep
straight on along a path fenced off from
a field to your left. At the end of the field,
at a footpath crossroads, *turn right on a
brick bridge over the railway line.*

5 metres beyond the end of the brick
wall of the bridge ignore a footpath to
the right and carry straight on towards
a fence of metal spikes 10 metres ahead.

*Cross a stile, hidden by a bush, just to
the right of the fence* to continue in the
same direction (240 degrees) as before
along the edge of a field, with a wood to
your right. Directly ahead at this point you
can see the rounded curve of Wolstonbury
Hill, which you will shortly climb.

In 100 metres, at the end of the field,
pass through a green metal gate with
a V-shaped stile to its right. In a further
50 metres pass through another green
metal gate, this time with a V-shaped
stile to its left. Follow a fenced track for
a further 40 metres to cross a stile and
emerge onto the road.

[!] Cross this road with care.
It may look like a country lane, but it
is a main road, and traffic can appear
suddenly over the hill to the right.
*Turn right onto the road for 30 metres
and then go left on a broad farm track*
following a green footpath sign, your
direction 260 degrees. In 25 metres a
hedge starts to the right-hand side.

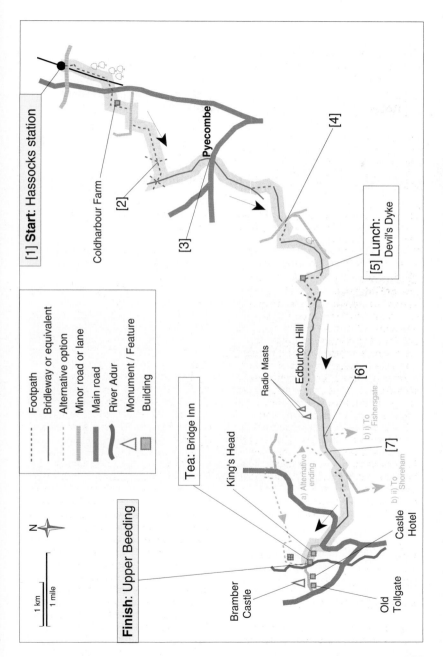

[1] **Start**: Hassocks station

Coldharbour Farm

[2]

[3]

Pyecombe

[4]

[5] Lunch: Devil's Dyke

Edburton Hill

Radio Masts

[6]

b) ii) To Fishersgate

[7]

a) Alternative ending

b) i) To Shoreham

Tea: Bridge Inn

King's Head

Finish: Upper Beeding

Bramber Castle

Castle Hotel

Old Tollgate

Footpath
Bridleway or equivalent
Alternative option
Minor road or lane
Main road
River Adur
Monument / Feature
Building

N

1 km
1 mile

Happy graze

Hard though it is to believe now, in their natural state the prehistoric **South Downs** would have been thickly forested like the rest of England. The first clearance came in the Neolithic period (the Stone Age), when the Downs were favoured by settlers for their easily cultivated soil and defensive advantage.

Later, the Downs were used for animal pasture, creating unique chalk grasslands. Grazing kept the grass short, enabling a wide range of wild flowers to grow. During World War II, and with the advent of modern farming, large areas of the Downs were ploughed up to grow cereals. The remaining pastures were often neglected, allowing the spread of bushes and reducing wild flower populations.

Conservation efforts today tend to focus on reintroducing grazing to the remaining grasslands: the sheep and cows you see on this walk are thus very much workers in the environmental cause.

In 140 metres you come to a stile and a three-armed footpath sign at the far end of the field. Go straight ahead, ignoring a faint path that forks half right across the field, with the field edge now on your left, your direction still 260 degrees

[!] *In 90 metres, 30 metres before you get to the end of the field, cross a stile to your left.* This is marked by a three-armed footpath sign, but it is hidden in the brambles to the left of the stile. *On the far side of the stile go right*, immediately crossing another stile and entering a wood. 5 metres beyond this the path turns half left downhill.

In a further 40 metres cross a V-shaped wooden stile and go left onto a car-wide path under an avenue of trees, your direction due south. In 70 metres pass to the right of a wood and brick barn, and carry straight on towards the farmhouse ahead, with a pond to your left. *Pass to the*

right of the farmhouse up a gravel drive between hedges, which climbs gently uphill. *In 230 metres this brings you out onto a road, where you turn right.*

Stay on the road for 280 metres as it crests a hill – giving a good view of Wolstonbury Hill half left – and then descends into a dip. At the bottom of the dip, *turn left up a tarmac drive,* marked with a footpath sign, your direction due south. To the left of the drive a sign says 'PRIVATE DRIVE. NO HORSES, NO CARS', but this is a public footpath.

In 70 metres, as the drive curves half right in front of a house, *go through a kissing gate to the right of a wooden five-bar gate,* and on up the broad track beyond, with a wood to the right and the house initially to your left. In 50 metres ignore a track to the right. A National Trust sign hidden in the bushes just before this announces Wolstonbury Hill.

Continue straight on uphill on the car-wide track. In 150 metres the trees end to the left, and in 50 metres more you emerge onto the saddle of the ridge. Ignore a metal gate and a V-shaped stile straight ahead and instead *follow the track to the right for 15 metres to a T-junction.*

Ignore the car-wide track to the left here and *go half right through a wooden gate* to the right of a seven-bar metal gate, and emerge onto the open hillside. Follow the broad grassy path straight ahead up the rounded **Wolstonbury Hill** in front of you, your direction 270 degrees.

In 300 metres the path crosses a stile and continues on upwards a bit more steeply. Be sure to look back on this ascent, for fine views of the Jack and Jill windmills and the Downs above Hassocks.

Near the top of the hill cross a low ditch and rampart (see p253 **Taking stock***).* Go straight on for 100 metres to the summit, marked by a concrete trigonometry post. **[2]** A fine view presents itself. The distant hill straight ahead topped by telecommunications masts is Truleigh Hill, which you will visit mid-afternoon.

Keep straight on from the trigonometry post, your direction 280 degrees, until you come in 70 metres to the far rampart of the fort. Keep straight on downwards following a grassy path. In 40 metres skirt a huge depression (a former gravel pit?) on your right.

In 100 metres, *just beyond the end of this depression, cross a stile to continue straight on downhill. 40 metres beyond this veer right to cross a ditch in another 40 metres.*

On the far side of the ditch turn left downhill, your direction 270 degrees. In 30 metres, just before you reach a line of thickets, you come to a substantial track, which at this point forks half right and right *at an old footpath post with a blue arrow. Take the fork that goes half right,* towards the thickets ahead.

In 60 metres pass through a gap in the thickets to carry on down an enclosed path that can be abominably muddy in winter. In 30 metres, *at a T-junction, go left through a gate and then left again onto a wide bridleway* between bushes and trees, your direction 130 degrees. This bridleway can be a complete quagmire after rain or in winter.

Ignore all ways off and carry on first gently uphill, then level or gently downhill for about 800 metres until the bridleway curves up to the left to join a broad car-wide track. Merge with this track, which mercifully has a much firmer surface. Carry on along the track down to the village of **Pyecombe**, where it becomes a road.

The road comes to a T-junction, with a phone box on your left, just before the noisy A23. **[3]** *Go straight ahead, crossing the A23 on a footbridge. On the far side go straight ahead uphill,* your direction 200 degrees, ignoring a tarmac pedestrian and cycle path left and right, up a stony path bounded to the left by a wooden fence. In 25 metres, pass through a wooden gate, and in 20 metres another, onto the open hillside.

Keep straight ahead up the hillside, with a fence and then a hedge to your left.

In 300 metres, *where the hedge curves away to the right, cross it at a four-armed footpath sign. Keep straight on in roughly the same direction as before* (250 degrees initially), curving gently left up the hill to the ridge ahead on a broad grassy path.

In 600 metres at the top of the hill pass through a line of thickets and through a wooden gate onto a broad grassy hilltop, marked by a National Trust sign for **New Timber Hill**. Beyond the gate *go left, following the hedge on your left-hand side*, your direction due south.

In 350 metres, *at the top of the hill, turn right at a footpath crossroads, following a fence downhill* and keeping it to your left, your direction 260 degrees. There is another sign for New Timber Hill here. On a clear day you see the sea and Brighton to your left.

In 300 metres, 50 metres from the bottom of the field, *ignore a faint path forking to the right and go straight down a steep bank*, still following the fence on your left-hand side. *Pass through a gateway* with a missing gate, marked by a blue arrow, and *carry on down the stony track beyond*, which soon passes into a cutting.

In 130 metres, as you emerge from the cutting, ignore a gate with a blue arrow right, and carry straight on for 25 metres to pass through a gate ahead and *out onto a concrete car-wide drive* that soon becomes gravel.

Ignore all ways off. Pass two houses to the right and a track to the left into a farm building complex opposite them. *60 metres beyond this ignore another track curving left into the farm complex and keep straight on, slightly uphill* on a car-wide track, following a blue arrow on a post, your direction 260 degrees.

[!] *In 40 metres fork half left off this track onto a path that descends steeply downhill, following a blue arrow on a post*, your direction 230 degrees. In 40 metres you come to a gate and cross one farm track to go straight ahead down another to reach a road in 30 metres. **[4]**

(If you are feeling tired at this point and want your lunch, you can cross the road, turn left and take the broad track that almost immediately rises half right from the road. This broad path takes you up through woods, eventually emerging at the top of Devil's Dyke, reaching a road, where you turn right for 100 metres to get to the pub. However, this route only gives you views of Devil's Dyke at the last possible minute. The suggested route is much more dramatic and involves only a little more effort.)

The recommended route is to *cross the road and go right. In 25 metres descend the steep bank from the road following a public footpath sign to cross a stile.* The public right of way (not a path as such: just a route) goes downhill alongside the tarmac track to the right, your direction initially 270 degrees.

In 140 metres you pass a mini pylon. **[!]** *30 metres beyond this, fork left from the tarmac track onto a grassy path* following a yellow arrow on a post, your direction 290 degrees. In 120 metres you pass a double-poled mini pylon, and carry on steeply downhill, with thickets to your right. In 70 metres the path *veers right into a ditch and* in 20 metres *you come to a stile hidden in the far right-hand corner of the field.*

Cross this and descend steeply 40 metres into a wood to a *T-junction, where you go left*, slightly uphill, on a broad track, your direction 200 degrees. In 100 metres you come to a gate, at which point the trees end and you have a dramatic view up the steep-sided valley of **Devil's Dyke**.

One track veers right along the bottom of the valley, but instead *take the left fork, a broad path, which climbs steadily on a narrow shelf* up the side of the valley, your direction initially 160 degrees.

In 150 metres ignore a faint path that forks uphill straight ahead to curve right with the main path. As you climb, the Devil's Dyke pub, the lunch stop, comes into view at the top of the Dyke half-right.

In 500 metres, near the lip of the Dyke, you come to a three-armed footpath sign, where you fork right, keeping just below the rim.

In 160 metres, when this path finally climbs over the lip, go straight ahead for 30 metres to meet a broad gravel track. *Turn right on this for 30 metres and then fork right off it again* on a faint path between bushes, your direction 290 degrees. (If you fail to find this faint path, stay on the main track until you get to the road, and then turn right to get to the pub)

In 60 metres the bushes fall away and you find yourself on a narrow track on the very lip of the Dyke. In 200 metres *this brings you to the neck of the Dyke, the uppermost point of the valley, and a footpath crossroads. Go straight across this* and on up the slope ahead, following a purple arrow on a post to a gate 30 metres up the hill.

Beyond the gate keep on uphill on a clear path, ignoring a path forking left at a footpath post in 30 metres. In 50 metres you climb a small bank and find yourself in the car park of the **Devil's Dyke** pub, the **lunch stop [5]**. The viewpoint is on the far side of the pub.

After lunch, emerge from the pub and, facing the escarpment and north, turn left, crossing the road that leads to the car park and walking straight ahead along the escarpment, roughly towards a brick structure on the hill to your left, your direction 230 degrees. In 50 metres cross over a stile and in 120 metres pass over a low ridge of earth.

(For the 45 minutes or so it will take you to walk from here to Truleigh Hill, easily identified in the distance by its tall telecommunications masts, it does not really matter which path you choose, so long as *you keep the escarpment in view on your immediate right.* Beware that some lower paths slant downhill to the villages below the escarpment, however.)

The recommended route is as follows. *100 metres after the low ridge broad grassy paths diverge. Keep on the higher, left-hand, one,* your direction 280 degrees, following the top of the escarpment to converge with another, higher path in 100 metres. The merged path goes through a metal gate, and past a National Trust sign for Fulking Escarpment.

Stay on this path as it rises over the top of the hill and descends the far side, your direction now 310 degrees. In 400 metres you reach a fenced field on your left-hand side and pass two low wooden barriers on your right to continue straight on, with the field fence on your left.

In 220 metres, as you start to climb out of the dip, pass through a gate to the left of what may be an open passageway or may be fenced off with metal barriers. *Just beyond this, where the path diverges into two car-wide tracks, take the right fork* towards the top of an electricity pylon visible over the rise ahead, your direction 290 degrees. In 300 metres, on the far side of the rise, this path descends to a pylon and rejoins the main path. Almost immediately, you pass through a double metal gate.

The main path now curves left on a broad stony track, and most other walkers follow it. But **the recommended route** – much better and less extra effort than it appears from this vantage point – is to *climb straight up the green hill in front,* your direction 300 degrees, keeping slightly to the right of the faint path that slants up the hill.

Near the top of this hill – **Edburton Hill** – a stile leads you into a fenced enclosure that surrounds the remains of earthwork defences. This is a fine, peaceful vantage point to sit and contemplate the scenery.

There is only one entrance to the enclosure, so to carry on cross back over the stile and follow the fence around to the right to *continue in your former direction, with the escarpment to your right,* heading for the three communications masts on Truleigh Hill, your direction 260 degrees. In about 200 metres the dip that separates

Edburton and Truleigh Hills comes into view and *you can see the main path curving in from the left to a gate. Head for this gate*, which is another 300 metres or so away.

Pass through the gate and *follow the main car-wide track, your direction initially 240 degrees, ignoring all ways off, as it curves left and then curves right* to climb to the top of **Truleigh Hill**.

In 580 metres, at the top of the hill, you pass a brick barn with a cylindrical metal tank in front of it on your right, and remain on the broad track as it crosses the top of the hill towards some houses 250 metres further on at the top of the next rise. 70 metres beyond the start of these houses, ignore a track to the left, marked by a footpath sign **[6]** to carry straight on.

(At this point, you can take option **b) (i)** the **Ending at a railway station** option to **Fishersgate** station; see directions at the end of this main walk text.)

In 60 metres ignore another track to the left to carry on downhill towards what looks like a white house with pine trees to its right. This turns out to be a Youth Hostel, and is in fact made mostly of brick.

Past the hostel the track is lined by pine trees. After you emerge from the trees the track becomes a tarmac road, and *shortly afterwards you see a rusted metal gate on your right-hand side*, marking the point at which a broad path (actually a grassy farm track) turns right off the road to climb the hill between two field fences. (There was once a three-armed footpath sign, and may well be one again, but at time of writing it had vanished). **[7]**

(At this point, you can, if you wish, take option **a)** the **Alternative ending via the valley**; follow the directions at the end of this main walk text. Note that this route is NOT advised during winter. At this point, you can also take option **b) (ii)**, the **Ending at a railway station** to **Shoreham station**; directions for this are also at the end of this main text.)

The **South Downs**.

Otherwise, to continue on the main walk, *ignore the footpath to the right at point [7] and carry on along the road.*

In 500 metres, 150 metres after the road curves to the right, cross a stile to the right, marked by a footpath sign and a yellow arrow. Descend directly downhill, your direction 320 degrees, for 70 metres to a line of thickets where the ground falls away sharply. *Turn left here, your direction 240 degrees, following the edge of the escarpment,* at first keeping level for about 90 metres, then gently descending on a path that curves right and then left, and *in 350 metres comes to a kissing gate.*

Beyond the gate the path descends for 30 metres to *a broad path in a deep cutting that slashes crossways downhill. Turn left onto this, and then in 15 metres turn right through a gate. Beyond the gate turn half left,* your direction 260 degrees, to follow a well-defined path that gently descends around the curve of the hill.

In 400 metres this comes to a gate at the edge of an area of thickets, and in 10 metres comes *to a T-junction with a track.* Ahead is a small Southern Water building. *Turn right down the track,* your direction 330 degrees, and follow it for 320 metres to the main road, the A2037.

Turn left along the A2037 for 500 metres, ignoring small side roads and tracks until you come to a mini roundabout, beyond which is a pub, the Rising Sun. Here, turn right, past a BP petrol station down the High Street.

40 metres beyond the BP garage, at the next mini roundabout, go left. You are now on the 2A and 20X bus route and, just beyond the mini roundabout, on the right-hand side of the road as you are walking, is the first possible bus stop: to check bus times here, look for times to Rottingdean or Old Steine.

For tea, stay on the road through **Upper Beeding** village. In 270 metres you come to the **Kings Head** on your left, the first of two possible tea stops. The bus stop back to Shoreham station is on the

opposite side of the road to the pub. 50 metres further on is the **Village Pharmacy and Store**, which sells cakes, and 50 metres beyond that, just before the bridge, is the **Bridge Inn**, the second possible tea stop.

(By carrying on across the bridge you can also continue into Bramber, a pretty and historic village dominated by its ruined Norman castle. In 200 metres you pass the half-timbered St Mary's House on your left and, 50 metres further on, the Castle Hotel and Inn on the left. 150 metres further on, also on the left, is the Old Tollgate Restaurant and Hotel, a possible alternative tea stop.

To get to Bramber Castle, cross the road from the Old Tollgate and climb the path to St Nicholas's Church. The entrance to the castle is immediately beyond it. To get back to Shoreham station from Bramber, take the 2A and 20X bus from the stop opposite the Castle Hotel: this is the same bus that serves Upper Beeding.)

Once on the bus, you pass for a short period through open country then under the Brighton bypass into Shoreham. You know you are getting close to the station when you pass down the substantial shopping street of Shoreham High Street, after which you see Shoreham harbour on the right. Just after an Esso petrol station, also on the right, the bus turns left up Eastern Avenue, curving back on itself. A few hundred metres after this it reaches a T-junction and goes right, almost immediately passing over the railway line on a level crossing. Get out at the bus stop just after this level crossing, and you will find yourself right by Shoreham Station. (If you miss the stop, the bus also goes via Portslade station and ends up in the centre of Brighton.)

Walk options

a) Alternative ending via the valley: *Follow main walk directions until* [7].

At point **[7]** *take the broad grassy path to the right between two field fences.* This climbs for 100 metres, and then starts to descend the hill on the far side. Pass a rusted gate and a stock pen on your right, and then another rusted gate.

In another 100 metres, when the fence ends to your left, at a footpath post with two arrows, *go three quarters right, your direction 50 degrees.* **[!]** The path that seems to go in this direction (a livestock track) is a little confusing. The actual route lies about ten degrees to the right of it, to the left of the faint remains of a field boundary (a small ridge and one or two old fence posts are all that mark it now).

Follow this route, roughly contouring along the ridge for 350 metres to a metal gate next to a metal five-bar gate. If you miss this gate, you will come to a broken down barbed-wire fence: follow it uphill to just before the crest of the hill, where you will find the gate.

Pass through the gate and follow a blue arrow three quarters left, directly down the ridge on an initially indistinct path, your direction 320 degrees, aiming straight for an artificial lake about 1.5km (0.9 miles) away in the valley below. A wonderful panorama of flat fields opens up below: **if they look flooded, however**, the onward route will be barred, and you should retrace your steps to the road and follow the Direct Route.

In 450 metres you will have descended to a saddle between the main hill and a spur that projects out ahead of you. You are approaching fences ahead and to the right. *In the corner of the two fences is a wooden gate. Go through it and steeply downhill, now on a bridleway between two fences.* Corrugated farm buildings are directly below you in the valley.

Descend steeply on this path, your direction initially 340 degrees, as it curves left through a rusted gate, then right in 60 metres, and later right into a wooded area after another 300 metres, before finally turning left and *down to the road* 180 metres later.

Turn left along the road. **[!] Take care on this road**. Though an innocent-looking minor road, cars come along it at

some speed. *In 350 metres you come to a T-junction with the A2037. Cross this to turn right along its far side* (a safer proposition than the road you have just left, as it has a broad grass verge).

In 50 metres you pass a house on the left named Burrells, and then 100 metres later, at the end of a tall hedge, one called Bramleys. 50 metres further on *turn left along a tarmac drive to Horton Hall Farm,* marked with a public footpath sign.

[!] In 100 metres, *near the end of the drive, ignore a footpath signposted right and carry straight on towards the closed metal gates of the house 30 metres ahead.* **Surprisingly, the onward route is through these gates. Unlikely as it seems, as you approach them they will open automatically to admit you into the garden of the house.** And yes, this is a public right of way.

Walk straight ahead towards a white dovecote 30 metres away, and then just beyond it turn left on the grass for 20 metres. Just opposite a metal gate marked 1964-1986 *turn right following a footpath sign,* which may be concealed by a hedge in summer. Almost immediately you pass a green metal tank and in 10 metres *go through a rusted metal gate.*

Beyond this turn left, following a footpath sign. In 15 metres when the field edge turns half left, follow it, your direction now due south, with Horton Hall's garden on your left. *In 120 metres, as the field ends without a hedge or fence, turn right following a footpath sign. Keep to the (unfenced) left-hand edge of the field.* In 130 metres cross a stile and keep straight on, still on the (now fenced) left-hand edge of the field.

In 160 metres the path curves half left with the fence, following a footpath sign, your direction now 220 degrees. *In 280 metres where the fence goes hard left, the path goes right* (NOT quite in the direction of the footpath sign), your direction 290 degrees. In 40 metres *it joins a small creek on the right and follows it for 60 metres to a stile on the right. Cross this stile and another straight away and then turn immediately left.* You are now following the bank of the larger creek, which is to your left.

In 110 metres cross a wooden footbridge over a side creek. Beyond it bear right a bit, your direction 290 degrees, and in 120 metres cross another footbridge, this one in a rather poor state of repair.

Go straight on, and in 70 metres in a field corner, *you go through a metal fieldgate and straight ahead (ignoring a footpath arrow that seems to point slightly right).* You can see two green farm buildings ahead: head for a point in the fence about 50 metres to the left of these, where you cross a stile after 120 metres.

40 metres beyond this the path converges with a hedge to the left, and you cross a stile to continue on a path fenced off from the field. *In 25 metres turn left with this path across two planks and through the hedge, after which you turn right and continue in the same direction as before,* a fence now on your left. *In 60 metres you emerge onto a car-wide tarmac track and go right.* It becomes a concrete and then a gravel track, curving slightly left.

In 200 metres at a three-armed footpath sign, and about 40 metres before the track turns left to a house, go left over a stile to the left of a wooden fieldgate. Beyond the stile go half left, following a creek on your right-hand side. In 650 metres *pass through a metal fieldgate* and in 70 metres

through a hedge, crossing a stream on two wood planks. *Cross a stile just beyond this and emerge onto the banks of a much larger water channel.*

Follow this channel as it curves right, but *when it curves right again in 150 metres, by a lone tree on its bank, keep straight on,* diverging from it, towards a line of thickets straight ahead. In 100 metres, *just before the thickets, cross a path and carry straight on for 5 metres up a track between hedges* that crosses a small water channel (not necessarily immediately visible in summer). The hedges end and you emerge into a broad meadow, where the path forks.

Go left onto a broad track that follows the water channel to your left, your direction initially 240 degrees.

In 60 metres the track curves left with the creek, and shortly after this you can see the **Priory of St Peters in Beeding** on a low hill ahead left. In 120 metres ignore a footbridge that crosses the water channel to your left, unless you want to go up and take a closer look at the priory.

In 110 metres climb up onto an embankment and you find yourself on the bank of the River Adur. *Turn left along this,* your direction 210 degrees initially. In 20 metres go through a kissing gate and just beyond this stay on the embankment, ignoring a track forking left. In 300 metres pass through a kissing gate and 120 metres beyond this, just before you reach a stone bridge, veer left

Taking stock

It used to be assumed that **Wolstonbury Hill** was an Iron Age (600-100 BC) fort, but recent research by the University of Bournemouth has cast doubt on that theory. The key factor is that the earth rampart is outside the ditch, and not the other way round, as might have been

expected if the structure was defensive. Instead, it seems more likely that it was a stock pen for cattle or other livestock. The researchers also concluded that the workings on the hill are probably a bit older than originally thought, perhaps dating from the late Bronze Age (1000-600 BC).

off the embankment to reach the road. Just ahead is the **Bridge Inn** in **Upper Beeding**, the first possible tea stop.

To reach the alternative tea stop and the bus stop for the return to Shoreham station, *turn left along the road*. In 40 metres you pass the **Village Pharmacy and Store** on the right-hand side of the road, which sells cakes and other snack items. 50 metres further on, the **Kings Head**, the alternative tea stop, is on your right.

The **bus stop** is opposite it, on the left-hand side of the road. For bus times to Shoreham station, look for the times for buses to Rottingdean or Old Steine: more details on the route are contained in the main walk directions above.

b) Ending at a railway station:
i) to Fishersgate station:
Follow the main walk directions until [6].

Turn left along the track mentioned at point **[6]** in the text and follow a well-defined route – a car-wide track and later a path – across the Downs to Thundersbarrow Hill and Southwick Hill. Just beyond the latter, pick up a line of electricity pylons, which you can follow first along a grassy ridge, and later on urban paths directly to Fishersgate Station, which is on the Shoreham to Brighton line (change at Brighton for London). This walk is 2.2km (1.4 miles) longer than the direct route into Upper Beeding described in the main text above. Note that the area around Fishersgate is drab and industrial, and something of a disappointing end to the walk: furthermore, the only tea option on this route is on or around Brighton Station.

ii) to Shoreham-by-sea station:
Follow the main walk directions until [7].

You can also follow the minor road at point [7] all the way into Shoreham. In 1.6km (1 mile) it turns sharp left and, 3.2km (2 miles) later, it crosses the A27 Brighton bypass to enter Shoreham. Keep straight on and in a further 1.6km (1 mile) you come to a point very near to Shoreham station.

Lunch & tea places

Bridge Inn *High Street, Upper Beeding, BN44 3HZ (01903 812773).* **Open** 11am-2.30pm, 4.45-11pm Mon-Fri; 11am-11pm Sat; noon-10.30pm Sun. **Food served** noon-2pm Mon, Tue, Sun; noon-2pm, 7-9pm Wed-Sat. The Bridge Inn serves hot drinks and the usual pub snacks. This is the suggested tea stop for the main walk.

Castle Inn Hotel *The Street, Bramber, Steyning, BN44 3WE (01903 812102).* **Open** 11am-11pm daily. **Food served** noon-2pm, 6.30-9.30pm Mon-Sat; noon-3pm Sun. Located close to the Old Tollgate, this place also serves tea and coffee, and is open all afternoon.

Devil's Dyke *Devil's Dyke Road, Poynings, BN1 8YJ (01273 857256).* **Open** 11am-11pm Mon-Sat; noon-10.30pm Sun. **Food served** 11.30am-10pm Mon-Sat; noon-10pm Sun. Located 8km (5 miles) into the walk is this large, family-oriented Brewers Fayre chain pub. It serves food all day. This is the suggested lunch stop for the walk.

Kings Head *High Street, Upper Beeding, BN44 3HZ (01903 812196).* **Open** 11am-3pm, 5-11pm Mon-Fri; noon-11pm Sat, Sun. **Food served** 11am-3pm Mon-Thur; noon-3pm, 6-9pm Fri, Sat; noon-3pm Sun. Hot drinks and pub snacks are available. An alternative to the Bridge Inn.

Old Tollgate Restaurant and Hotel *The Street, Bramber, BN44 3WE (01903 879494).* **Open/food served** noon-2pm, 6.45-9pm daily. A possible tea stop in this picturesque village. Note that cream teas are served all day, providing it is not catering for major private functions: phone ahead to check on the day.

Village Pharmacy, Store and Post Office *High Street, Upper Beeding, BN44 3HZ (01903 813218).* **Open** 8.30am-1pm, 2-5.30pm Mon-Fri; 8.30am-1pm Sat. Located between the village's two pubs, it sells, among other snack items, some bakery-fresh cakes.

Picnic: This walk also affords many excellent places for a picnic – in many ways a better option in such fine scenery – including Wolstonbury Hill, the rim of the Devil's Dyke itself, the area in front of the Devil's Dyke pub and Edburton Hill.

Lewes via Rodmell Circular

The South Downs Way and Virginia Woolf country.

Start and finish: Lewes station

Length: 15.2km (9.5 miles). For a shorter walk and other variations, *see below* **Walk options**.

Time: 4 hours 45 minutes. For the whole outing, including trains, sights and meals, allow at least 9 hours.

Transport: Twice hourly trains run between London Victoria and Lewes (journey time: 1 hour 5 minutes).

From London Bridge and other Thameslink stations, you can change at East Croydon for the train from Victoria. For those driving, park centrally in Lewes; the train station has a car park.

OS Landranger Map: 198
OS Explorer Map: 122
Lewes, map reference TQ416098, is in East Sussex.

Toughness: 4 out of 10.

Walk notes: This rewarding walk follows the South Downs Way along ridges of chalk grassland with panoramic views in all directions, keeping in sight of Lewes Castle almost throughout. The walk starts in the historic town of Lewes then quickly rises to follow the ridge of the South Downs Way. After lunch back down in the picturesque village of Rodmell, it follows the banks of the River Ouse back to Lewes.

Walk options: The directions for the following variations appear at the end of the main walk text (*see p260*).

a) Alternative return to Lewes via Northease Manor: This route, which is lower-lying than the main walk route, takes you inland via Northease Manor. It is almost exactly the same length (and walking time) as the main walk route. You follow the main walk directions to point [5], then follow the directions for this option at the end of the main walk text.

b) Shorter walk ending at Southease: You can reduce the length of the walk to 12.5km (7.8 miles) by ending at Southease and returning by train to Lewes from there. Follow the main walk directions until point [6], then follow the directions at the end of the main text.

c) Lewes to Seaford walk (via South Downs): For the ultimate, invigorating long walk (24.8km/15.5 miles) from Lewes to Seaford, you can take the short walk option (b) above, ending at Southease station, then take the separate **Southease to Seaford** (walk 26, option (a) in this book) which starts at Southease station.

Saturday Walkers' Club: Take the train nearest to 9.15am (before or after) from London Victoria to Lewes.

Walk directions

[1] Numbers refer to the map.
Coming out of **Lewes station** (past the ticket office), cross the road and *turn right*

on Station Road, which crosses the railway. In 100 metres turn left on Southover Road, your direction west. In 120 metres cross over Garden Street and enter the flint-walled arched gate to **Southover Grange Gardens** on your left.

Continue on the path inside the gardens with the flint wall to your right, your direction still west. Then after 70 metres take the path off to the left to pass **Southover House** across the lawn on your right-hand side. (You might consider visiting the house for coffee before continuing.) Then after 40 metres turn right just before the water course (20 metres before the public conveniences), your direction west, to enter the walled garden through the arched entrance.

Turn left on the red-brick path to cross the footbridge over the water channel, then bear right to take the path west to exit the gardens through the metal gate in the far corner opposite Elm Tree House.

Turn left on the road (Southover High Street), your direction 150 degrees, to continue for 50 metres up to the mini roundabout. Once there, with the **Kings Head** pub on your left, turn right, still on Southover High Street. Continue west passing **Southover Parish Church** on your left and after 200 metres pass **Anne of Cleves House** on your right.

In 400 metres cross a mini roundabout to continue in the same direction as before, passing the **Swan Inn** on your right, with a three-armed road sign on the left-hand side marked 'Kingston, Rodmell, Piddinghoe'. In 20 metres turn right on Juggs Road. In 350 metres the road veers left and you continue to cross over the A27 deep below on a metal single-track road bridge.

Continue on this tarmac lane uphill following it round as it bears to the left in 200 metres. In a further 200 metres, at the top of the hill, the lane becomes a car-wide track, signposted by a blue arrow. Keep straight on down this, your direction due west.

In 300 metres go through a wooden fieldgate and follow the path in the same direction as before, initially due west with a barbed-wire fence on your right. Take the path across the centre of the field towards the direction of the V-shaped paths ahead on the downs, visible after about 100 metres. In 500 metres exit through the gate (to the left of a wooden fieldgate) on the opposite side of the field.

Continue in the same direction, passing small stables on your right and then a mock-Tudor house on your left. The path becomes a tarmac lane with houses to your left. In 140 metres you cross over a road with a sign on your left telling you this is Kingston [2]. Continue on up the tarmac path opposite with 'The Lodge' on your left and a red postbox on your right.

In 400 metres where the road ends at a junction of tracks and at a three-armed bridleway sign, continue in the same direction with a barbed wire fence to your left and fence posts to your right (and in summer bushes on both sides) to continue uphill along a potentially muddy car-wide track, your direction 240 degrees.

In 300 metres go through a metal gate (to the left of a fieldgate) and continue uphill for 80 metres to where the path divides (the 'V' shape). Take the left-hand fork to follow this path upwards, your direction 230 degrees, until after 600 metres at the top of the hill it merges with the South Downs Way [3] indicated by a post with a blue arrow.

Go left on the South Downs Way ignoring all ways off for the next 3.8km (2.4 miles) until the asterisk below [*].

In more detail: In 70 metres go through a wooden gate (to the left of a fieldgate) and continue uphill with a barbed wire fence to your right. In 100 metres pass a cattle grid on your right to continue up along the South Downs Way, still keeping the wire fence to your right.

In 600 metres pass a double metal fieldgate on your right and ignore a major path running off left downhill to continue along the top ridge with the fence on your right.

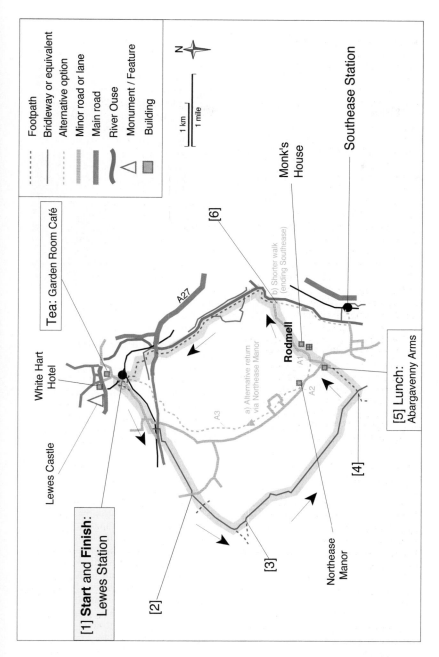

Lewes via Rodmell Circular

Legend:

- - - - - Footpath
———— Bridleway or equivalent
- - - - - Alternative option
▓▓▓▓ Minor road or lane
———— Main road
〰〰 River Ouse
△ Monument / Feature
▓ Building

N

1 km
1 mile

[1] **Start** and **Finish**: Lewes Station

White Hart Hotel

Lewes Castle

Tea: Garden Room Café

A27

A3

a) Alternative return via Northease Manor

Rodmell

A1

A2

Monk's House

b) Shorter walk (ending Southease)

Southease Station

[6]

[5] Lunch: Abargavenny Arms

[4]

[3]

[2]

Northease Manor

Twin peaks

Lewes Castle, which is visible for much of this walk, is a rare example of a Norman fortress with two mottes (castle mounds) within its bailey (surrounding wall). It was built around 1070 by William de Warenne, one of William the Conqueror's most distinguished lieutenants at the Battle of Hastings.

The most significant military action to take place in the area came in 1264 when, at the Battle of Lewes, the rebel Earl of Leicester, Simon de Montfort's army defeated Henry III, leading to England's first parliamentary meeting at Westminster in 1265.

The castle remained in the de Warenne family until the death of the last of their line in the mid 14th century. At around this time it was finally completed, with the erection of its magnificent barbican. In the 17th century much of the castle was pulled down and sold off as building material, though the barbican remains.

The Barbican House Museum contains both the archaeological collections of the Sussex

Archaeological Society and a sound and light show telling the story of the town of Lewes.

Lewes Castle & the Barbican House Museum

169 High Street, Lewes, BN7 1YE (01273 486290/ www.nationaltrust.org.uk). **Open** 11am-5.30pm Mon, Sun; 10am-5.30pm Tue-Sat. **Admission** £4.30; £2.15/£3.80 concessions. **Credit** AmEx, MC, V.

In 140 metres go through a wooden gate on your right, then initially go right uphill for 60 metres passing a wooden log on your left (which is actually a bench made by school pupils – this might not be very obvious in summer). *Then turn left*, still on the South Downs Way, on a concrete track, your direction 130 degrees.

In 1.5km (0.9 miles) at a footpath crossroads cross over a car-wide track to go through a wooden gate opposite with a white post to its left. In a further 300 metres go straight on at a crossroads of paths, through a wooden gate to

continue in the same direction. In 400 metres go through a wooden gate to continue along a path corridor.

In 200 metres at a crossroads of paths at **Mill Hill [4]** (indicated on the black wrought iron gates of the big house on your right) *turn left* on a semi-tarmac lane (broken up) leaving the South Downs Way, following the route of mini pylons, your direction east. (This is Mill Lane)**[*]**.

In 500 metres pass a lane on your left and a sign to your right saying, 'Private Lane, access and bridle path only. No parking, no through road'. Continue as before, your direction 50 degrees. The path becomes a lane and ends at a T-junction with a road. This is the village of **Rodmell**. *Cross the road and turn left* to come to the **Abergavenny Arms [5]**, the suggested lunch stop.

[At this point, you may take option **a)**, the **Alternative return to Lewes via Northease Manor**. Follow the directions at the end of this main text.]

Otherwise, to continue on the recommended route: after lunch, *coming out of the pub, turn left down the lane*, your direction 30 degrees. In 40 metres you pass a National Trust sign on your right saying 'Monk's House 400 yards'. In 400 metres, ignoring ways off, pass **Monk's House** on your right (*see p262* **Woolf's lair**). (If you want to visit the church take the footpath to the right just before Monk's House, opposite the small road leading off to the left 'To Barley Field'.)

In 80 metres just before the road veers left, after passing Navigation Cottages on your left, take the signposted car-wide track straight ahead, crossing through a brown metal fieldgate with Monk's House car park on the right-hand side. The track curves right in 50 metres and in 150 metres passes rough corrugated buildings on your left. 20 metres beyond the buildings go through a wooden gate (to the right of a metal fieldgate), with a water treatment works building on your right, and carry straight on along the car-wide track with a ditch on your right.

Follow this track for 700 metres through two further gates until you come to the raised bank of the River Ouse. Climb up this raised bank **[6]**.

[At this point, you can choose to take option **b)** the **Shorter walk ending at Southease** option. Follow the directions at the end of this main walk text. You should also take this option if you are doing the long **Lewes to Seaford** option **c)**.]

Otherwise, *to continue on the main walk* back to Lewes:

Turn left to follow the path along the banks of the Ouse. You now follow the river all the way into Lewes for 4km (2.5 miles).

In more detail: In 100 metres cross two stiles at a pumping station. In 700 metres cross a stile. In 1km (0.6 miles) cross another stile. In 400 metres descend the bank around a metal barrier passing a sign on your left 'Warning Outfall submerged structure, deep water', and then get back up onto the bank.

In 500 metres go over a stile. In 200 metres cross another stile. In 40 metres go over a stile where a barbed-wire fence starts to your left. In 250 metres go over a stile as the barbed-wire fence ends, and turn left passing a sign indicating 'Rise Farm'. In 5 metres turn right and in 100 metres *pass underneath the A27 road bridge*.

The path now diverges from the River Ouse to your right and passes between bushes to either side. In 100 metres the path veers first right and then in 50 metres left, and *in 10 metres you pass through a gap to the right of a metal fieldgate* to emerge on a road to the left of Lewes household waste recycling site.

In 80 metres pass another metal fieldgate and go under a yellow metal barrier. Keep on the road and in 100 metres it bends right and then in 80 metres left, with a sports field to your left.

In 300 metres the road bends to the right. *In 120 metres you come to a T-junction where you turn left. In 180 metres, at the mini roundabout, go right* (leaving Mountfield Road). In 100 metres you come to **Lewes station** on your right for trains to London. For tea continue on Station Road to cross the railway then after 100 metres cross Lansdown Place and after 50 metres come to the **Garden Room Café**, the suggested place for tea, on your right. If this is closed continue on the road for 100 metres up to the traffic lights. *Turn left* to come to the **White Hart Hotel** in 30 metres on your left.

Walk options

a) Alternative return to Lewes via Northease manor:
Follow the main walk directions until point [5].

Coming out of the pub turn left down the lane, your direction 30 degrees. In 40 metres pass a National Trust sign on your right saying 'Monk's House 400 yards'.

[!] [A1] *In 300 metres turn left off the road following the public footpath yellow arrow opposite a triangular road sign indicating 'School 30mph',* crossing through the kissing gate to the right of the brown-stained wooden fieldgate marked 'Denholme'.

In 30 metres go through a squeeze stile. Continue straight ahead across a small field (an open space), your direction 300 degrees. In 50 metres cross a brick-stepped stile over a flint wall and continue in the same direction with tennis courts to your left and a hedge to your right.

In 50 metres enter a field, passing a wooden fence to your right and a footpath post with yellow arrows, to continue in the same direction to pass under mini pylon cables after 20 metres, your direction 280 degrees. You are following a footpath across the middle of the field.

In 350 metres emerge to the left of the field to rejoin the road. *Cross the road and turn right* to continue in the same direction as before. Follow the narrow grassy pavement on the left-hand side of this road.

In a further 250 metres pass the main gates of **Northease Manor** School on your left at which point the pavement becomes tarmac. **[!]** In 50 metres cross back over the road **[A2]** *to turn right through a double metal fieldgate* onto a car-wide track. *In 10 metres turn left* on the footpath by a post marked 'Public footpath, Iford ¼ mile, Lewes 2½ miles', to enter a field, your direction 340 degrees.

In 280 metres cross a stile into the next field. Walk across this field aiming for the left corner post of a small orchard ahead,

your direction 310 degrees. In 150 metres, on reaching the corner post, continue in the same direction, now with a barbed wire fence on your right. *In 60 metres turn right to cross a stile* (to the right of a metal fieldgate). Come out onto a lane with Charlemore House on your right. *Turn left along the lane.*

In 25 metres, as the lane curves to the left, enter a field via an old metal kissing gate (to the left of a metal fieldgate) with a public footpath sign to your left. Pass under telegraph wires, continuing in the same direction as before, your direction 320 degrees, keeping the hedge and barbed-wire fence to your right as you cross this field.

In 100 metres exit through a metal kissing gate to cross a car-wide track and after 15 metres go through another metal kissing gate. Continue in the same direction as before with a barbed-wire fence on your right, your direction 300 degrees. In 100 metres pass to the left of a redundant stile with a 2.5 metre-high brick wall on your right-hand side.

In 120 metres go over a stile and cross a tarmac lane to continue on the footpath indicated by a sign on the opposite side, between a one metre-high flint wall.

In 30 metres cross a stile on your left to continue in the same direction along the right edge of a small field. In 60 metres cross a stile in the right corner of this small field to cross it along the left edge. In 10 metres pass under a pylon and continue in the same direction. In 180 metres cross over a stile and continue on the footpath through the middle of the field, your direction 330 degrees.

In 180 metres the footpath divides as marked by a wooden footpath post. There is also a circular drain set in concrete between the paths. *Turn right*, your direction 10 degrees. In 350 metres just after passing under mini-pylon cables cross a stile. *Descend some steps and after 15 metres turn right*, as indicated by a footpath signpost to your right, down a concrete car-wide track, your direction 60 degrees **[A3]**.

In 20 metres turn left following the direction of the yellow arrow on the wooden footpath post, your direction 330 degrees. In 30 metres cross a stile and after another 30 metres continue along a narrow footpath between a barbed-wire fence on your left and trees on your right. In 80 metres go over a stile and pass a pen of wooden hutches on your left (where there might be geese).

In 150 metres emerge into a field and veer slightly to the right, your direction 10 degrees. In 300 metres go through a wooden kissing gate, continuing in the same direction. *In 100 metres the path brings you close to the main road on your left, but you veer right following the direction of the footpath* indicated by faded yellow arrows on an old post with a ditch stream to its left, your direction 70 degrees.

In 40 metres pass under mini-pylon cables. In 160 metres go through a wooden kissing gate. In 500 metres the stream goes underground to your left and you *turn left through a wooden gate (to the left of a metal fieldgate) to go in the direction of the busy A27*, your direction 20 degrees. *In 50 metres go through another wooden gate and turn right.*

In 10 metres turn left to take the underpass under the A27 to veer right on the tarmac road, your direction 100 degrees. *In 70 metres turn left at a T-junction*, your direction 350 degrees.

In 50 metres pass the entrance to Southdown Sports Club on your right. *Immediately after, turn right into Priory Ruins, 'Ancient Monument'.* Cross the lawn towards the ruins of the **Priory of St Pancras**. In 150 metres pass to the right of the ruins. In 80 metres pass the knight's helmet-shaped monument on your right 'to mark the 700th anniversary of the Battle of Lewes fought on the 14th May 1264 unveiled by the Duke of Norfolk'.

In 50 metres exit through a 1.5 metre-wide gap in the brick wall leading out onto Convent Field. *In 7 metres turn left up towards a flint wall.* In 20 metres, on reaching the wall (where there is a water tap), *turn right along a tarmac path* with a playing field on your right, your direction east. *In 70 metres turn left, your direction north*, passing a large grass mound behind a wall to your left, and Lewes Football Club to your right.

In 120 metres come out onto the road, where there is a fine view of Lewes Castle on your left-hand side. *Cross this*

Not known at this address

Lewes proudly trumpets **Anne of Cleves House** as one of its prime tourist attractions. The fine 16th-century Wealden building was part of Henry's 1541 divorce settlement with Anne. It's only when you get to the small print that you discover that the unfortunate queen (referred to unflatteringly by Henry VIII as his 'Flanders mare'), never lived here and possibly never even saw the house.

Today, much of the original Tudor splendour of the house has been restored, and the kitchen and a bedroom have been furnished in 16th-century style. There are also displays of Sussex-related crafts and artefacts, including some pottery and ironware.

Anne of Cleves House

52 Southover High Street, Lewes, BN7 1JA (01273 474610/ www.sussexpast.co.uk). **Open** 11am-5.30pm Mon, Sun; 10am-5.30pm Tue-Sat. **Admission** £2.90; £1.45/£2.60 concessions. **Credit** AmEx, MC, V.

Woolf's lair

In 1919 the novelist Virginia Woolf and her husband Leonard bought the modest weather-boarded **Monk's House** in the village of Rodmell as a country retreat. In contrast to the exuberance of nearby **Charleston** (01328 811265), where Virginia's sister Vanessa Bell lived in bohemian conviviality with the artist Duncan Grant, novelist David Garnett and her two sons, Monk's House is a sober, peaceful, introspective place. During their years here the Woolfs entertained many of the leading literary and artistic lights of the time, including EM Forster, TS Eliot and Vita Sackville-West. Yet Monk's House will forever have melancholy associations for Woolf fans. Close by is the desolate spot on the River Ouse where Virginia drowned herself in 1941, wading into the chilly waters, her pockets full of stones. Her ashes are buried in the garden.

Monk's House
Rodmell, Lewes, BN7 3HF (01372 453401). **Open** *Apr-Oct* 2-5.30pm Wed, Sat. **Admission** £2.80; £1.40 children. **No credit cards.**

---

road and turn left. In 20 metres you come to a mini roundabout. Turn right and after 100 metres you come to **Lewes station** on your right for trains back to London. For tea, continue past the station on Station Road to cross the railway, then after 100 metres cross Lansdown Place and after another 30 metres you come to the **Garden Room Café**, the suggested place for tea, on your right.

b) Shorter walk ending at Southease:
Follow the main walk to point [6]. Having climbed the raised bank of the River Ouse *turn right onto a footpath* and cross a wooden stile to follow this path along the west bank of the river.

Follow this path for 1.6km (1 mile), passing wooden gates at 700 metres, then cross a stile after 300 metres, then go through a gate after a further 300 metres. 30 metres from the last gate you *go through a wooden gate to turn left onto a tarmac road crossing the green swing bridge over the Ouse.* In 300 metres you come to **Southease station**.

From here, you can return by train to London, changing at Lewes.

c) Lewes to Seaford walk (via South Downs):
Follow the main walk to point [6]. *Then follow the above short walk option to Southease station.*

From Southease station, you start the separate Southease to Seaford walk (walk 26, option a) in this book).

Lunch & tea places

Abergavenny Arms *Newhaven Road, Rodmell, BN7 3EZ (01273 472416).* **Open** 11am-3.30pm, 5.30-11pm Mon-Fri; 11am-11pm Sat; noon-10.30pm Sun. **Food served** noon-2pm, 6-9pm Mon-Fri; noon-3.30pm, 6-9.30pm Sat; noon-3.30pm Sun. This large friendly pub has a log fire and a wide menu advertising 'traditional english wholesome home-made food'. This is the suggested lunch stop for the main walk. It also offers cream teas during July and August on Wednesdays and Saturdays from 2.30pm to 5.30pm.

Garden Room Café & Gallery *14 Station Street, Lewes, BN4 2DA (01273 478636).* **Open** 10am-5pm Mon-Sat. Situated close to the station, this is the suggested tea stop for the main walk.

White Hart Hotel *55 High Street, Lewes, BN7 1XE (01273 476694).* **Open** 10am-10pm, 12.30-2.15pm, 7-10.15pm daily. One of several alternatives for tea in the centre of town.

Lewes via West Firle Circular

A historic town, the South Downs and the River Ouse.

Start and finish: Lewes station

Length: 23.3km (14.5 miles). For shorter walk variations, *see below* **Walk options**.

Time: 6 hours walking time. For the whole outing, including meals, breaks and trains, allow 11 hours.

Transport: Twice hourly trains run between London Victoria and Lewes (journey time: 1 hour 5 minutes).

From London Bridge and other Thameslink stations, you can change at East Croydon for the train from Victoria. For those driving, park centrally in Lewes; the train station has a car park.

OS Landranger Map: 198
OS Explorer Maps: 122 and 123 Lewes, map reference TQ416098, is in East Sussex.

Toughness: 7 out of 10.

Walk notes: Each of the three sections of this walk make fine walks in themselves. Put together they add up to a grand day's circuit in stunning scenery. The main walk starts in the historic town of Lewes, with the early section having fine views over the town and castle. After reaching a secluded valley, skylarks can often be heard high above. The middle section along the South Downs Way offers extensive views both inland and towards the port of Newhaven with the Channel beyond. The final stretch re-enters Lewes along the levee beside the River Ouse.

The walk has 360 metres of ascent spread over three steepish hills, but in between there are long sections that are mainly level. The main walk, being fairly long, is not well suited to December and January owing to the limited daylight.

Walk options: This walk is in three sections, each with a station at the beginning and end, and each section can therefore be done individually, or

in any other combination. Lewes to Glynde is 5km (3 miles), Glynde to Southease is 11.8km (7.4 miles) and Southease to Lewes is 6.5km (4 miles). The latter section is completely flat, but is perhaps the least interesting. Glynde and Southease are on separate train lines but each has trains daily to Lewes.

Saturday Walkers' Club: Take the train nearest to 9.15am (before or after) from Victoria direct to Lewes.

Walk directions

[1] [Numbers refer to the map]

[Lewes station to Glynde station section.]
From the main exit of **Lewes station** *turn right to head towards the centre of town.* 100 metres from the station entrance *turn right on Lansdown Place* in front of the White Star Inn. Continue down Lansdown Place; after 100 metres pass a church on the left that has been converted into an arts centre. In another 180 metres, at a mini roundabout, go straight on.

After 60 metres *turn right at Boots into the pedestrianised High Street.*

Go straight on and after 80 metres go over the river bridge; on the left you can see **Harveys Brewery**. Continue straight along Cliffe High Street until it ends at a junction with Malling Street (the parish church of **St Thomas a Becket** will be on your left). *Cross Malling Street to go essentially straight on* up a small road called Chapel Hill (this is slightly to the right of the junction by the church).

Walk up the hill; soon you will have views behind you over Lewes. After 200 metres ignore a footpath sign pointing to the left and continue up the drive of Lewes Golf Club (by a 7'-00" width restriction sign up a road with speed ramps). In 70 metres take the path parallel to the roadway on the right-hand side giving good views of Lewes.

[2] In 300 metres, at the start of the Club House car park, *follow the footpath around the right-hand side of the car park.* After 40 metres go through a wooden gate and follow a clear path past a water trough, your direction 70 degrees. Pass the trough and in 320 metres go through disued gate posts and then *bear slightly right with the main path* to go downhill, due east, ignoring a faint path to the left. 100 metres past the posts go through a gate and follow the path gently downhill.

After 200 metres ignore a path coming in from the right by a waymark post and in a further 25 metres, at another waymark post, go down to your right and through a gate. Continue gently downhill on a clear path, your direction 120 degrees. Proceed along the path towards the valley bottom, passing a waymark post after 200 metres.

In 140 metres, at a waymark post in the valley bottom, *bear left with the footpath, which then turns to the right,* and in 40 metres cross a stile or pass through a wooden gate to the left of a metal fieldgate (the gate may be hidden by nettles). In 20 metres pass a circular concrete pond on your left. In a further 20 metres *bear right,* ignoring a track leading uphill and

passing a waymark post on your left. You are walking along the floor of the valley and your initial direction is 150 degrees.

300 metres from the post you come to a stile beside an information board for Mount Caburn nature reserve. Cross this stile and *veer right to take the path steeply uphill* (ignoring a footpath further to the right alongside a fence), your direction 130 degrees. The route is essentially straight all the way from here to Glynde.

In more detail: go uphill and after 700 metres cross a stile. At this point a detour is recommended to the hill fort of **Mount Caburn**, which is 250 metres to your right; the views from the fort are excellent. Returning to the main route, at the stile, continue in almost the same direction as you came up the hill to head towards Glynde, which is soon visible in the distance, your direction 110 degrees.

After 450 metres cross a stile in a fence, 20 metres to the left of a fieldgate. Go down a step and then follow the path down in a similar direction to before (100 degrees), with a wire fence on your right, towards a house with white windows. To the left the cupola of **Glynde Place** can be seen. In 500 metres cross a stile between two fieldgates then *bear half right downhill* with the main path, your direction 120 degrees. In 150 metres cross a stile to a road, where you *turn left to pass the post office* after 15 metres.

In 30 metres, at the main road, *turn right* to pass the **Glynde Forge General Smith**. If this is open you can pop in for a look. Continue along the road for 180 metres to pass **Glynde station**.

[Glynde station to Southease station section now follows.]

[3] From the station go uphill on the road, over the railway, following the road round to the right to pass the **Trevor Arms** pub, a possible lunch stop. [!] *20 metres beyond the pub, and just after Trevor Gardens nos.11-16, turn right on a small path.* Pass gardens, cross a track, pass more gardens and go over a footbridge to follow a hedge, keeping it on your right.

Lewes via West Firle Circular

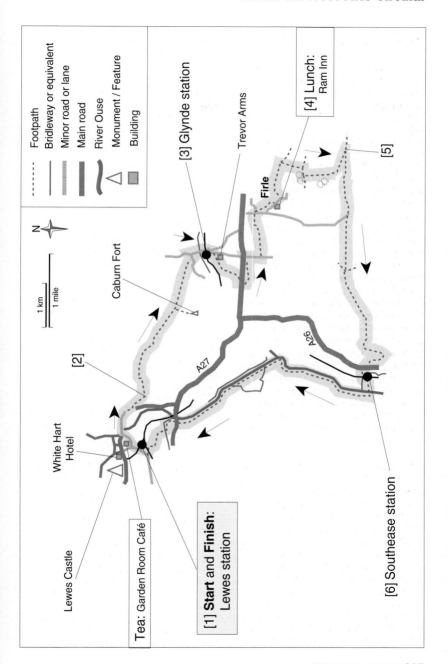

Lewes Castle

Tea: Garden Room Café

White Hart Hotel

[2]

Caburn Fort

[3] Glynde station

Trevor Arms

Firle

[4] Lunch: Ram Inn

[5]

A27

A26

[1] **Start** and **Finish**: Lewes station

[6] Southease station

N

1 km
1 mile

- - - - Footpath
──── Bridleway or equivalent
▦▦▦ Minor road or lane
████ Main road
〰〰 River Ouse
△ Monument / Feature
▪ Building

In 250 metres at the end of the hedge follow a waymark to cross a field, your initial direction 220 degrees. The exit to the field is 450 metres away through an overgrown stile beside a gate in the hedge opposite. These are located in the hedge about 300 metres to the left of woods. Pass over this stile and *follow the path half left* towards an underpass going under the busy main road.

In 70 metres go through the tunnel. Emerging from the tunnel your direction is essentially straight onto a quiet old road, passing to the right of a complex

No Paine, no gain

Lewes's most (in)famous resident was the 18th-century radical propagandist **Thomas Paine**. Born in Thetford, Norfolk, in 1737, Paine was initially educated at the local grammar school before his cash-strapped Quaker corset-maker father was forced to apprentice his son to his trade. Young Tom, however, grew tired of corsets and went to sea aged 19. He failed to find his fortune and returned to land, eventually settling down in Lewes in 1768, where he worked as an excise officer and shopkeeper.

It was in Lewes that Paine started to develop his radical ideas. He was highly active in local affairs and founded a debating club in the inn that is now the White Hart Hotel. He campaigned tirelessly on behalf of his profession, publishing *The Case of the Officers of Excise* in 1772 to argue for a pay rise, and frequently travelling to London to lobby his case. The result, though, was that he was dismissed from his post for being so often absent from Lewes.

However, Paine's life was soon to be transformed. While in London he had met Benjamin Franklin, who helped him to emigrate to America in 1774. He settled in Philadelphia, where he turned to journalism, and in 1776 published the hugely influential pamphlet *Common Sense*, which argued the case for American independence from Britain. It sold more than half a million copies.

Paine joined the American army but (as with virtually every job he ever did) did not thrive, yet his pamphlet *The Crisis* proved a significant inspiration for Washington's soldiers in their darkest hours.

After independence had been won Paine turned to private concerns, attempting to design an iron bridge and invent a smokeless candle, before returning to Europe in 1787.

The global cataclysm provoked by the French Revolution in 1789 drew him back to the political fray, inspiring his most influential work, the *Rights of Man* (1791-92). This passionate defence of democratic republicanism and call for radical social legislation to tackle the atrocious condition of the poor led to him being hounded out of Britain and declared an outlaw.

He settled in France in 1792 and became a French citizen, but fell foul of the Terror and spent a year in prison. During his incarceration Paine wrote *The Age of Reason*, a bitter atheistic attack on established religion that made the outspoken writer yet more enemies.

Eventually he outstayed his welcome in Paris and returned to the United States in 1802, where his final years were scarred by alcoholism, poverty and ostracism. Thomas Paine died in 1807.

The **South Downs** in autumn.

of barns. At the old road *turn left* and then in 300 metres *turn right up a small road*, away from the busy main road.

250 metres away from the main road turn left onto a tarmac track with a sign saying 'Preston Court'. Continue straight along the farm track and 150 metres from the road pass between a barn with a corrugated roof on the left and a house and garage on your right. Pass through blue-painted gates and, 3 metres beyond these, *go over a stile in the fence to the left.* Follow roughly the right-hand edge of the field towards a metal fieldgate. In 200 metres go through this gate and in a further 40 metres pass through a small gate and continue along a small ridge in the field.

After 100 metres pass just to the right of a clump of trees and barns. Immediately beyond the barns *turn left on a track and then in 20 metres turn right on a track heading towards houses*, your direction 100 degrees.

After 200 metres cross a tarmac road and *turn half right* into the grounds of **Firle Place**. In 30 metres pass a cattle grid and *immediately turn half right*, almost along the field edge. In 60 metres cross a stile to continue, your direction 150 degrees, and *head towards the left-hand edge of tennis courts 200 metres away*, just beyond a row of young trees surrounded by protective fences.

Just to the left of the tennis courts go over a stile, ignore a path signposted to the left and walk 15 metres to the edge of the cricket ground. *Turn right* and in 15 metres take a track between walls, emerging after 60 metres at the road with the **Ram Inn** on your right. [4] This is the suggested lunch stop.

Leaving the pub *turn left and then bear right with the road to go into the village*. In 200 metres, at Firle Stores Post Office, *turn left down a small private road*, your direction 40 degrees. After 200 metres pass through a wooden kissing gate into the grounds of **Firle Place**.

[!] *From here the path curves round to the right on a bend a little tighter than the track ahead. The route follows waymarked posts all the way through the grounds. The first post is about 70 metres from the entrance to the grounds and to the right of the track ahead.* From this post, after 70 metres, the route next crosses the main driveway to Firle Place at a two-armed sign. At times you can see the top of a round tower poking through trees ahead of you. You will pass in front of Firle Place.

700 metres after entering the grounds you exit them through a small gate and *turn right up a car-wide track.* In 250 metres, at a junction of tracks, go straight on uphill (as indicated by a blue arrow on a post on the left) and in a further 220 metres pass through a gateway to reach a T-junction where you *turn right along a track through trees*, your direction 260 degrees. In 200 metres you come to a line of trees going

uphill; *turn left immediately before these trees to take the track uphill.* (The path heads uphill with a row of trees just to its right; it's not the path through these trees.)

After 500 metres pass through a gate to the right of a metal fieldgate. Continue directly uphill for 40 metres, going slightly left with the path between trees and climb up the side of the hill.

[5] In 300 metres, as the path starts to level off near the top of the hill, *turn right at a post* to go directly uphill for 60 metres to another post by a fence. *Turn right at the fence* and head towards two radio masts, your direction due west. The walk now stays on the South Downs Way all the way to Southease station. For the first 4km (2.5 miles) remain on the ridgeway (passing the radio masts after 2.5km/1.5 miles and a concrete trigonometry point after a further kilometre).

When the path starts to go steeply downhill, note the farm buildings below as this is where you will cross the main road. In order to get there *follow the path round to the left, heading for a wooden sign and post.* Then follow a fence on your left for 300 metres. At the fence corner go slightly right towards a post and after 30 metres, at the post, turn right down a track, eventually coming to the main road.

At the main road *turn right and after 60 metres cross and turn left* into a road downhill towards Southease station. You will pass a tap for drinking water 40 metres from the main road and arrive at the station after 200 metres.

[Southease station to Lewes station section now follows.]

[6] From Southease station you can catch a train back into Lewes or continue for the last 6.5km (4 miles), completely flat and mostly beside the river.

In more detail: cross the railway line at the station and continue on the road to cross the river on a bridge. *10 metres beyond the bridge turn right on a path* signposted to Lewes. Follow the bank of the river for 5km (3 miles) until you go under a road bridge. Near the start of the

section by the river, to the left, can be seen the village of **Rodmell**. It was from here that Virginia Woolf left her country home **Monk's House** (*see p262* **Woolf's lair**) to cross the water meadows to the river and end her life in 1941.

60 metres after going under the bridge *follow the path round a corner to the right,* and after a further 30 metres *turn left to pass just to the left of some recycling banks.* Walk along the tarmac road, with the recycling banks to your right. In 200 metres, at a T-junction, *turn right* on a road, crossing a small stream and then passing low buildings on the right and then playing fields on your left. Near the end of the playing fields *turn right with the road* and, after a further 100 metres, *turn left at the junction.* After 250 metres, at a mini roundabout, *turn right* towards the railway station.

To reach either of the tea stops, continue past the station and then go up hill. The **Garden Room Café** is on the right. To get to the **White Hart Hotel**, continue up to the traffic lights, turn left and the hotel is 20 metres on the left.

Lunch & tea places

Garden Room Café & Gallery *14 Station Street, Lewes, BN4 2DA (01273 478636).* **Open** 10am-5pm Mon-Sat. The suggested tea stop for the main walk.

Ram Inn *The Street, Firle, BN8 6NS (01273 858222).* **Open** 11.30am-11pm Mon-Sat; noon-10.30pm Sun. **Food served** noon-5.30pm Mon-Thur; noon-9pm Fri-Sun. Real ale and wholesome food at reasonable prices, plus two pleasant gardens and a no-smoking snug. The suggested lunch stop for the main walk.

Trevor Arms *The Street, Glynde, BN8 6SS (01273 858208).* **Open** 11am-11pm Mon-Sat; noon-10.30pm Sun. **Food served** noon-2.15pm, 6-9.15pm daily. Located 5km (3 miles) into the walk, the Trevor Arms is an alternative for lunch if starting the walk later.

White Hart Hotel *55 High Street, Lewes, BN7 1XE (01273 476694).* **Open** 10am-11pm daily. **Food served** 12.30-2.15pm, 7-10.15pm daily. One of several alternatives for tea. It was at this inn that Thomas Paine was wont to expound (*see p266* **No Paine, no gain**).

Southease to Seaford

From the Downs to the sea via Rodmell and Bishopstone.

Start: Southease station
Finish: Seaford station
Length: 18.1km (11.3 miles). For a shorter walk and other variations, *see below* **Walk options**.
Time: 5 hours 40 minutes. For the whole outing, including trains, sights and meals, allow at least 10 hours.
Transport: Two trains an hour run from London Victoria to Lewes, where you change for Southease (journey time: 1 hour 17 minutes). Trains back from Seaford run twice hourly (one per hour on Sundays), changing at Lewes (or sometimes Brighton; journey time: about 1 hour 30 minutes). Buy a day return ticket to Seaford. For those driving, it is probably best to park at Lewes station and use trains as appropriate from there.
OS Landranger Map: 198
OS Explorer Maps: 122 and 123 Southease, map reference TQ432055, is in East Sussex, 5km (3 miles) south-east of Lewes.
Toughness: 6 out of 10.

Walk notes: This walk offers a wealth of contrasting scenery, passing alongside a river, then rising to the heights of the South Downs to command views both inland and out to the coast, before descending to pass through pretty villages en route to the seaside. It begins at Southease station then follows the banks of the River Ouse to Rodmell for an early lunch. Afterwards the route returns to Southease via an alternative way, which passes its picturesque village centre, then ascends to follow a ridge of the South Downs Way before heading south to the village of Bishopstone and the coast. It finally follows the seaside esplanade to the sleepy seaside town of Seaford with its cafés, pubs and restaurants.

Walk options: Directions for these variations are given at the end of the main walk text (*see p274*).

a) Shorter walk (not via Rodmell): By not doing the round trip to Rodmell for lunch at the start, but instead heading straight off to Seaford from point [3], you can reduce the length of the walk to 12.3km (7.7 miles). If taking this approach, it is wise to take a picnic or other refreshments.

b) Alternative ending at Bishopstone: You can reduce the length of the walk, whether going via Rodmell or not, by ending the walk at Bishopstone station. Follow the main walk directions until point [7], then follow the directions for the alternative ending at the end of the main walk text. This reduces the length of the walk by 1.8km (1.1 mile).

c) Lewes to Seaford walk (via river): This is a slightly different and gentler walk from the Lewes to Seaford walk option (c) detailed in walk 24 in this book (which takes a higher route along the Downs). This is a long walk of

20.8km (13 miles), so be sure to leave plenty of time if attempting it. Directions are given at the end of the main walk text.

Saturday Walkers' Club: Take the train nearest to 9.50am from Victoria station to Lewes, then change for Southease.

Walk directions

[1] [Numbers refer to the map]
Coming off the train from Lewes at **Southease station** *cross the footbridge over the railway and turn left onto a tarmac road* parallel to the railway line, your direction due south. In 90 metres the road curves to the right, your direction 260 degrees, and in a further 250 metres it crosses a green swing bridge over the **River Ouse**. *15 metres beyond the bridge turn right through a wooden gate and follow the footpath to the left (west bank) of the rive*r, your direction north.

Follow this footpath for 1.6km (1 mile). In more detail: Pass wooden gates in 30 metres, then go to the right of a redundant stile in a further 300 metres, then over a stile in a further 300 metres. In 900 metres cross over a stile (with a water safety ring on the other side), *then descend the steep riverbank to turn left away from the river onto a car-wide earth track*, your direction west. There is a ditch stream on your left.

[If you followed the **Lewes to Seaford (via river)** walk option **c)** detailed at the end of the main text, continue from this point.] **[*]** In 160 metres go through a metal fieldgate (to the right of a metal fieldgate). The track passes under mini pylon cables in 120 metres, after which it veers to the left.

In 140 metres go through a wooden gate (to the right of a metal fieldgate). In 30 metres the path goes under mini pylon cables and in a further 160 metres it veers to the left to pass under more pylons. (You are following the line of pylons to your left.)

In 300 metres go through a wooden gate (to the left of a metal fieldgate) with a water treatment works building on your

left. In 20 metres the track passes a collection of rough corrugated metal buildings on your right. In a further 250 metres you come to the end of the lane and pass through an open metal fieldgate with a public bridleway sign to your right and Monk's House car park on your left, to emerge on a tarmac road.

Veer left on the road opposite Navigation Cottages to continue in the same direction as before. In 100 metres pass **Monk's House** (*see p262* **Woolf's lair**) on your left. (If you want to visit the church take the concrete footpath off to the left just after Monk's House, opposite the signposted 'To Barley Fields' on your right. In 70 metres pass a school to your right, then at the end of the path enter the churchyard of **St Peter's, Rodmell** through the lychgate.) Otherwise, continue on this lane until after 400 metres it ends at a T-junction with a road. This is **Rodmell [2]** and immediately on your right is the **Abergavenny Arms**, the suggested lunch stop.

After lunch turn left from the pub door, crossing over the lane you arrived on earlier to continue along the main road. There is a pavement or grass path next to the road all the way to the Southease turn-off if you stay on this side. In 100 metres ignore the public footpath to your left, after which the pavement becomes grass. In 250 metres ignore a public bridleway to your right and in 40 metres the pavement becomes gravel.

In 100 metres pass a road sign to your right indicating Telscombe Village. In another 100 metres pass the turn-off to Telscombe and a YHA sign on your right. *In 60 metres leave the main road and turn left downhill on the road signposted to Southease Village and as a 'No through road',* your direction 100 degrees (there is also a South Downs Way signpost). This road has no pavement but is fairly quiet.

In 100 metres pass **St Peter's, Southease** on your right-hand side, followed by a large village green and a thatched house set back on your right. (To visit the church turn right,

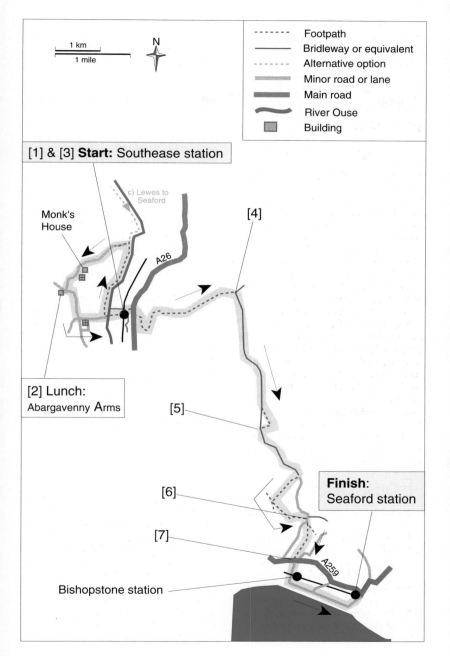

1 km
1 mile

N

Footpath
Bridleway or equivalent
Alternative option
Minor road or lane
Main road
River Ouse
Building

[1] & [3] **Start:** Southease station

c) Lewes to Seaford

Monk's House

A26

[4]

[2] Lunch: Abargavenny Arms

[5]

Finish: Seaford station

[6]

[7]

A259

Bishopstone station

with the churchyard wall on your right and the green on your left, and in 30 metres you come to the entrance of the overgrown churchyard.)

After passing the village green you pass buildings on each side of the road and a lake behind a wire-netting fence to your right. Continue on this road and in 400 metres once again cross the green swing bridge over the River Ouse. In 300 metres you are back at Southease Station **[3]**. [Option **a)**, the **Shorter walk** option, starts here.]

Continue over the level crossing, passing, in 200 metres, Itford Farm and Kington Cottage on your left. In another 50 metres the lane ends at a major road, the A26. *Turn right and in 80 metres carefully cross this busy road to turn left uphill on the South Downs Way*, your direction initially due east.

Follow the South Downs Way for the next 3km (1.9 miles).

In more detail: In 200 metres go through a wooden fieldgate. In 600 metres **[!]**, *just before a cattle stockade ahead of you, fork left following a blue South Downs Way arrow on a post*, your direction 30 degrees. In 60 metres ignore a field opening to the right and stay to the left of a barbed-wire fence.

In 220 metres, when the fence bends right, curve right uphill following a blue arrow on a post, your direction 60 degrees. Climb to the top of the hill, curving gently

right all the time. At the top there is a wire fence on your right and you follow a ridge in an easterly direction, with fine views of Newhaven and the twisting course of the River Ouse on your right and of Lewes back to the left.

In 380 metres go through a fieldgate and keep straight on, still with the wire fence to your right, ascending all the while. In 200 metres you pass a trig point on your left and just beyond this the dried-up hollow of the **Red Lion Pond** (which is marked on OS maps).

Continue, keeping the wire fence to your right, your direction 25 degrees, heading towards radio masts. After 600 metres go through a wooden gate with sheep pens to your right and veer slightly right with the path.

In 250 metres pass through another gate with a four-armed footpath sign to its left (the radio masts are now on the hill immediately ahead). **[4]** *Here you turn right to leave the South Downs Way, crossing over a cattle grid and then crossing a car-wide track* to continue in the direction of the cattle grid on the faint path indicated by two parallel tracks that descend across a field, your direction 165 degrees. **[!]** [Note that this path may sometimes be blocked by metal barriers to keep grazing sheep in. However, despite this, it is a public right of way.]

In 250 metres go through a wooden gate. The buildings of **America Farm**

Episcopal haven

The peaceful village of **Bishopstone** gained its name as a retreat for the Bishops of Chichester until the 1600s. One bishop entertained Edward II here in 1324, and a predecessor commissioned the building of the first windmill in Sussex (and possibly in England) here in 1199. The mill has long since disappeared and, today,

Bishopstone's main draws are its superb Saxon church of St Andrew's (parts of its original eighth-century structure remain) and the cutesy cottages that crowd around its village green, known locally as 'the Egg'. The church hosts two summer fêtes, on the first Saturday of May and the first Saturday of August.

(marked on the OS map) can be seen ahead to the left.

In 950 metres, where the path narrows at a gate just before a hill, the path divides and you take the left-hand fork with a barbed-wire fence still on your left, your direction 140 degrees. In 260 metres, where the fence ends at the top of the hill, the path veers right across the field passing slightly to the left of the line of the ridge, your direction 170 degrees. It soon begins to descend across a large dip towards a gate between two bushes near the far left-hand corner of the field.

In 650 metres you pass through this gate and continue on a series of faint parallel paths between two unfenced fields, roughly following the line of the ridge, your direction 210 degrees. In 330 metres you come to a footpath with a blue arrow.

[!] The official path veers right across a field to your right at this point, roughly following the line of the ridge. However, this path appears to have fallen into disuse, so simply follow the field edge downhill, your direction 160 degrees, for 440 metres, until you reach a sunken track (not visible until you are immediately on top of it at the bottom of the field). *Turn right on this sunken track, uphill, to reach a footpath crossroads after 170 metres.* [5] *Turn left here, your direction 160 degrees.*

(If you have taken the official route across the ploughed field you will arrive at this point, in which case your route is straight on at this junction, which you will have arrived at after crossing to the far side of the field).

You are now descending between a barbed-wire fence to your left and a bank of trees to your right (later there are trees right and left) into a well-defined valley, **Poverty Bottom**, on a path that later becomes a car-wide track. In 670 metres ignore a track uphill to the left and in 250 metres you pass the buildings of the South Eastern Water treatment works, where the track becomes a tarmac lane. Continue on this for 1.3km (0.8 miles) to the village of **Norton**.

When you get to the village you come to a junction with a car-wide gravel track to the left and a pale cream house on the corner.

[If you want to take a short cut, continue on this quiet road, keeping to the right as it forks, and continue to the village of Bishopstone. Resume the directions at the asterisk [**] below.]

[If you want to visit the pretty hamlet of Norton, take the left fork and then return to this point to resume the main walk.]

The main route at this point, however, is to leave the lane and *turn right at the junction and cross over a stile* to follow a car-wide farm track beyond as it curves right and then left up the hill ahead.

In 700 metres, at the top of the hill, pass under pylons and go straight ahead for 40 metres to arrive at a spot affording a fine view of the port of Newhaven. Do not cross the stile through the barbed-wire fence ahead, however, *but turn left following the top of the ridge.* [!] As you follow the ridge, keep to a faint path that curves left aiming slightly to the right of **St Andrew's Church**, now in sight in the village below. In 150 metres you see a gate in the line of bushes rising up the hill from the valley to the left, which on closer inspection is marked 'In memory of Dick Dennis'.

Pass through this gate and continue downhill on a path under trees, your direction 150 degrees. *In 300 metres go left through a wooden kissing gate* by a post with the yellow circular marker signs of the East Sussex County Council footpath, your direction 50 degrees.

Keep to the left-hand edge of the field beyond, following a flint wall to your left and crossing over a potentially muddy ditch. In 40 metres go over a stile to the left of a flint wall and *on the far side take the path half right across the field towards the church visible ahead*, your direction 110 degrees. In 270 metres cross over a stile and *turn left on a car-wide track.*

In 20 metres go right uphill on a concrete path and in 15 metres turn left up some wooden steps, your direction east and cross a grassy space to enter the churchyard through an iron gate. Turn right to follow the path around the church and turn left onto the paved path to exit the churchyard through the lych-gate [6].

Turn right on the gravel path down to the road for 25 metres and then turn right onto the road [**].

In 70 metres, where the road bends right, there are two footpaths marked by a post to the left of a wooden gate. Take the right-hand path, your direction 200 degrees, following the direction for 'Bishopstone Station ¾ mile', your direction south. In 280 metres in the far corner of the field cross an unusual stile made of tree trunks over a flint wall and bear half right to walk in a valley with a hilly bank on your left-hand side and hedging and metal fencing on your right, your direction 220 degrees.

In 400 metres cross a stile and ascend the bank ahead to emerge onto and cross a busy road, the A259. **[7]** [At this point, you can take option **b)**, the **Alternative ending at Bishopstone**. Follow the directions at the end of this main walk text.]

Otherwise, *to continue on the main walk* for tea and to reach the coast and Seaford, *turn right on the A259 for 50 metres, then turn left on Marine Parade*. In 180 metres go under a railway bridge, then pass Sunnyside Caravan Park on your left and 60 metres further on Buckle Caravan Park on your right. *In another 150 metres you reach the coast and veer left*, your direction 210 degrees.

Cross the road to the seashore and follow the esplanade at the back of the shingle beach, starting opposite the Martello tower-shaped cream house opposite the sign on the beach saying 'Warning Submerged structure'. Continue towards Seaford now visible ahead.

In 1km (0.6 miles) pass Salts Recreation Ground on your left (with a café that might be open in the summer). *Just after the* **Beachcomber Bar** *turn left on Dane Road*, where you will be able to get coffee if it is too late for the café. In 100 metres, opposite Safeway's, you come to **Hardy's**

Coffee House, the suggested tea place, on your left. Continue to the end of this road to a T-junction with Church Road. *Turn immediately left onto Station Approach* to arrive at **Seaford station** to take the train back to London via Lewes.

Walk options

a) Shorter walk (not via Rodmell): If you are following this option, which goes directly east rather than returning to Rodmell for lunch, go to point [3] in the main walk text to start this walk, exiting the station and heading east towards the Downs (as opposed to heading towards the green swing bridge).

b) Alternative ending to Bishopstone: *Follow the main walk directions until [7].* To end your walk at Bishopstone, *continue straight on a tarmac path for 25 metres to cross Hawth Hill then follow Station Road to come to* **Bishopstone station** *at its end.*

From there, you can catch a train back to London, changing at Lewes.

c) Lewes to Seaford walk (via river): *From Lewes station, turn left and in 100 metres at the mini roundabout turn left on Mountfield Road*, marked 'No through road'. Go past Lewes Football Club and in 180 metres turn right on Ham Lane, your direction 160 degrees.

In 120 metres the road bends to the left (note there is no pavement on this road). In 300 metres cross a narrow tributary after following the road as it veers to the right. Pass a scout's hut on the right-hand side. Turn left where there is boarded-up works on your right-hand side with a sign announcing: 'Automatic machinery may start without warning. Risk area'.

In 120 metres go past Lewes household waste recycling site on your left, following the road to its right-hand side.

Go through a gap to the left of a metal fieldgate and turn right, your direction 220 degrees. The footpath passes between bushes to either side. *In 140 metres pass underneath the A27 road bridge.*

*From here just follow the footpath
for 3.4km (2.1 miles) alongside the River
Ouse, which is to your left, until you reach
the major path on which you turn right
(west) towards Rodmell.*

In more detail: In 100 metres you come
to a sign for Rise Farm and turn left for
10 metres to cross over a stile, then follow
the path, with a barbed-wire fence to the
right and the river to the left.

In 250 metres you cross over a stile and
the barbed-wire fence ends. In 40 metres
cross over another stile. In 200 metres
go over a stile. In 500 metres descend
briefly from the bank around a metal
barrier passing a sign on your right
saying 'Warning Outfall submerged
structure, deep water' and then get back
up onto the bank.

In 400 metres cross a stile. In 1km (0.6
miles) cross a stile. In 700 metres cross
two stiles at a pumping station. *In 100
metres, just before the next stile (with a
water safety ring), turn right to descend
the steep banks of the Ouse. Turn right
away from the river onto a car-wide earth
track, your direction west. There is a ditch
stream on your left [*].* From this point
continue from the point marked by an
asterisk in the main text.

[At this point if you would rather go
directly towards Seaford without having
lunch at Rodmell, then continue on the
footpath alongside the Ouse for a further
1.6km (1 mile) until reaching the tarmac
road on which you turn left to cross the
green swing bridge over the Ouse. 300
metres further on you come to Southease
station and then continue from point [3]
in the main text.]

Lunch & tea places

Abergavenny Arms *Newhaven Road,
Rodmell, BN7 3EZ (01273 472416).*
Open 11am-3.30pm, 5.30-11pm Mon-Fri;
11am-11pm Sat; noon-10.30pm Sun. **Food
served** noon-2pm, 6-9pm Mon-Fri; noon-
3.30pm, 6-9.30pm Sat; noon-3.30pm Sun.
This is a large friendly pub with a log fire
and a wide menu advertising 'traditional
English wholesome home-made food'. It is

Monk's House, Rodmell.

open all day during July and August, and is
the suggested lunch stop for the main walk.

Beachcomber Bar *Corner of the seafront
(Marine Parade) and Dane Road, Seaford,
BN25 1DX (01323 892719).* **Open**
10.30am-midnight daily. **Food served**
noon-2pm Mon-Sat; noon-2.30pm Sun. A
possible option for refreshment in Seaford.

Hardy's Coffee House *Dane Road,
Seaford, BN25 1DN (01323 894877).* **Open**
May-Sept 8.30am-5pm Mon-Sat; 10am-5pm
Sun; *Oct-Apr* 8.30am-5pm Mon-Sat. Opposite
Safeway on the way to the station, this is the
suggested tea place for the main walk.

Old Plough *Church Street, Seaford, BN25
1HG (01323 872921).* **Open** 11am-11pm
Mon-Sat; noon-10.30pm Sun. **Food served**
noon-2.30pm, 5.30-9pm Mon-Sat; noon-
2.30pm Sun. Serves food, tea and coffee.

Trawler's Fish and Chip Restaurant
*Church Street, Seaford, BN25 1LD (01323
892520).* **Open** 11.30am-2pm, 5-8.30pm
Mon; 11.30am-2pm, 5-9pm Tue-Thur;
11.30am-2pm, 5-9.30pm Fri, Sat. Opposite
and to your right as you come to the end of
Dane Road, this is an option for grabbing a
bite to eat before catching the train home.

Note that there are no refreshment
possibilities between Rodmell and Seaford.

Picnic: Almost anywhere on the South
Downs makes a good picnic spot, as does the
green outside St Andrew's in Bishopstone.

Berwick to Eastbourne

The Long Man of Wilmington and smugglers' villages.

Start: Berwick station
Finish: Eastbourne station
Length: 18.5km (11.6 miles). For a shorter walk and other variations, *see below* **Walk options**.

Time: 5 hours 50 minutes. For the whole outing, including trains, sights and meals, allow at least 12 hours.

Transport: Hourly trains go from London Victoria to Berwick, changing at Lewes (journey time: 1 hour 33 minutes). On Sundays trains are direct (journey time: 1 hour 23 minutes). Trains back from Eastbourne are approximately twice hourly (journey time: 1 hour 29 minutes, 10-25 minutes slower on Sunday). Buy a day return ticket to Eastbourne. For those driving, the best place to park is Berwick station; trains back from Eastbourne take 15 minutes, and are approximately hourly.

OS Landranger Map: 199
OS Explorer Map: 123
Berwick, map reference TQ524068, is in East Sussex, 12km (7.5 miles) north-west of Eastbourne.

Toughness: 7 out of 10.

Walk notes: This long but rewarding walk heads from inland Sussex to the coast, taking in a variety of scenery along the way. From Berwick the walk cuts across to the peaceful birdwatchers' paradise of Arlington Reservoir before crossing farmland towards Wilmington, with the huge chalk figure of the Long Man frequently in sight. From here the route continues to the historic smuggling village of Jevington for lunch. Then afterwards it ascends the South Downs to follow ridges of chalk grassland with views in all directions, before heading towards the seaside resort of Eastbourne and the possibility of extending the walk to the dramatic heights of Beachy Head.

Walk options: Directions for these variations are given at the end of the main walk text (*see p284*).

a) Short walk to Polegate via Folkington: You can reduce the length of this walk by finishing at Polegate. To go via Folkington, a walk of 10.3km (6.4 miles), follow the main walk directions until point [5], then pick up the directions at the end of the main walk text.

b) Short walk to Polegate via Jevington: You can also go to Polegate via Jevington, a walk of 14.4km (9 miles). However, be aware that this route includes approximately 300 metres of road walking with no pavement, followed by sections of footpaths that are steep, narrow and slippery, including a rather treacherous section before reaching Wannock. On the plus side, this route does directly pass Filching Manor Motor Museum. Follow the main walk directions until point [6] (the Eight

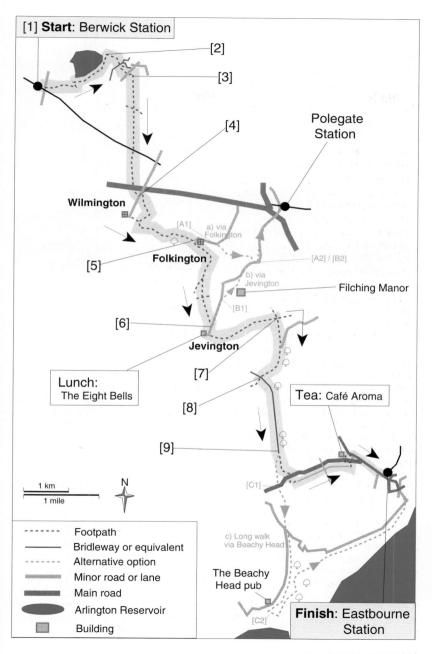

[1] **Start**: Berwick Station

[2]

[3]

Polegate
Station

[4]

Wilmington

[A1]

a) via
Folkington

[5]

Folkington

[A2] / [B2]

b) via
Jevington

Filching Manor

[B1]

[6]

Jevington

Lunch:
The Eight Bells

[7]

[8]

Tea: Café Aroma

[9]

1 km

1 mile

N

[C1]

c) Long walk
via Beachy Head

The Beachy
Head pub

[C2]

Finish: Eastbourne
Station

---- Footpath
——— Bridleway or equivalent
---- Alternative option
▬▬▬ Minor road or lane
▬▬▬ Main road
⬭ Arlington Reservoir
◻ Building

The Long Man of Wilmington

Bells pub), then pick up the directions at the end of the main walk text.

c) Long walk via Beachy Head: You can lengthen the walk to visit Beachy Head by following the South Downs Way all the way down. This creates a walk of 24.4km (15.3 miles). Follow the main walk directions until just before point [9], then pick up the Long walk directions where indicated at the end of the main walk text.

Saturday Walkers' Club: Take the train nearest to 9am from Victoria station to Berwick.

Walk directions

[1] [Numbers refer to the map]
Leaving platform 2 of **Berwick station,** *exit by the green wooden gate and turn right to emerge on the road opposite Berwick Stores. Cross the road here and turn left for 20 metres.*

[!] *Turn right on an unmarked path running between the car park for Berwick Stores and the Proteus garage* to head to the left of a red-brick house, your direction 100 degrees.

In 40 metres go over a dilapidated stile. Continue straight ahead across a field on a faint grass track, with a barbed-wire fence to your right, your direction 100 degrees. In 90 metres, at the corner of the field, follow the field edge round to the left, passing the remains of a flint wall of a derelict building on your right, your direction due north.

In 30 metres turn right to cross a stile (to the right of a metal fieldgate) and continue on the faintly marked grass footpath across the next field, heading to the left of a row of bushes on the far side and to the left a line of mini pylon cables, your direction 80 degrees.

In 140 metres cross two wooden stiles each side of a ditch stream and continue uphill, with a barbed wire fence to your right, your direction east. *In 120 metres at the top of the hill turn right to follow the fence,* your direction 140 degrees. *In 40 metres cross a stile and turn left downhill, still with a barbed wire fence on your right,* your direction east. There is now a clear view of **Arlington Reservoir** to your left.

In 140 metres cross a stile in the bottom right-hand corner of the field (which may be hidden by trees). *In 5 metres turn left on a tarmac lane*, your direction initially 330 degrees. In 50 metres ignore a stile on your right. *In 100 metres, at a sign saying 'South East Water, No Parking', as indicated by a circular walk footpath signpost on your left-hand side at the junction, turn right towards the reservoir.* In 10 metres go through a wooden kissing gate (to the right of a wooden fieldgate) to continue on a tarmac path that follows the right-hand perimeter of the reservoir. (There are two information signposts on your left after going through the gate.)

In 800 metres, at the end of the reservoir, the tarmac path ends and there are two footpaths. *You take the right-hand footpath to go over a stile* (to the right of a metal fieldgate) with a sign saying 'Footpath to Arlington Village' [2]. *Turn immediately right to head towards the church*, your direction initially 100 degrees, then in 40 metres bear right with the path, your direction 140 degrees.

In 250 metres cross a metal car-wide bridge flanked by two stiles over the **River Cuckmere**. Follow the yellow arrow on your left on the second stile towards the church, your direction 80 degrees.

In 60 metres go right across a stile into the next field and continue along the left-hand edge of the next field, your direction initially 150 degrees. In 60 metres, at a crosspaths, go right, signposted 'Wealdway', to head towards a wooden fence, your direction 220 degrees.

In 70 metres, just before a stile [!] *(don't cross it), turn left, keeping the fence to your right-hand side*, your direction 120 degrees. In 100 metres cross a wooden plank over a ditch stream, then go over a dilapidated stile to continue on a very narrow and potentially overgrown footpath between a wire fence to your right and a tall hedge to your left.

In 80 metres go over a stile to turn left onto a lane, your direction 40 degrees. *In 60 metres turn right* following a yellow arrow on a post, initially up two

steps then between a high wooden fence to your right and a hedge and barbed-wire fence to your left [3].

In 30 metres go through a wooden gate and in 25 metres turn right to go through another wooden gate where there is a public notice indicating 'Alternative 37a route' and other messages. *Head diagonally across the field following a yellow arrow*, your direction due south.

In 60 metres cross a stile over an electric fence to continue in the same direction. In 40 metres cross another stile over an electric fence and in 50 metres cross a further stile. Then continue to head half right, your direction due south, on a very faint path across a field.

In 160 metres go over a stile. In 120 metres cross another stile, still heading south to cross the next field, heading for the mid-point of the southern edge of the field. In 240 metres go over a stile marked 'Public footpath and bridleway'. *Turn left on a track for 5 metres then go over a high stile on your right to follow your former direction south.* Continue across the next field towards the Downs.

In 100 metres cross an (unstable) stile over a ditch stream and the remains of a metal pipe to continue as before, your direction south, rising uphill. In 120 metres go over a stile (to the left of a wide metal fieldgate). There is now a good view of the **Long Man of Wilmington** ahead of you on the Downs.

In 140 metres descend into a dip to go through a fieldgate entrance and then pass the remains of an old stile into the next field (ignoring the other crossing over the stream), your direction still south, with a ditch stream to your left. In 50 metres cross over the stream (there is an unofficial crossing to the left) following the footpath, and in 10 metres cross over a stile to go uphill.

In 10 metres ascend a bank and turn left to follow the left edge of the field as it curves round, your direction initially 130 degrees. In 300 metres go over a stile and climb the banks of

Jiggery-pokery

In the 1780s **Jevington** was infamous as a centre for smuggling. At the heart of the trade was the local innkeeper James Pettit, known as '**Jevington Jigg**'. His gang would unload their cargoes at nearby Birling Gap and Crowlink, and then store the contraband in the inn now called the Eight Bells (the suggested lunch stop for this walk) and in the cellar of the village rectory. His activities are well documented in reports and newspaper accounts of the time. In 1788 an attempt was made to arrest Jigg by a party of armed constables as he played cards inside the inn. The resourceful smuggler escaped by quickly donning women's clothes, dashing outside and feigning hysterics. The constables were too slow to realise the ruse and he made his escape by horse. Jigg soon returned, however, and was not so lucky. This time he was captured, after being discovered hiding in the loft of the inn. After various other adventures he was convicted of horse stealing in 1799 and sentenced to 14 years at Botany Bay.

the railway embankment to (carefully) cross the railway line.

Descend steps on the far side of the track and then go over a stile, keeping the hedge on your left. In 50 metres cross a second stile and a wooden plank over a ditch stream between trees and a wire fence. *Follow the yellow arrow on a post to turn left*, your direction 150 degrees, with a barbed-wire fence to your left.

In 120 metres the path ends at a gravel car-wide track and you turn right, your direction initially 280 degrees. In 50 metres pass black metal gates on your right. *In 10 metres turn left through a metal gate to continue along a corridor of high wire fences* (this is deer protection fencing), your direction 170 degrees. (Ignore the padlock on the gate. It opens at the right.)

In 100 metres go through another high metal gate to cross over a grassy track, then in 5 metres continue through another high metal gate on the opposite side. In 150 metres exit through the (last) metal gate.

In 4 metres cross a stile, your direction 160 degrees, following the direction of an arrow across the next field. In 180 metres cross another stile. In 150 metres, after passing through an overgrown field, go over a dilapidated stile on the opposite side and in 30 metres cross another stile, which is often overgrown in summer.

Emerge onto the A27 and take care crossing this very fast road, with a sign for Wilmington on your left-hand side, then descend a steep bank opposite by wooden steps and go over another stile signposted 'Please don't feed the animals'.

In 20 metres go over a footbridge flanked by two stiles *and then descend steps to cross the next field diagonally*, your direction 160 degrees. In 50 metres cross a stile and follow a corridor of hedges between gardens to emerge after 50 metres at a road T-junction with the **Giants Rest** pub on your right, a possible early lunch stop. This is **Wilmington [4]**.

[You now have a **choice** of going through Wilmington village or continuing on footpaths.]

To go through the village:

Turning right on Wilmington High Street, pass the pub, then ignore the footpath sign to your left at Stable Cottage. Pass the village hall on your right and 400 metres after the pub take the elevated pavement on the right-hand side of the road until it ends at the church of **St Mary and St Peter's**. *Then cross the road to follow the Weald Way opposite,* signposted 'To Folkington 1 mile'. Keep on this path until the point marked by the asterisk **[*]**.

Otherwise, by footpaths:

Cross the road (Wilmington High Street) and turn left on the road (towards the A27), then in 40 metres, after passing a flint-walled house on your right, turn right on a footpath alongside its wall, running parallel to the A27, your direction 110 degrees.

In 20 metres turn right and go over a stile (to the left of a metal fieldgate) opposite to continue on the footpath, your direction south. In 110 metres pass through an opening between a hedge. In a further 35 metres pass through an opening to the left of a wooden stile and in 50 metres veer left to go over a stile (to the right of a metal fieldgate), still heading south.

In 30 metres cross a stile between a hedge. In 200 metres cross another stile in the corner of the field. **[!]** *Cross the field, your direction initially 240 degrees, veering half right, towards the Long Man, aiming for the right-hand corner of the field.* There is no footpath visible.

In 250 metres, at the right-hand field corner, exit this field through a wooden gate, which, after going through, you see has a sign 'Bridleway only' on the other side. *After exiting through the gate turn immediately left, your direction 110 degrees* **[*]**.

Until the asterisks **[**]** *below your way is to follow the Weald Way to Jevington for the next 3.5km (2.2 miles) on a car-wide bridleway and then on footpaths.*

In more detail: In 30 metres the path veers right with the Long Man directly on your right. The path rises steadily between bushes.

In 400 metres ignore the steep uphill turnoff to the right marked 'Folkington Estate 1 mile', to continue bearing to the left. (However, if you take this turnoff, in 30 metres it leads to a lovely

viewpoint ideal for a **picnic** spot). This bridleway is potentially muddy.

In 900 metres, where the left turn becomes a road at the church of **St Peter's, Folkington,** and *there is a sign for 'Folkington Estate' behind you on your right, fork right down a car-wide track to continue on the Weald Way* with a flint wall to your left (and church beyond), your direction 160 degrees **[5]**.

[At this point you may choose to visit the church, in which case fork left onto the road. You can also take option **a)**, the **Short walk to Polegate via Folkington** option, at this point: refer to the directions at the end of this main text.]

Otherwise: in 30 metres ignore a track off to the right through a gap in the hedge. In 300 metres ignore a yellow arrow signposted footpath to your right. You are following a path between trees and a high bank to your right.

[!] *After 700 metres ignore a conservation path to your left. In a further 300 metres, 15 metres after a partially obscured footpath indicated by a yellow arrow running back on your right, leave the Weald Way by turning left on a footpath indicated by a yellow arrow, your direction south.* In 60 metres go over a stile to continue along a fenced-in footpath, continuing in the same direction.

In 250 metres go over a stile and turn right up a bridleway, your initial direction 220 degrees. *In a further 70 metres turn left off the bridleway,* your direction south, and in 10 metres go over a stile to continue in the same direction, your direction 160 degrees. In 80 metres cross a stile to immediately cross another stile over an electric fence. (The way to cross through these electric fences safely is to lift the blue handle.)

Cross the next field veering half left heading towards houses. In 300 metres go through a metal fieldgate. *In 50 metres cross a stile and turn right and in 60 metres turn left onto the earth car-wide track of the Weald Way.* You will see a footpath sign on your left indicating the way you have just come saying 'Folkington footpath 1½ miles'.

In 100 metres the lane ends (Green Lane) and *you emerge onto the High Street* **[**] [6]**. This is **Jevington**.

[If you missed the turn-off from the Weald Way you would just continue to the end of the path to a T-junction, then turn left following the red arrows and continue on the lane to the High Street].

Turn right, your direction 190 degrees, and in 200 metres you come to the **Eight Bells** pub on your right, the suggested lunch stop.

[At this point, you can take option **b)**, the **Short walk to Polegate via Jevington** option. Follow the directions at the end of this main walk text.]

After lunch leave the pub and retrace your steps left on the road for 10 metres. Then cross the road to go up concrete steps opposite, where there is a sign saying 'Weald Way, Butts Row 1 mile and Willingdon 2 miles', your direction initially 120 degrees, passing up between barbed-wire fences. In 250 metres go over a stile and continue up the footpath towards the next stile visible ahead. In 120 metres cross another stile.

In 250 metres, as the footpath forks, take the right fork following the line of gorse bushes to your right. In 150 metres cross a stile signposted 'Weald Way' to continue up along a footpath, your direction 70 degrees.

In 400 metres cross another Weald Way signposted stile to continue between bushes. In 500 metres the ridge curves round to the right and two tracks join in from the left. You have fine views of Polegate, Eastbourne and the coast ahead **[7]**. Stay on this ridge on the main track veering right, passing to the right of a wooden seat in 80 metres. This is another spot suitable for a **picnic**.

20 metres after the first wooden bench you pass a second bench on your left. There are now two paths and you *follow the less distinct left-hand path heading towards the car park visible ahead.*

In 240 metres go through a wooden swing gate into the car park next to a five-armed footpath sign.

Follow the direction of the blue arrow on the post saying 'Beachy Head 3 miles'. Cross over the rough gravel lane of the car park and take the path marked by the big stone for 'Beachy Head' to go straight ahead. There is a gravel track running parallel on your left, but your path gradually diverges away from it, your direction 200 degrees. In 100 metres, just after passing a (second) wooden bench on your left, a path merges from the left.

As you continue on this path you see a car-wide track following a barbed-wire fence to your right. In 200 metres, where paths merge and diverge, *keep to the right on a broad chalk path, your initial direction 230 degrees, to join the car-wide track following the barbed-wire fence in 200 metres.* (There is a footpath post 1066/WW at the path junction.)

In 140 metres after the paths merged you come to a T-junction with the South Downs Way. *Turn left to join the South Downs Way, your direction 150 degrees* **[8]**. There is another stone marker on your left-hand side and you follow its direction for 'Old Town Eastbourne'. (The paths to your left on the ridge would also have brought you to the South Downs Way but at a point further east.)

In 80 metres you pass a white trig point away to your left. *You now stay on the South Downs Way with the barbed-wire fence on your right-hand side for the next 1.7km (1.1 miles) until turning off on the bridleway for Eastbourne YHA.* In more detail: In 500 metres pass a South Downs bridleway and Weald Way sign where a path merges from the left.

In 600 metres pass a concrete drinking trough and a small round pond on your left. In 170 metres the path becomes gravel for the next 50 metres. *In 200 metres you turn left off the South Downs Way in the direction indicated by a*

Church Lane, **Jevington**

two-armed bridleway sign on your left indicating 'Eastbourne YHA', your direction 100 degrees **[9]**.

[At this point, you can take option **c)**, the **Long walk via Beachy Head** option, which continues on the South Downs Way, ignoring this turnoff via the Eastbourne YHA. See the directions at the end of this main walk text.]

After 50 metres this path descends. In 600 metres you go through a wooden gate to arrive at the main East Dean Road with **Eastbourne YHA** on your right.

Cross this road and continue in the same direction to descend on a footpath signposted 'Jubilee Way'. In 40 metres pass through two wooden barriers and in 70 metres go down steps and through two more wooden barriers. In a further 35 metres turn left down an unmarked path leading towards a whitewashed house, your direction 160 degrees.

In 50 metres the path ends at a wooden fence where you turn left for 20 metres down an earth path and exit through a gate onto the road opposite a Tudor-style house. *Turn right down the road,* which initially veers to the left and then runs straight after 50 metres, your direction

now 70 degrees. (You are following the direction of the busy East Dean Road that you crossed at the YHA but this is a quieter route.)

In 600 metres on this road (Pashley Road) you come to a crossroads where you cross over the main road (Summerdown Road) to continue in the same direction as before, now on Vicarage Drive. *In 200 metres at the end of this road veer right,* then cross over Love Lane and Glebe Close to continue on Vicarage Road. In 220 metres this ends at a road T-junction.

Cross over this road (Borough Lane) to enter **Manor Gardens** opposite through a wrought-iron gate set within flint walls. Then continue ahead through an inner archway (also within flint walls). *In 8 metres turn left on a crazy-paved path,* your direction north. In 30 metres descend steps and head towards a house (an art gallery). *Then turn right and in 25 metres turn left down steps to exit the gardens* on a main road (the High Street) opposite Safeway. Descend more steps and cross the main road (at the zebra crossing). *Then turn left* towards the church of **St Mary's**

The historic village of **Jevington**, with its Saxon church tower and smuggling past...

and, just after the 14th-century **Lamb Inn**, now on your right (and before the church), *turn right down the initially pedestrianised Ocklynge Road.*

In 50 metres the road forks and you stay on the right fork, then in 100 metres the road comes to a T-junction with Crown Street. Across this road and slightly to the left is **Café Aroma**, the suggested tea place. *If you are not going to the café turn right here* (on Crown Street).

Otherwise, if you have visited the café, on leaving it turn left. In 25 metres pass the Crown pub on your left and in 200 metres the road ends and you cross Moatcroft Road to continue in the same direction, now on the main A270 towards the town centre. Now continue for 1km (0.6 miles). At a major road junction continue straight on and in 100 metres reach the **Deep Pan Pizza** restaurant on your right where you cross the road and continue to **Eastbourne station** on Terminus Road on your left for trains back to London.

Walk options

a) Short walk to Polegate via Folkington:

Follow the main walk directions until point [5].

From the point indicated in the main text, turn left down the lane, your direction 70 degrees. In 30 metres you pass the church of **St Peter's**, Folkington, on your right. Continue on the lane. In 100 metres the lane curves sharply to the right; you now have a 2 metre-high concrete wall on your left. After 100 metres, as the lane levels out and the concrete wall ends, pass the entrance to the Old School House on your left.

In 110 metres the lane reaches an open field on your right. After 80 metres pass a double metal fieldgate on your left. *In 70 metres leave the lane by turning right to cross a stile* with a wooden footpath post to the left of it and a yellow arrow engraved on a footpath post, indicating 'Wannock 1 mile' [A1]. *Go diagonally up across a field heading towards the top left corner of the field,* your direction 115 degrees.

... is the ideal place to stop for lunch.

After 160 metres, at the top left corner, cross a stile to enter a wooded area. In 20 metres go up some steps. In 15 metres go through a wooden gate to emerge from a wooded area into a field. Veer slightly to the right to continue along an unfenced (but obvious) field boundary, your direction 120 degrees. In 50 metres, having been following fairly level ground, the field boundary edge descends.

In 250 metres you reach the right-hand corner of the field on your left, with the corner of a small wood immediately ahead on the left. The field on your right continues. Continue ahead up along the left edge of the field, with the small wood on your left.

After 40 metres turn left over a stile and turn right to continue up a path along the edge of woodland in the same direction as before, aiming for a stile (at the corner fencing of the field ahead) 40 metres distant.

Cross the stile to walk along the upper right-hand edge of the field, your direction 80 degrees. In 100 metres you reach the corner where the field edge turns 90 degrees right uphill. *Leave the field edge*

to continue straight ahead, your direction east along the DEFRA conservation path (a black dotted line on the OS map) to link up with the main (green dotted on the map) footpath. (This may be difficult to find if the field has been recently ploughed or harvested.)

Continue up across the field. After 100 metres you reach the brow of the field and continue on, aiming for the double metal fieldgate 15 metres to the left of the right-hand corner of the field. In 200 metres go through a (usually open) double metal fieldgate (with a stile to the left) to continue along a car-wide track with housing on your left behind fences and hedges, your direction 150 degrees.

In 100 metres you come out to a road and turn left. This is **Wannock**, as confirmed by a sign to your left **[A2]**. *Now continue from point* **[B2]** *in the option below.*

b) Short walk to Polegate via Jevington:
Follow the main walk directions until point [6]*.*

From the **Eight Bells** *pub turn left on the road.* In 200 metres you pass Green Lane on your left (the lane from which you previously emerged). After 250 metres you pass a wooden fieldgate on your left. *After a further 100 metres leave the road by turning right to cross over a stile* (to the left of a metal fieldgate, with a footpath post marked 'Filching Manor' to the left of the stile) **[B1]** *and turn left along the lower side of a field*, your direction 40 degrees. In 50 metres go over a stile.

Continue on in the same direction, keeping the field edge about 30 metres to your left. In a further 200 metres the path becomes almost invisible but you keep the barbed-wire fence in sight to your left-hand side.

In 500 metres exit the field by going over a stile on your left. Descend some steep steps and follow a steep, potentially slippery path, which meanders and has some occasional steps, for 150 metres to eventually cross a stile and emerge onto the road opposite a big house.

Turn right along the road and in 50 metres, and 30 metres before the entrance to* **Filching Manor Motor Museum** (open by appointment at certain times of the year; phone 01323 487838 for information) on your right, cross the road and go through a gap to the right of a wooden fieldgate saying 'South East Water – Do not obstruct' to follow in the same direction as the road, your direction 50 degrees.

In 40 metres follow the footpath up some steps to the left past a sign for 'Wannock ½ mile'. From here the way becomes steep, narrow and potentially very slippery. A watercourse appears on your right-hand side and in 600 metres, where there is an electric fence and farm buildings on your left, turn right to cross over the watercourse on a wide concrete platform to emerge on the road. *Then turn left to continue on the grass verge alongside the road.* This is **Wannock**, as confirmed by a sign to your left **[B2]**.

After 100 metres cross over Old Mill Lane to continue in the same direction along a tarmac pavement. In 200 metres you reach the end of Jevington Road and continue on Wannock Road, where there is a three-armed road sign on your right. Follow the direction for Polegate. The pavement is now on the right-hand side.

In 1.2km (0.75 miles) cross the A27 at the traffic lights to follow the High Street, with the Horse and Groom pub on your left. In 120 metres you pass St John's church on your right.

In a further 80 metres you pass Polegate Fisheries fish and chip shop on your left and in 70 metres, *just before the level crossing, turn right up a tarmac path*, which leads onto platform 1 of **Polegate station** for trains back to London.

c) Long walk via Beachy Head:
Follow the main walk directions until point [9].
In 25 metres pass a sign for Eastbourne Downs golf course on your left. Continue on this path until after 1km (0.6 miles) you reach the main A259 where there is a sign for Eastbourne Downs golf club also on your right **[C1]**.

Cross this road and continue on the South Downs Way directly opposite, with a barbed-wire fence to your right, and after 300 metres pass a three-armed footpath sign to 'Beachy Head, Willingdon Hill and Paradise Drive', where you carry straight on towards Beachy Head, your direction 140 degrees.

In 80 metres pass a stone trig point on your left. In 30 metres pass a circular pond on your left with wooden benches. Continue on the path as it veers to the right. In 70 metres pass a four-armed footpath sign and follow the direction signposted 'To Beachy Head 1¼ miles'.

[!] Veer left around the curve of the hill taking the lower of three paths, with a large wooded area to your left and several small clumps of trees on your right, your direction 210 degrees initially. Continue until you reach the busy B2103 and in 40 metres carefully cross this to follow the direction of the road sign to 'Birling Gap and Beachy Head Countryside Centre' to continue on another road running straight ahead.

Continue on the grass verge to the left of the road. (Any path off to the left will now take you down to Eastbourne.) In 1.9km (1.2 miles), as you reach the coast and as the road veers to the right, pass the **Beachy Head** pub on your right-hand side opposite a paragliding area to your left on a grassy bank. This is the suggested tea place for the long walk. (It is possible to take a bus here back to Eastbourne pier.)

To get a view down to the famous lighthouse, do not follow the Peace Path Circular Walk and Viewpoint, but instead continue along the road. *In 100 metres veer left towards the sea*, where there are benches set within a round brick structure, to reach the highest part of the cliff overlooking the lighthouse. **[C2]** (Take care looking down as this part of the cliff is prone to erosion.)

To return to Eastbourne, retrace your steps, now with the coast on your right, and in 400 metres, opposite a small lay-by for cars marked by a post, turn right where there is a two-armed footpath post and a wooden bench, following the direction of the signposted 'Seafront, South Downs Way'.

In 700 metres you pass another footpath post to your left; the path then descends steeply. In 300 metres, after the path becomes stepped, emerge onto a road at the foot of the Downs. (You had initially been walking through a corridor of trees, and as you descend you get good views of Eastbourne.) There are two interesting information boards here, one describing the 160-km (100-mile) South Downs Way to Winchester, and the other detailing the 131-km (82-mile) Weald Way to Gravesend.

Follow the direction for the town centre signposted on the four-armed footpath post '1 ½ miles via the seafront' on a road called Duke's Drive. In 250 metres, just after the bus stop and signpost for 'Meads

Village shops', *follow the direction of the pedestrian sign off to the right to Holywell Promenade Western Parade.*

Descend a steep tarmac road (with pavement). You can then take any path to get down to the seafront. Continue on the promenade *and in 1.5km (0.9 mile) you come to the Wish Tower (a round Martello tower) on your left and then turn left away from the promenade to get back up to the road.* (The bus from Beachy Head would have delivered you to the pier, which is now in sight.)

Continue towards the pier and, in 400 metres *just before the bandstand, take the steps to your left and follow the direction of the signposted tourist information inland to the town centre. Turn left on Devonshire Place.* At the end of this road, having passed many (Italian) restaurants, cross over Cornfield Terrace then continue over Lushington Road to **Eastbourne station**.

Lunch & tea places

Beachy Head *Beachy Head Road, BN20 3JY (01323 728060).* **Open** 11am-11pm Mon-Sat; 10am-10.30pm Sun. **Food served** 11.30am-10pm Mon-Sat; noon-10pm Sun. This pub is a good tea option; it serves meals, and tea and coffee all afternoon and evening, and offers views back over the walk from its windows.

Café Aroma *54 Ocklynge Road, Eastbourne, BN21 1PR (01323 640263).* **Open** 10am-4pm Mon-Sat. Serves coffee and afternoon teas. There are plenty of other eating options in Eastbourne.

Eight Bells *High Street, Jevington, BN26 5QB (01323 484442).* **Open** 11am-11pm Mon-Sat; noon-10.30pm Sun. **Food served** noon-3pm, 6-9pm Mon-Sat; noon-9pm Sun. The Bells is a very popular pub and gets quite crowded inside, but has a reasonably sized garden. It is the suggested lunch place for the main walk.

Giants Rest *Wilmington, BN26 5SQ (01323 870207).* **Open** 11.30am-3pm, 6.30-11pm Mon-Fri; 11.30am-11pm Sat; noon-10.30pm Sun. **Food served** noon-2pm, 7-9pm daily. This welcoming pub is the suggested lunch place for the walk via Folkington.

Seaford to Eastbourne

The Seven Sisters and Beachy Head.

Start: Seaford station
Finish: Eastbourne station
Length: 21km (13.1 miles)
Time: 7 hours walking time. For the whole outing, including trains and meals, allow 12 hours.

Transport: Two trains an hour (one an hour on Sunday) go from London Victoria to Seaford, changing at Lewes (journey time: 1 hour 27-34 minutes). There are two direct trains hourly (only one is direct on Sunday; change at Brighton for the other) back from Eastbourne to Victoria (journey time: 1 hour 29 minutes/10-25 minutes longer on Sunday). For those driving, it is best to park at Seaford, and catch the bus (*see below* **Walk options**) back there from Eastbourne. You could also park at Lewes, and catch trains to Seaford and back from Eastbourne.

OS Landranger Map: 199 (a small section at the start is on 198)
OS Explorer Map: 123
Seaford, map reference TV481991, is in East Sussex, 13km (8.1 miles) west of Eastbourne.

Toughness: 10 out of 10.

Walk notes: This classic clifftop walk – one of the finest coastal walks in England – affords stunning (and very famous) views of the white cliffs of the Seven Sisters and Beachy Head, before ending in the seaside town of Eastbourne. En route, you can swim in the sea at Cuckmere Haven or Birling Gap (provided that the tide is up – and watch out for underwater rocks at Birling Gap). Note, however, that this is a **very strenuous** walk. Apart from the start, finish and a short section around Cuckmere Haven, almost none of it is flat, and there are several steep climbs. The very scenic section between Cuckmere Haven and Birling Gap, in particular, is a series of steep ascents and descents, and it is a long, though relatively gradual, climb up to Beachy Head. Also note that the cliffs on this walk are eroding fast,

and you are advised to keep well away from the edge at all times.

Walk options: A very useful bus, the 712, runs from Seaford to Eastbourne (both railway station and the pier) via Exceat and East Dean four times an hour from Monday to Saturday, enabling you to start or finish the walk at either of these two intermediate stops. On Sunday and bank holidays, when the bus becomes the 713 and the frequency is three times hourly, it also calls at Beachy Head and Birling Gap. In both cases, the last bus from Eastbourne is about 7.30pm. To get up-to-date details for this route, phone 0845 121 0170/0180 or see www.stagecoachbus.com. Using the bus, you could opt for the following sections of the main walk:

a) Seaford to Exceat: This short but pretty walk makes a fine 6.2km (3.9

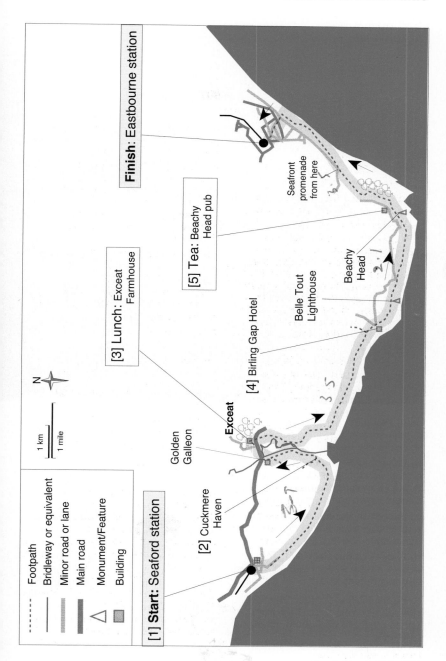

N

1 km
1 mile

Footpath
Bridleway or equivalent
Minor road or lane
Main road
Monument/Feature
Building

[1] **Start**: Seaford station

[2] Cuckmere Haven

Golden Galleon

Exceat

[3] Lunch: Exceat Farmhouse

[4] Birling Gap Hotel

Belle Tout Lighthouse

Beachy Head

[5] Tea: Beachy Head pub

Seafront promenade from here

Finish: Eastbourne station

Cuckmere River near Seaford.

mile) excursion on a summer's day, combined with a swim and a picnic at Cuckmere Haven.

b) Exceat to Eastbourne: This is a total walk of 14.8km (9.2 miles), though it misses the fine Seven Sisters views earlier in the walk.

c) Exceat to Birling Gap: This makes a total walk of 5.8km (3.5 miles); see bus details above.

d) Exceat to Beachy Head: This makes a total walk of 9km (5.6 miles); see bus details above.

Saturday Walkers' Club: Take the nearest train to 9.15am from London Victoria to Seaford, changing at Lewes.

Walk directions

[1] [Numbers refer to the map]
Leaving Seaford station, *turn right*. In 40 metres *turn right down Church Street*, heading towards the church, ignoring a road (Dane Road) sharp right.

In another 60 metres you pass the church of St Leonard's on your left and in a further 80 metres, *as the road curves to the left, leave it to continue straight on down a side road* (still called Church Street).

In 60 metres, *at a T-junction, turn left and, in 10 metres, turn right* along The Causeway. In 100 metres *you come to the seafront, where you cross the road and turn left* along the seafront promenade towards the chalk cliffs.

In 250 metres you pass a **Martello tower**. In a further 300 metres, *at the start of the cliffs, turn left at a two-armed Vanguard Way signpost up the left fork of the gravel path. In 80 metres turn right to climb steps* made from railway sleepers. You are now on the cliff edge, climbing uphill. *You follow this clifftop path for 3.2km until you reach some cottages at Cuckmere Haven.*

In more detail: Initially there is a golf course to your left. In 800 metres, as the course ends, you pass a sign for **Seaford Head Nature Reserve**, with the white cliffs of the **Seven Sisters** now visible in the distance and a radar station to your left.

2km later, *after a long steady descent, the latter part of which is in a shallow valley, you reach* **Hope Gap**, where some steps lead down to the sea and there is a sign explaining the geology of the landscape. *Bear left here*, following the clifftop path up a steep slope, your initial direction 40 degrees. The path soon levels out and in 450 metres *you come to a row of cottages.*

Turn right downhill here on a car-wide gravel track past the cottages. In 100 metres *pass through a wooden fieldgate onto the shingle beach of* **Cuckmere Haven. [2]** Ignore a path to the left (the Vanguard Way) and instead *continue straight ahead across the shingle*, passing a pool on your left, to reach the bank of the **Cuckmere River**.

Though the onward route lies over the cliffs ahead, you now have to make a 4.5km detour inland to cross the river (and get to lunch at Exceat).

[Note that, tempting though it looks just to wade the river, *the Cuckmere is deeper than it looks and surprisingly fast flowing*; trying to cross it is NOT recommended. However, there are occasions at very low tide when it fans out in shallow rivulets across the lower reaches of the shingle beach and can be crossed with relative ease. If you do this, however, you will miss lunch at Exceat.]

To continue the walk, *turn left along the river*, your direction 340 degrees initially.

In 2km, about 150 metres before the green road bridge, the bank makes a sharp turn left along a hedge, your direction due west. *80 metres later, at a crosspaths, go right* to follow a path between two barbed-wire fences, your direction 10 degrees.

In 200 metres pass through a wooden gate to enter the car park of the **Golden Galleon** pub, a possible lunch stop. Carry on across the car park for 70 metres to reach the A259. Cross this very busy road with care and *turn right to follow the pedestrian path across* **Exceat Bridge**. At the other side of the bridge, re-cross the road to continue along the tarmac roadside footpath.

In 400 metres, *where the main road curves to the right*, ignore a minor road to the left, but 10 metres further on *go straight ahead up a tarmac drive*. In 50 metres, when level with the car park, *turn right for 10 metres* to reach the entrance to the **Exceat Farmhouse Restaurant and Tea Room**, the recommended lunch stop, on your left-hand side. **[3]**

After lunch, *come out of the tearoom and turn left* (or if you have not stopped for lunch here, go straight on past the entrance). In 40 metres a wooden fence blocks your way to the main road. Just on the right here is the **Exceat Visitor Centre**, which among other things has interesting historic pictures showing just how rapidly the cliffs of the Seven Sisters are eroding. But to continue the walk, *turn left along the fence to reach the main road in 20 metres.*

Cross the road with care and go straight ahead through a wooden fieldgate with a cattle grid. Carry on straight ahead on the concrete car-wide track beyond (or the grass beside it).

In 1.4km, just after passing around the spur of a hill to your left, you come to a three-way footpath signpost. Ignore multiple gateways immediately on your left to carry straight on through a wooden gate marked with a yellow South Downs Way arrow. 60 metres further, *at another three-armed footpath sign, take the left*

Big sisters

Between Cuckmere Haven and Birling Gap you'll find the undulating cliffs known as the Seven Sisters. They are thought to have been formed by glacier meltwater at the end of the last Ice Age: the meltwater carved steep-sided valleys, which were then truncated by sea erosion into the cliffs we see today. The original Seven Sisters are the Pleiades, a constellation of seven stars, which Greek mythology portrayed as sisters. There are in fact now only six Pleiades, one having exploded in antiquity, and from the approach to Cuckmere Haven there seem to be only six humps on the Seven Sisters too. But there are in fact seven: one is hidden from view from this angle.

fork, signposted 'South Downs Way', your direction 160 degrees. In 70 metres pass through a wooden gate and carry on up steps, your direction 100 degrees initially. Ignore a stile immediately on your right and *carry on uphill, with a wire fence to your right.* You now stay on the South Downs Way all the way to the outskirts of Eastbourne.

But in more detail: *follow the fence uphill for 600 metres* as it curves gently right. Eventually it loses itself in bushes to the right and you *carry straight on uphill to cross a stile in 150 metres.* 250 metres later *you come to the summit of* **Haven Brow**,

the first of the **Seven Sisters**, which is marked with a three-armed signpost.

Bear left, following the signpost to Birling Gap, your direction 110 degrees. The path now descends for 230 metres to reach **Short Bottom**, rising 100 metres to **Short Brow**. 50 metres further on you cross a stile and then descend for 230 metres to **Limekiln Bottom**.

Here the path rises for 200 metres to reach **Rough Brow** and then descends for 150 metres to **Rough Bottom**. Next, ascend steeply for 150 metres to reach **Brass Point**, where you cross a stile beside a National Trust sign for Crowlink.

The path now gently descends for 380 metres to **Gap Bottom** before rising for 160 metres to reach the peak of **Flagstaff Point**, which is marked by a low Sarsen stone monument.

Keep straight on along the clifftop path for 1.9km to Birling Gap, whose buildings are visible ahead. You pass over three more humps – one minor one, and two major ones – **Bailey's Hill** and **Went Hill**.

150 metres after the summit of Went Hill you pass through a wooden kissing gate. In 60 metres you pass between a fence right and bushes left down a path, which in 25 metres brings you to another kissing gate and a T-junction. Turn right here for 25 metres and then left with the path, past a wooden fieldgate, onto what is now a car-wide gravel track.

Carry on down this track and in 250 metres, 30 metres before you come to a road, turn right at steps leading down to a toilet block, and across the car park to the **Birling Gap Hotel** and café, a possible lunch or tea stop. It is worth going to the top of the steps just in front of the café for a fine view of the Birling Gap beach. **[4]**

From the clifftop at Birling Gap, *turn inland and go half right across the car park to the left of the red telephone box to rejoin the clifftop path.*

You now follow this path, the South Downs Way, for 1km to reach the **Belle Tout Lighthouse**. At the start of the climb out of Birling Gap, look back for fine views of the Seven Sisters. When you get to the lighthouse, *pass to the left of its perimeter wall on a broad grassy path.*

Where the wall ends keep straight on across the grass. In 80 metres *you come to a tarmac footpath, where you turn left* to continue into a large dip. *In 250 metres, at the bottom of the dip*, you pass a sign giving information about the lighthouse and the Eastbourne Downland Path. Here leave the tarmac path, which curves left to the road, *and carry straight on up the next rise in the cliff path.*

You now climb solidly for 2.8km to Beachy Head, the one exception being a sharp and unexpected dip after about 1km. You know you have reached Beachy Head proper when you come to an eight-sided memorial to armed forces personnel involved in the World War II defences that were sited here. Across the road 130 metres away half left is the **Beachy Head** pub, if you want to stop for tea here. **[5]**

Otherwise, *from the memorial carry on for 100 metres to a shallow dip and then turn right on a tarmac path* that skirts around the seaward side of a small hill. In 120 metres, *where the path swings right to a viewpoint, continue straight on a gravelly section of path toward a post with a yellow arrow.*

In 20 metres, *just before the arrow post, you re-cross the tarmac path and carry straight on* in the direction of the arrow along a footpath that runs just below the tarmac path initially, your direction 20 degrees.

Stay on this path, the **South Downs Way**, *keeping just below the lip of the ridge to your left* and ignoring all ways off. *In 650 metres, at a fork in the path, take the leftmost path, which climbs up onto the ridge* and passes a bench to your left in 50 metres, followed by a post with a yellow arrow on it.

Follow the direction of the arrow, skirting along a line of hawthorn bushes to your right. *In 200 metres, at a footpath sign, veer right following the sign to 'Seafront SDW',* your direction 30 degrees.

This car-wide grassy path descends gradually, at first between bushes and small trees and then across open hillside, for 1km all the way to the edge of **Eastbourne**. The last part is a steep descent of a hillside to a bend in a road, the B2103 or Foyle Way. When you reach the road there should be a refreshment kiosk on your right.

When you get to the road keep straight on along the right-hand side of it. In 100 metres you cross the driveway to St Bede's Preparatory School and, in 70 metres, the entrance to Helen Gardens on your right. In a further 70 metres, *turn right, into Holywell Drive,* signposted: 'Holywell and Promenade (Western Parade)'.

Continue downhill, ignoring turnings off, and *in 300 metres you reach the seafront promenade.*

Follow this promenade all the way to Eastbourne Pier, a distance of 2km. The stop for the 712 or 713 bus is to be found

10 metres beyond the pier entrance. But to go to Eastbourne railway station, *120 metres before the pier, climb steps to your left, to reach a pedestrian crossing across the seafront road.*

Cross here and turn right then immediately left down Terminus Road. In 200 metres, at a crossroads, go straight on up Eastbourne's pedestrian shopping street (still Terminus Place), crossing Pevensey Road and curving left with it in 100 metres.

In 80 metres you pass the entrance to the Arndale Centre on your right and in 150 metres another entrance to the same place. 150 metres further on you come to **Eastbourne station** on your right.

Lunch & tea places

Beachy Head *Beachy Head Road, BN20 3JY (01323 728060).* **Open** 11am-11pm Mon-Sat; 10am-10.30pm Sun. **Food served** 11.30am-10pm Mon-Sat; noon-10pm Sun. This pub is a good tea option; it serves meals, and tea and coffee all afternoon and evening, and offers views back over the walk from its windows.

Birling Gap Hotel *Seven Sisters Cliffs, East Dean, BN20 0AB (01323 423197).* **Open** 10am-11pm daily. **Food served** noon-2.30pm daily. Situated 12.2km (7.6 miles) into the walk, this place offers a basic lunchtime menu in its Thatched Bar. The rather run-down café next door also does simple meals with chips, as well as sandwiches.

Exceat Farmhouse Restaurant & Tea Room *Seven Sisters Country Park, nr Seaford, BN25 4AD (01323 870218).* **Open** 10am-4pm Mon-Sat; 10am-5.30pm Sun. **Food served** (hot) noon-2pm daily. 6.2km (3.9 miles) into the walk, this spot has a charming open-air courtyard and serves a varied home-made hot lunch menu, and after that sandwiches, ploughman's lunches and teas until around 5pm (or 4pm if custom is light). This is the suggested lunch stop for the main walk.

Golden Galleon *Exceat bridge, Exceat, BN25 4AB (01323 892247).* Half a kilometre before the Exceat Farmhouse Restaurant & Tea Room is this busy, popular pub, with a garden looking seawards. It has a relatively varied menu, and tends to pack out at weekends, with people queuing to order at times.

Hastings to Rye

One Cinque port and two ancient towns.

Start: Hastings station
Finish: Rye station
Length: 19km (11.8 miles). For a shorter variation, *see below* **Walk options**.
Time: 6 hours. For the whole outing, including trains, sights and meals, allow at least 11 hours.
Transport: Two trains an hour (one on Sunday) run from Charing Cross to Hastings (journey time: 1 hour 31-42 minutes). Trains back from Rye run once an hour, changing at Ashford (journey time: 1 hour 43-53 minutes). Buy a day return to Rye. For those driving, park centrally in Hastings. Trains back from Rye to Hastings are hourly and take 20 minutes.
OS Landranger Maps: 189 and 199
OS Explorer Maps: 124 and 125 Hastings, map reference TQ814097, is in East Sussex.
Toughness: 7 out of 10.

Walk notes: This rewarding walk starts with a fine clifftop coastal walk with steep climbs along the way. This section is the most strenuous part of the walk. Lunch is at Pett Level, after which the terrain levels out, before leading up through the New Gate into Winchelsea for tea. After tea, just east of the town, you reach the Look Out, offering panoramic views across the whole of Romney Marsh and the Kent Downs beyond. From here it is down and along to Ferry Bridge, following an easy flat route north-east to Rye.

Walk options:

a) Shorter Hastings circular walk: You may reduce the length of the main walk to 9.5km (6 miles) by following the main route directions as given until [2]. Then follow the directions for this option at the end of the main walk text. This route goes past the Caves and the castle to finish at Hastings.

You could also reduce the length of the walk by 2.4km (1.5 miles) by finishing at Winchelsea station.

Saturday Walkers' Club: Take the train nearest to 9am from London Charing Cross station to Hastings.

Walk directions

[1] [Numbers refer to the map]
Coming out of **Hastings station**, *go down Station Approach*. After 130 metres *cross Devonshire Road to go down Havelock Road*, your direction south. In 200 metres Havelock road intersects with a six-way crossroads, four roads of which are pedestrianised. *Bear left along Wellington Place*, a pedestrian zone, your direction 100 degrees. In 160 metres you *pass through a subway* and 70 metres further on *bear left to join the main A259 coastal road*, your direction east.

After 250 metres fork left along George Street through Hastings old town. In 300 metres you come to the High Street. Cross over to join the East Street, ahead and slightly to the right. After 90 metres cross over The Bourne and continue in the same direction, along Rock-A-Nore, with the tall black net huts away to your right.

[!] In 100 metres *turn left up Tamarisk Steps*, immediately before the Dolphin Inn.

After the initial flight ignore a narrow flight of steps ahead to follow the steps round to the right *to come out onto Tackle Way. Turn left and, after 25 metres, turn right up a long flight of steps to East Hill.* At the top of these steps you reach a sign 'Welcome to Hastings Country Park – East Hill'. Turn right to go up a short flight of steps. To your right is the East Hill funicular railway.

There is a large footpath post (No.1) on your left indicating cliff walks, with 'Fire Hills 3½ miles', pointing east along the cliff.

If you are taking the **main walk** to Rye you now *follow the cliff walk for 5.6km (3.5 miles) to Fire Hills at the end of Hastings Country Park* [3], which is clearly signposted by large wooden footpath posts. [If you are taking the **Shorter circular walk**, the route diverges from the cliff walk at footpath post No.8 ([2] below).]

In more detail: Head east as indicated by the large footpath post along the cliff with a wooden fence on your right, keeping to the lower route, your initial direction 80 degrees.

In 700 metres you start to go more steeply downhill, with a fence to your right. After 100 metres go through a wooden kissing gate to reach a large footpath post (No.2), with a footpath arrow to the right indicating 'Ecclesbourne Glen 1 mile, Firehills 3 miles'. Turn right to go down some steps, your initial direction 80 degrees.

After 80 metres, at the bottom of the steps, you come out to a level. Ignore a main turning off to the left and continue straight ahead to then go down a second flight of steps. 150 metres further on, at the bottom of the steps in the middle of the gorge, you pass a large footpath post on your left (No.3) to follow the footpath arrow for Firehills pointing ahead.

Continue up a flight of steps to reach the top of the steps after 200 metres to go through a wooded area. In 25 metres you emerge from the wooded area and bear right to reach a viewpoint after 25 metres. Turn left and continue along the coastal path, with a wooden fence on your right. Stick to the wider grassy path rather than the narrower one through the brambles.

In 750 metres you pass a large footpath post (No.4a) on your left, with a footpath arrow for Firehills pointing ahead.

After 600 metres, just after ignoring a fork to the left, you reach a large footpath post (No.7), with a footpath arrow for Firehills pointing ahead, to then enter a wooded area, your initial direction 70 degrees. After 100 metres you go down some steps. 100 metres further down the steps you reach a large footpath post (No.8) on your left, with a footpath arrow pointing ahead to 'Fairlight Glen (lower) ¼ mile, Warren Glen ¾ mile, Firehills 1¼ miles' and left to 'Fairlight Glen (upper) ¼ mile, Fairlight picnic site 1 mile, North's Seat 1¼ mile'. **[2]**

[At this point, you can choose to take option **a)**, the **Shorter Hastings circular walk** option. Follow the directions at the end of this main text.]

Otherwise, *for the main walk, continue straight ahead down the steps*, your direction 130 degrees.

After 40 metres, at the bottom of the steps, the path levels out. In 60 metres you emerge from the wooded area to commence a steep descent. After 150 metres, at the foot of the hill, you enter a wooded area. In 45 metres, at a footpath junction with a large footpath post (No.10) on your left, follow a footpath arrow pointing right to Firehills, your initial direction 50 degrees. In 30 metres you pass a Hastings Country Park notice board on your right.

Continue uphill to eventually emerge from the wooded area. In 500 metres, at a footpath junction marked by a large footpath post (No.11), turn right for Firehills, up some steps into another wooded area, your initial direction 50 degrees. In 80 metres, at the top of the steps, continue on the level to emerge from the wooded area after 20 metres.

In 110 metres you pass a large footpath post (No.12) on your left, with a footpath arrow pointing ahead for Firehills.

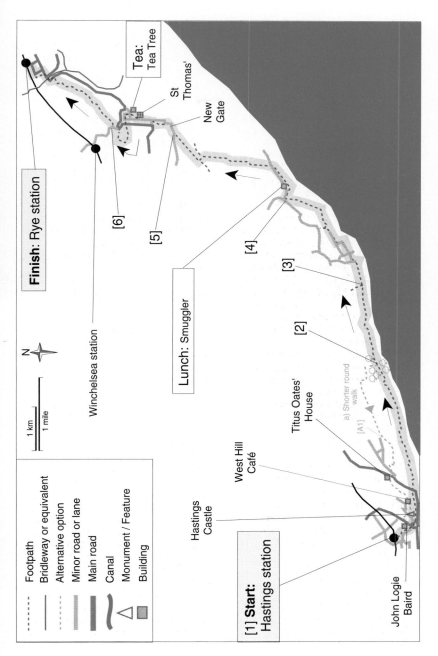

Legend:

- Footpath
- Bridleway or equivalent
- Alternative option
- Minor road or lane
- Main road
- Canal
- Monument / Feature
- Building

[1] **Start:** Hastings station

John Logie Baird

Hastings Castle

West Hill Café

Titus Oates' House

Lunch: Smuggler

[2]

[3]

a) Shorter round walk

[A1]

[4]

[5]

New Gate

St Thomas'

Tea: Tea Tree

[6]

Winchelsea station

Finish: Rye station

N

1 km
1 mile

The beach at **Hastings**.

After 90 metres you enter a wooded area and go down some steps. In 100 metres at the bottom of the steps you emerge from the wooded area to pass a large footpath post (No.13) on your right with a footpath arrow pointing ahead to Firehills.

After 140 metres of going downhill the footpath narrows and becomes steeper. In 200 metres you pass a large footpath post (No.13a) on your left, with an arrow for Firehills pointing ahead, to enter a sparsely wooded area, your initial direction 60 degrees.

In 20 metres you cross a stream and start to go uphill and after 220 metres you go up some steps. In 40 metres, at the top of the steps, you reach a footpath junction, with a bench and a footpath post on your left. Turn right, following a yellow arrow on the post, your direction 130 degrees.

In 500 metres go through a wooden kissing gate and pass a large footpath post (No.14) on your left with a Firehills arrow pointing ahead. There is also a radar station up to your left. Continue straight ahead and take the lower path, which forks downhill to the right.

In 120 metres the path levels out. After 350 metres you come to the end of Hastings Country Park to go through a wooden kissing gate. **[3]** Follow the path between fences to come out onto a shingle road (Channel Way) after 100 metres, with houses and bungalows to your left.

In 250 metres you pass Gorsethorn Way on your left. After 260 metres, *at a road junction, turn left down the tarmac Shepherds Way*, your direction 350 degrees.

In 120 metres *turn right along Bramble Way*. After a further 120 metres you pass Blackthorn Way on your left and Heather Way on your right. In 75 metres ignore Smugglers Way on your left to continue along the shingle Rockmead Road, passing a sign on your left 'Unsuitable for large vehicles'. In 200 metres the lane curves to the left and then to the right, as you pass a wooden fieldgate entrance to No.15 on your left.

After 80 metres the lane now curves to the left to go slightly downhill, your direction 330 degrees. In 40 metres the shingle lane becomes tarmac.

In 170 metres (having ignored a footpath off to your right) you *reach a road junction where you turn right*, your initial direction 50 degrees. After 180 metres you pass Cliff Way on your right with a sign 'Sea Road closed'. 40 metres further on you pass Primrose Hill on your left and 180 metres further on you pass Briar Close on your left.

[!] In 150 metres, *where the lane curves round to the left and Sea Road leads off up to the right, continue straight on through a narrow entrance onto a footpath*, passing a two-armed wooden footpath signpost after 10 metres, and turn right as indicated, your initial direction 120 degrees.

In 100 metres the footpath bears round to the left. Follow the fenced-in footpath for 100 metres to come out with the cliff edge away to your right. Continue up the footpath, with a field fence on your left.

After 140 metres go up some steps. In 300 metres ignore a stile on your left and after a further 300 metres, at the end of the field on your left, go downhill along a narrow path.

Continue downhill, ignoring any turnings off for the next 450 metres to then *go down some steps to join a lane. Continue down for a few metres to a T-junction* [4] *and turn right onto a road*, your direction east. In 150 metres you pass some public conveniences on your right and a three-armed public footpath signpost.

[!] After 15 metres, *where the road curves to the left, continue straight on to go through a wooden gate to the left of a driveway entrance.* Go along the driveway for 40 metres and *then turn left*, marked by a wooden public footpath signpost, to go up a small flight of steps and then down some steps.

Follow an arrow on a post to bear right. In 50 metres you *climb up some steps to cross a beach rampart and turn left along the promenade* with the rampart on your left and a metal railing to your right.

After 220 metres you pass a bench and *go through some sea defence gates to bear left*, passing the fieldgate entrance to Pett Level caravan park on your left. You then *join a car-wide track off the promenade, which descends down to the* **Smuggler** pub, the suggested lunch stop.

After lunch, *retrace your steps back up to the promenade and turn left. In 400 metres ignore a car-wide track veering down to the left* towards the main road *and continue along a narrow path* with a grass slope on your left and the shingle beach to your right.

[!] *After 180 metres turn left down the easy to miss steps to the road. Cross over the road into a field and turn right* next to a Pett Level Preservation Trust sign on your left, your direction 350 degrees.

In 50 metres you *join the Military Canal, with the canal on your left.* Cross a car-wide track, ignoring a bridge over the canal to the left, and continue straight ahead alongside the canal.

In 100 metres you cross over a stile to the left of a wooden fieldgate. After 550 metres ignore a footbridge to your left at the canal junction. Continue along the canal in a northerly direction, crossing two more stiles to the right of metal fieldgates along the way.

In 1.2km (0.75 miles) you *reach a footbridge on your left (30 metres before a metal fieldgate). Turn left to cross over the footbridge. Then bear right* for 20 metres *to cross a concrete footbridge over the junction of the canal.*

Continue straight ahead for 120 metres to Wickham Cliff, the old coastline, your direction north, where you *bear right along the base of the old cliff on your left.* In 150 metres bear left to cross over a stile and continue along the base of the cliff for another 400 metres to then cross over a stile to the left of a metal fieldgate.

Bear left to follow the edge of the field round and up for 80 metres to its top corner. **[5]** *Cross over a stile and turn right onto a lane,* your direction 60 degrees.

After 300 metres you pass through the **New Gate** of Winchelsea to continue up the lane. *In a further 300 metres, as the lane curves round to the right, take an unmarked footpath that forks off to the left,* your direction 350 degrees. *In 200 metres, at a footpath junction* where the 1066 Country Walk crosses your path, go *over the stile on your right,* to join the 1066 Country Walk.

Turn half left, diagonally up across the field, heading towards a stile 20 metres to the left of the remains of an old stone wall on the far side of the field, your direction 20 degrees. (This gable is all that remains of St. John's Hospital.)

After 160 metres cross the stile and cross the road and turn right along the pavement into **Winchelsea** (*see p301* **High and dry**), with a stone wall on your left.

In 500 metres, having come into Winchelsea, you reach a crossroads. Go over to *enter the south-west kissing gate entrance to* St Thomas' churchyard, to visit the church of **St Thomas**.

Coming out of the church, turn right for 80 metres to exit via the north-east kissing gate. Turn right to go down the High Street for 50 metres to reach the **Tea Tree** tearoom on your right.

On coming out of the tearoom *turn left* to go back up the road *for 50 metres to the crossroads and turn right,* your direction 10 degrees. After 100 metres *turn left at the crossroads* to go up (Mill Road), your direction 280 degrees. After 220 metres you *reach a T-junction with the main road. Cross over to go along a lane,* passing a two-armed wooden footpath signpost on your right, indicating the 1066 Country Walk.

After 160 metres, where the lane comes to an end, cross a stile between two fieldgates to follow a yellow footpath arrow *towards a fire beacon,* your direction 260 degrees.

After 140 metres you reach the **Look Out**, with the remains of Winchelsea windmill to the right of the fire beacon. *Veer right to go 40 metres downhill to cross a stile* and follow a yellow footpath arrow *downhill through a cutting,* your direction 300 degrees.

In 160 metres continue down the cutting as it veers to the right to cross a stile 30 metres further on at the bottom corner of the field. Continue straight ahead along the top edge of the field, with an embankment up to your right, your direction 20 degrees.

After 250 metres, at the corner of the field, *cross over a footbridge.* In 30 metres cross a stile and after a further 100 metres you come out onto a car-wide concrete track.

After 40 metres pass round to the right of a wooden fieldgate. In 20 metres you *come out onto the main road and turn left. In 10 metres continue straight on, leaving the main road to go along a slip road* (signposted to Winchelsea station), your direction 20 degrees.

After 200 metres *the road crosses Ferry Bridge. Immediately past the bridge on the right you reach a stile* with a metal footpath signpost. **[6]** [If you wish to cut the walk short then ignore this stile to continue along this lane for 600 metres to **Winchelsea station**.]

High and dry

Visiting **Winchelsea** today, with the sea more than two kilometres (1.25 miles) away, it is curious to think that 700 years ago it was one of England's leading ports. But this is not the first Winchelsea – that was sited on a massive shingle spit, somewhere out towards Dungeness (probably offshore from the village of Camber). The old town was devastated by storms in the 13th century, with the great storm of 1287 causing its final destruction. At the time, the loss of Winchelsea was as great a blow as, say, Portsmouth disappearing beneath the waves would be today, such was its maritime significance.

King Edward I ordered a new port to be built and work started in the 1280s, from the Strand to the New Gate (where you can see the deepest section of the town ditch around Winchelsea, part of the town's defence), with the streets being laid out on a grid system.

The wealth of new Winchelsea in its heyday was based largely on the lucrative wine trade. (There are 47 known cellars in the town.) Other prominent industries included wool, timber, iron, shipbuilding and repair. Along with Rye, Winchelsea emerged as one of the key ports in south-east England. As one of the Cinque Ports (the others were Rye, Romney, Hythe and Dover), it held trading privileges in return for (in the days before a national navy) providing maritime protection in the Channel. In effect, the Cinque Ports were given a Royal licence for piracy.

However, new Winchelsea's heyday lasted only a few generations. By the middle of the 14th century the town was in terminal decline. In the 1340s it started to suffer from shingle drifts, and when ships were no longer able to reach the town its livelihood dried up and it returned to being just another obscure little coastal town.

Otherwise, for the main walk, cross over the stile and turn half left to cut the corner of the field, your direction 80 degrees. *In 70 metres cross over into the next field (not the field on your left) and veer left, diagonally across this field*, aiming for a wooden railed footbridge on the far side (also in the direction of Rye, visible 3km/1.9 miles ahead), your direction 40 degrees. (However, depending on the time of year and the state of the field you may prefer to follow its left-hand edge all the way round to the footbridge.)

In 260 metres *cross the wooden footbridge* into the next field and continue along in the same direction (40 degrees) across the field. In 120 metres you pass by the corner of a ditch stream on your right and veer slightly to the right (aiming just to the right of the peak of Rye) and continue across the field, your direction 50 degrees. In 200 metres you reach a bend in another ditch stream on your left to now go along the right-hand bank of this ditch stream. After 220 metres turn left to *cross over a metal-railed wooden footbridge and veer slightly to the right to head towards a not clearly visible footbridge*, your direction 40 degrees. (If you can't make out the footbridge or the path continue straight ahead aiming just to the right of the peak of Rye in the distance.)

After 50 metres a small embankment starts on your left. Veer left to continue along this embankment. In 250 metres you *cross over the metal-railed wooden footbridge and continue straight ahead* in the same direction (40 degrees). *After 60 metres, with a metal fieldgate off to your left, go straight ahead and cross over some low wire fencing* (this is a public footpath) *to continue with the ditch stream on your left*. In 500 metres you pass a wooden footpath post with a yellow public footpath arrow indicating your direction ahead, with the ditch stream on your left.

After 180 metres you pass a yellow 'roofed' wooden footpath post with a yellow public footpath arrow, indicating your direction ahead. In 140 metres

go over a stile to the right of a metal fieldgate and continue straight ahead, your direction 20 degrees. In 200 metres go through a (usually open) metal fieldgate to continue along a car-wide track, which curves to the right just before it becomes tarmac after 240 metres.

In 240 metres you *come out to a main road. Turn left* to follow the main road round to the right to cross a road bridge over the river Tillingham after 60 metres. After 150 metres you reach Cyprus Place on your left.

If you wish to head straight back to the station, turn left, your direction 300 degrees, *and follow the road round to the right after 70 metres* to reach a T-junction after 30 metres, with a level crossing on your left. Cross over the road to reach **Rye station** after 150 metres.

However, Rye is a town well worth visiting. Cross over Cyprus Place to turn right along Wish Ward to head into the historic part of Rye.

Walk options

a) Shorter Hastings circular walk: *Follow the main walk directions to [2].* *At the large footpath post (No.8)* on your left, with a footpath arrow pointing ahead to 'Fairlight Glen (lower) ¼ mile, Warren Glen ¾ mile, Firehills 1¼ miles' and left to 'Fairlight Glen (upper) ¼ mile, Fairlight picnic site 1 mile, North's seat 1¼ mile', *turn left*, your initial direction 50 degrees; go along the level through a wooded area.

After 350 metres you emerge from the woods to *reach a path T-junction. Turn left uphill*, your initial direction 310 degrees. In 250 metres you pass a flight of steps down to the right (leading down after 25 metres to a small dripping waterfall). In 30 metres you reach a *footpath junction with a large footpath post on your left.*

[!] *Turn sharp left uphill*, your direction 210 degrees. In 100 metres, *at the top of the hill*, you come out of Hastings Country Park to *continue along a car-wide earth track* and in 20 metres turn right with the track *along the right-hand edge of*

Hastings Castle.

the field, your direction west. In 200 metres cross a stile (to the right of a metal barrier) and *continue down a car-wide earth track between hedgerows*, your initial direction 300 degrees.

In 150 metres the car-wide track curves to the right. In 160 metres, *at a T-junction, turn left onto a shingle lane*, your direction 250 degrees.

In 400 metres you pass round to the right of a metal fieldgate with a sign saying 'Private Road to Fairlight Place and Farm only'. Beyond the gate a driveway leads to the left. Continue along the lane. In 300 metres you pass the entrance to Shear Barn Tourer and Tent Park on your right.

In 150 metres you pass the entrance to Shear Barn caravan and camping ground on your left. After 270 metres *take the slip road* [A1], *Rocklands Lane, forking off to the left*, your direction 210 degrees. In 60 metres the tarmac lane becomes shingle.

After 400 metres you pass the entrance to Rocklands Holiday Park on the left, with a car barrier ahead to continue slightly uphill along a shingle track. In 20 metres ignore a footpath forking

off downhill to the right. After 60 metres *the shingle driveway leads out into open parkland*, with a Hastings Country Park notice board on the right.

Veer right down the right-hand edge of the open parkland in the direction of Hastings (visible ahead), your direction 260 degrees. In 150 metres you pass a brick pavilion on your right and after a further 30 metres, *at a two-armed footpath signpost to the left of a bench, take a path down a steep hill*, your direction 250 degrees.

In 40 metres you emerge into an open space and *continue downhill along the right-hand edge of the open space. In 100 metres, at the bottom of the open space, turn left at a 'Welcome to Hastings Country Park – East Hill' sign*, your direction 190 degrees.

After 50 metres take an unmarked footpath forking down off to the right, your direction 230 degrees. In 100 metres, *at a T-junction, turn right down some steps for 10 metres to reach another T-junction. Turn right* as marked by a yellow arrow on a post and *continue along this main lower path along the side of the hill*, with the slope dropping to your left, your direction 20 degrees.

In 300 metres turn sharp left down a tarmac footpath. After 150 metres the tarmac footpath *comes out to a road. Continue down the road for 60 metres to then turn right across the road via a zebra crossing. 15 metres further on cross over the main A259 via a zebra crossing and turn right*, passing the house on your left where notorious fraudster Titus Oates (1649-1705) once lived (in 1678 he claimed to have discovered a Popish plot to kill Charles II and replace him with his Catholic brother James; 80 people were rounded up and several executed before Oates admitted that he'd made the whole thing up). *After 20 metres turn left up an unmarked public footpath*, your direction 290 degrees.

In 30 metres, *where the footpath forks, fork left* alongside a brick wall on your left. In 100 metres ignore some steps leading up to the right and continue uphill. After 150 metres, *at a path T-junction, bear left down a tarmac footpath.*

In 100 metres turn right uphill along an alleyway (Salters Lane). After 70 metres *go up some steps to then turn left* onto Croft Road. *After 10 metres fork right to go up a tarmac footpath.* In 100 metres *at the top of the footpath you come out into open parkland and turn left.* In 100 metres you pass the entrance to the **Caves** on your left. Continue along this path, which curves to the right and up towards West Hill Café. In 200 metres, *at the end of the path, turn left for 30 metres to* **West Hill Café**, the recommended refreshment stop at the top of the West Cliff railway.

Coming out of West Hill Café, turn left along a tarmac footpath, which leads up onto the cliffs. In 60 metres you *emerge onto a green and turn half right across the green*, your direction west. In 60 metres, at a footpath post, *go down some steps and follow the path, which leads to* **Hastings Castle** entrance after 60 metres.

Turn right to go down a lane. After 80 metres, *at a T-junction, turn left* to go down Castle Hill Road. After 30 metres

pass Castle Down Avenue on your right. In 60 metres *cross over a main road and turn right for 20 metres to then turn left down Portland Steps.*

At the bottom of Portland Steps turn left onto Portland Terrace. *In 30 metres go down some steps and turn right downhill along a narrow road* (Castle Hill Passage). *In 70 metres you reach Queen's Road*, with a Marks & Spencer's on the opposite side.

Cross this main road via the pelican crossing and turn left. In 120 metres you *reach a pedestrianised zone and continue straight on. After 100 metres you reach a six-way crossroads. Turn half right to go up Havelock Road*, your direction 300 degrees. In 20 metres you reach the **John Logie Baird** pub on your right, a recommended refreshment stop.

Coming out of the John Logie Baird, turn right up Havelock Road for 200 metres to then cross Devonshire Road. Veer left to go back up Station Approach to **Hastings station**.

Lunch & tea places

John Logie Baird *29-31 Havelock Road, Hastings, TN37 1BE (01424 448110).* **Open** 10am-11pm Mon-Sat; 10am-10.30pm Sun. **Food served** 10am-10pm Mon-Sat; 10am-9.30pm Sun. Located at the end of the shorter circular walk, this is a decent pub option.

Smuggler *Pett Level Road, Pett Level, nr Hastings, TN35 4EH (01424 813491).* **Open** 11am-3pm, 6-11pm Mon-Fri; 11am-11pm Sat; noon-10.30pm Sun. **Food served** noon-2pm Mon-Sat; noon-3pm Sun. Located 10km (6.25 miles) from the start of the walk, this pub serves homely food and is the suggested lunch stop for the main walk.

Tea Tree *12 High Street, Winchelsea, TN36 4EA (01797 226102/www.the-tea-tree.co.uk).* **Open** Feb-Dec 10am-5pm Mon-Fri; 10am-6pm Sat, Sun. Situated halfway through the walk, this is the recommended tea stop for the main walk.

West Hill Café *Castle Hill Road, Hastings, TN34 3RD (01424 429636).* **Open** Nov-Feb 10am-4pm daily. *Mar-Oct* 9am-5.30pm daily. 1km (0.6 miles) from the end of the walk, this café is recommended as a tea stop if doing the shorter circular walk.

Dover to Deal

Along the White Cliffs of Dover.

Start: Dover Priory station
Finish: Deal station

Length: 16km (9.9 miles). For a shorter walk and other variations, *see below* **Walk options**.

Time: 5 hours walking time. For the whole excursion, including meals and trains, allow 11 hours.

Transport: Two trains an hour run from London Charing Cross and two per hour from Victoria to Dover Priory (one an hour from both stations on Sundays; journey time: 1 hour 34-53 minutes). Hourly trains from Deal pass through Dover to Charing Cross (journey time: 2 hours 5-14 minutes). For those driving, parking centrally in Dover is best. Trains from Deal go back to Dover Priory, taking 15 minutes from Deal.

OS Landranger Map: 179
OS Explorer Map: 138 (the last mile or so is on 150)
Dover, map reference TR313414, is in Kent.

Toughness: 3 out of 10.

Walk notes: This simple walk (it should be impossible to get lost if you keep the sea on your right-hand side) is nevertheless one of the finest coastal walks in England, taking you right along the top of the famous White Cliffs of Dover. On a clear day, you will enjoy stunning views of the English Channel, the ferries buzzing in and out of Dover Harbour, and the French coast from Boulogne to Dunkerque. On hazier days, the dramatic (though dangerously crumbling) cliffs afford exciting views of the inaccessible beaches below.

Surprisingly, for a walk that seems to spend much of its time on the airy heights, not much exertion is involved. There are only two significant climbs, one out of Dover and the other out of St Margaret's Bay. Otherwise, the terrain is level or gently undulating. The last quarter of the walk, indeed, is totally flat, along a tranquil coastal path behind the pebble beach to Deal. Though less dramatic than the White Cliffs, this section of the walk is full of historical and natural interest, passing Walmer and Deal castles and examples of rare coastal flora.

Walk options: Directions for these variations are given at the end of the main walk text (*see p312*).

a) Short walk to St Margaret's Bay: You can also simply cut the walk short by ending at St Margaret's Bay, creating a walk of 7km (4.4 miles), or just over 2 hours walking. There is an efficient bus service from here back to Dover, which incidentally passes right by Dover Castle en route. For details on where to catch the bus, see the details for this option at the end of the main text.

b) Short walk to St Margaret's at Cliffe: If choosing not to end the walk at Deal, you can also walk on from St Margaret's Bay to the historic village of St Margaret's at Cliffe. For a suggested route see the directions at the end of the main text. This route adds 3.5km (2.2 miles) to the walk from Dover to St Margaret's Bay, making a total walk of 10.5km (6.6 miles) or 5 hours walking time.

You could also trim 3km (1.8 miles) off the main walk by getting a bus from Walmer Castle to Deal. Buses run hourly until about 5.45pm Monday to Saturday (phone 0870 243 3711 for exact times).

Saturday Walkers' Club: Take the train nearest to 9am (before or after) from London Charing Cross to Dover .

Walk directions

Special note: *Take care near the cliff edges on this walk, as they are crumbly and liable to collapse: the official advice is to keep 5 metres from any cliff edge. Even on the route described, you should use your judgement at all times and follow local warnings.*

[1] [Numbers refer to the map] *Leave* **Dover Priory station** *on platform 1*, the main exit, and turn right following the taxi sign. *In 20 metres curve left* up the station approach, your direction 80 degrees.

In 35 metres ignore a road to the left and 20 metres further on *merge with the main road to carry on downhill*. There is soon a fine view of **Dover Castle** on the hill ahead.

In 170 metres *go straight ahead across a large roundabout* (curving to the left to pass around metal barriers and across a pedestrian crossing) and *go straight ahead up Priory Street* (NOT Priory Road or Priory Place), which is *the road to the left of the Golden Lion pub*.

In 60 metres, *at a T-junction with Biggin Street, go right* into Dover's main shopping street. In 80 metres this street becomes pedestrianised and in another 100 metres you pass the church of St Mary on your left.

90 metres after this *you come to the Market Square. Walk straight ahead across this, passing just to the right of the fountain, and on into King Street,* the traffic-bearing road that runs along the square's left-hand side. In 45 metres the traffic swings right into Queen Street, but you *go straight on into the pedestrian underpass* ahead, signposted 'Sea front'.

Keep straight on through the underpass. *At the top of the steps at the far end go straight on through a circular plaza and across a road to get to the sea front promenade, where you go left.* Dover Eastern Docks – the main ferry terminal – is ahead of you, and Dover Castle is on the hill to your left. Note the small stone tower to the left end of the church by the castle: this is the **Roman Lighthouse**.

Signal success

South Foreland Lighthouse was built in 1843 to protect shipping from the Goodwin Sands (*see p310* **The real Deal**), which at low tide can be seen just offshore in the later part of this walk. The lighthouse is famous, though, for playing a key role in the history of radio. It was from its 21-metre (69-foot) tower in 1898 that Guglielmo Marconi first successfully made a ship-to-shore transmission, making contact with the Goodwin lightship, ten miles offshore. The

following year, the world's first international radio transmission was made from the lighthouse, the signal being picked up in Wimereux near Boulogne.

South Foreland Lighthouse
The Front, St Margaret's, Dover CT15 6HP (01304 852463/ www.nationaltrust.org.uk). **Open** *Mar-Oct* 11am-5.30pm Mon, Thur-Sun. **Admission** £2; £1 child; £5 family. **Credit** MC, V.

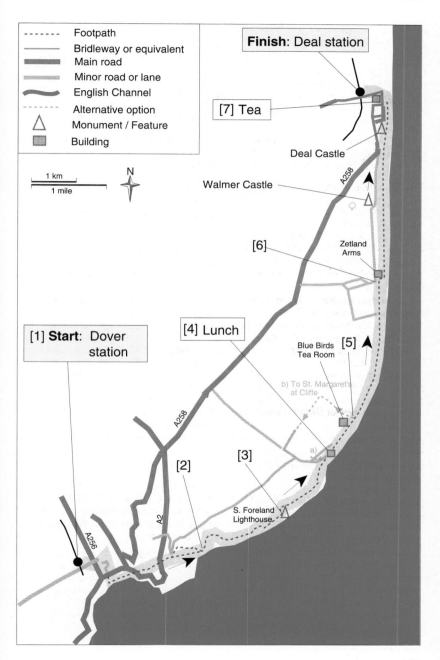

Footpath
Bridleway or equivalent
Main road
Minor road or lane
English Channel
Alternative option
Monument / Feature
Building

1 km
1 mile

N

Finish: Deal station

[7] Tea

Deal Castle

Walmer Castle

[6]

Zetland Arms

[1] **Start**: Dover station

[4] Lunch

Blue Birds Tea Room

[5]

b) To St. Margaret's at Cliffe

a)

[2]

[3]

S. Foreland Lighthouse

A258

A258

A2

A256

Stay on the promenade for 350 metres
until a point just after the cliffs start to
your left, and before a toilet block on the
promenade, where you *fork left, following
the green cycle path to the main road.*

Cross the road at the pedestrian lights
and *go straight ahead up East Cliff*, a
narrow road between the cliff to the left
and the rear of some houses to the right.

*In 250 metres you come to an open
area*, with the entrance to the ferry
terminal now right in front of you. *Go
straight on by a line of houses (Athol
Terrace) as it curves slightly left.* In 70
metres the *road becomes a concrete path.*
Follow this, with the cliff to your left and
the port to your right.

In 200 metres *pass under a road flyover*
and go straight ahead up several flights
of steps, ignoring a path to the left
halfway up. *50 metres after this you
come to another double flight: ignore
the left-hand one that leads to some
houses and take the right-hand one.*
This brings you up onto a tarmac path
that climbs the hill in shallow steps.

In 60 metres, *at the top of the hill* and
just before a wooden barrier that leads
into a car park, *turn right following a
green Saxon Shore Way sign.*

In 5 metres turn left, ignoring two
fainter paths forking off right downhill,
to follow a path contouring along the
slope, your direction 40 degrees. Almost
immediately you pass a wooden footpath
post on your right and soon after the
path passes into hawthorn thickets.

In 40 metres it emerges into an open
space for another 40 metres and then
goes into thickets once more. In 90 metres
you come into a much larger open space,
with the car park uphill to the left and a
telescope downhill to the right. *Walk to
the telescope. Just beyond it you will find
a clear metre-wide path, again contouring
along the slope. Turn left on this*, your
direction now 70 degrees. (If in any doubt
at this point, simply walk up to the car
park and turn right until you get to the
White Cliffs Visitor Centre.)

In 60 metres this path goes into
thickets again. In 50 metres ignore steps
to the left and keep straight on, now on
a wide, straight shelf, your direction due
east. In 10 metres you see the **White
Cliffs Visitor Centre** about 30 metres
uphill to the left. Even if not making a
refreshment stop, you might like to look
at the informative exhibits in the Centre
on the cliffs and their wildlife.

Staying on the broad shelf, *250 metres
beyond the Visitor Centre, a concrete
path merges from the left and you come
to a telescope and a bench. Ignore the
barricaded path that forks right just
beyond here* (it is a dead end) and stay
on the main track, now stony. In 70
metres you find yourself on a thrilling
shelf cut high into the chalk cliff, at the
end of which, in 230 metres, *you pass
through a kissing gate.*

*(If this shelf makes you vertiginous,
return to the telescope and instead take
the grassy slope to the left of the path.
In 200 metres you come to a kissing
gate, 130 metres to the right of the
radar tower of the Dover Coastguard
facility. Beyond the kissing gate there
is a wire fence to your right. Follow
this for 80 metres to a kissing gate.
You can now follow the directions in
the following paragraph.)*

Beyond the kissing gate, *keep straight
on, following the wire fence on your right-
hand side*, your direction 10 degrees.

In 120 metres *the wire fence gives way
to a wooden one and the path descends
for 80 metres onto a car-wide grassy track*
(actually an old railway line used to bring
goods down to the port). **[2]** *Cross this
track to follow an earth path straight on*,
your direction 80 degrees.

In 50 metres the path curves left
around a hillock and descends into a dip
for 70 metres, before climbing again. The
big depression in the cliff you are now
crossing is **Langdon Hole.**

Stay on the clearly defined path,
ignoring a stile uphill in the fence to the
left after 70 metres. 80 metres later the

The much-celebrated **White Cliffs of Dover**.

path comes up alongside the fence and
follows it for 100 metres to a stile.

*Cross this stile to keep straight on,
initially skirting a now fenceless arable
field to your left*, your direction initially
100 degrees. *Keep to this path as it curves
around to the left and uphill*, ignoring
alternatives to the right (unless you
want, at your own risk, to have a closer
look at the sea below).

In 270 metres, at the top of the hill,
the South Foreland Lighthouse comes
into view ahead. *You now walk along the
clifftop towards this for 1.6km (1 mile) on
a clear path*, in 500 metres skirting to the
left of a large depression. Along this route
there are several places where large areas
of the cliff have been undermined and are
about to fall into the sea.

Just after you come level with the
lighthouse, *your way forward is blocked
by a wire fence. Turn left inland here up
a clear path*, following a Saxon Shore
Way arrow. In 100 metres this brings you
to the entrance to the **South Foreland
Lighthouse** (*see p306* **Signal success**)
and a car road **[3]**.

Do not go down the road but *turn
immediately right after the entrance to
the lighthouse*, following the right-hand
edge of a grassy space, your direction 50
degrees. In 70 metres *turn right onto a
gravel lane*, your direction 90 degrees.

In 370 metres, just after a high wooden
fence ends to your right, *turn right through
a kissing gate*, which has a White Cliffs of
Dover information board next to it. Walk
downhill for about 40 metres and then *turn
left to follow the cliff edge. In 500 metres,
where your way is blocked by a rusty fence*
(the cliff path here fell into the sea about 20
years ago), *turn left though a kissing gate*
to emerge onto a chalky car-wide track.

*Walk straight ahead downhill along
this track*, following a Saxon Shore Way
arrow on a post, curving left with the
track after a few metres. *In 90 metres,
at a track crossroads, go right*, with
formal gardens to your left. In 150 metres
the track becomes a car-wide road and in
70 metres you pass the **St Margaret's
Museum** on your right, which also has
a tearoom. On the left here is the entrance
to the **Pines Garden**.

The real Deal

Deal has a rather sleepy air these days, but the town was a major port in the days of sail. Great concentrations of ships used to collect in the area just off its beach, which offered a protected anchorage due to the presence of the sandbanks of the Goodwin Sands offshore, and cargo would be loaded or offloaded using rowing boats.

Because of the sandbanks, the area was known among sailors as the Downs (the word deriving from the same Saxon word as 'dune'). At times, up to 1,000 ships could be seen in the bay, and the town still retains many fine buildings from this era.

The economic and strategic importance of this part of the coastline in Tudor times led to Henry VIII building a series of defensive fortifications in 1539-40 against the threat of a French invasion. These became known as the 'Castles in the Downs', and include Walmer Castle (*see above*) and Deal Castle. They were never permanently occupied and saw only minor military action.

Since 1708, Walmer has been the official residence of the Lord Warden of the Cinque Ports. For the past couple of centuries this title has been largely ceremonial, but it was at one time a position of some power, with the holder controlling the five greatest ports of Medieval England. Two famous wardens – the Duke of Wellington, victor of Waterloo, and WH Smith of newsagents fame (*see p79* **Keeping up with the Smiths**) – died here. The simply furnished room in which the former expired (in his armchair at 3.25pm on 14 September 1852) has been left much as it looked in those days. Walmer also has fine gardens, which include 19th-century terraces, lawns, a kitchen garden, woodland walk and wildflower meadow.

Deal Castle

(01304 372762/www.english-heritage.org.uk). **Open** *Apr-Sept* 10am-6pm daily. *Oct-Mar* closed. **Admission** £3.50; £1.80-£2.60 concessions. **Credit** MC, V.

Walmer Castle

(01304 364288/www.english-heritage.org.uk). **Open** *Apr-Sept* 10am-6pm daily. *Oct* 10am-4pm Wed-Sun. *Nov-Mar* closed. **Admission** £5.80; £2.90-£4.40 concessions. **Credit** MC, V.

75 metres beyond this, at a T-junction, turn right downhill on a broad gravel track, following the Saxon Shore Way sign. *In 45 metres you come to a road, where you go straight on, steeply downhill.* In 120 metres you come to the sea front. The **Coastguard** pub, the recommended lunch stop, is on your immediate right **[4]**. (Note that if the pub is full, there is a seasonal **tea kiosk** in the car park, 50 metres to the left along the beach, which serves sandwiches and chips.)

[At this point, if you are taking option **a)**, the **Short walk to St Margaret's Bay**, refer to the directions at the end of this main walk text.]

After lunch, *turn left out of the pub along the sea front.* In 90 metres, *where the public slipway bisects the beach promenade, turn left up steps*, following a green Saxon Shore Way footpath sign.

Climb these steps in zigzags all the way to the top of the cliff and then turn right on an earth path. Keep to this path, ignoring ways off uphill to the left. In 100 metres you pass through a kissing gate and in 40 metres more you emerge into an open space.

Keep straight on, following the wire fence to your right. In 420 metres, *where the fence ends, fork left uphill towards a tall obelisk about 100 metres away*, your direction 340 degrees

In 75 metres pass through a gate to turn right onto a tarmac road. Almost immediately you pass the obelisk, which is a memorial to sailors in the merchant marine and Royal Navy who died in the Dover Strait during the two World Wars.

30 metres further on you pass the **Blue Birds Tea Room** on the right in an old coastguard station. 40 metres beyond the tearoom you come to a path crossroads **[5]**.

[At this point, you can take option **b)**, the **Short walk to St Margaret's at Cliffe**. Follow the directions at the end of this main walk text.]

Otherwise, *keep straight on*, following two arrows on a post. This path descends very gradually, between the cliff edge and

a huge field to the left for just over a kilometre, eventually passing through a wood and wire fence, which marks the end of the National Trust-owned Bockhill Farm.

Cross this fence by a low stile and then pass into a gentle dip before starting to climb gently. In 500 metres a track joins from the left and becomes a tarmac road and you pass a National Trust sign for Kingsdown Leas. Keep straight on, with the road and houses now to your left, for about 600 metres until you come over the top of the rise to see the long, flat beach stretching away ahead towards Deal.

Descend the hill, with the cliffs, ever-diminishing in height, still to your right and, in 400 metres, you pass a golf clubhouse and car park to your left. Shortly after this the path descends more steeply and in 160 metres passes into thorn bushes, from which it emerges 30 metres later to descend concrete steps to a road **[6]**.

Go left along this road (Undercliffe Road), keeping to the sea front, ignoring a turning left inland almost immediately.

In 600 metres you come to a triangular road junction (in fact, a crossroads), 40 metres after passing some public toilets on your left. *Turn right here, down South Road*, a gravel track with pretty houses to the left, following a green Saxon Shore Way footpath sign.

In 130 metres, as this track comes out to the sea front, turn left at the **Zetland Arms**, a possible early tea stop.

You now stay on this path, just inland of the beach, all the way into Deal, a distance of about 5km (3 miles). (Interest on this walk is provided by the pebble beach right, which is covered with interesting shore plants in spring, and which is a good place for a **picnic** tea stop, as well as by the endless architectural variations on the sea front house theme to the left and, towards Deal, by fishing boats drawn up on the beach. You might also like to imagine the scene more than 2,000 years ago when Julius Caesar's legions came ashore at this point.)

In slightly more detail, for the first kilometre you have houses to your left and you pass several turnings inland. The route is a car-wide gravel track for 60 metres, then a narrow path of deteriorating tarmac and gravel and then a broad car-wide track again (Wellington Parade).

When the houses end you cross an open space on a tarmac foot and cycle path. 400 metres after this you pass **Walmer Castle** (*see p310* **The real Deal**) on your left. It is possible to end the walk here by going to the road to the left and getting a **bus** into Deal (*see below* **Walk options**).

400 metres after passing the castle, the path forks. Straight ahead takes you to the road in 50 metres, but instead fork right with the cycle path to keep along the edge of the beach.

In 500 metres you pass the premises of the Downs Sailing Club to the right and shortly afterwards there are two buildings on the green to the left: the Café on the Green (which never seems to be open) and the lifeboat station. 100 metres beyond the lifeboat station, in the parade of shops across the road to the left, there is a **fish and chip shop** if you fancy dinner on the beach.

Keep on the sea front and in 500 metres you come to **Deal Castle** on your left (if you want to visit the castle, the entrance is on the far side; *see p310* **The real Deal**). 300 metres further on, just after passing the **Port Arms** and **Old Kings Head** pubs to the left, and 30 metres before you reach the pier, you come to a roundabout **[7]**, marking the junction with Broad Street, which goes inland.

The recommended tea stop, **Dunkerley's Hotel**, is on the left-hand corner of Broad Street, with **Debs** café on the opposite corner. For other tea options, continue along the sea front. 60 metres beyond the pier on the left is the **Deal Beach Parlour** and 40 metres beyond this on a corner is the **Caterer** café.

After tea, *to reach the station* from Dunkerley's Hotel or the roundabout, *walk inland up Broad Street*. In 80 metres you cross the pedestrianised High Street and in a further 170 metres you come to a five-way road junction. **Deal station** is up the second road to the right.

However, *if you want a brief flavour of the atmospheric narrow streets of old Deal*, the following **short detour** (15 minutes or so) might be of interest. Coming out of Dunkerley's Hotel, turn left along the sea front, in 230 metres passing the Royal Hotel right and in another 45 metres the Star and Garter pub to the left. 60 metres beyond this *go left up Brewer Street*. At the top of this, in 60 metres, *go left along Middle Street* (there is another small fish and chip shop on the left here) and in 35 metres *right up Oak Street*. This brings you in 50 metres to the *High Street, where you go left*. The High Street is full of small, old-fashioned shops and has an air of the 1950s about it.

In 160 metres you come to a pedestrianised section of the High Street and go straight on for 110 metres until this is crossed by a car road, Broad Street, where you go right. In 170 metres you come to a five-way road junction. **Deal station** is up the second road to the right.

Walk options

a) Short walk to St Margaret's Bay:
[Follow the main walk directions until point [4].
To catch the bus back to Dover from St Margaret's Bay, *retrace your steps up the road* from the Coastguard pub for 120 metres until you get *to a junction with a broad gravel track on the first hairpin bend*. On the left at this point is South Sands House.

Do not go up the gravel track but instead *go up a flight of steps to the right of the track at the point where it joins the road* and to the right of a Saxon Shore Way sign, your direction 300 degrees.

The steps climb steeply uphill. *At the top* ignore a fork to the right 10 metres after a green metal fence starts to your left and *keep straight on along the fence* (whose railings are now blue) for 80 metres *to merge with a road.* Keep straight on up the road and, in a further 110 metres, *as you come to a roundabout and Granville Road on your right, the bus stop is to the left.*

Buses run hourly to Dover until around 8pm Monday to Saturday, while on Sunday there are buses every two hours, with the last around 6pm. Phone 08702 433711 to find out exact times. Note that buses from this stop also serve Deal, so be sure to get the right one.

Once you are on the bus, the journey into Dover takes around 20 minutes. On the way into the town, the bus stops right outside Dover Castle and then slants downhill on Connaught Road, before turning left into Park Avenue, a residential street. At the traffic lights at the end of this street it turns left onto a broad one-way road and then right into Pencester Road, where it stops at the bus station, which is marked by a large ticket kiosk at the side of the road, and which is opposite South Kent College.

Getting off the bus, continue straight ahead down the road for 110 metres and then right into Biggin Street, Dover's central shopping street. *In 80 metres turn left down Priory Street for 60 metres to a large busy roundabout.*

Go straight across this, using the pedestrian crossing to the right, *and go straight ahead up Folkestone Road.* The slip road to **Dover Priory station** is 170 metres up on the right.

b) Short walk to St Margaret's at Cliffe:
Follow the main walk directions until point [5].
At the footpath crossroads 40 metres beyond the Blue Birds Tea Room, instead of going straight on as for the main walk, *turn left inland* between two unfenced fields, your direction 340 degrees.

In 140 metres pick up a hedge on your left-hand side. In 160 metres, at a

crossroads where a farm track merges from metal barns to the left, go straight on, your direction due north, with a small wood now on your left-hand side. In 60 metres ignore a footpath to the left to stay on the main track and in 50 metres more *curve left and then right through the line of trees to emerge onto a car-wide track between two huge unfenced fields.* Cross the valley between these two fields, your direction 330 degrees.

In 300 metres, as you are climbing up the far side of the valley, ignore a footpath to the right. In a further 260 metres, *just over the top of the ridge, go left at a T-junction following a yellow arrow on a post* (though this may be obscured by a bush), your direction 240 degrees. In 15 metres cross a stile to the left of a wooden fieldgate.

In 75 metres *merge with a tarmac lane and continue straight on,* still bearing 240 degrees.

You now keep on this lane for 1.5km (0.9 miles), ignoring ways off. In 1.1km the road becomes a residential street (Kingsdown Road) and 400 metres later *you come to the main road and the centre of* **St Margaret's at Cliffe**. The **Red Lion** pub is on your right at this point.

Turn left on the main road, in 50 metres passing the post office on your left. Just beyond this is the **Smugglers Free House** (01304 853404), which has an extensive food menu seven days a week and a garden.

In another 30 metres you pass the church of **St Margaret of Antioch** on your right (locked, but the key is available from the Post Office during office hours). There is a memorial window in the church to those who died in the Zeebrugge ferry disaster.

10 metres beyond the church you pass the **Cliffe Inn** on your left and 30 metres later the **Hope Inn** ('Sorry, no muddy boots'). 20 metres further along on the right-hand side, opposite Chapel Lane, is the **bus stop for buses to Dover**.

Note that buses from this stop also serve Deal, so be sure to get the right one. Note also that though this is not the same bus stop as is mentioned in the **Short walk to St Margaret's Bay** instructions above (it is about 600 metres further along the route), the onward details of the bus route described in that section also apply if you get the bus from here.

If you miss the last bus on a Sunday, a walk of 2.3 kilometres down the road from St Margaret's at Cliffe brings you to **Martin Mill station**, which has direct trains until about 9pm to Dover and on to London. To get to Martin Mill station, go north-west, that is inland, on the road out of the village and *ignore a road forking to the left signposted to Dover to keep straight on.*

The road is quite busy as far as its junction with the A258 in 1.5km (0.9 miles) but has a pavement on its right-hand side for about half of the way and fairly wide verges thereafter. *After crossing the busy A258 turn right for 10 metres and continue on Station Road.* Note that though this road is fairly quiet, it has *no pavement and no grass verges, so care is needed with oncoming traffic.* Follow this road for 800 metres to its very end (the road goes into a dip and then up again and has hedges and farmland on either side) until you get to the **Ugly Duckling** pub on your left-hand side.

Cross the road (Martin Mill) and *follow the sign to the train station through the pedestrian blue iron gate* and along a path with blue iron railings on either side. At the end on your left is Martin Mill station.

Lunch & tea places

Blue Birds Tea Room *Granville Road, St Margaret's Bay (no phone).* **Open** 10.30am-4pm Tue-Sun. Romantically situated in an old coastguard station on the clifftops just beyond St Margaret's Bay, this place is highly recommended, and the suggested stop if doing the short walk option to St Margaret's at Cliffe.

Coastguard *The Bay, St Margaret's, CT15 6DY (01304 853176).* **Open** 11am-11pm Mon-Sat; noon-10.30pm Sun. **Food served** 12.30-2.45pm, 6.30-8.45pm daily. 7km (4.4 miles) into the walk, the Coastguard describes itself as Britain's 'closest pub to France'. Food is served at lunchtime and drinks, including coffee and tea, are available all afternoon. It has a pleasant open-air terrace directly overlooking beach. This is the suggested lunch stop for the main walk.

Dunkerley's Hotel *19 Beach Street, Deal, CT14 7AH (01304 375016).* **Open/food served** 7-9.30pm Mon; noon-2.30pm, 7-9.30pm Tue-Fri; noon-2.30pm, 6-10pm Sat; noon-3pm, 7-9.30pm Sun. Situated at the end of the walk in Deal, Dunkerley's has a small but very comfortable lounge. The hotel is right by the roundabout near the pier (see walk text for exact location). Open to non-residents, and offering comfortable leather armchairs and classical music, it serves cream teas and teacakes until at least 10pm.

St Margaret's Museum tearoom *Beach Road, St Margaret's Bay, CT15 6DZ (01304 852764).* **Open/food served** Apr-Sept 10am-5pm Wed-Sun. The museum tearoom serves sandwiches and cakes.

White Cliffs Visitor Centre *Upper Road, Langdon Cliffs, nr Dover, CT16 1HJ (01304 202756/www.nationaltrust.org.uk).* **Open** *Mar-Oct* 10am-5pm daily. *Nov-Feb* 11am-4pm daily. On the cliff above Dover Eastern Docks, the Centre's coffee shop has a view of the sea.

Zetland Arms *Wellington Parade, Kingsdown, Deal, CT14 8AF (01304 364888).* **Open** 11am-2.30pm, 6-11pm Mon-Sat; noon-3pm, 7-10.30pm Sun. **Food served** noon-2pm, 7-10pm Mon-Sat; noon-3pm, 7-10pm Sun. Located at the start of the Deal beach section of this walk, this pub serves tea and coffee and has some outside tables overlooking the sea. Note that it is open during the afternoon on bank holiday weekends and for the six weeks of the school holidays in the summer.

Deal is also full of seaside cafés, such as **Debs**, the **Deal Beach Parlour** and the **Caterer**, and cosy old pubs, of which the **Old Kings Head** and the **Port Arms** are possibilities. **Walmer Castle** has a lovely café too, where sandwiches and simple hot meals are available.

Index